MW00329863

THE I TATTI
RENAISSANCE LIBRARY

James Hankins, General Editor

FICINO

COMMENTARIES ON PLATO

VOLUME 2, PART II

ITRL 52

MARSILIO FICINO

✦ ✦ ✦

COMMENTARIES ON PLATO

VOLUME 2 ✦ *PARMENIDES, PART II*

EDITED AND TRANSLATED BY

MAUDE VANHAELEN

THE I TATTI RENAISSANCE LIBRARY

HARVARD UNIVERSITY PRESS

CAMBRIDGE, MASSACHUSETTS

LONDON, ENGLAND

2012

Series design by Dean Bornstein

Library of Congress Cataloging-in-Publication Data

Ficino, Marsilio, 1433–1499.
[Selections. English & Latin. 2008]
Commentaries on Plato / Marsilio Ficino ;
edited and translated by Michael J. B. Allen.
p.   cm. — (The I Tatti Renaissance Library ; 34)
Includes bibliographical references and index.
ISBN 978-0-674-06472-0 (cloth : alk. paper)
1. Plato   I. Allen, Michael J. B.   II. Title
B395.F4713   2008
184 — dc22   2008037878

Contents

❦❦❦

COMMENTARY ON THE *PARMENIDES*

Chapters 50–111

Note on the Text   341

Notes to the Text   343

Notes to the Translation   349

Bibliography   374

Index   376

COMMENTARY ON
THE *PARMENIDES*

De unitate super essentiam, de unitatibus in essentiis, de diis,
de communi intentione Parmenidis in suppositionibus suis.

1 Sicut ipsa simpliciter unitas est super ens universum, ita in ordine
rerum sua cuiusque entis unitas quodammodo est essentia sua
superior, ad quam essentia eamque comitantia ita se habent ut cir-
culus se habet ad centrum. Ubique profecto unitas essentiam sibi
familiarem modo quodam coaguli continet sibiquemet uniendo et
ab alienis secernendo perficit atque firmat, tamquam essentiae
cardo quidam atque praestantior. Neque ipsa quidem unitas adae-
quatur enti, sed entis unio. Latior enim ente unitas privationem
etiam quamlibet declarat unam, sicut et habitum quemlibet unum,
ipsamque materiam ferme non minus unam quam formam atque
compositum, quamvis materia longius ab ente et esse et essentia
cadat. Unum ergo bonumque solum communicatum omnibus testatur, ut diximus, ipsum simpliciter unum bonumque omnium
esse principium, siquidem ad primum pertinet proprium symbo-
lum in singulis potenter exprimere.

2 Ubi vero ens est non verum, ut in rebus omnino caducis, unitas
non est divina, at ubi essentia vera, ut in substantiis sempiternis,
scilicet in animabus rationalibus etiam particularibus caelisque,
unitas iam est divina, sed quoniam haec non sunt proxima deo,
tamquam mobilia et quasi composita, unitas eorum non est deus.
Sed ubi essentia verissima est, ut in mentibus separatis vel caelestibus animabus, unitas earum iam est deus, quotve essentiae illae
sunt, totidem et excelsae earum sunt unitates, totidem et dii vocantur. Unitas ergo proprium est dei nomen — unitas omnino su-

On unity above essence, on unities in essences, on the gods,
on the general purpose of Parmenides in the hypotheses.

Just as the absolute Unity transcends universal being, so in the 1
order of nature the unity proper to each being somehow transcends its own essence. Essence and essential things are related to
unity like a circle to its center. Surely unity always contains the
essence that is related to it through some sort of bond, and by
uniting essence to itself and separating it from the others it perfects and strengthens it, as though it were the pole of essence, as it
were, and superior to it. This unity is not equal to being, but is the
unifying principle of being. For unity, by extending further than
being, reveals the unity of any privation, as well as that of any
disposition; matter itself, falling very far from being, the act of being, and essence, is hardly less one than the form and the composite. So the fact that the One and the Good are the only principle
to be communicated to all things bears witness, as we said, that
the absolute One-and-Good constitutes the principle of all things,
since it pertains to the first principle to powerfully imprint its own
character on individual things.

In things where being is not real, such as in things that are 2
completely corruptible, unity is not divine; in things where essence
is real, such as in eternal substances, that is, the rational souls
(even the particular ones), and in the heavens, unity is already divine, but as these are not the closest realities to God, being mobile
and quasi-composite, their unity is not God. In things where essence is most real, however, such as in the separate intelligences
and the celestial souls, their unity is already that of God, or rather,
there are as many superior unities as there are essences of that
kind, and all these unities are called gods.[1] Thus Unity is the
proper name of God — the Unity that utterly transcends essence,

per essentiam, deus unicus atque primus. Unitates in essentiis sublimibus eminentes dii multi sunt atque secundi, atque propter unitates eiusmodi quasi expressiores unitatis primae characteres, essentiae illae deorum nomina susceperunt providentiamque universalem sortitae sunt divinae propriam bonitatis. Unitates illae ita sunt unitati primae semper unitae, sicut radii luci et lineae centro coniunctae sunt et invicem. Cum enim per unitatem in caeteris fiat unio, multo artius invicem unitae sunt unitates, sed interim inter se distinctae, siquidem unitatis virtus est naturam sibi familiarem prius sibimet unire quam caeteris. Ideo cum unione communi semper unitatem propriam servat distinctamque ab aliis proprietatem.

3   Quamobrem Parmenides, dum versatur multipliciter circa unum, propter mirabilem unitatem omnium ad primum unum et invicem unionem, aliquando, ut Platonici quam plurimi voluerunt, primum tangit unum extra entis terminos universi ibique omnes entium de illo negat proprietates, aliquando de uno loquitur quod comitem habet essentiam ibique entis et entium munera iam affirmat, et omnia quidem, ubi de essentia prima, alia rursus prae caeteris atque alia, ubi de essentiis tractat aliis et ubique divinis.

4   Putat ergo Proclus, ut supra tetigimus, significationem ipsius unius, quod repetitur ubique, in variis suppositionibus variari quidem, sed interim ipsum suppositionis antecedens quodammodo idem videri posse propter mirabilem illam divinarum unitatum invicem unionem, sed multo magis passim consequentia variari, ut ostendatur interim unitatum earundem sincera distinctio. Quan-

the unique and first God, while the eminent unities within the sublime essences are multiple and secondary gods. And it is by virtue of these unities, which are the more express imprints of the first Unity, that these superior essences have received the names of gods and have been allotted the universal providence that is proper to divine Goodness. These unities are always joined to the first Unity, just as the rays are joined to their light, the lines to their center and conversely. For since union occurs by virtue of unity in all the other realities, unities are even more firmly joined to one another, yet at the same time they remain distinct from one another, since the power of unity is to unite to itself the nature that is close to it before uniting it to the others. So unity always preserves, together with the communion of all things, both the unity that is proper to each thing and the property that distinguishes each thing from the others.[2]

For this reason, according to most Platonists, when Parmenides 3 concerns himself with unity in various ways, thanks to both the wonderful unity of all things with respect to the first One and their union with one another, he sometimes goes beyond the limits of universal being and refers to the first One, and in that case he negates of the One all the properties of beings; at other times, he refers to the unity that is the companion of essence, and in that case he asserts of the one the properties of being and beings — all of these properties, when the term "one" corresponds to the first essence; some properties more than others, when the term "one" refers to the other utterly divine essences.

Proclus considers, therefore, as we mentioned above, that the 4 sense of the term "one," which is repeated in each hypothesis, varies in the different hypotheses; the antecedent of the hypothesis can be considered the same in each hypothesis, on account of the wonderful union between the divine unities, but the consequents vary to a much greater extent, so as to reveal from time to time the pure distinctness of each of these unities. For some time "whole" is

doque enim in consequenti ponitur ipsum totum, quandoque pars, quandoque figura, et alias quidem affirmativum consequens est, alias negativum. Addit alibi quidem unum super ens, ut diximus, pertractari, alibi vero unum et unitates multas in ente vero ibique per gradus entium late procedi, alibi vero cursim unum in ente non vero perstringi, unde tamen ad divina commodius subito reddeatur. Omnino vero dialogi totius intentionem esse tractare, aliquo posito vel non posito, quid sequatur ipsi ad seipsum et ad alia, quidve non sequatur, atque rursus quid sequatur vel non sequatur aliis invicem et ad illud. Itaque in prima suppositione perquiri, posito quidem uno, quae non sequantur uni ad seipsum atque alia; in secunda vero quae consequantur; in tertia quae et consequantur et non consequantur; in reliquis duabus agi quae consequantur aliis invicem et ad suppositum et quae non consequantur ad se invicem similiter et ad illud; in quattuor vero caeteris suppositionibus (sunt enim cunctae novem suppositiones) simili quodam ordine, uno non posito, variantur. Putat vero passim per suppositionum similitudinem significari miram divinarum unitatum unionem, primo uni radicitus inhaerentium, per dissimilitudinem vero discretionem earundem, quatenus ab uno aliter aliterve procedunt. Operae pretium esse, inquit, animadvertere per priores quinque suppositiones vera concludi posito uno, per quattuor vero posteriores ostendi quae absurda uno sublato sequantur, quoniam Parmenidi propositum sit ostendere quomodo existente uno omnes entium gradus inde procedant et quomodo non existente omnes

posited in the consequent, at another, "part," at another "shape," sometimes affirmatively, sometimes negatively. In some passages, he adds, Parmenides treats of the One above being, as we have said; in others, he treats of the one and the many unities within real being, and proceeds from there through the whole extent of beings; elsewhere, he briefly mentions the unity in nonreal being, from which he promptly and more appropriately returns, however, to the divine realities.[3] In fact, Proclus says, the purpose of the whole dialogue is to postulate that something is or is not, and to examine what follows for this thing in relation to itself and to the others, and what does not follow, and again what follows for the others in relation to one another and to the postulate. So in the first hypothesis Parmenides examines, after having postulated the existence of the One, what does not follow for the One in relation to both itself and the others; in the second hypothesis, what follows; in the third, both what follows and what does not follow. In the next two hypotheses he examines what follows for the others in relation to one another and to the postulate, and what does not follow for themselves in relation to one another and to the postulate. In the remaining four hypotheses (for there are nine hypotheses in total) the arguments vary similarly when postulating that the one [being] is not.[4] Proclus considers that the overall similitude between the hypotheses reveals the wonderful union between divine unities, which are attached by their roots to the first one, while the difference between the hypotheses reveals their distinctness, inasmuch as they proceed differently from the One.[5] It is noteworthy, he says, that the first five hypotheses produce true conclusions when positing the existence of the one [being], and the last four demonstrate the absurdities that follow if the One does not exist. For Parmenides' purpose is to demonstrate how, if the One exists, all the degrees of being proceed from it, and how, if the one [being] does not exist, all are eliminated. And Parmenides reveals this in the whole dialogue, partly through the

auferantur; totoque tractatu id declarare, partim quidem ponendo
vera, partim vero falsa interimendo, perinde ac si ita de providentia
disseratur: 'si providentia sit, erunt omnia recte disposita; si vero
non sit, sine ordine omnia. Est igitur providentia, siquidem ordi-
nata sunt omnia.' Denique in quinque suppositionibus disponi
vult principia rerum, in quattuor vero sequentibus non tam novas
poni substantias quam demonstrari interempto uno multa impossibilia sequi. Istud denique unum, quo et posito ponuntur omnia
et sublato tolluntur, non est nomen a logico fictum, sed ipsum
universi principium. Solius enim principii omnium hoc est proprium.

: LI :

Dispositio propositionum Parmenidis
apud Plutarchum.

1 Dialogum hunc divinum apud veteres iudicatum testis est Plutarchus, qui post multos expositionum modos ipse quem mox narra-
bimus introduxit, partim ex antiquorum, partim ex sententia sua
componens, quem et Proclus comprobat ea forma quam perstrin-
ximus in prooemio.

2 Sed ad Plutarchi sensum iam pergamus, hunc imitaturi quam
plurimum nec usquam, nisi forte circa suppositiones ultimas, ali-
quantulum mutaturi.[1] Prima suppositio de primo tractat deo; secunda de intellectu primo et ordine prorsus intellectuali; tertia

postulation of true propositions and partly through the refutation of false ones, just as if one said about providence: if providence exists, all things will be disposed as they should be; if providence does not exist, all things will be disposed without order. Therefore, providence exists, since all things are disposed in order. Finally, according to Proclus, the first principles of things are disposed in the first five hypotheses, whereas the last four hypotheses intend not so much to postulate the existence of new substances as to demonstrate the various impossibilities that result from the nonexistence of the one [being].[6] Lastly, the One, the existence of which causes the existence of all things, and the nonexistence of which causes the nonexistence of all things, is not a name fabricated by logic,[7] but the principle of the universe. For such is the function of the unique principle of all things.

: LI :

*The arrangement of the dialogue's hypotheses
according to Plutarch.*

That this dialogue was considered divine among the ancients is   1
attested by Plutarch [of Athens], who, following different ways of interpreting the dialogue, established the interpretation that we are presently going to describe, which he developed partly from the teaching of the ancients and partly from his own theory, and which Proclus approves in the form that we have summarized in the introduction.

Let us describe, then, Plutarch's interpretation, and let us imi-   2
tate it as far as possible without modifying it in any way, except perhaps a little in the final hypotheses.[8] The first hypothesis is about the first God, the second is about the first intellect and the

de anima suoque similiter ordine; quarta de materiali specie; quinta de informi materia. Haec enim quinque rerum principia sunt. Tria quidem illa principia separata, duo vero sequentia intrinsecus complent opus. Parmenides interim Pythagoreorum suorum more unum communiter appellat propter simplicitatem substantiam quamlibet separatam, aliud autem et alia nominat, propter fluxum diversitatemque a divinis longe distantem, materiam formamque corpoream, praesertim quia duo haec non tam sui ipsorum sunt quam aliorum nec tam causae quam concausae, ut in *Timaeo* dicitur et *Phaedone*. Merito igitur tres quidem suppositiones quaerentes quomodo unum se habet ad seipsum atque ad alia, de principalibus causis tractare putantur; reliquae vero duae investigantes quo pacto alia se habeant invicem et ad unum, speciem et materiam videntur inducere. Itaque in quinque his suppositionibus principia haec, et quae in eis vel circa ea sunt, uno posito confirmantur, uno inquam super ens, in ente, sub ente.

3   In reliquis quattuor demonstratur, si non est illud quod intra entia unum, quot absurda sequantur, ut intellegamus multo magis absurda sequi, si quis negaverit ipsum simpliciter unum. Sexta igitur probat, si non sit quod in entibus unum, id est intellegibile, ita ut partim quidem sit, partim vero non sit, solum fore in rerum ordine quod est sensibile. Cum enim intellegibile non sit quod est unum cum ente vero, reliquum est sensibile solum quod esse quodammodo dicitur, nullaque ulterius erit cognitio praeter sensum, quod quidem in suppositione sexta absurdum esse convincitur, scilicet solum in ordine cognitionis esse sensum, solum quoque in

whole intellectual order, the third is about the soul and its order, the fourth is about material species, the fifth about formless matter. For these are the five principles of things. Three separate principles and two dependent principles, which are immanent in things, constitute the work. Following the custom of his Pythagorean colleagues Parmenides commonly calls "one" any separate substance on account of its simplicity, and "other" or "others" matter and incorporeal form, on account of their flux and their remoteness from divine realities. This is especially so because these two realities belong to others rather than to themselves, and are contributory causes rather than real causes, as stated in the *Timaeus* and the *Phaedo*.[9] These theologians rightly consider, therefore, that the first three hypotheses, which examine what relation the one has to itself and to the others, concern the first causes, while the remaining two, which examine what relation the others have to each other and to the one, introduce species and matter. In this way, the first five hypotheses confirm the existence of these principles, both those that are external to beings and those that are in or about them,[10] on the assumption that the one (and I mean the one above being, in being, and under being) exists.

In the remaining four hypotheses it is shown that a number of absurdities follow if the one present in beings does not exist. This will make us realize that even more absurd consequences will follow if the absolute One does not exist. Thus the sixth hypothesis shows that if the one present in beings, that is, the intelligible one, does not exist (in the sense that it partly exists and partly does not exist), there will only be sense objects in the order of things. For if the intelligible world does not exist, that is, the one united to real being, there remains only the sensible world, which is said to exist in a certain way, and there will be no knowledge besides sense perception, a consequence that is shown to be absurd in the sixth hypothesis — that only sense perception would exist among the modes of knowledge, and only sense objects among the objects of

ordine cognobilis esse sensibile. Suppositio septima probat, si non sit illud in entibus unum, ita ut nullo prorsus modo sit, nullam omnino cognitionem fore, cognobile nullum, quod stultum dictu fore septima haec suppositio docet. Tum vero alia, si unum illud partim sit, partim vero non sit, ut sexta suppositio modo fingebat, somniis et umbris similia fore, quod tamquam absurdum suppositio octava redarguit. Sin autem nullo modo sit, alia iam minus erunt quam umbra vel somnium, id est nihilum, quod tandem quasi monstrum suppositio nona convincit.

4   Quamobrem suppositio prima ad suppositiones reliquas ita se habet, quemadmodum ad caetera principium universi. Reliquae vero quattuor mox sequentes primam de his quae post ipsum unum principiis agunt. Quattuor autem quae his subduntur convincunt, sublato uno, omnia quae in quattuor superioribus ostensa fuerant penitus peritura. Cum enim secunda demonstret . . .[2] si sit unum quod habet cum ente coniugium, omnem animae ordinem esse, septima declarat, si non sit illud unum, virtutem omnem cognoscendi perire, rationem et imaginationem atque sensum. Rursus cum quarta declaret, si est illud ens unum praeter ipsum simpliciter unum, quodammodo et species materiales existere, quae sane unius entis quomodolibet sint participes, octava ostendit, si non sit illud ens unum, umbras tantum et somnia fore quae nunc sensibilia nominantur nec ullam formalem distinctionem vel substantiam habitura. Praeterea cum quinta moneat, si est illud ens unum, fore materiam (unius quidem entis non participem,

knowledge. The seventh hypothesis shows that if the one present in beings does not exist (in the sense of absolute nonexistence), there will be absolutely no knowledge and no object of knowledge, and the seventh hypothesis teaches us that this is a foolish thing to say. As to the others, if the one present in beings partly exists and partly does not exist, in the sense supposed by the sixth hypothesis, they will be like dreams or shadows, a consequence that the eighth hypothesis rejects as absurd. Conversely, if the one present in beings does not exist in the sense of absolute nonexistence, the others will be less than shadows or dreams, that is, nothing, a consequence that the ninth and last hypothesis shows to be against nature.

In this way, the first hypothesis has the same relation to the other hypotheses as the principle of the universe toward the rest of reality, while the four remaining hypotheses immediately following on the first concern the principles following on the One, and the four hypotheses after these show that if the one [being] does not exist, all the things indicated in the former four will not exist. For while the second hypothesis shows <that if the one exists, the order of the intellect exists, the sixth hypothesis shows that if this one does not exist, then only sense perception and sense objects exist in the order of knowledge. While the third hypothesis shows>[11] that if the one united with being exists, the whole order of soul exists, the seventh hypothesis shows that if it does not exist, every cognitive power will perish, including reason, imagination, and sense perception. Likewise, where the fourth hypothesis shows that if the one being exists (separately from the absolute One), then material species also have an existence of a sort, since they in some way participate in the one being, the eighth hypothesis shows that if the one being does not exist, then the things that we now call sense objects will be mere shadows and dreams, having no formal distinction nor any substance; where the fifth hypothesis shows that if the one being exists, matter will exist (al-

4

qua ratione ens, quamvis eiusdem compotem qua ratione unum),
nona tandem explicat, si non sit illud ens unum, nec umbram quidem rei ullius usquam fore. Hactenus Plutarchus.

: LII :

Quid significent in suppositionibus negationes,
quid affirmationes, quae et quo
ordine tractentur in eis.

1 Quoniam vero suppositio prima colit ipsum simpliciter unum ente
superius, ideo omnes ab eo entium conditiones negat. Est enim
ab omnibus absolutum, tamquam principium finale, praecipue et
eminenter efficiens. In omni vero finalium efficentiumque causarum ordine, illa est potissima quae a propriis effectuum conditionibus maxime distat, ut principalior causa hominis caelum est vel
idea quam aliquis homo, principalior caloris vitalis causa sol quam
ignis. At vero cum secunda suppositio agat iam de uno non simpliciter, sed uno ente, in quo praeter simplicem et eminentem unitatis rationem est et essentiae ratio a simplicitate degenerans, merito
iam de hoc uno ente primo omnes entium formales proprietates
affirmat. Hoc enim est entium non tam finis quam efficiens, neque
tam efficiens quam exemplar et quodammodo forma uniformis
pariter atque omniformis. Quapropter negationes quidem illae
circa primum non sunt privationes merae, sed significant ipsum
esse causam omnium, non quomodolibet, sed ineffabiliter eminentem, adeo ut nedum forma quaedam horum sit in illo, sed neque

though not by participating in the one being insofar as it is being, but insofar as it is one), the ninth hypothesis finally shows that if the one being does not exist, there will nowhere be even a shadow of anything. Thus much is Plutarch's interpretation.

: LII :

The significance of the negations and the assertions
in the hypotheses, what things are dealt with
in them, and in what order.

The first hypothesis concerns the absolute One that is superior to   1
being. Therefore, it denies of it all the conditions of beings. For the One transcends all things, as the final principle and the first and eminently efficient cause. At every level among the final and efficient causes, the cause that is furthest apart from the conditions proper to its effects is the most powerful. For instance, as causes of man's existence, the heavens, or the Idea, have precedence over any individual man; as cause of life's heat the sun has precedence over fire. By contrast, since the second hypothesis no longer concerns the absolute One but the one being, in which the rational principle of essence, which falls away from simplicity, exists alongside the simple and eminent rational principle of unity, it rightly asserts of the first one being all the formal properties of beings. For the one being is not so much the final as the efficient cause, and not so much the efficient as the paradigmatic cause, and in some way is the uniform and multiform form. So the negations about the One are no mere privations, but rather they indicate that it is the eminent cause of all things — not eminent in any manner whatever but ineffably. In this way, at the level of this One,

exemplar in plura distinctum neque proportio ad haec vel ulla similitudinis habitudo. Sed de his una cum Dionysio Areopagita in commentariis in eum nostris saepe tractamus. Affirmationes vero circa secundum non compositionem vel conditionem horum propriam illi adhibent, sed exemplares horum species virtutesque effectrices inter se formaliter ibi et absolute distinctas.

2   Proinde si Proclum sequimur, dicemus omne principium alicuius multitudinis supereminens et maxime unum procreare prius multitudinem sibi similem, id est unitates quasdam eminentes sibique similiores, quam multitudinem longe distantem et uniones singulorum in multitudine proprias. Sicut igitur intellectus primus intellectus primo puros procreat separatos, deinde vires in animabus intellectuales, ita ipsum simpliciter unum unitates primo excellentes procreat et divinas, quae et dii vocantur, deinde uniones rebus insitas iamque cognatas et proprias unitorum. Differt autem ipsum unum ab unitatibus illis, quoniam ipsum ab omnibus proprietatibus est absolutum, illae vero sub proprietatibus inde variis derivantur. Quapropter varia nomina et officia sunt deorum.

3   Observandum praeterea monet (quod equidem, ut verum fatear, difficillimum arbitror observatu) quomodo in secunda suppositione eiusmodi ordines divini tradantur, deincepsque proprietates ipsorum, totidem designatae quot et conclusiones ibi sunt, singulae singulis ordinibus competentes. Tertiam vero suppositionem non simpliciter de qualibet anima, sed de omni divina anima

there is no paradigm for distinguishing the plurality of things, nor any proportion or similitude between the principle and that plurality, let alone a particular form of things. But we have frequently treated of these matters, together with Dionysius the Areopagite, in our commentaries on his works. The assertions concerning the second principle do not provide it with any composition or condition proper to beings, but rather with the paradigmatic species and efficient powers related to these beings, which in the intelligible realm are distinct in a formal and absolute way.

Likewise, following Proclus we will say that every principle of 2 any multitude, being utterly eminent and one to the highest degree, first generates the multitude that is like the principle itself (that is, some eminent unities [or henads] that are very similar to it), and then the multitude that is far distant from it, as well as the unions between individuals within the multitude. Therefore, just as the first intellect generates the unmixed and separate intellects before creating the intellectual powers of the souls, so the absolute One generates the excellent and divine unities [or henads], which are also called gods, before creating the unions immanent in things, which are akin to these things and unify them.¹² But the One differs from these unities [or henads], because it transcends all their properties, while these unities [henads] take on various properties as they derive from the One, for which reason the gods have different names and functions.

Proclus also invites us to observe (something which, to tell the 3 truth, I myself find extremely difficult to observe) the way in which these divine orders are introduced in the second hypothesis, as well as their properties, and he considers that the number of divine orders is the same as the number of conclusions in the second hypothesis, each conclusion corresponding to a single order of gods.¹³ As to the third hypothesis, they consider that it is not simply about any soul whatever, but about the whole divine soul.¹⁴

esse putant. Illic agi de anima Parmenides ipse testatur, dicens unum ibi temporis esse particeps, primum vero tempus in anima, mentibus vero superioribus non convenit 'erat' aut 'erit,' sed esse praesens semper aeternum. De his quidem mentibus et de anima, si qua prorsus est dea, in secunda suppositione tractari, in tertia vero de anima, non dea quidem, sed divina.

4   Summatim vero, ut saepius eadem repetam, suppositio prima tractat, si antiquis licet credere, quomodo primus deus singulos deorum ordines procreat atque disponit. Secunda vero, de divinis ordinibus, quomodo processerunt ab uno et de qualibet essentia unicuique deo unitati videlicet coniugata. Tertia, de animabus deitatem quidem ipsam substantialem non habentibus, sed similitudinem ad deos expressam. Quarta, de formis materialibus, quomodo proficiscuntur a diis, et quae proprie ab unoquoque deorum ordine pendent. Quinta, de materia prima, quomodo formalium unitatum non est compos, sed desuper ab unitate superessentiali dependet. Nam usque ad materiam ultimam unius primi actio provenit, interminatam illius naturam per quandam unitatis participationem quoquomodo determinans. Suppositio prima et quinta per negationes incedunt, sed illa quidem, de primo rerum omnia negans, per negationes significat virtutem causae ab omnibus absolutae incomparabilemque excessum; haec autem de ultimo negans omnia privationes significat atque defectum. Secunda et quarta suppositio affirmationibus dumtaxat utuntur, sed illa quidem exemplaria continet, haec imagines. Tertia, tamquam media, cum anima rerum media congruit ac propter eiusmodi congruentiam ex affirmationibus negationibusque componitur habetque negationes affirmationibus quodam consortio coniugatas.

Parmenides himself attests that this hypothesis[15] concerns the soul when he states that the one there partakes of time [151E–55C] — time first manifesting itself in soul — whereas neither "was" nor "will be" befit the superior intellects, but rather the eternally present "is." The second hypothesis concerns these divine minds and the goddess soul (if indeed there is such a goddess), while the third hypothesis is about the soul that is divine but not a goddess.[16]

In sum, to repeat once more the same thing, if one may trust the ancients, the first hypothesis concerns how the first God generates and arranges the individual orders of gods. The second is about the divine orders, how they have proceeded from the One, and the essence that is joined to each god, or unity [henad]. The third is about the souls that have no divine substance, but bear an express likeness to the gods. The fourth is about material forms, how they proceed from the gods, and which forms specifically depend on each order of gods. The fifth is about first matter, how it has no share in formal unities [henads], but depends on the supraessential Unity above. For the action of the first One extends as far as the lowest principle, matter, determining its indeterminate nature through its participation in unity.[17] The first and fifth hypotheses both proceed by negations; the first, which negates all things of the first principle, expresses through negations the power of the cause that is separate from all things and its incomparable excess, while the fifth, which denies everything of the last principle, expresses privations and deficiency. The second and fourth hypotheses use solely assertions; the second comprises these attributes asserted as paradigms, while the fourth comprises them as images. The third, intermediate hypothesis corresponds to the soul, which is the center of nature, and on account of this correspondence is composed of both assertions and negations, the negations being in some way coordinate with the assertions.[18]

: LIII :

Intentio, veritas, ordo suppositionis primae.

1   In *Sophiste* demonstratur cum omnia participent unum, oportere
ipsum unum vere esse, quandoquidem et caetera tanto verius sunt,
quanto magis participant unum, et cum quodlibet participantium
propter multitudinem aliquam sibi propriam non sit vere unum,
tamen revera haec existant, oportere ipsum verum unum, id est
nullius particeps multitudinis, vere in natura rerum existere, et
tanto prius esse quam caetera, quanto est et verius unum. Ubique
enim quod secundum aliquam naturam verum est, est prius et
ante illud quod ibi falsum. Denique concluditur inde nulla entia
fore, nisi sit ipsum vere unum. Vere autem unum esse penitus impartibile. Hoc autem quod accipimus ex *Sophiste* a Melisso Parmenidis auditore tractatum, profecto simillimum est suppositioni
Parmenidis primae, ipsum unum probanti primo multitudinem vel
partes nullas habere. Ex qua quidem conclusione omnes deinceps
conclusiones necessaria quadam serie contexuntur. Ex quo patet,
sicut nec in *Sophiste*, ita nec in *Parmenide*, de uno quodam tantum
nomine ita logice ficto vel de ente conficto, sed de uno et ente, ut
ita dixerim, existente vel subsistente tractari. Immo et ubi de ipso
uno negat essentiam, necessario asserturus est ipsum esse super
essentiam summumque esse deum. Non enim de uno quod tanti
facit essentiam ideo negat quia vel nihil esse putet (quod si forte
non sit, nihil superesse probat) vel quia infra essentiam esse iudi-
cet, infra hanc enim esse vult temporalia et fluxum atque mate-

: LIII :

The purpose, truth, and structure of the first hypothesis.

In the *Sophist* it is shown that since all things partake of the One, the One must truly exist, given that the truer all other things are, the more they partake of the One, and that since all the beings that partake of the One are not truly One (for they each possess their own multitude), yet truly exist, the true One, that is, the One that does not partake of multitude, must truly exist in the nature, and the more precedence it has over all the rest, the more truly one it is. For in every case what is true according to a certain nature always has precedence over that which is false. In the end, the *Sophist* concludes that there will be no beings if the true One does not exist, and that the true One is completely indivisible.[19] Yet the doctrine which, according to the *Sophist*, has been developed by Parmenides' disciple, Melissus, corresponds exactly to the first hypothesis, which first shows that the One has no multitude and no parts [137C–D],[20] and all the conclusions deriving from this first conclusion are interwoven in a series which unfolds in a necessary sequence. As a result, it is clear that both the *Parmenides* and the *Sophist* do not treat of a certain one that would only be a name imagined for the sake of logic, and of a being that would simply be the product of imagination, but of the One and being that have, as it were, existence or subsistence.[21] Moreover, even when Parmenides denies essence of the One [141E–42A], he necessarily intends to assert that the One is above essence and is the supreme God. Since he holds the One in such high esteem he does not deny essence of the One because he considers that the One is nothing (since he shows that if the One does not exist, nothing else exists), or because he thinks that it is below essence (since he thinks that below essence there lie temporal things, flux

1

riam, a quibus ipsum unum excellenter absolvit. Sit igitur suppositionis huius fundamentum: unum ipsum non nomen quidem a disputante confictum, sed universi principium, quod quidem praecipue comprobat Dionysius Areopagita sedulus Parmenidis observator. Quotiens enim in ipsius unius mentionem venit, quod frequenter efficit, totiens super essentiam collocat atque hoc nomine ubique significat universi principium.

2   Nonnulli Platonicorum existimaverunt suppositionem primam sub hoc unius ipsius nomine non modo deum primum, sed cunctos pariter introducere, quippe cum dii omnes communiter unitates eminentes sint atque vocentur, sed profecto non par est unitatis ratio circa primum atque sequentes. Sequentes enim dii unitates quidem sunt superessentiales quodammodo, in essentiis tamen consistunt essentiarum omnium perfectissimis. Primus vero deus nullam coniugatam habet essentiam, quocirca prima suppositio de uno, quod introducit essentiam, ut diximus, negat et esse, quod de caeteris unitatibus negari non potest. Ex quo patet de unico simpliciter uno per se hic agi, de caeteris autem non per se, sed quatenus derivantur et superantur a primo.

3   Oportet sane super omnem naturam in alio iacentem velut in suo quodam ordine imperfectam ascendere ad naturam eiusdem vel similis ordinis aut saltem nominis in se existentem iam perfectam, ut a specie materiali ad immaterialem; a vita quae penitus est addicta corpori ad vitam, id est animam, separatam vel separabilem; ab intellectu qui est in anima ad intellectum purum atque substantialem. Sed numquid ab intellegibili quod est in intellectu, ad intellegibile quod extra intellectum sit more Procli ascendemus? Profecto ubicumque in aliquo intellectu est intellegibile non omnino universum, sed intellegibile quoddam, nec idem re ipsa cum

and matter, from which the One is totally separate because of its excellence). So the principle of this hypothesis is as follows: the One is not a name imagined for the sake of the discussion, but the principle of the universe, as Dionysius the Areopagite, the respectful interpreter of the *Parmenides* has principally shown. For each time Dionysius mentions the One — which he often does — he places it above essence, and on each occasion he uses this term to designate the principle of the universe.

Some Platonists considered that by the term "one" the first hypothesis not only introduces the first God, but also all the gods, since the gods are, and are called, eminent unities [henads].[22] But the unity of the first God is surely not equal to that of the rest of the gods. For if indeed the other gods are in some way superessential unities [henads], they nevertheless reside within essences, even if these are the most perfect of all. By contrast, the first God has no link with essence, for which reason the first hypothesis also denies of the One the act of being, which it cannot deny of the other unities [141E–42A], since the One ushers in essence. It is clear, then, that the first hypothesis is about the unique and absolute One in itself; it is not about the others in themselves, but inasmuch as they derive from, and are transcended by, the One.

Surely one should rise above any nature that resides in another than itself (since such a nature is imperfect within its own order) and ascend toward the nature that resides in itself and is perfect within the same or similar order (or at least with the same name). For instance, we must ascend from the material species to the immaterial species; from life that is closely linked to body to the separate or separable life (that is, the soul); from the intellect that is within the soul to the pure and substantial intellect.[23] But will we be able to ascend from the intelligible object that is within the intellect, to the intelligible object that is beyond the intellect, in the manner of Proclus? Surely, in the case where any given intellect contains an intelligible object that is not fully universal, but

substantia mentis, ibi excellentius intellegibile perquiremus. Postquam vero ad intellectum primum pervenerimus, ubi intellegibile est universum et intellectui penitissimum, ut sit ipsamet intellectus huius essentia, intellegibile nullum ultra desiderabimus.

4   Sed quoniam unitas hic non est ipsa simpliciter unitas, sed essentialis, intellectualis, intellegibilis unitas numerumque formalem consortem habet, pergemus hinc ad ipsum simpliciter unum, inde vero velut ex specula divinas unitates, id est deos profluentes suo quodam ordine, contemplabimur.

5   Hic nobis peropportunum, ut videtur, succurrit exemplum. Linea, quoniam primum continuum est atque dividuum, ideo est individui particeps, id est puncti. Quod quidem punctum, etsi super linearem conditionem est atque individuum, in linea tamen est et aliquid caputque lineae. Item lineae multae in circulo per puncta quaeque sua contingunt circuli centrum. Similiter intellegibilis intellectualisque essentia, quoniam primum multiplicabile est, ideo excellentis unitatis est compos. Quae quidem unitas, etsi non est essentia vel essentiali obnoxia multitudini, tamen in essentia permanet vel potius extat ut apex. Per quam unaquaeque intellectualis essentia deus est, divina videlicet perfruens unitate, atque sicut per formam unumquodque in sua specie collocatur et nos per animam sumus id quod sumus, ita unusquisque deorum per unitatem id ipsum quod est potissimum, id est deus, esse censetur.

6   Intentio denique primae suppositionis erit ipsum simpliciter unum ab omnibus passim intellectualium unitatum, id est deorum, proprietatibus conditionibusque absolvere et absolvendo significare omnium inde processum.

has a measure of universality, and is not truly identical to the substance of this intellect, we will be looking for a more excellent intelligible object. But when we have reached the first intellect, within which the intelligible object is universal and innermost to the intellect, we shall not desire to find any intelligible object beyond that one, inasmuch as this is the very essence of the intellect.[24]

But since the unity in question is not the absolute Unity, but is essential, intellectual, and intelligible, and since it shares in formal number, we shall then proceed from there to the absolute One and from there, as from a watchtower,[25] we shall contemplate the divine unities [henads], the gods that proceed from it, each according to his own order.   4

It might be helpful to illustrate this point with an example. The line, as the first continuous and divisible reality, partakes of the indivisible, that is, the point.[26] This point, although it is superior to the condition of the line and indivisible, is nevertheless on the line; it is "something" of the line, and its extremity. Likewise, in a circle each line touches the center of the circle through its own point. The same goes for the intelligible and intellectual essence: as the first multiple reality, it possesses the most excellent unity. Although this unity is not an essence and does not undergo essential multitude, it nevertheless resides within essence, or rather it resides within essence as a summit, and it is through this unity that each intellectual essence is a god and fully enjoys divine unity; and just as through its form each thing is located in its own species and through our soul we are what we are, in the same way through his unity each god is considered to be that which he is most — god.   5

Finally, the purpose of the first hypothesis will be to separate the absolute One from all the properties and conditions of the intellectual unities [henads], that is, the gods, and to make clear by this separation that all things proceed from it.   6

7   Intentio vero nostra ad haec mysteria consequenda fuerit per logicos rationis nostrae discursus ad simplices entium intellegentias pervenire, per has autem excitare unum ipsum quod nobis inest, immo praeest divinum, ut hoc ipsum simpliciter unum percipiamus. Postquam enim per discursiones intellegentiasque conditiones omnes proprias entibus rite de primo principio negaverimus, periculum imminebit ne forte, imaginatione decepti, post negationes rerum munerumque quam plurimas opinemur nos vel ad nihilum vel ad exile vanumque aliquid vel indeterminatum et informe confusumque devenisse, nisi quatenus negamus, eatenus divinum unitatis nostrae vigorem affectu quodam amatorio suscitemus, nos in ipsam supra nos unitatem e vestigio translaturum, per unitatem nostram fruituros unitate divina, quando et motum rationis et multiplicatem intellegentiae dimiserimus, unitate sola ad ipsum unum et ad ipsum bonum amore nitentes.

: LIV :

Ubi entium proprietates de uno negantur, significatur
ipsum haec omnia antecellere atque procreare.

1   Affirmationes circa summum deum fallaces admodum periculosaeque sunt. Solemus enim in quotidianis affirmationibus nostris certam quandam speciem proprietatemque concipere et applicare aliquid alteri atque definire. Hoc autem agere circa primum nefas. Negationes vero contra indefinitum semper reliquunt illud et in sua amplitudine liberum, animam quoque aptius deo praeparant, dum hanc ab humanis conditionibus definitionibusque segregant

But let our purpose be, in order to attain these mysteries, to 7 reach, through the discursive logic of our reason, the simple intelligences of beings, and through them to stir up the one that is within us (or rather transcends us, since it is divine) in order to perceive this absolute One. For after having in due form denied of the first principle, through discursive reason and intelligence, all the conditions that are proper to beings, we might find ourselves in danger of being deceived by our imagination, and think that, after having denied so many divine realities and powers, we have reached nothingness, or something that is void and vain, indeterminate, formless and confused—unless we balance our negations by stimulating the divine force of our unity through an erotic affect, a force that will immediately transport us to the very Unity that transcends us, and enable us to enjoy divine Unity through our own unity, when we have let go of the motion of reason and the multiplicity of intelligence, striving solely through unity toward the One, and toward the Good through love.[27]

: LIV :

When the properties of beings are denied of the One,
it signifies that the One transcends and creates all these things.

Assertions about the highest God are utterly false and dangerous. 1 This is because our everyday assertions usually serve to designate some particular species and property, to attribute something to something else, and to establish a definition. Yet it is not right to do so regarding the first principle. By contrast, negations always leave the first principle without definition and free with respect to its extension; they also prepare the soul for a better apprehension of God, by separating the soul from human conditions and defini-

et quasi iam incircumscriptam deo prorsus incircumscripto committunt.

2   Neque vero nos latet quod et saepe cum Dionysio dicimus: negationes circa deum non defectum significare, sed excessum. Quando enim dicimus deum non esse mentem nec vitam nec essentiam, intellegi volumus ipsum his omnibus esse praestantiorem horumque principium. Iam vero negare artifici manus defectum significat, caret enim sibi necessariis instrumentis; negare vero naturae manus excellentiam naturae declarat non indigentis manibus ad agendum. Profecto sicut primum illud est omnium causa, sic artificiosae circa ipsum negationes sequentium affirmationum causae sunt. Quamobrem quotcumque de uno prima suppositio negat, affirmat suppositio sequens, ut videlicet declaretur ab illo omnia propterea fieri, quia illud nullum est omnium, sed super omnia pariter. Sicut enim anima vel natura, quoniam non est corpus, generat regitque corpus, et intellectus, cum non sit anima, procreat animam, sic ipsum unum, quia non multiplicatum, non numerosum, non figuratum, multitudinem et numerum procreat et figuram. Nullum enim eorum quae procreat ipsum esse potest. Neque enim alia quaevis excellens universalisque causa vel eadem est cum effectibus vel cognata. Quando igitur formam vel figuram deo negamus, non defectum aliquem suspicamur, qualem cum cogitamus infiguratam informemque materiam, sed deum nullo circumscriptum materiam formis atque figuris circumscribere contemplamur, siquidem de deo sicut de materia negantes omnia per similitudinem quandam dissimilem, volumus eadem de utriusque negata. Solemus et animam naturamque dicere, quoniam nec oculos neque pedes habet eadem conditione qua corpus, ideo haec in corpore generare. Similiter unum ipsum dicit neque totum esse neque partem neque idem neque alterum neque stare neque mo-

tions, and, as though it were now uncircumscribed, place it before God, who is utterly uncircumscribed.[28]

Nor are we unaware, either, that the negations about God do 2 not signify a defect, but an excess, as we often say in agreement with Dionysius.[29] When we say that God is neither mind, nor life, nor essence, we mean that He transcends all of them and is their principle. Now denying of the artisan his hands signifies a defect, for the artisan needs instruments to be an artisan; however, when we deny "hands" of nature, we disclose the excellence of nature, which requires no hands to act. Surely, just as the first principle is the cause of all things, so skillful negations made about the first principle stand as causes of the assertions made about secondary ones. For this reason, all the things that the first hypothesis denies of the One are asserted in the second hypothesis to reveal that all things are created by it, for the very reason that it is not any of these things, but equally transcends them all. Indeed, even as the soul or nature generates and governs the body because they are not a body, and just as the intellect creates the soul because it is not a soul, even so the One creates multitude, number and shape precisely because it is neither multitude, nor number, nor shape. For it cannot be any of the things that it creates. Indeed no other eminent and universal cause is the same as, or akin to, its own effects. So when we deny of God form or shape, we do not conceive this as a defect, as in the case of shapeless and formless matter, but we contemplate a God who is circumscribed by nothing circumscribing matter by means of shapes and forms: by denying all things of God as well as of matter — the two being similar in their dissimilarity[30] — we wish to deny the same things of both of them. We also usually say that soul and nature generate corporeal eyes and feet precisely because they do not possess eyes or feet according to a corporeal condition. Likewise, Parmenides says that the One is neither whole nor part, neither same nor different, neither at rest nor in motion, neither any one of these opposites nor any pair of

veri neque simpliciter oppositorum aliquod neque ambo ut possit
haec omnia pariter agere, nec ipsum est alicui simile, ne cogatur
cum aliquo in superiore quadam similitudinis causa convenire,
immo ut omnem similitudinem possit efficere, nec ullis opponitur,
ne forte alicui oppositionis causae sit subiectum, immo ut oppositiones omnes ab ipso dependeant.

: LV :

De uno ente, de ipso simpliciter uno, de intentione
Parmenidis hic et in poemate, intentio
et epilogus negationum.

1 Operae pretium forte fuerit repetere breviter in praesentia quod
saepe iam diximus, rationem unitatis a ratione entis esse diversam.
Illa enim omnem respuit multitudinem, hoc vero non renuit. Illa
rursus non minus competit informi passivaeque potentiae quam
caeteris, hoc autem multo minus. Est denique propter necessariam
simplicitatem unitas prior ente, et qui negat unum latius negat
quam qui negat esse. Hinc sapientes nominum conditores inte-
gram privationem non appellavere οὐδ'ὄν, quod non ens Graece
significaret, sed οὐδ'ἕν, quod significat non unum, id est penitus
nihilum. Non praedicant proprie de uno 'est' aut 'ens' aut 'essentiam,' sed 'existit' potius atque 'existentiam,' significantes per haec
efficacem et simplicem ipsius unius actum atque praesentiam,
quamquam neque hanc praedicationem esse volunt, ne qua compositio fiat, sed simplicem prorsus intuitum.

opposites, to allow for the fact that the One equally creates all these things. The One itself is not like anything else, lest it be compelled to converge in some higher principle by means of some cause of likeness — or to be more precise, so that it can create all likeness, and not be in opposition to something, lest it chance to be subject to some cause of opposition — or to be yet more precise, so that all oppositions may depend on it.[31]

: LV :

On the one being, the absolute One, and the purpose of Parmenides in this dialogue and in his poem. The purpose and summary of the negations.

It might be worth repeating briefly here what we have already said   1 many times: the rational principle of unity is different from that of being. The former rejects all multitude, while the latter does not; the former is as much in accordance with passive and formless potentiality as it is with any other potentiality, while the latter is much less so. Finally, by virtue of its necessary simplicity, unity has precedence over being, and a person denies more by denying the existence of unity than by denying that of being.[32] Hence the wise inventors of names did not call pure privation *oud'on*, which means "not-being" in Greek, but *oud'hen*, which means "not-one," that is, total nothingness. They do not properly predicate of the One "is," "being" or "essence," but rather "exists" and "existence," whereby they designate the One's efficient and simple act as well as its presence, although they do not mean this as a predication, lest this imply some composition, but they only mean this as simple intuition.

2   Proinde Melissus Parmenidis discipulus in *Sophiste* ante multa entia unum ens excogitat. In quolibet enim ordine multa talia ad unum tale superius reducuntur. Unum vero ens ad unam simpliciter unitatem refert, cuius unum ens tamquam posterius est necessario particeps, neque contra fingendum est unitatem similiter entis esse participem, alioquin non simplex iam foret unitas, sed multiplex aliquid atque compositum. Probat deinde hoc unum ens esse totum quiddam atque multiplex, in quo alia sit entis ratio, alia unitatis, idque universum ens omnium quidem entium fontem existimat iudicandum, sed posterius uno. De hoc quidem uno ente proprie librum teste Melisso Parmenides poetico stilo composuit, tamquam de secundo principio (primum enim ineffabile), affirmans[3] de ipso multa quae hic in prima suppositione de uno negantur, in secunda de uno ente similiter affirmantur. Itaque cum Parmenides ait se incepturum ab uno, discrimen significat inter se atque Zenonem in exordio disputandi (Zeno enim a multitudine cepit, hic ab uno) atque cum de uno negentur hic omnia, quando Parmenides hic ait se a suo illo uno facturum disputationis exordium, non debemus intellegere proprie ab uno ente, sed ab ipso simpliciter uno, cuius hoc unum ens est compos, ideoque ab hoc e vestigio scandit ad illud, in illo primum omnia negaturus, in hoc deinde affirmaturus, omnia quae et affirmaverat in poemate, esse scilicet universum, intellegibile, sphaericum atque similia. Primum quidem, quoniam est ipsa simpliciter unitas, id est suprema simplicitas atque virtus, quod proxime generat, maxime generat unum, et quoniam genitor ad nullum omnium habet propriam habitudinem, sed aeque se habet ad omnia et pariter est super omnia, aut nullum facit, quod dictu nefas, aut in illo, quod modo dicebamus,

In the *Sophist* Parmenides' disciple Melissus develops the notion 2
that the one being is prior to the multiplicity of beings, since any
given multiplicity in each order is reduced to its own, superior
"one," while the one being is reduced to the absolute and unique
Unity, which the one being is inferior to and necessarily participates in. One must not imagine the contrary, i.e. that Unity would
partake of being, otherwise Unity would cease to be simple and
would be something multiple and composite. Melissus next demonstrates that the one being is a whole and multiple, in which the
rational principle of being differs from that of unity, and this universal being must be considered, he says, the source of all beings,
but is inferior to the One.[33] According to Melissus, Parmenides
composed a poem about this very one being, as though it were the
second principle (for the first principle is ineffable), asserting of it
many things which are denied of the One in the first hypothesis,
and are similarly asserted of the one being in the second hypothesis. So when Parmenides declares that he will start from the One
[137B], he indicates right at the beginning of the discussion the
issue at stake between himself and Zeno, for Zeno starts from the
many, Parmenides from the One. Since all things are denied of the
One in the first hypothesis, when Parmenides here declares that he
will start the discussion from his own "one," we should not understand that he properly starts from the one being, but from the
absolute One, on which depends the one being, and so he immediately ascends from the one being to the One, in order to first
deny in the first hypothesis, and then assert in the second, all the
attributes that he had asserted in his poem: "universal," "intelligible," "spherical" and so on. Since the first principle is the absolute
Unity, that is, the highest simplicity and power, the thing it most
closely generates is "one" to the highest degree, and because the
Creator has no proper relation with anything among his creation,
but is equally disposed toward all things and transcends them all
equally, then either He does nothing, which is a wicked thing to

uno simul efficit omnia. Dicimus itaque cum Plotino simul atque Parmenide primum quidem esse unum super omnia, secundum vero unum omnia, ut perfectissimi genitoris progenies sit omnium perfectissima. Quomodo autem genitor genitumque sit unum in *Christiana Theologia* tractamus. Plato, quem nunc interpretamur, duo putavisse videtur. Sed pergamus ad reliqua.

3   Negationes vero circa primum fiunt non tam propter imbecilitatem intellegentiae nostrae non valentis aliter circa illud agere (nam et neque aliter circa idem agit intellectus primus), quam quia nec aliter illud attingi potest aut debet, nec aliter intellectus attingere, quam sua multiplici proprietate posthabita unitati unitatem simpliciter offerendo.

4   Epilogus autem et ordo negationum in prima suppositione est eiusmodi: ipsum unum neque multitudo est neque totum neque partem habet. Rursus nec habet principium nec medium neque finem aliquem aut terminum, neque figuram nec est in alio nec in seipso neque stat neque movetur nec idem est nec alterum, vel sibimet vel aliis, neque simile neque dissimile nec aequale nec inaequale neque maius neque minus. Item non senius, non iunius neque generationem participat neque tempus neque est particeps ipsius quod dicitur esse nec est nominabile nec effabile nec opinabile neque scibile.

say, or He creates all things simultaneously within the one being, as we have just mentioned. So we say, in agreement with Plotinus and Parmenides, that the first One is beyond all things and that the second one is all things, as the most perfect progeny of the most perfect Creator. In our treatise *On Christian Theology* we examine the way in which the Creator and his progeny are one.[34] Plato, whom we are now interpreting, seems to have considered that there were two substances. But let us pass on to what remains.

Negations are made of the One less because human intelligence, 3 which is unable to grasp the One in any other way, is too weak (indeed, even the first intellect [only] knows the One through negations), than because the One cannot and must not be grasped in any other way, nor can the intellect know it in any other way than by leaving aside the multiplicity proper to itself, and by simply offering its own unity to Unity.

Here, in conclusion, is the order of negations in the first hy- 4 pothesis: the One is not many; it is neither a whole nor a part; it has neither beginning nor middle nor end nor limit; it has no shape; it is neither in anything else nor in itself; it is neither at rest nor in motion; it is neither the same as, nor different from, itself and the others; it is neither like nor unlike, neither equal nor unequal nor greater nor smaller. Likewise it is neither older nor younger; it does not partake of generation or time; it does not partake of that which is said "to be"; it is neither nameable nor expressible; it is the object neither of opinion nor knowledge.[35]

: LVI :

*De universo ente et proprietatibus eius, et quomodo
negantur de primo et quae multitudo
negatur et quare negatur.*

1 Saepe probavimus in commentariis in Plotinum, quem in hoc
sicut et in pluribus libentius quam Proclum sequor, intellectum,
intellegibile, ens primum, essentiam, vitamque primam re ipsa
unam esse substantiam, haec autem ibi quadam ratione differre in
qua et quinque rerum genera ideaeque sunt formali inter se ratione
distinctae. Essentia enim prima cum omnes perfectiones essentiae
habeat, vitam habet et intellectum (primam inquam vitam intellectumque primum), si perfectus intellectus est perfectam habens intellegentiam, intellegibile quoque possidet penitissimum. Quod si
quis ipsum intellegibile ab hoc separet per essentiam, cogemur
deinde confiteri intellegibile primum tamquam perfectum sibi ipsi
intellegibile fore, igitur intellegentiam in se habere. Utrimque igitur redimus ad idem, utrobique videlicet intellectum cum intellegibili in eadem essentia copulare coacti, in qua omnia intellegibilia atque entia intellegibiliter et intellectualiter comprehendantur.
Hunc mundum appellamus intellegibilem; universam hanc sphaeram intellegibilem Parmenides in poemate canit unumque ens
inscribit, quod in *Sophiste* esse quidem ens primum, sed non esse
vere unum, quia non sit impartibile dicitur, itaque nec esse primum unum, quod tamquam vere unum est penitus impartibile,[4]
nullius particeps multitudinis, alioquin et unius foret particeps,
itaque nec esset verum primumque unum, ad quod tandem ab uno
minus vero pervenire ratio cogit, quemadmodum et compellit supra non veras formas, non veram vitam, non veram cognitionem

: LVI :

On the universal being and its properties, and how these are denied of the first principle. Which multitude is denied of the One, and why.

We have often shown in our commentary on Plotinus (whom I 1
follow more readily than Proclus on this matter, as well as on
many others) that the intellect, the intelligible, the first being, essence, and the first life constitute in reality one single substance,
but that they differ in the intelligible realm in that the five genera
of things and the Ideas are formally distinct from one another.[36]
Since the first essence possesses all the perfections of essence, it
also possesses life and intellect (I mean the first life and the first
intellect); since the perfect intellect is that which possesses perfect
intelligence, it also possesses its innermost intelligible object. Yet if
someone distinguishes the essence of this intelligible object from
that of the intellect, one will then be forced to admit that the first
intelligible, because it is perfect, will be intelligible to itself and
thus possess intelligence within itself. Thus in both cases we come
back to the same starting-point: we are led to unite the intellect
and the intelligible within the same essence, which contains all intelligibles and beings in an intelligible and intellectual way. This
we call the intelligible world; this is the universal intelligible sphere
that Parmenides celebrates in his poem and labels the one being.
As stated in the *Sophist*,[37] it is the first being, and not the One,
since it is not indivisible; it is not, therefore, the first One, since
the real One is completely indivisible and thus partakes of no multitude. Otherwise it would also partake of the One, and would
therefore not be the real and first One. This argument ultimately
forces us to reach beyond the one that is less real, just as we are
compelled to proceed beyond the forms, life and cognition that are

progredi ad veras formas, id est ideas, ad vitam cognitionemque
veram.

2   Si mundus intellegibilis est ens primum atque formale principiumque[5] entium omnium et exemplar, forma naturaque sua omnia generans atque formans, quaecumque sibi sunt propria, eadem
entibus cunctis, qua entia, competunt, atque vicissim quaecumque
entibus, qua ratione formaliter entia sunt et in sua quaeque specie
perfecta, conveniunt haec, sed excellentius sunt in illo. Iamblichus et Syrianus et Proclus oppositionales[6] generum idearumque
differentias in primo ente non ponunt, quia cum proxime sit ab
ipso uno ideoque[7] sit unitissimum, oppositiones admittere nequit,
praesertim quia[8] in primo ente nihil sit non entis, ergo nec oppositiones illae per quas idem non est alterum, status non est motus,
rationale non est brutum, ignis non est aqua, homo non est equus.
Item quia ens simpliciter de quolibet praedicatur, nullum vero oppositorum, nulla idea de quolibet affirmatur, ut traditur in *Sophiste*,
igitur eiusmodi differentias in sequente quadam post essentiam
simplicem, intellectuali essentia, collocant; in illa vero tantum originem numeralem. Nos autem antiquiores secuti dicimus differentias illas in ente primo ponendas, sed eas non primo quidem
gradu, quo simpliciter ens est, sed sequente quodam gradu, quo
per vitam intellegentiamque progreditur explicari. Sic enim obiec-
tiones quas narravimus devitantur et in primo ente entium omnium propria tamquam illud mox consequentia collocantur. Quinque sane genera in essentia iam vivente, ideae potius in vivo iam
intellectuali, latius explicantur; vix enim in essentia discernuntur.
Insunt tamen ibi propria cunctis entibus communiter necessaria.
Propria vero haec generatim omnia Parmenides in prima supposi-

not real, toward the real forms, that is, the Ideas, and to real life and cognition.

If the intelligible world is the first and formal being, as well as 2 the principle and model of all beings, if it generates and forms all things according to its own form and nature, then whatever properties belong to it also belong to all beings *qua* beings, and conversely all the properties belonging to beings, inasmuch as they are formally beings and each perfect in their own species, are in agreement [with each other], although they exist in the intelligible world in a more eminent way. Iamblichus, Syrianus and Proclus[38] do not locate the differentiae and contradictions among genera and Ideas within the first being, because the first being, as it is the closest to the One and thus the most united, cannot admit any contradictions, especially as there is no not-being in the first being, and thus none of those contradictions either whereby the same is not the other, rest is not motion, the rational is not brute, fire is not water, man is not horse. Likewise, because simple being is predicated of everything, whereas no contradiction nor any Idea is asserted of everything, as stated in the *Sophist*,[39] they locate these differentiae in an essence that follows simple essence, the intellectual essence; they place only the origin of number in simple essence.[40] By contrast, we declare, following older authorities, that these differentiae should be located in the first being, but that they do not unfold at the first level, where the simple being lies, but at the following level, where being proceeds through life and intelligence.[41] In this way, the objections mentioned above are avoided and the properties of all beings are placed within the first being, as immediately consequent upon it. Surely the five genera [of being] unfold more widely in the essence that is already alive, while the Ideas unfold more widely in the intellectual order that is already alive; for within essence, genera and Ideas are hardly distinct from one another, whereas in the first being there are the necessary properties that are common to all beings. Parmenides enumerates

tione numerat, ut in capite superiore narravimus, in uno quidem negans, sed in uno ente mox affirmans, ut postquam omnia universi entis propria de uno primo negaverit, demonstret inde ipsum universo ente superius, quod et prope suppositionis primae finem manifeste confirmat, negans ipsum quod dicitur esse atque ens de uno, alioquin quaecumque esse ensque ipsum comitantur atque sequuntur competitura primo, quae tamen propter diversitatem suam simplicissimo, immo ipsi simplicitati, competere nequeunt. Quo enim pacto multitudo universitasque differentium inter se idearum, quomodo generum oppositio, scilicet identitas, alteritas, status, motus, item simile, dissimile, aequale, inaequale, atque similia, quae ibi ideales inferiorum proprietatum rationes sunt, absolute inter se differentes primo consentanea sunt?

3   Syrianus inter haec et Proclus omnium conclusionum capita deos quosdam seorsum existentes esse putant, ut et multitudo sit deus quidam et ipsa pars sit deus alius, alius quoque totum, rursus recta figura et sphaerica et iuventus atque senectus, similitudo, dissimilitudo, caeteraque sint numina quaedam, quae per omnes consequentias negativas quidem decernantur inferiora primo, affirmativas autem deinceps suo quoque ordine disponantur. Sed inventum hoc poeticum potius quam philosophicum esse videtur. Nobis vero satis esto haec tamquam propria quaedam entis universi recipere, quae et in primo ente suo modo sint atque sequentibus, meminisseque Parmenidem a proprietatibus magis universalibus, ubi negat incipere, deincepsque ad minus universales consequenti quadam serie progredi. Sic enim negatis illis consequenter negantur et ista, quemadmodum si quis neget hoc esse

all these properties in their several kinds within the first hypothesis, as expounded in the previous chapter, by denying their existence in the One and then asserting their existence in the one being. In this way, after having denied of the first One all the properties of universal being, he then demonstrates that the One is superior to universal being, as he also clearly confirms nearer the end of the first hypothesis, when he denies of the One the attributes "to be" and "being." If this were not the case, all the things that follow or accompany "to be" as well as "being" would be in accordance with the first principle. Yet because of their diversity they cannot be in accordance with that which is the simplest, or rather that which is simplicity itself. How, indeed, can the multitude and the universality of Ideas which differ from one another, how can the contradictions between genera (sameness, otherness, rest, motion, like, unlike, equal, unequal, and so on), which yonder are the ideal rational principles of properties inferior to it — how can these be in accordance with the first principle, while they differ from one another in an absolute way?

As to Syrianus and Proclus, they consider that the chapters of 3 all the conclusions correspond to separate gods. For instance, they consider that "multitude" is a god, "part" is another god, "whole" another, and likewise the attributes "straight" and "spherical," "youth" and "old age," "similitude" and "dissimilitude" and so on, correspond to some divinities, which are shown to be inferior to the first principle through all the negative conclusions of the first hypothesis, then arranged each in its own order through assertions.[42] But this contrivance seems more poetic than philosophical. It suffices to accept these realities as the properties of universal being, which exist in their own way in the first being and in the beings that follow, and to remember that in the negations Parmenides passes from the most universal to the less universal properties in a logical sequence, so that by denying the former he consequently denies the latter too. For instance, when one denies that

animal, negaverit esse hominem, neque e converso; affirmando
vero contra contingit, nempe si affirmes hominem, affirmaveris
animal, neque fit vicissim. Quoniam vero a notioribus ubique rite
incipiendum est ut per ea possimus facile minus nota dinoscere,
merito in conclusionibus negativis negat primo, quod ab uno manifestius est alienum, scilicet multitudinem, per hanc consequenter
quae aliena minus post plurima negat essentiam aut esse, quod
quasi videbatur idem neque tamen idem est, ac si adhibeatur uni
compositionem vel proprietatem affert. Postremo negat ipsum
unum esse aliquid unum, ne forte sit vel duo quaedam, scilicet
aliquid simul et unum, aut certe sit in genere quodam vel ordine
unum atque definitum. Plato igitur in *Epistolis* vetat de ipso omnium primo quaerere, quale sit vel quale quid sit. Conditiones
enim eiusmodi eminentiam ubique deiciunt atque definiunt, sicut
qualis vita, qualis essentia, quale bonum, similiter quale vel quid
unum.

4   In conclusionibus autem affirmativis id prius affirmabit de uno
ente, id est de illo intellegibili mundo, unum atque ens, mox praeter essentiam unitatemque suam, quod ipsi potissimum est cognatum, scilicet multitudinem, multitudinem inquam idealium specierum atque generum. Per haec apprime familiaria tamquam
evidentissima quaedam affirmabit quae familiaria minus deinceps
atque minus. Ideo suppositio prima non est 'si universum ens est
unum, quid sequatur,' alioquin semel posito quod sit ens et universum, id est omnia, mox inferendum esset, ergo habet in se
multitudinem, partes, terminos, et caetera essentiamque postremo.
Contra vero negantur haec omnia, quia suppositio non est 'si om-

something is an animal, one also denies that it is a man, but not the opposite; and conversely in assertions the contrary occurs: when one asserts that something is a man, one also asserts that it is an animal, but not the opposite. But since one should rightly first consider, in relation to the One, the attributes that are more familiar to us, which will in turn help us consider more easily its relation with the attributes that are less familiar, in the negative conclusions Parmenides rightly denies first what is more clearly alien to the One, that is, multitude, and then, as a consequence, what is less clearly alien to it: after having denied multitude, he denies essence, or being. Essence appeared to be the same as the One, as it were, yet it is not, since attributing essence to the One would be to add a composition or apply a property to the One. Finally, he denies that the One is some one thing, lest it be two, that is, both "something" and "one," or at any rate something that is one and defined within a given genus or order.[43] So in the *Letters* Plato forbids inquiry about anything regarding the first principle of all things, of what quality it is,[44] for conditions such as "which life," "which essence," "which good," "which or what one" always undermine and limit the One's eminence.

By contrast, in the affirmative conclusions Parmenides will first 4 assert of the one being (that is, the intelligible world) the attributes "one" and "being," and then, after its essence and unity, he asserts what is most akin to it, that is, multitude, and by multitude I mean the multitude of Ideal species and genera. Through these attributes, which are the most easily understandable to us, he will assert the attributes that are progressively less akin to the one being.[45] So the first hypothesis is not "if the universal being is one, what follows?" Otherwise, once we postulate the existence of that which is being and universal, that is, all things, we would then have to infer that it possesses within itself multitude, parts, limits and so on, and essence in the last instance. Instead, all these attributes are denied, because the hypothesis is not "if all things are

nia sint unum,' sed 'si ipsum unum sit,' cuius oppositum post
quinque suppositiones[9] etiam supponetur, scilicet 'si unum non sit,
quid inde[10] sequatur?'

5   Sed ubi multitudinem negat uni, quam potissimum multitudinem? Non rerum quidem sensibilium aut etiam seminalium rationum aut rursus animalium cogitationum (neque enim decebat in
his reiciendis elaborare quae de primo nullus assereret), sed multitudinem illam de primo negat quam asseret de secundo, id est intellectualem intellegibilemque[11] multitudinem, id est multiplicitatem talem, qualis convenit intellectui primo seipsum intellegenti,
idearum generumque pleno,[12] eademque sequentibus convenit[13]
intellectibus puris atque divinis. Primo tamen omnium principio
minime competit, si modo multitudo quaelibet sit unitate posterior, si etiam in ipso vere primo nihil debet esse non primum, si
rursus in immensa virtute unitas et simplicitas vigeat infinita, si
denique in illo quod seipso perfectissime fruitur, nihil oporteat
esse non ipsum. Sed de mira simplicitate primi et de formali mul-
tiplicate secundi saepe et multa diximus cum Plotino.

6   Quaeret forte quispiam an multitudo uni sit opposita. Respondemus opposita versari circa subiectum idem, ut circa numerum
par et impar, circa dimensionem aequale et inaequale, circa qualitatem simile et dissimile, circa substantiam idem atque alterum,
circa motum velox atque tardum, circa essentiam unum atque
multitudo. In qua quidem, sicut multitudo non est seorsum ab
unione, ita nec unum seorsum a multitudine. Est enim unum hoc
multitudinis unum, quod quidem non est multitudo, quamvis in
multitudine situm, neque qua ratione unum est esse potest multa,
sed qua conditione est multitudinis unum, hac utique unum multa
nominari potest. Ipsum vero super essentiam et extra numerum
essentialem simpliciter unum adeo est absolutum, ut multitudo

one," but "if the One exists," the opposite of which is also postulated in the sixth hypothesis, that is, "if the one does not exist, what follows?"

When he denies multitude of the One, which multitude does 5 he deny above all others? Surely not the multitude of sensible realities, seminal reasons, or even that of thoughts in the soul (for it would not make much sense to attempt to deny attributes that no one would assert of the first principle) — but he denies of the first principle the multitude that he asserts of the second principle, that is, the intellectual and intelligible multitude, that is, a multitude such as befits the first intellect (which knows itself and is full of Ideas and genera), as well as the pure and divine intellects that follow.[46] This multitude does not, however, befit the first principle of all things: firstly, every multitude is inferior to unity; secondly, there must be nothing in the truly first principle that is not first; thirdly, unity and simplicity are infinite in the immensity of their power; finally, within the principle that enjoys itself most perfectly there is nothing that could not be the principle itself. But we have often discussed in our commentary on Plotinus the admirable simplicity of the first principle and the formal multitude of the second.

We might wonder whether multitude contradicts the one. The 6 answer is that contradictories are related to the same subject. For instance, odd and even are related to number, equal and unequal to dimension, like and unlike to quality, the same and the other to substance, quick and slow to motion, one and multitude to essence. Within essence, the one is not separated from multitude, just as multitude is not separated from union: in this case the one is the unity of a multitude; it is not itself a multitude, but is *within* a multitude; as one, it cannot be many, although as the unity of the multitude it can be called one and many. But the simple One beyond essence and essential number is so absolutely One that multitude is not so much considered contradictory of, as different

huic non tam opposita iudicetur quam diversa. Sicut enim primus calor, prima lux, prima essentia, primum bonum nihil habent frigidi vel tenebrosi vel non ens vel non bonum, ita primum unum nihil non unum admittit, multitudinem omnem prorsus expellit sibi diversam. Si enim multitudo sit in eo, ut Platonice loquar, non unum ipsum erit, sed unitum, nec a seipso unitum, sicut et quod formatum est aliunde formatum, igitur ab ipso simpliciter uno superiore erit unitum. Quomodo vero Platonicae rationes multitudinem primo tollentes Christianae trinitati non detrahant, in qua, servata penitus simplicitate et unitate naturae, relatio quaedam sola quandam distinctionem facit, compositionem vero nullam, Nicolaus theologus Graecus Methones episcopus[14] evidenter ostendit ac nos in adnotationibus quibusdam in eum breviter designamus.

7   Concludamus denique cum Platonicis, ubi Plato multitudinem negat uni, nihil aliud velle quam et ipsum supra quam cogitari possit simplicissimum secretissimumque esse, et universam ab eo rerum multitudinem, ferme[15] sicut ab unitate numeros, proficisci. Quod autem hic unum nominat ente superius, in *Republica* nominat bonum similiter super essentiam. Ut autem accipimus ex *Phaedone* simul atque *Parmenide,* idem est proprium unius atque boni, scilicet perficere omnia atque continere et pariter per omnia propagari. Praeterea nihil ipso bono melius, nihil ergo superius, nihil etiam simplicius uno, nihil igitur super unum, alioquin quod superius fingitur aut nihil est aut multitudo unionis expers infiniteque infinita. Cum vero duo esse principia nequeant, idem est penitus unum atque bonum, sed unum quidem, ut alibi diximus, propter singularitatem et excellentem simplicitatem, bonum vero propter fecunditatem communicationemque amplissimam nominamus.

from it. Just as the first heat, the first light, the first essence, and the first good do not possess anything cold, dark, not-being or not-good, in the same way the first One does not admit anything that is not-one, and it utterly rejects all multitude, because multitude differs from it. If indeed multitude exists within a "one," to speak Platonically, it will not be the One itself, but united; it will not be united by itself (in the same way that what is formed is formed by another) and consequently it will not be united by a superior principle, the absolute One. But the Platonic reasoning that abolishes multitude from the first principle is not in disagreement with the Christian Trinity, wherein, while preserving nature's simplicity and unity, there is only a sort of relation that creates a distinction, but no composition. This has been clearly shown by the Greek theologian and priest Nicholas of Methone and briefly indicated in the annotations I have made on his work.[47]

Let us finally conclude, together with the Platonists, that when 7 Plato denies multitude of the One, he means precisely that the one is the utterly simple and unknowable and hidden One, and that the universal multitude of things proceeds from the One in almost the same way as numbers proceed from unity. What he calls here the One superior to being, he calls the One above essence in the *Republic*.[48] Yet as we have learned from the *Phaedo*[49] and the *Parmenides*, the One and the Good have in common the ability to perfect and contain all things, and to propagate themselves equally through all things. In addition, nothing is better than the Good, and thus nothing is superior; nothing is simpler than the One, and thus nothing is superior to it, otherwise what is imagined to be superior would either be nothing or a multitude deprived of unity and infinitely infinite. Given that there cannot be two principles, the One and the Good are the same principle, and, as we have said elsewhere, the first principle is called "One" on account of its singularity and excellent simplicity, and "Good" on account of its most extended fecundity and communicability.[50]

: LVII :

Per negationem multitudinis negantur de uno partes et totum.
Numerus est ante entia,[16] *omnis multitudo particeps*
unitatis. Idem est prima essentia, vita, mens.

1   Ubicumque Parmenides aliquid de uno negat, memento, ut alibi
monui, significari non modo deum non esse illud tamquam super
illud, sed etiam illud a deo fieri, deo interim propter effectum
nullo modo inclinato vel aliter se habente. Cum ergo primum multitudo negetur, designatur et deum nullo modo esse multiplicabilem et primum quod fit ex deo multitudinem esse atque universam
in uno collectam, in uno scilicet intellegibili mundo, sicut ab unitate duitatem[17] in qua omnes numeri continentur. Cum rursus
secundo negetur deum esse totum aliquod partesve habere, designatur, praeter id quod nullo modo compositus est, omnem
compositionem praesertim primam ab eo fieri. Nempe propter ipsum simpliciter unum et quaelibet partium unum aliquid est et
invicem omnes in unam totius formam conciliantur. Prima vero
compositio inde in ipso intellegibili mundo conficitur ex infinitate
et termino, tamquam ex materia quadam atque forma, item ex
essentia, vita, intellegentia, rursus quodammodo ex generibus primis entium et ideis.

2   Praeterea, ut alibi diximus, in negativis conclusionibus rite a
propositionibus magis universalibus debemus incipere (si non est
animal, ergo nec homo), in affirmativis vero contra (si est homo,
ergo animal). Itaque cum Parmenides per ipsam multitudinis ne-

: LVII :

*By denying multitude we also deny "parts" and "whole" of the
One. Number precedes beings; every multitude partakes of
unity. The first essence, life, and mind are identical.*

Whenever Parmenides denies something of the One, you should   1
bear in mind, as I suggested elsewhere, that this not only signifies
that God *is not* the thing denied, in the sense that He is superior
to it, but also that the thing denied is created by God, while God
is by no means affected or altered by the effect He has caused.
Therefore, since multitude is the first attribute to be denied of the
One [137C4–5], it means that God is by no means manifold, that
multitude is the first thing to come into existence from God, and
this first multitude is gathered as a whole into a one, that is, the
intelligible world, just as duality, which contains all numbers, derives its existence from unity. Since whole and parts are the second
attributes to be denied of God [137C5–6], it means that, separately from that which is not composite, every composition (especially the first) comes into existence from God. Surely it is thanks
to the absolute One that every part is some one thing, and that all
parts are united to one another within the single form of the
whole.[51] The first composition, which comes into existence in the
intelligible world from God, results from the mixture of infinity
(as matter) and limit (as form), as well as essence, life, intelligence,
and also the first genera of beings and the Ideas.[52]

In addition, as we have said elsewhere, in the negative conclu-   2
sions we must appropriately begin first with the more universal
propositions (for instance, the proposition "if this is not an animal,
it is not a man") and, conversely in the assertive conclusions, one
must first deny the less universal propositions (for instance, "if this
is a man, it is an animal"). So when Parmenides denies the attri-

gationem consequenter neget totum atque partes, declarat multitudinem esse universaliorem partibus atque toto. Inquit enim si
unum est aliquid totum ideoque habet et partes, necessario erit
multa. Merito dum affirmat, a rebus magis particularibus incipit
(ut si est homo, ergo est et animal; similiter si est totum, necessario partes habens est et multa sive multitudo). Hoc enim consequens antecedente universalius est. Quo rursus negato, scilicet
unum non est multa, statim negatur quod modo fuerat antecedens, dum infertur 'si non est multa, ergo non totum est neque
partes habet.'

3   Quod autem multa vel multitudo sit universalius atque prius,
hinc patet quia quodlibet totum ex partibus conficitur multis. Partes quoque sunt ubique multae et hae referuntur ad totum atque
vicissim (non tamen omnia multa videlicet, si seiuncta sint); sunt
partes alicuius conficiuntve totum. Accedit ad haec quod multitudo, qua ratione multitudo est, nullum certum decernit sibi
finem, immo suapte natura occurrere videtur deinceps multiplica-
bilis infinite. Partes autem ad unam totius formam conditione
propria conspirantes sunt sub terminata quadam totius specie
terminatae. Denique multa etiam, si numquam coeant, simpliciter
multa sunt, partes vero fiunt totumque conflant, quando coierint,
et certa quadam ratione coierint. Multitudo igitur in ordine rerum
totum antecedit et partes.

4   Quomodo vero sicut unum antecedit ens, sic et multitudo vel
numerus in mundo intellegibili antecedat entia numerosa et com-
positiones totorum quaslibet, sive ibidem sive in sequentibus subinde fiant, satis in libris *De Ideis* et *Generibus entis* et *Numeris*
diximus cum Plotino. Nisi enim in primo ente formali entium

butes "whole" and "parts" as a consequence of denying the attribute "multitude," he means that "multitude" is more universal than "parts" and "whole." For he says that if the one is a whole and thus possesses parts, it will necessarily be many [137C8–10]. When using assertions, he rightly starts with the more particular things: for instance, "if this is a man, it is therefore an animal"; likewise, "if this is a whole, it necessarily possesses parts and is many or a multitude." For the consequent is more universal than the premise, and, when the consequent is denied (i.e. when it is said that the one is not many), we immediately deny what was initially the premise, since we infer that "if the one is not many, it is not a whole and it does not have parts."53

That the attributes "many" or "multitude" are more universal   3
and superior is clear from the fact that every whole is composed of a multitude of parts. In addition, the parts are always many; they are related to their whole and vice versa (they would not all be many if they were detached and separate); they are parts of something and form a whole. Moreover, multitude *qua* multitude does not provide itself with a fixed limit, but seems to be infinitely manifold by virtue of its own nature, while the parts, which act in concert under the single form of the whole, are encompassed and limited by the species of the whole by virtue of their own condition. Finally, if the many are never united, they are simply many; but when they are united (and are united in a particular way), they become parts and form a whole. Therefore, multitude precedes the whole and parts in the order of things.54

The way in which, just as the One precedes being, multitude or   4
number in the intelligible world precede the multiplied beings and all the compositions that result in wholes (whether in the intelligible world or at the following levels), we have amply discussed in our commentary on Plotinus' treatises *On the Ideas, On the Genera of Beings* and *On Numbers*.55 Indeed, if the rational principles of nature did not reside in the first formal being, which is the source

multorum fonte naturales quaedam rationes inessent atque praecederent, ad quarum quasi normam distribueretur entium multitudo, omnis utique turba rerum vel hic vel ibi sorte quadam absque ordine certoque numero vel termino vel fine contingeret.

5   Proinde si primam[18] quaerimus causam multitudinis, eandem inveniemus huius atque unionis originem. Quod enim res quaelibet atque cunctae quodammodo unum sint, extra controversiam habent ab ipso simpliciter uno, quod et saepe unitatem ipsam cognominamus; quod rursus multae sint accipiunt ab eodem. Multae namque sunt per ipsam multitudinem, sicut unum per unitatem. Ipsa vero multitudo non, inquam, haec vel illa aut horum aut illorum, sed ipsa per se simpliciter multitudo, nihil est aliud quam unitates quaedam ab ipsa simpliciter unitate fecundae, propagatae passim atque distributae. Non recipient ergo Platonici Peripateticum illud, unitatem multitudinemve ad ens ipsum quasi conditiones quasdam eius quodammodo sequi, sed praecedere potius, quatenus ex ipso simpliciter uno ad ens et entia derivantur latiusque unum praedicari quam ens, siquidem privationes quaelibet ita ut habitus dicuntur unum. Sicut enim visus unus, vox una, ita caecitas una unumque silentium, opinio vera unum aliquid, falsitas unum aliquid. Amplius quoque multitudinem quam ens praedicari, quippe cum non res ipsae solum multae, sed rerum etiam privationes multae dicantur, non solum praesentia multa, sed et futura pariter atque praeterita, multae opiniones verae, multae falsae. Unitas igitur unitatumque multitudo, quae et simplex primaque multitudo est, videtur ordinem entium antecedere. Quod igitur haec entia sint non solum efficienter ab uno, sed etiam a primo

of the multitude of beings, and had no precedence over them, then the whole mass of things (whether in the intelligible or in the sensible world) would exist by chance, without order, number, end or limit, because the rational principles of nature constitute the norm, so to speak, according to which the multitude of beings is distributed.

So if we are looking for the first cause of multitude, we will find 5 that it is also the origin of union. The fact that things have unity both individually and collectively can indisputably be inferred from the existence of the absolute One, which we also frequently call Unity. Conversely we can infer the fact that things are many from the existence of the One, since many exist by virtue of multitude as such, just as a one exists by virtue of unity — and by multitude I do not mean any multitude of any given things, but multitude as such, simply in itself, which is nothing other than certain fecund unities [henads] that are propagated everywhere and distributed by the absolute Unity itself. Thus the Platonists will reject the Peripatetic doctrine according to which unity and multitude, inasmuch as they are the conditions of being, somehow come after being.[56] In reality, unity and multitude precede being, inasmuch as they are derived from the absolute One into being and beings, and "one" is predicated more extensively than "being," since both privations and dispositions are said to be "one." For example, blindness and silence are "one," just as vision and voice are "one"; true opinion is some one thing, and falsity is some one thing. "Multitude" too is predicated more extensively than "being," since not only are the things themselves many, but also the privations of these things; not only the things that are present, but also those that are future and past; there are true opinions that are many and false opinions that are many. Thus unity, as well as the multitude of unities [henads], which are also the simple and first multitude, appear to precede the order of beings. Therefore, beings not only obtain the fact that they exist from the One, which is their efficient cause,

ente formaliter habent; quod autem multa sint ab ipso solum simpliciter uno, a quo et unitatum numerus entibus est infusus.

6   Si quis multitudinis entium causam assignaverit ipsam simpliciter multitudinem, a Platonicis minime dissonabit, simplicis vero
multitudinis causam si aliunde quaesiveris praeterquam ab uno
nimium aberrabis. Unde enim vis ipsam multitudinem proficisci?
Numquid ab alia multitudine, ut clam labaris in infinitum, an
forsitan a nulla causa, ut ita multitudo sit causa rerum prima nullaque futura sit in rebus unio, nullus ordo? Denique si multitudo
quaelibet est necessario particeps unitatis, nimirum ab ipsa unitate
tamquam a causa superiore dependet. Nisi vero sit unitatis compos, nec aliqua partium erit aliquid unum neque partis particula
rursus unum, sed in infinitum deinceps pars quaelibet infinita,
neque rursus partes cum partibus unionem ullam habebunt, neque
cum toto cognationem neque forma totius erit certa, sed, ut ita
dixerim, infinities infinita, nec ex suis partibus copulata, cum careat uno, sed usquequaque divulsa. Ipsum igitur unum multitudinis omnis compositionisque et ordinis principium est et servator
et finis.

7   Gregorius Nazianzenus Nicolausque theologi divinam trinitatem ab eiusmodi conditionibus exceptam volunt. Multitudinem
enim illam esse participem unitatis et post unitatem, quae numerus quidam est partium quarundam aliquid componentium, trinitatem vero divinam non esse numerum vel multitudinem aut acci-
dentalem aut essentialem, sed super essentiam. Neque componere
ibi quicquam, praeterea totum, neque extra unitatem ipsam existere, sed esse proprietatem ipsi unitati naturae divinae naturaliter
necessariam. Haec itaque trinitas unitatis quidem propria est,
nec[19] tamen particeps unitatis nec per participationem eius unita,
sed unitati naturaliter penitissima, naturalem unitatem non divi-

but also from the first being, which is their formal cause, whereas the fact that they are "many" they obtain only from the absolute One, because the number of unities [henads] is infused into beings from the One.

If we identify simple multitude as the cause for the multitude of beings, we will by no means disagree with the Platonists; but if you are looking for another cause for the simple multitude than the One, you will commit a serious mistake. From what source, then, do you want multitude to come? Does it proceed from another multitude, so that you inadvertently fall into infinity,[57] or could it derive from no cause at all, which would make multitude the first cause of things, with the result that there will be neither union nor any order in nature? Finally, if every multitude necessarily partakes of unity, it surely depends on unity, which is its superior cause. Without sharing in unity, none of its parts will be some one thing, nor any particle of part, but every part will then be infinitely infinite, and parts will have no union with other parts, nor any kinship with the whole; the form of the whole will not be limited but infinitely infinite, so to speak; it will not be linked by the union of its parts since it lacks unity, but everywhere will be torn apart. Thus the One is the principle, conservator and end of all multitude, composition, and order.[58]

According to the theologians Gregory of Naziance and Nicholas [of Methone], the divine Trinity is exempt from these conditions. Indeed, the first multitude partakes of unity, it comes after unity, and is a certain number of certain parts that compose something, whereas the divine Trinity is neither a number nor a multitude, whether accidental or essential, but is beyond essence. It is not something composed yonder, but is a totality, nor does it exist outside it own unity; it is rather the propriety that is naturally necessary to the unity of God's nature. So the Trinity is the property of unity, without, however, partaking of unity or being united through partaking of it; it is naturally the innermost part of unity;

dens, sed conservans. Platonici quidam nihil aliud moliuntur quam ut dei summi naturam asserant simplicissimam. Proprietates autem personales, quae super ingenium nostrum sunt, numquam cogitaverunt. De simplicitate vero naturae divinae nulla est inter Christianos et Platonicos controversia.

8   Praeterea Proclus et Syrianus trinitatem quandam substantiarum trium extra primum introduxerunt, scilicet primam essentiam, primam vitam, intellectum primum, et essentiam quidem illam esse rebus essendi principium, vitam vero vivendi, intellectum intellegendi. Essentiam praeposuere vitae quoniam latius extenditur essendi quam vivendi munus, vitam simili ratione intellectui praefecerunt. Dispositionem eiusmodi, si Dionysium Plotinumque sequimur ut utrobique diximus, non admittemus, quoniam cum superioris causae donum perfectius esse debeat quam sequentis, praestantius erit esse quam vivere, vivere quam intellegere, neque verum hoc est effectu, neque igitur illa principiorum dispositio vera. Praeterea vanum est plura ad haec efficienda principia fingere, cum et sufficiat et deceat unum. Nempe cum essentia prima omnes sibi naturales perfectiones habeat, vita vero sit intimus motus vel actus essentiae primae, intellegentia denique sit quaedam vitae reflexio in essentiam, merito in ipsa essentiae primae natura simul vita est et intellegentia prima. Latius autem extendi esse quam vivere rursumque vivere quam intellegere respondebimus, non quoniam illa tria principia sint per substantiam inter se distincta, et in ordine graduum universi essentia sit superior vita et vita superior intellectu, sed quoniam, ut vult Plotinus, in mundo intellegibili, dum ipse generatur a primo secundum quendam generationis illius

it does not divide up natural unity, but preserves it. Some Platonists content themselves with asserting the utter simplicity of the supreme God, but they never considered the properties of the persons of the Trinity, a doctrine which transcends human intelligence. Regarding the simplicity of God's nature, however, there is no disagreement between Christians and Platonists.

In addition, Proclus and Syrianus have established a sort of trinity composed of three substances besides the first principle: the first essence, the first life and the first intellect. Essence is the principle of being for things, life that of living, and intellect that of intelligizing. They placed essence before life, because the gift of being is extended more widely than that of living, and for the same reason they placed life before intellect. Following Dionysius and Plotinus, we do not accept this arrangement, as we have said in our commentaries on both philosophers:[59] since the gift of the superior cause must be more perfect than that of the following cause,[60] being will be superior to living and living to intelligizing, something that is not true as regards the effect, and thus this disposition of principles is not true either. Moreover, it is vain to imagine several principles for creating things, while the One is both sufficient and fitting [to create all realities]. Surely, just as the first essence possesses all the perfections that are natural to itself, while life is the innermost motion or act of the first essence,[61] and intelligence is finally a sort of reflection of life within essence,[62] it is right to say that the first life and the first intelligence simultaneously reside within the very nature of the first essence.[63] We shall answer that being extends further than living, and likewise living extends further than intelligizing — not because these three principles are distinct from one another in substance, not because in the hierarchy of the universe essence is superior to life and life is superior to intellect, but rather because, according to Plotinus, when being is generated by the first principle within the intelligible world, following some order of generation, the essence of the first

ordinem, prius quodammodo sit essentia illa primi entis, mox
vero vivat, mox intellegat. Prius enim est quam moveatur, prius
movetur quam per motum in se reflectatur. Summatim vero intellegibilis illa substantia, si primo sui gradu perfecta esset, per nullum appetitum converteretur ad principium et ad ipsum bonum.
Necessarium tamen est ad illud entia cuncta converti. Nascitur
igitur illa nondum penitus absoluta, sed ulterius a quo est effecta
perficienda. Quod ergo primum ibi genito datur, tamquam quod
ad vitam referatur accipiendam, in sequentibus quoque illinc effectibus prius est communiusque quam vita, similiterque cum vita
ibi ad intellegentiam adnitatur quasi perfectiorem, pluribus subinde priusque vivere quam intellegere est concessum. Donum
vero ipsius unius atque boni, tamquam effectoris omnium poten-
tissimi, per cuncta procedit et omnium optabilissimum est dono-
rum. Quamobrem unum ipsum bonumque omnes universi gradus
et ordines mirabiliter antecellit. Quod autem hoc sit super intellegentiam, vitam, essentiam non solum Platonici disputant, sed
Dionysius etiam Areopagita saepe confirmat. Sed satis iam di-
gressi sumus. Redeamus ad institutum.

: LVIII :

Opinio affirmans abstractorum abstracta de deo.
Item tutiores sunt negationes relationesque
circa deum.

1   Antiquiores nonnulli Platonici absolutis quibusdam affirmationibus utebantur circa deum, existimantes cum deus omnino sit omnium causa, praecipue amplissimorum atque priorum, merito vires

being first exists, then lives and then intelligizes.[64] For it *is* before being in motion, and it is in motion before reflecting upon itself through motion. In sum, if the intelligible substance was perfect at its first degree, it would have no desire to turn itself toward its principle and supreme Good. Yet all beings must necessarily turn themselves toward the Good. Thus this substance does not come into existence completely separate, but aspiring to be perfected by its creator. So, in the intelligible world, what is first given to each creature, inasmuch as it relates to life (since life receives it), also has precedence over life; and in the effects that proceed from it, it is more general than life. Likewise, since in the intelligible world life tends toward intelligence, inasmuch as intelligence is more perfect than life, it is generally agreed that at the subsequent levels life also precedes intellect. But the gift of the One-and-Good, which is the most powerful creator of all things, proceeds through all things and is the most desirable of all gifts. This is why the One-and-Good precedes all the levels and orders of the universe in a marvelous way. As to the fact that it transcends intelligence, life and essence, not only do the Platonists state this, but Dionysius the Areopagite also frequently confirms it. But enough digression; let us return to our subject.

: LVIII :

The opinion according to which one can assert abstractions
of abstracts about God. Also, negations and comparisons
are safer for characterizing God.

Some of the older Platonists[65] used absolute assertions to charac- 1
terize God: they assumed that since God is the absolute cause of
all things (especially the most extended and first ones), He rightly

radicesque horum in se prorsus habere, per quas affirmari de deo absolutissima quaeque possint—nullo quidem pacto concreta, videlicet quod deus sit ens aut vivens aut intellegens, neque rursus proxima his abstracta, ceu quod deus sit essentia vel vita vel intellectus, sed abstractorum potius abstractiones ipsae, ut (si pronuntiari possit vel extra risum audiri) essentialitas, vitalitas, intellectualitas caeteraque similiter generatim perfectissima quaeque. Esse autem haec in deo ratione quadam, ut aiunt, quam unitissima, quam secretissima nobis soli deo cognita. Opinabantur forsan abstracta concretis proxima nonnullas concretorum conditiones habere, abstracta vero remota sive abstractorum abstractiones ab omnibus concretorum passionibus absolutissimas esse, ut affirmata de deo nihil ibi angustiae, nihil mutabilitatis, nihil multiplicitatis vel divisionis compositionisve ullius afferant, sed eminentissimam ad optima quaeque perficienda significent potestatem, ut cum essentialitatem dicunt, non formam quandam sive speciem intellegant a vita vel vitalitate distinctam, similiter cum vitalitatem nominant, non speciem fingant ab essentia vel intellegentia differentem, rursus cum intellectualitatem aiunt, non speciem ab essentia et vita discretam. Haec enim tria et praeter haec sapientia veritasque et virtus et similia his abstracta ita se habent, ut unumquodque horum distinctum sit a caeteris neque sit id ipsum quod sunt illa. Unumquodque igitur definitum est certumque bonum, non simpliciter omne bonum. Volunt ergo per illa quae diximus abstracto-

possesses within Himself the powers and the roots of these things, by virtue of which some utterly absolute attributes can be asserted of God—not by any means concrete appellations (for instance, God is being, living or intelligizing), nor abstract appellations, which are very close to concrete appellations (for instance, God is essence, life or intellect), but rather the very abstractions of these abstract appellations—for instance (if one can say or hear these neologisms without laughing), "essentiality," "vitality," "intellectuality" and so on for all the other eminently perfect appellations in their several genera.[66] They say that these attributes are within God in the most unified way, a way that is utterly hidden from us and known only to God. Perhaps their reasoning was that the abstract appellations, being so close to concrete attributes, might possess some of the conditions of concrete attributes, whereas the abstracts less close to these concrete attributes, or "abstractions of abstracts," are totally separate from all the passions pertaining to concrete attributes. As a result, these older Platonists considered that by being asserted of God these appellations would not introduce any limitation, change, multitude, division, or composition within God, but manifest God's utterly eminent power to accomplish the best things. In this way, when they call Him "essentiality," they do not conceive a form or species distinct from life or vitality; likewise, when they talk about His "vitality," they do not conceive a species different from essence or intelligence, and when they speak about "intellectuality," they do not speak of a species separate from essence and life.[67] The triad being, life and intellect, as well as that of wisdom, truth and power[68] and similar abstracts, are disposed in such a way that each is distinct from the others and is not that which the others are. Therefore, each is a defined and particular good, and not the whole absolute Good. So when

rum abstracta significari non bonum in hoc genere aut illo nec rursus bonorum cumulum differentium, sed absolute, singulariter, eminenter, omne bonum. Quod generum omnium limitibus omnino subtractis omnique adempta multiplicitate omnium generum bona producat, per unicam videlicet potestatem ad essentias, ad vitas, ad mentes, sapientias, veritates, virtutes efficiendas. Haec inquam antiquiores Platonici forsan meditabantur.

2   Posteriores vero Platonici post negationes quas cum Platone prae caeteris eligunt, non absolutas quidem affirmationes admittunt, sed solummodo relativas. Non absolutas, inquam, quia verentur ne quid penes deum forte definiant, ne quid interim deo adhibeant naturae nostrae cognatum, quod quidem in *Epistola ad Dionysium* Plato providentissime prohibet, asserens hunc circa deum errorem errorum omnium originem esse. Relativas autem affirmationes tradunt non significare quid vel qualis sit ipse deus, neque nomen eius notitiamve exprimere (haec enim nobis impossibilia Parmenides inquit), sed quo pacto res ad deum se habeant declarare, ut quando principium dicimus et medium atque finem intellegimus res a deo fieri, servari, perfici, quando bonum tamquam finem ab omnibus expeti omnium perfectorem. Quid vero? Si etiam quando unum videmur affirmare, tunc vel ad ipsum nostra referimus quasi haec uniantur inde, vel forte negamus ipsum esse multiplicem vel aliqua ratione compositum.

they use these "abstractions of abstracts," as we call them, they do not wish to manifest the good of any given genus, nor the accumulation of different goods, but the whole, absolute, singular, and eminent Good. Once the limits proper to all genera are abolished and all multitude is suppressed, the Good creates the goods of all genera through a unique power that enables it to create essences, lives, intelligences, wisdoms, truths and powers. Such might have been, as I said, the thoughts of the older Platonists.

As to the later Platonists, after the negations, which they privilege more than anything else, like Plato, they admit the use of assertions—not the absolute ones, but only the relative ones [i.e. comparisons].[69] They do not admit the absolute ones, I say, lest these define something within God, or attribute to God what is akin to us, something that is with great foresight forbidden by Plato in his *Letter to Dionysius*, where he says that this error is the source of all errors regarding God.[70] They consider, however, that relative assertions [i.e. comparisons or analogies] do not signify what God is and what His nature is, nor express His name or concept (which, according to Parmenides is impossible for us), but they reveal the way in which realities are related to God. For instance, when we call God beginning, middle and end, we understand that nature is created, preserved and achieved by God; when we call Him Good, we understand that, as an end, He perfects all things and is desired by all things. Well then, even if we sometimes appear to assert that He is One, then either we relate things in our experience to God, inasmuch as they are united by Him, or we deny that He is many and composed in any way.[71]

: LIX :

*Si unum non habet partes, consequenter nec
habet principium vel finem aut medium.*

1   Quemadmodum vero per negationem multitudinis tamquam uni-
versalioris, mox partes habere tamquam particularius negavit uni,
ita deinceps per negationem partium negat habere principium mediumve et finem, tamquam illud quoque universalius sit quam istud, sed primo quidem affirmative concludit a particulari hunc in
modum ad universale: si habet principium, medium, finem, consequenter habet et partes. Deinde vicissim negando concludit, non
habet partes, ergo non habet illa.

2   Universalius quidem esse partes habere quam illa patet ex eo
quod prius quidem partes concipis tamquam communius aliquid
atque facilius quam eo prorsus ordine discernas atque disponas, ut
hanc quidem ibi obtinere principium, illam vero finem, istam inter
utrasque mediam animadvertas. Praeterea in binario partes quidem quodammodo sunt, discretio vero principii, finis, medii non
est in binario, sed in ternario. Prima et in pluribus numerorum
distinctio eiusmodi non est facilis. Denique quid prohibet multitudinem partium in infinito innumerabilem cogitare? Non licet
tamen ibi terminos et medium machinari. Sed ubi Parmenides
inquit haec tria, si sint, in uno erunt et partes unius, linea scrupu-
lum nobis obicit. In hac enim duo quaedam puncta principium

: LIX :

*If the One has no parts, it has consequently
no beginning, end, or middle.*

In the same way that, by denying the attribute "multitude," which   1
is more universal, Parmenides then denied of the One the fact of
having parts, which is more particular, so in the same way, by denying parts, Parmenides then denies of the One the fact of having
a beginning, a middle and an end [137D], inasmuch as the former
attribute is more universal than the latter. But he first brings in an
affirmative conclusion based on a deduction from the particular to
the universal: if the One has a beginning, a middle and an end, it
consequently also has parts. Then he brings in a negative conclusion: the One has no parts; therefore it does not have a beginning,
a middle and an end.

   Having parts is clearly more universal than having a beginning,   2
a middle and an end, for we first conceive of "having parts" as
something more common and easier to conceive than the distinguishing of these parts and disposing them so as to make one part
the beginning, another the end, and a third the middle between
the first two. Moreover, parts exist somehow in a dyad, whereas
the distinction between beginning, end and middle does not occur
in a dyad, but in a triad.[72] Such a distinction, both the first distinction into three parts and the distinction into more than three
parts, is not easy. What prevents us, after all, from conceiving a
numberless multitude of parts *ad infinitum?* By contrast, it is not
possible to imagine an infinite number of beginnings, ends and
middles. But when Parmenides declares that these three elements,
if they exist, will be in a one and will be parts of a one [137D6–7],
someone could object to this statement with the following example. On a line, the beginning and the end are two points, and the

finemque faciunt, inter quae punctum quoque medium designatur, neque tamen puncta sunt lineae partes. Non enim ex individuis magnitudo conficitur et partes quidem lineae non sunt infinitae. Puncta vero nihil ibi prohibet innumerabilia cogitare. Respondemus ad haec: in linea quidem res diversae qualitatis esse posse, ut aliud quidem sit pars eius, aliud vero terminus; in uno vero maxime omnium sibimet conformi, si quid principii mediive vel finis sortem habuerit, pars quoque unius erit. Sed quis Parmenidi vetuit partes alicuius appellare quicquid illius est aliquid, quicquid ipsum quodammodo complet, quicquid commercium habet in ordine? Sic igitur et puncta partes lineae poterit nuncupare. Denique etsi puncta non intellegantur ut lineae partes, qua ratione simpliciter linea cogitatur, qua tamen ratione terminata supponitur, puncta eius termini quodammodo lineae terminatae partes esse censentur. Sed haec utcumquelibet accipito.

3   Dubitatur iterum quomodo in *Legibus* quidem affirmat deum habere principium, mediumque et finem omnium, hic vero negat. Respondemus breviter aut de alio quidem deo, id est de intellectu conditore mundi huius, ibi loqui, in quo distincta sunt principiorum mediorumque et finium mundanorum omnium exemplaria, hic autem de primo simpliciter uno, in quo nullae sunt absolutae idearum distinctiones, sed simplicissima fecunditate sua universum mox intellegibile procreat, ut Platonice loquar, per ipsum vero universum quoque sensibile. Aut forte si de primo in *Legibus* quoque tractat, non vult quidem primum illud in seipso tamquam sui

middle is another point between these two extremities; however, these points are not parts of the line, since magnitude does not consist of individual points, and the parts of the line are not infinite. Yet nothing prevents us from considering that in the intelligible world the points are infinite. In reply to this objection we say that the line can have elements of different quality, by virtue of which one element would be part of the line and another one of its extremities. By contrast, if someone were to postulate the existence of a beginning, a middle or an end within a one, which of all things is that which most conforms to itself, these would also be parts of a one. Who would prevent Parmenides from calling "parts of something" everything that is *of* this thing, everything that somehow completes this thing, everything that is linked to it within its order? In that case, Parmenides will also be able to consider the points as parts of the line. Finally, even if the points are not considered to be parts of the line when the line is considered simply *qua* line, when the line is considered as something limited, the points making up this limit are in some way considered to be parts of the limited line.[73] One can adopt whatever side of the reasoning one wishes.

Another question concerns the fact that Plato says in the *Laws* 3 that God holds the beginning, middle and end of all things,[74] whereas he denies this in the *Parmenides*. In reply to this objection, we briefly say that either the passages in the *Laws* concern another god, that is, the intellect and creator of this [intelligible] world, which contains distinct models of all the beginnings, middles and ends of the [sensible] world, whereas the *Parmenides* is concerned with the first, absolute One, within which there are no absolute distinctions among the Ideas, but which then creates, by virtue of its utterly simple fecundity, to speak like Plato, the intelligible world, and through it the sensible world. Another possibility is that, supposing that Plato is also referring to the first principle in the *Laws*, he does not mean that the first principle possesses

partes habere principium et medium atque finem, sed suo quodam cardine principia et fines et media rerum omnium continere atque ad ipsum omnia ut ad principium suum et finem atque medium se habere. Omnia enim inde proficiscuntur, omnia illud appetunt, omnia in illius centro, dum sua centra figunt, firmata servantur.

: LX :

Quomodo ipsum unum dicatur infinitum omniumque finis.

1 Probavit in superioribus unum, quia non habeat partes, consequenter terminos non habere. Probat in praesentia, quia careat terminis, interminatum, id est infinitum, esse. Sed non videtur prima fronte magnum aliquid assequi. Forte enim simili ratione quis convincet unitatem quoque mathematicam, quae est principium numerorum, item punctum, quod est quasi dimensionum principium, quia partes non habeant ideoque nec terminos esse, similiter infinita. 'Parturiunt ergo montes, nascetur ridiculus mus.' Respondemus unitatem hanc et punctum in suo quodam genere infinita quodammodo dici posse, quia nec unitas numerales nec punctum dimensionales partes vel terminos habet, et utrumque nihil prohibet per numeros infinitos inde sequentes vel dimensiones quaslibet inde productas innumerabiliter se diffundere. Hinc igitur utrumque quodammodo videbitur infinitum. Sed in universo rerum ordine est utrumque finitum partesque quodammodo suas habet et terminos. Neutrum enim simpliciter est omnino, sed est utrumque res quaedam in genere quodam et per

within itself, as parts of itself, a beginning, a middle and an end, but rather that the One contains by its pivotal position, as it were, the beginnings, ends and middles of all things and that all things are in relation to it as their beginning, end and middle. For all things proceed from it, all desire it, all are firmly maintained in its center, while they fabricate their own center.[75]

: LX :

How the One is said to be infinite and the limit of all things.

Parmenides has just shown that since the One has no parts, it has 1 no limits. He now shows that since the One has no limits, it is indeterminate, that is, infinite [137D]. At first sight this does not appear to be a particularly groundbreaking conclusion. Surely one could use similar reasoning to show that since mathematical unity, which is the principle of numbers, and the point, which is the principle of dimensions, do not possess parts and are therefore not limits, they are also infinite. In other words, "the mountains are in labor, and bring forth a silly little mouse."[76] In reply to this objection we say that in their own genus the unity and the point can somehow be said to be infinite, since unity possesses no numerical parts or limits, and the point possesses no dimensional ones, and nothing prevents both of them from propagating infinitely through the infinity of numbers that come after them or through the dimensions that are created by them; thus both of them will somehow appear to be infinite. However, in the universal order of nature both unity and point will be limited and have somehow their own parts and limits, for neither of them is absolutely simple, but they are each individual things, because they reside within a particular genus; they are both composed, through their own

differentiam propriam componitur in specie quadam et consequenter proprietates habet et accidentia subit terminaturque a natura vel causa superiore et a certo quodam fine dependet vimque
ad aliquid habet determinatam. Igitur eiusmodi partes terminosque habentia merito sunt finita. Similiter caetera omnia praeter primum composita sunt atque finita. Ipsum vero simpliciter
unum nihil habet eiusmodi. Nullam enim multiplicitatem admittit, conditionem nullam.

2 Res omnes praeter primum, quemadmodum probavimus in
commentariis in *Philebum*, ex infinito componuntur et termino,
id est ex potentia quadam passiva, per se informi vel deformi,
aliorsum vergente, ulterius progressura, aliunde formabili, atque
insuper ex forma vel actu potentiam eiusmodi inclinationemque
terminante. Hoc infinitum, hic terminus, elementa rerum sunt
creatarum, inter se opposita, conciliabilia desuper ab ipso simpliciter uno, quod quidem nec eiusmodi quaedam infinitudo est, alioquin foret desuper terminandum nec sequentibus infinitis terminum ullum tamquam sibi oppositum adhiberet, nec insuper est
quidam eiusmodi terminus, alioquin et cohibitum esset in rebus et
infinita iam tamquam sibi opposita procreare non posset. Est igitur super haec et omnia quomodolibet inter se opposita, ut possit
omnia regere pariter atque conficere. Est itaque infinitum, quia
nec terminos habet intus nec subit exteriores, per quos vel a causa
vel fine vel subiecto vel comprehendente vel conditione quavis defi-
niatur, gradusque virtutis et actionis eius nullum numerum subeunt vel mensuram. Est et terminus, non aliquis vel alicuius vel
in aliquo, sed tamquam terminorum quorumlibet auctor.

3 Syrianus et Proclus duo illa rerum elementa, finitum et infinitum, existimant ante omnes entium gradus, in seipsis, infra pri-

difference, within an individual species, and consequently possess properties, undergo accidents, are limited by nature or by a superior cause, depend on a certain end, and possess a specific power that tends toward something. By virtue of having these parts and limits, the unity and the point are indeed limited. Likewise all the other things besides the first principle are composed and limited, whereas the absolute One possesses nothing of the sort, since it admits no multiplicity and no condition of any sort.

As we have shown in our commentary on the *Philebus*, all 2 things, except the first principle, are composed of the infinite and the limit: in other words, they are composed [firstly] of a potentiality which is passive in itself, formless or deformed, which tends toward another reality, is destined to proceed further and receives its form from another, and [secondly] of a form or act which limits this potentiality and inclination. The former is the infinite, the latter is the limit, which are the elements of things that are created; they are opposed to one another, but can be unified from above by the absolute One, which is neither an infinity like this (otherwise it would be limited by a superior principle and would not give a limit to the infinites that come after it, lest it be opposed to itself), nor a limit like this (otherwise it would remain within the things it limits, and would not be able to create the infinites, which would be opposed to it). The One transcends, therefore, the infinite and the limit, as well as all opposites, so that it can govern and perfect them all. So the One is infinite, because it possesses no limits from within, nor does it undergo any limit from the outside by virtue of which it would be defined by a cause, an end, a subject, a receptacle, or any condition. Moreover, the degrees of its power and action are not subject to any number or measure. It is also limit, not a particular limit of something or in something, but it is limit inasmuch as it is the creator of all limits.[77]

According to Syrianus and Proclus, these two elements, the 3 limit and the infinite, precede all the levels of beings, exist in

mum, abstracta et inter se separata subsistere, quoniam ante composita atque etiam ante opposita invicem confusa existere simplicia debeant in seipsis et oppositum seorsum ab opposito purum. Ego vero arbitror cum Plotino non esse duo haec a compositione qualibet, praesertim a prima, aliter separata quam ratione formali. Nam in ente primo prima infinitudo eius, id est formabilitas eius; qua ratione formabilitas est, neque terminus ipse est, id est prima et universalis ipsius forma, neque eiusmodi terminum adhuc habet neque huius termini quicquam. Rursus nec eiusmodi terminus, qua ratione terminus est formalis, est ipsa infinitudo formabilis nec proprietates illius habet sed oppositas. Iam vero Socrates, ut significaret duo haec non esse substantias seorsum duas, non dixit deum haec duo fecisse vel generavisse, sed ostendisse. Compositum vero ex his ens primum, inquit, ab ipso deo genitum atque factum, quasi hoc ipsum sit subsistens, illa vero nequaquam. Ex his elementis ita distinctis componuntur reliqua omnia, his invicem iam conflatis, ideae scilicet et mentes et animae et caelestia et quae sub caelo sunt omnia. Vanum vero videtur infinitatem hanc, id est formabilitatem imperfectam, nondum formatam necdum finem optabilem consecutam opinari per se et in se seorsum posse subsistere, ceu si quis a forma informem materiam separaverit. Stultum quoque fingere terminum illum, qui intimus huius infinitatis est finis, similiter segregatum, veluti si quis materialem formam a materia forte seiunxerit. Materiam quidem re ipsa numquam a forma seiungere potes. At vero si formam ab ea cogitaveris separatam, praeteristi iam formam tibi prius obviam, transcendisti genus, nec formam iam habes eiusmodi, sed idealem. Similiter si infinitatem et terminum quae sunt in ente, praeterea infini-

themselves immediately after the first principle, separate from the others and separate from one another. They reason that before the composites and even the opposites mixed with one another there must exist elements that are simple in themselves, each unmixed and separate from its opposite.[78] I myself consider, like Plotinus, that these elements are only formally separate from every composition, especially the first composition.[79] For the first infinity of being resides within the first being, and is the being's capacity to form; as a capacity to form, it is neither the limit, that is, the first and universal form of the first being, nor does it yet possess any limit or anything pertaining to a limit. Likewise, a limit like this, since it is formal, is neither an infinity receiving form nor does it possess any of the properties of infinity, but rather the opposite properties. In fact, Socrates shows that these two elements are not two distinct substances by saying that God has "revealed" rather than "created" or "generated" these two elements, whereas he says that the first being, which is composed of these two elements, has been generated and created by God, which clearly indicates that being subsists in itself, but that the two elements do not.[80] Of these two elements thus distinguished, once they are mixed with one another, all the other beings are composed: the Ideas, the intellects, the souls, the celestial and all sublunar things. It seems vain to consider that infinity, that is, the potentiality to receive form, which is imperfect, is not yet formed and has not yet reached the end that it desires, can exist separately, by itself and in itself, as if someone separated formless matter from form; it seems equally foolish to imagine that limit, which is the end and the innermost part of infinity, is also a separate principle, as if one separated material form from matter. Yet matter can never really be separate from form. However, if one conceives form as separate from matter, leaves aside the first form that comes to mind and goes beyond the genus [of form], one does not reach the form just mentioned, but ideal form. Likewise, if one goes beyond the infinite and the

tum tibi prorsus occurret non eiusmodi, non formabile, sed
formarum omnium auctor. Occurret et tibi terminus non illius-
modi, non terminus addictus terminati, sed hanc supereminens[20]
terminosque infinitati cuique suos ex alto distribuens. Infinitum
igitur atque finis, quae sunt in rebus opposita, extra res sunt ipsum
simpliciter unum.

: LXI :

Quomodo negatur de uno figura
et rectum atque rotundum.

1 Terminatum est universalius quam figuratum. Quicquid enim
figura praeditum est finibus est inclusum, neque tamen quicquid
finibus est astrictum, ut linea, est etiam figuratum. Negavit ergo
unum habere terminos, tamquam universalius, priusquam habere
figuram atque ex universali negatione rite negationem adduxit par-
ticularem, rursusque prius negavit figuram, quasi generale aliquid,
quam species e medio tolleret, rectum scilicet et rotundum. Atque
vicissim dum negavit unum rectae figurae esse particeps vel rotun-
dae, non solum has duas figurarum extremas e medio sustulit, sed
medias etiam participes extremarum, conum, cylindrum, triangu-
lum et quadratum. Tametsi ridiculum foret, si quasi magnum aliquid moliretur, negare scilicet mathematicas de uno figuras, quod
quidem certum est super omne continui genus, immo super uni-

limit that are in being, one will not then reach the infinite just mentioned, nor that which is able to form, but the creator of all forms, nor will one reach the limit just mentioned, not that which is added to the limited, but that super-eminent limit which distributes from above their limits to each infinite. In sum, the infinite and the limit, which are opposites within things, are, outside these things, the absolute One.

: LXI :

How the attributes "shaped," "straight," and "round" are denied of the One.

The attribute "limited" is more universal than the attribute 1 "shaped." For everything that has a shape is comprised within some limits, while everything that is circumscribed by limits, such as the line, does not necessarily possess a shape. So Parmenides first denied that the One has limits before denying that it has any shape, because the first proposition is more universal, and he has appropriately introduced a particular negation deriving from this universal negation. Likewise Parmenides first denied "shape," which is a general attribute, before denying the more specific attributes "straight" and "round." And similarly after denying that the One participates in the straight or the round, he not only suppressed these two opposite shapes, but also the intermediate shapes that partake of these two: the cone, the cylinder, the triangle and the square.[81] It would be ridiculous, however, if one wished to undertake a demonstration of some importance, to deny mathematical shapes of the One, because the One surely transcends the whole genus of the continuum, transcending, indeed, universal being.[82] So Parmenides denies shapes that are more sublime than the

versum ens existere, sublimiores ergo figuras quam mathematicas
uni negat, dum has quoque evidentissime negat.

2   Inter haec nota quod monuimus alibi: Parmenidem per opposita semper versari negando per ens unum et multitudinem uni
huic oppositam, per partes atque totum, per principium atque
finem, per rectum atque rotundum, per situm in seipso vel in alio,
per statum atque motum atque similia, ut ubique significet ipsum
unum nec esse utrumque oppositorum, alioquin foret multiplex,
non simpliciter unum, nec rursus alterum oppositorum esse, alioquin non faceret alterum oppositionemque pateretur, tamquam
non simpliciter absolutum.

3   Iuvat hic cum Proclo saepe nostro parumper investigare utrum
Plato sub eadem significatione figuram hic quidem de uno negaverit, in *Phaedro* autem de loco supercaelesti, id est de natura intellegibili. Ibi enim per locum sub caelo sensibilem vel ad summum
animalem designat naturam, per locum vero caelestem, intellectualem, per supercaelestem, intellegibilem, quam sane naturam appellat infiguratam. Cum vero de illa affirmet ibi multa, scilicet essentiam et intellegentiam et alia, quae hic de uno negat, merito et alio
quodam sensu illam infiguratam et unum inquit infiguratum.
Respondeo vero non tam cum Proclo quam Plotino essentiam
primae mentis sibi mox intellegibilem nondum habere figuram,
id est exactam idearum distinctionem quam in seipsa concipit intellectualis mentis eiusdem virtus, mox in suam substantiam se
reflectens. Ipsum vero unum non habere figuram significat nullum
habere vel habiturum in se discrimen idearum absolutis inter se

mathematical ones, although he of course also denies the mathematical ones.

However, one must note, as we have observed elsewhere, that in the negations Parmenides always proceeds through opposites: the one being and the multitude that is opposed to it, parts and whole, beginning and end, straight and round, what is situated in itself and in another, rest and motion, and so on. In this way, he shows in every case that the One is neither of the two terms of an opposition, otherwise it would be many rather than the absolute One, nor one of the opposites, otherwise it would not create the other term of each opposition and would itself undergo opposition, rather than being simple and separate.

It is worth briefly investigating here, following Proclus, as we often do, the question whether Plato has denied the attribute "shaped" of the One by giving to the term "shape" the same meaning as in the *Phaedrus* regarding the supra-celestial world (that is, the intelligible nature). In Plato's *Phaedrus* the "place under the heavens" refers to sensible nature, or at most psychic nature; by the "celestial place," he refers to the intellectual nature; by the "super-celestial place," he refers to the intelligible nature, and he calls the latter "shapeless nature." However, in the *Phaedrus* Plato asserts many attributes of the intelligible nature, namely, essence, intelligence, and others, whereas in the *Parmenides* he denies these attributes of the One. So it must be right to conclude that the attribute "shapeless" that is employed in reference to the intelligible nature and the One is not the same.[83] In reply to this objection, I respond, following Plotinus rather than Proclus, that the essence of the first intellect, which is immediately intelligible to itself, does not yet possess any shape (that is, the precise distinction between Ideas that the intellectual power of this same intellect conceives in itself as soon as it turns itself toward its own substance). However, the fact that the One possesses no shape signifies that it does not and will not possess in itself any distinction between Ideas, which

proprietatibus differentium, alioquin nec foret simpliciter unum et iam in qualibet idea determinatum esset atque finitum. Item non habere figuram in se rectam declarat processum nullum intus ab hoc in illud pati nec aliunde pendere neque vergere aliorsum. Denique non esse rotundum docet non ea per intellegentiam multiplicem reflexione uti, qua intellectus in seipsum utitur et in causam. Sed de hoc saepius in Plotino.

4   Profecto Parmenides ubi in poemate de uno ente, id est de mundo intellegibili, loquitur, sphaerae comparat et ipsa sphaerae definitione describit idemque confirmat hic in suppositione secunda, de eodem videlicet uno ente verba facturus. Negat autem in prima circulare simul atque rectum de ipso simpliciter uno, quasi duo haec intellegibilis intellectualisque naturae sint propria. Nemo utique dubitat orbicularem sui ipsius vel causae animadversionem esse intellegentiae propriam. Rectitudo quoque praecipua eiusdem propria est. Rectitudo enim processum significat non quemlibet re vera, sed nusquam declinantem vel obliquum, immo firmiter prorsus intentum. Eiusmodi vero processu procedit intellectus a patre summo. Item intus ab essentia sua procedit vita, ab hac intellegentia, rursus a natura virtus, ab hac operatio, ab hac opus externum.

5   Processus quidem discretionis principium est. Per hunc enim discernuntur rerum ordines, tum a causa producente, tum invicem, quatenus hi quidem usque ad primos universi gradus, hi vero ad medios, hi autem ad infimos processerunt, atque ita in eius-

differ from one another through distinct properties, otherwise it would not be the absolute One and would already be particular and limited within each Idea. Likewise, the fact that the One does not possess any straight shape shows that it does not undergo any procession from within itself between two points, that it does not depend on another principle, and that it does not turn itself toward another. Finally, the fact that the One is not round indicates that it does not employ reflection through a multiple intelligence, in the way the intellect employs reflection to turn itself toward itself and its cause. But we often speak about this in our commentary on Plotinus.[84]

Certainly, when Parmenides speaks in his poem of the one being, that is, the intelligible world, he compares it to a sphere and describes it by using terms that define the sphere,[85] and he also confirms this same doctrine in the second hypothesis of the *Parmenides*, where he is also going to talk about the one being. In the first hypothesis, however, he denies the attributes "round" and "straight" of the absolute One because these two elements concern the intelligible and intellectual nature. Doubtless the circular motion of conversion to oneself and to one's cause pertains to intelligence. Straight motion also specifically pertains to intelligence, because straight motion does not actually designate any given procession, but the procession that nowhere falls or goes astray and remains firmly directed: it is through this procession that the intellect proceeds from the highest Father.[86] Likewise within the intellect life proceeds from essence and intelligence proceeds from life; again, power proceeds from nature, action proceeds from power, and external creation proceeds from action.

Procession is the principle of distinction: it is by virtue of procession that the orders of things are distinguished, both from the cause that produces them and from one another, inasmuch as some have proceeded to the first levels of the universe, others to the middle levels, and others, finally, to the lowest levels; in this

modi recto scilicet processu medium utraque praecedit extrema, sive enim descendas praecedit ultima, sive ascendas praecedit summa. Conversio autem quae per circulum designatur conficit unionem. Per hanc enim et res quaelibet sibimet unitur, quatenus ad intimum sui centrum singula colligit et cuncta invicem congregantur, dum enim communi quadam aviditate boni ad ipsum bonum cuncta contendunt, invicem quoque conspirant.

6   Sicut autem vera rectitudo est in natura intellectuali per processum indeclinabilem qualem diximus, sic verus est circuitus in eadem, non solum quia haec potissimum ad seipsam causamque convertitur, sed etiam quia quaecumque in ea sunt praeter suum centrum quasi per circumferentiam aeque distant a centro, aeque convertuntur ad ipsum perque ipsum pariter ad commune centrum atque bonum. In caeteris vero eiusmodi paritas non servatur. In ipso denique simpliciter uno neque processionem possumus designare per quam vel ipsum a causa, vel aliud ipsius ab alio procedat eiusdem, neque rursus conversionem per quam vel convertatur ad causam aliudque bonum, vel extima sui convertantur ad intima, alioquin neque primum omnium foret, neque simpliciter unum. Ipsum vero unum esse universi principium, ex eo patet quia nihil usquam unitate et unione melius inveniri potest; si qua vero super ipsum causa, foret melius aliquid unione rebus afferret.

way, during a procession like this, which is rectilinear, the mid-point precedes both extremities: in the descent it precedes the inferior levels and in the ascent it precedes the superior levels. The conversion, which is designated by the circle, perfects union: through it each thing is united to itself, inasmuch as it unifies all the individual parts to its innermost center, and all things are united to one another, because it is indeed through their common desire for the good that they all tend toward the Good and are in accordance with one another.

However, just as true straight motion exists in the intellectual 6
nature through the inflexible procession we mentioned above, even so true circular motion also exists in the intellectual nature, not only because it turns toward itself and toward its cause above all, but also because all the things that it contains besides its center, inasmuch as they are equidistant from the center through their place on the circumference of the circle, turn equally toward it, and through it toward the common center and good. But this equality is not preserved at all the other levels of reality. Finally, in the absolute One we cannot designate any procession through which it would proceed from a cause, or another than itself would proceed from another than itself, nor any conversion whereby it would turn toward a cause or another good, or its outward parts would turn toward its inward parts, otherwise it would not be the first principle of all things nor the absolute One. The One is the principle of the universe, as demonstrated by the fact that we can nowhere find something better than unity and union. If there was a cause superior to the One, it would bring something better than union to things.

: LXII :

Ipsum unum nusquam est quia nec est in seipso
nec in alio. Item quomodo separata dicuntur
ex seipsis existere vel produci.

1 Parmenides in poemate quidem affirmavit unum ens in seipso et
circa se manere. Hic autem negat ipsum simpliciter unum in
seipso manere vel in alio, attribuens ei proprie nusquam esse. Neque enim in causa est, quod est causa causarum, nec in sequentibus, quod nullam ad haec inclinationem habet vel habitudinem. In
loco enim vel subiecto vel tempore vel genere vel in toto tamquam
partem, vel ut totum[21] in partibus esse quod est primum nemo
utique suspicatur, neque est insuper in seipso simplicissimum illud, in quo non est aliud atque aliud, ut propterea alterum adhae-
reat alteri vel toti partes insint vel totum sese complecti nitatur.
Unum vero ens, id est intellectus primus, est ubique. Primo quidem est in causa, id est ipso bono intellegentiae patre, deinde
etiam in seipso, penes quem est intellegentia in vita, haec in essentia, ideae in ipsa intellegentiae distinctione consistunt. Est insuper
in sequentibus, singula providenter ubique dispensans formasque
quodammodo similes exemplari ubique disponens, sed et in hoc
officio, quia nusquam proprie cohibetur, ideo singulis ubique pariter adest. Proprium quidem est intellectus ipsius, dum in alio est,
scilicet patre suo, interim in seipso manere, id est et ad seipsum
perfecta quadam animadversione reflecti et sequentibus nullis co-
herceri vel affici. Id vero intellegentiae proprium, id est esse in alio

82

: LXII :

*The One is nowhere, because it is neither in itself nor in
another. Similarly, the way in which separate things
are said to exist or be produced by themselves.*

In his poem Parmenides asserted that the one being remains in   1
itself and by itself,[87] whereas here he denies that the absolute One
remains in itself or in another, and properly attributes to the One
the fact of being nowhere [138A2–3]. For the One is neither in a
cause, since it is the cause of causes, nor in the subsequent realities, because it possesses no desire or disposition toward them.
Surely nobody would imagine that the first principle resides in a
place, a subject, a period of time, a genus, is in a whole as a part or
in parts as a whole; moreover, what is utterly simple is not in itself
either, since it does not contain different things, so that therein it
is not possible for one thing to adhere to another or the parts to be
in the whole or the whole to strive to embrace itself. By contrast,
the one being (that is, the first intellect) is everywhere: firstly, it is
in its cause, that is, the Good itself, father of the intelligence; secondly, it is also in itself, because within the intellect intelligence is
in life, life in essence, and the Ideas consist in the very distinction
of intelligence. It is also in the realities that derive from it, because
it distributes its providence to every reality and everywhere arranges the forms in a way similar to their model. However, even
when it performs this function, the intellect is everywhere equally
present to every individual thing, because it is properly contained
by nothing. It is proper to the intellect, while being in another
(that is, in its father), to remain at the same time within itself
(that is, to turn toward itself in a perfect movement of reflection,
without being restrained or affected by any of the realities subsequent to it). However, this property of intelligence — to be in an-

simul atque intellectualiter habitare secum, non convenit ipsi simpliciter uni, sed praestat ipsum esse nusquam, quod quidem sufficienti divisione probatur. Si enim alicubi est, vel in se est, vel existit in alio. Cum vero neque in se neque in alio sit, consequenter dicitur esse nusquam.

2   Proinde ubi probat unum non esse in alio, quia videlicet circum per multas partes tangeretur ab eo tangeretque similiter, videtur quidem negare tantum non esse in alio tamquam loco vel vase, quod profecto leve quiddam foret et commune rebus etiam omnibus quomodolibet individuis atque incorporeis. Putandum tamen est Parmenidem hic negare sic unum esse in alio, ut hoc proprium sit unius nec ullo modo sit in alio, cum multifariam esse aliquid in alio possit. Dicemus igitur una cum Syriano hic negari ipsum unum in alio esse eodem sensu quo in suppositione secunda affirmatur unum ens in alio esse, siquidem unum ens, id est prima illa intellegibilis vel etiam intellectualis essentia, est in alio ut in causa, id est in ipso uno atque bono, quod quidem quasi circulo quodam comprehendit eam, tamquam principium finisque eius mediumque conservans, excedensque ipsam undique, quia hinc quidem eminentius est, inde vero latius ac longius operatur. Haec vero tangit illud multis, ut Parmenides ait, id est per plures sui partes, vires, ideas, actus se applicat illi et numero quodam utcumque potest unicam illius fecunditatem imitari conatur. Est autem proprium intellegibilis huius essentiae esse in primis in uno, siquidem est uni quam proxima ipsique indistanter et indeclinanter inhaeret. Est et proprium esse in seipsa revera penitusque se complecti

other while residing intellectually in itself—does not befit the absolute One; it is best that the One be nowhere, as is sufficiently shown by the method of division: if the one is somewhere, it is either in itself or in another, but since it is neither in itself nor in another, it is consequently said to be nowhere.[88]

As a result, when Parmenides shows that the One is not in another because all round it would have many contacts with this other thing at many points [138A3–7], he appears solely to deny that the One is in another as in a place or container, which would assuredly be a trivial statement and common to all the things that are somehow indivisible and incorporeal. One must consider, however, that Parmenides here denies that the One is in another inasmuch as this constitutes the property of the One and inasmuch as it is *absolutely not* in another, since something can be in another in many different ways.[89] Thus we shall say, together with Syrianus, that Parmenides here denies that the One is in another in the same way as he asserts that the one being is in another in the second hypothesis, since the one being (that is, the first intelligible or even the intellectual essence) is in another inasmuch as it is in its cause, that is, the One-and-Good, which envelops it as though in a circle, preserving it as it is the first intelligible essence's beginning, end and middle, transcending it at every point, since on the one hand it is more eminent, and on the other it operates with greater extension and length.[90] According to Parmenides, the first intelligible essence is in contact with the One at many points [138A4–5]. This means that it brings itself to contact with the One through many of its parts, powers, Ideas and acts, and it strives in a multiple way to imitate as much as possible the unique fecundity of the One. It pertains to the intelligible essence to be primarily in the One, since it is as close as possible to the One and is linked to it without discontinuity or change. It is also proper to this intelligible essence to really be in itself and to completely em-

propter reflexionem virtutis, intellegentiae, voluntatis in se reflexionum omnium exactissimam. Similiter ipsius unius maxime proprium est nec esse in alio ullo modo, praecipue sicut in causa, nec esse in seipso per ullam sui ipsius comprehensionem intellectui alicui notam, alioquin in eo duae quaedam partes aut vires aut rationes diversae forent, saltem videlicet ratio quidem altera comprehendentis, altera vero comprehensi. Quae quidem diversitas immo et oppositio ab ipsa ratione unius est admodum aliena. Non enim potest aliquid per idem ac simul et secundum se totum opposita pati. Igitur si simul haec admittit quae modo narrabam, certe secundum aliud aliudque sui vel saltem per aliam et aliam rationem se continet atque continetur. Nam et quod movetur ex se, quamvis non per duas sui partes id agat, tamen per virtutes duas expedit differentes.

3   Praeterea in seipsa esse non modo per quandam sui ipsius animadversionem intellegibilis illa substantia dicitur, sed etiam qua ratione seipsam quoquomodo producit.²² Sicut enim quaedam moventur ab alio, ut corpora quaedam, a semetipsis, ut animae, ita quaedam solum producuntur ab alio, ut corpora et corporea cuncta, quaedam non modo sunt ab alio, sed etiam cum primum inde sunt quodammodo etiam a seipsis existunt, ut separatae separabilesque substantiae. Quantum igitur se sua quadam virtute producunt, se continent; quatenus producuntur a se, pariter continentur.

4   In omnibus profecto substantiis intellegentia praeditis duae sunt virtutes: altera quidem generativa, altera conversiva. Per generativam atque fecundam explicant in seipsis ulteriorem formam et

brace itself through the movement of reflection undertaken by its power, intelligence and will, a movement which is the most exacting of all the movements of reflection. Similarly, it primarily pertains to the One to be absolutely not in another, especially in a cause, nor to be in itself by comprehending itself in a way that could be known by any intellect, otherwise there would be within the One two different parts, powers or rational principles, with at least one rational principle for the enveloping and one for the enveloped. Yet this difference, or rather this opposition, is totally alien to the very rational principle of the One. For nothing can undergo two opposites by virtue of the same thing, simultaneously and in its totality. So, if [*per impossibile*] the One simultaneously admits the opposites mentioned above, it surely contains itself and is contained, through one of the two opposites, which are other than itself, or at least through one of the two rational principles. Indeed, that which is moved by itself, even if it does not act through two parts of itself, nevertheless acts by means of two different powers [138A7–B7].

Moreover, the intelligible substance is said to be in itself, not 3 only by virtue of reflection upon itself, but also because it somehow produces itself. Just as some things are moved by another (as in the case of bodies), or by themselves (like the souls), in the same way certain things are only produced by another, like the bodies and all the bodily things, others are not only produced by another, but they also exist by themselves as soon as they proceed from their principle (for instance, the separate or separable substances). So inasmuch as they produce themselves by virtue of their own power, they contain themselves, and inasmuch as they are created by themselves they are also contained by themselves.[91]

Assuredly, there are two powers in all the substances that pos- 4 sess intelligence: one is cause of generation and the other is cause of conversion.[92] By virtue of their generative and fecund power they unfold within themselves a further form, life and act, and, as

vitam atque actum, unde videntur generare et quasi regenerare seipsas. Explicant insuper simile nonnihil in aliud, ubi videntur foras se quoque producere. Per conversivam vero virtutem ad se et ad causam reflectuntur, ubi etiam se reformare et conformare videntur. Intellectuales ergo substantiae hac apud Platonicos ratione ex seipsis et in seipsis existere vel produci dicuntur. Quae sane conditio non competit uni, penes quod, praeter actualem existentiam ipsam, non est praeterea virtus aliqua ab existentia differens, sicut in caeteris omnibus quae inde dici possint[23] existere, vel per quam explicetur intus ulterior forma vel actio, nec ulla rursus conversione opus est illi in quo nulla penitus diversio vel diversitas fingi potest.

: LXIII :

Quomodo unum neque moveri neque stare dicatur,
et quomodo sit motus et status in omnibus
praeter primum.

1 Parmenides in poemate quidem de uno ente statum motumque affirmat, quemadmodum affirmabit in suppositione secunda. Hic autem in suppositione prima motum de ipso simpliciter uno statumque negat. In poemate profecto primo quidem inquit ens primum unum immobileque consistere, deinde intellegentiam huic adhibuit intellegibili summo coniunctam. In sequentibus addidit intellegentiam esse sine motu non posse, ubi ultra statum videtur motum quoque tribuere, quoniam videlicet intellegentia versatur in vita, vita vero est quidam motus essentiae, vegetus videlicet actus ex essentia pullulans omnis vitae motusque principium, intel-

a result, they seem to generate and regenerate themselves, so to speak. They also unfold something similar within another, whereby they also appear to produce something outside themselves. By the power of conversion they turn toward themselves and their cause, whereby they seem to form themselves again and conform themselves to their cause. So, following the principle established among the Platonists, the intellectual substances are said to exist or to be produced by themselves and in themselves. Surely this condition does not befit the One, which besides its actual existence, contains no power that would differentiate it from its existence (as in the case of all the other things, which can be said to derive their existence from it), or whereby another form or action would unfold from within itself. The One does not need conversion, because it is impossible to imagine any difference or diversity within it.[93]

: LXIII :

How the One is said to be neither in motion nor at rest
and how motion and rest exist in all things
but the first principle.

In his poem Parmenides asserts rest and motion of the one being, just as he will do in the second hypothesis. But here, in the first hypothesis, he denies motion and rest of the absolute One [138B–39B]. In his poem he first declared that the first being is one and unmoved,[94] then he attributed to it the intelligence that is united to the highest intelligible.[95] In the next lines he added that intelligence cannot be without motion;[96] after rest he also appears to attribute motion to it, since intelligence concerns itself with life and life is the motion of essence: life is a vital act which brings forth from essence the principle of every life and motion, while

legentia vero est vitalis huius motionis terminus quidam reflexio-
que naturam suam animadvertens. Itaque intellegentia, quatenus
versatur in vita discernitque iam plurima, motus quidam esse videtur; quatenus vero quasi terminus progressum vitae sistit centro-
que refigit, status etiam iudicatur.

2   In *Theologia* nostra probavimus in omni re post primum quattuor haec inter se differre, essentiam et esse et virtutem et actionem. Hic igitur videtur essentia quidem ad suum esse perduci,
virtus autem hinc protinus egredi atque ad actionem e vestigio
progredi. Id totum motus quidam videri potest. Ubi et status
adesse putatur, quatenus, dum sequentia progrediuntur, interim
prima consistunt ac denique in suo quodam fine quiescunt. At
vero penes ipsum unum praeter simplicem existentiam non licet,
ut diximus, virtutem vel actionem aliquam adhibere, per quam
progressum aliquem possimus effingere vel quietem quandam
praeterea progressioni oppositam cogitare. Profecto potentia, actio,
motus differentem ab uno rationem habent. Non igitur applicanda
sunt uni, ut per haec unum efficiat omnia. Certum est interea non
per motum facere, ne forte omnia sint mobilia; item ne vel motum
efficiat per motum, vel ponere motum cogamur in uno. Iam vero
tria haec modo dicta ad bonum ubique contendunt, quasi non sint
ipsum bonum. Ipsum itaque bonum unumque non per aliud, sed
ipsa unitate bonitateque facit et perficit omnia. Si enim ubique
quod magis unum bonumque est magis et maiora efficit atque
plura, sequitur ut ipsa proprie unitate bonitateque omnia fiant.
Mitto nunc qua ratione Proclus uni auferat actionem, quia videlicet sicut quaecumque sunt ab ente ens habent, sic quaecumque
sunt[24] ab uno unum necessario habeant. Itaque materiam ab uno

intelligence limits this vital motion by making it turn back toward its own nature. So, inasmuch as intelligence concerns itself with life and then distinguishes a large number of things, it appears to be in motion, but to the extent that, as a kind of limit, it interrupts life's progression and brings it back to the center, it is also considered to be at rest.

We have shown in our *Theology* that there are four different elements in all the things that follow the first principle: essence, being, power and action.[97] The process is as follows: essence is led toward its own being, it seems, and from this movement power immediately springs forth and directly proceeds toward action. The whole process can be seen as a sort of motion. The process also appears to include rest: while the inferior realities proceed, the first realities, meanwhile, stand fast and are eventually at rest within their own limit. But, as we have said, no power or action should be added to the One's simple existence, so that it is impossible to imagine a procession within the One or conceive some rest that is opposed to this procession. Surely, potentiality, action and motion possess a rational principle that is different from that of the One. Therefore, they cannot be applied to the One, as if the One created all things through them. Clearly the One does not use motion to create. Otherwise, all things would be in motion; by using motion the One would create motion and we would need to place motion within the One. In addition, the three elements that we just mentioned always tend toward the Good, inasmuch as they are not the Good. So the One-and-Good does not create and perfect all things through the agency of another, but by virtue of their very unity and goodness. Indeed, it is a universal fact that the more "one" and "good" a thing is, the greater and more effects it creates. It follows that all things, properly speaking, are created by Unity and Goodness. I leave aside the way in which Proclus denies any action of the One on the grounds that, just as the things that derive their existence from being possess being, so all the things

procedentem unum esse, nullam tamen actionem in se habere, alioquin habituram, si per actionem aliquam uni propriam ab uno processerit.

3   Praeterea etsi videtur Parmenides solos hic motus corporeos uni negare sub nomine alterationis atque lationis, meminisse tamen oportet levem fore operam et puerilem, si hos solos uni sustulerit. Sed profecto sub horum appellatione sustulit omnes, tam videlicet incorporeos quam corporeos. Ait enim hos solos esse motus, item unum nullo motu moveri. Motus quidem alterationis in anima est, quando affectum et vitam et formam et actionem vel superiorum vel inferiorum subit, quasi facta iam altera, localis autem rectus, tum intus rationalis a superioribus ad inferiora discursus vel vicissim, tum extra mutatio loci et ipsa corporis vegetatio. Circuitus quoque fit in ea, quando vel seipsam animadvertit vel repetit eadem. In mentibus vero puris alteratio quidem est ex intellectuali potentia in obiectum intellegibile transformari; localis autem est circuitus ad seipsos pariter atque causam. Forte vero rectum quoque motum agunt, quatenus per aliam speciem aliam intuentur. His igitur motibus omnibus absolutum est ipsum simpliciter unum. Tu vero ubi alterationem audis, intellege non de qualitate tantum in qualitatem, sed de omni praeter localem transmutatione, scilicet generatione, corruptione, augmento, decremento, qualitatum commutatione atque similibus.

4   Denique sic argumentatur: quicquid movetur aut alteratur aut fertur, ipsum unum neque alteratur neque fertur. Quamobrem

that derive their existence from the One necessarily possess the One, and so matter, which proceeds from the One, is one, but possesses no action within itself; it would possess an action, if it proceeded from the One by virtue of an action of the One.[98]

In addition, even if by using the terms "alteration" and "spatial motion" [138B9–C1] Parmenides appears to deny solely corporeal motions of the One, let us bear in mind that it would be of little consequence, and facile, to suppress only these motions. In reality, Parmenides includes all motions in these terms, both the incorporeal and the corporeal ones, for he declares that "these are the only types of motions" [138C1], and likewise that "the One is moved by no motion" [139A].[99] The motion of alteration occurs in the soul, when the soul undergoes emotion, life, form and action caused by superior or inferior realities, since it is altered by these; rectilinear local motion also occurs within the soul, both from within when discursive reasoning proceeds from the superior realities to the inferior realities and conversely, and from without when it changes place and gives life to the body. Circular motion also occurs within the soul, when the soul becomes conscious of itself or when it repeats the same circuits.[100] Alteration occurs in pure minds when they transform themselves from intellectual potency to intelligible object; local circular motion occurs when they turn toward themselves and toward their cause. They might also engage in rectilinear motion when they contemplate one species through another. So the absolute One is separate from all these kinds of motion. However, when you hear the term "alteration," you must understand that this term not only concerns a quality within a quality, but also any transformation besides local motion: generation, corruption, increase, decrease, change of qualities and so on.

Finally, the argument goes as follows: anything that is in motion either moves spatially or undergoes alteration. The One neither moves spatially nor undergoes alteration. So it is not in mo-

nullo modo movetur. Primo quidem probat non alterari, deinde neque ferri probabit. Ita vero si alteratur, aut transmutatur totum aut ex parte mutatur. Si totum omnino, vel transit in multitudinem unius expertem, quae quidem nusquam esse potest, vel in nihilum, unde nihil in rebus amplius erit uno non existente; sin autem per aliquid sui mutatur, in eo iam aliud erit et aliud, quorum alterum quidem manet, alterum vero movetur, rursumque recipitur aliquid peregrinum. Itaque non unum est, sed multitudo quaedam est et fit, quod ita movetur. Animam vero concessimus alterari, dum se rebus aliis aliisque per affectum modumque actionis et vitae conformat; intellectum quoque, dum se ad intelligibile conferens et formatur illo et interim vel rem distinguendo vel se applicando intellegibilibus pluribus conformatur. Sic itaque et anima et intellectus, dum id ipsum quod sunt permanent, multiplicia fiunt, quod tamen de uno cogitari nefas.

5 Post haec unum neque loco ferri probat hunc in modum: quicquid loco movetur sive localiter, ut ita dixerim, aut circa locum eundem versatur in orbem, aut locum pro loco mutat in rectum, vel mixto quodam ex his obliquo motu mutatur. At unum nec in orbem nec in rectum mutari ullo modo potest, ideoque neque mixtum ex his sibi alienis subire motum. Quapropter nullo motu mutatur.

tion. Parmenides first shows that the One does not undergo any alteration, then he will show that it is not moving spatially. So, if the One undergoes alteration, it does so by changing as a whole or in one of its parts. If it moves as a whole, then either it transforms into a multitude which is deprived of unity and which cannot be anywhere, or into nothing, and in that case there will be nothing left in nature, given the nonexistence of the One. But if it undergoes some change in a part of itself, there will be one thing and [then] another in it, one motionless and one in motion, and again the One will be taking in something adventitious. So it is not the One, but a multitude that is and is created, because it undergoes this kind of motion. We have conceded that the soul undergoes alteration when it conforms to changing stimuli owing to emotion and its mode of action and life; the intellect also undergoes alteration, whenever, uniting to its intelligible object, it is formed by it and, when distinguishing something or applying itself to something, it conforms itself to the multiplicity of intelligible objects. For this reason both the soul and the intellect, so long as they remain what they are, become multiple. Yet it is wrong to think this about the One.

Parmenides then shows that the One does not move spatially as 5 follows [138C]: anything that is moved spatially or locally, so to speak, turns round in the same place, shifts from one place to another in a rectilinear motion, or undergoes a change through an intermediate, oblique motion. Yet the One can by no means undergo circular or straight motion, and cannot, therefore, undergo an oblique motion,[101] which results from the mixture of two motions that are alien to it. Therefore it is not altered by motion.

: LXIV :

Unum neque circulo movetur nec in rectum.

1 Probat unum ita circulariter non moveri: quod circulo fertur necessario medium et extrema circa medium habet, mediumque manet in eo, caeteris permutatis. Itaque et partes habet et totum. Haec autem uni propter supremam simplicitatem eius competere nequeunt. Igitur circulo non movetur. Circularem hic motum uni demens non solum corporeum circulum adimit, sed etiam incorporeum. Nempe in anima et intellectu permanet ipsum eius centrum et unitas ipsa virtusque praecipua sive substantia, dum caeterae partes et vires actionesque illinc effluunt atque refluunt et quomodolibet multipliciter operantur. Quod quidem circuitum quendam referre videtur, ab ipsa unius simplicitate penitus alienum.

2 Probat praeterea unum non moveri in rectum hac forma: quod movetur in rectum ab hoc loco transit in illum, aut igitur totum simul hic est et ibi, aut totum neque hic neque ibi est, aut pars quidem eius hic est, ibi vero pars alia. Si concedatur primum, iam non movetur, sed simul utrobique permanet. Si secundum, nihil ad ipsum locus hic vel ille pertinere videtur. Si tertium, iam est partibile. Unum igitur, cum sit individuum, hoc motu moveri non potest. Probatum quidem est in superioribus unum in aliquo non existere, quoniam conditio eiusmodi sit dignitate unius inferior. Cum vero in aliquo fieri, id est nuper alicui contingere, vel aliquo

: LXIV :

The One is not moved in a circle or in a straight line.

Parmenides shows that the One is not moved in a circle as follows   1
[138C–D]: what is moved in a circle necessarily possesses a center
and extremities around its center; the center remains immobile
within the circle, while the other parts undergo permutation. So it
possesses parts and a whole. Yet these conditions cannot befit the
One given its supreme simplicity. Therefore, it is not moved in a
circle. When denying circular motion to the One Parmenides not
only removes corporeal circular motion, but also that which is incorporeal. Surely what constitutes the very center, unity and first
power, or substance within the soul and the intellect remains immobile, while the other parts, powers and actions flow forth from
them and back again, and operate in some sense in a multiple way.
This, which seems to be related to circular motion, is totally es-
tranged from the One's simplicity.

Parmenides then shows that the One is not moved in a rectilin-   2
ear motion as follows: that which is moved in a rectilinear motion
moves from one place to another. Thus it is, at the same time, totally in two different places, or totally in none of these two places,
or part of it is in one place and part of it in another [138E]. In the
first case, the One is not in motion, but it remains at rest simultaneously in both places. In the second, neither of the two places
appears to befit the One. The third case implies that the One is
divisible. Therefore, since the One is undivided, it cannot be
moved in a rectilinear motion. Now it has been shown above that
the One is not "in" anything, since such condition is inferior to the
One's transcendence. Yet since "coming to be in something" (that
is, to happen to something, be moved toward something or to

ferri, vel quomodolibet alterari etiam deterius sit quam in aliquo esse, multo minus id uni competere iudicatur.

3 Dici quidem potest aliquid simul totum in loco et extra locum existere, ut mens et intellectualis anima, multo magis unum. Fieri vero per motum et intro simul et extra totum, dictu ridiculum.

4 Hic iterum te admoneo ut, dum motiones partesque corporeas uni detrahit, simul etiam incorporeas existimes esse sublatas. Anima, siquidem vel divina per multiplices formas intellegentiasque intellegibili superno se admovet circa aeternum temporaliter mobiliterque se versans, et quasi recto quodam incessu, modo per hanc formam actionemque suam, modo per illam transiens, illud attingit similiter quidem, non tamen temporaliter, distributum. In hac ergo progressione recta, anima neque tota in illo intellegibili fit,[25] neque est tota seorsum, sed partim quidem fit ibi, dum actu illud attingit, partim vero nondum est ibi, per actiones videlicet alias in posterum explicandas. Possumus et in mente divina processum quasi rectum auspicari, qua ratione e suo quodam centro progrediuntur multiformes ideae. Ubi sane pars quidem mentis vel intellegentiae suae in hac idea, pars in illa videtur existere, quamvis tota simul essentia sit in cunctis. Conditiones tandem eiusmodi non solum corporibus, sed animabus etiam atque mentibus attributae uni competere nequeunt.

5 Omnia denique, in quibus virtus et actio ab essentia quomodolibet distinguuntur, quodammodo moveri videntur, quia et ab essentia virtus et a virtute progreditur actio. Sed penes ipsum unum, quemadmodum supra diximus, propter supremam simplicitatem, non possunt duo haec ulla ratione ab existentia fingi distincta,

undergo any kind of change), is even inferior to "being in something," it is considered to be even less suitable to the One.

Surely a thing can be said to be totally and simultaneously in and outside a place, such as the mind and the intellectual soul and, even more so, the One. But it is a foolish thing to say that the One comes to be totally inside and outside a place through motion.[102]

Again, here one must bear in mind that when Parmenides denies corporeal motions and parts of the One, he also simultaneously denies incorporeal motions. When the divine soul moves itself toward the higher intelligible world through the multiplicity of forms and intelligences, turning around eternity through time and motion, and moving as though in a rectilinear progression, at one time by way of one form and action, at another time by way of another form and action, it reaches the intelligible world, which is divided in the same way, except that it is not temporal. During this rectilinear progression, the soul neither comes to be totally in the intelligible world nor is totally separate from it, but one part of it comes to be in the intelligible world by actually reaching it, and a part of it is not yet in it, in the sense that it will be through other actions that will unfold later on. One can also assume the existence of a kind of rectilinear procession within the divine intelligence, inasmuch as the multiform Ideas proceed from its center. In this case, surely, one part of mind or of its intelligence seems to be in one Idea, and another in another Idea, although its whole essence is simultaneously present in all parts. Finally, conditions like these, which are not only attributed to bodies, but also to souls and minds, cannot befit the One.

Ultimately all the things in which power and action are somehow distinguished from essence appear to be in motion in some way, because power proceeds from essence and action from power. But as we have said above, given the One's supreme simplicity, we cannot imagine that there exist in the One two things that are in any way distinct from existence, especially since in that case, the

praesertim quoniam si ita finxeris, interrogabimus numquid ipsum unum produxerit virtutem actionemve suam per virtutem aliam actionemve procedentem, an per ipsam potius existentiam. Si forte primum concesseris, mox infinito cuidam progressui aditum patefeceris. Si secundum dederis, ipsum quidem unum sola cum existentia pones a virtute sequente procul et actione secretum. Quod vero penes ipsum sub quadam virtutis et actionis forma confinxeras nec ipsum erit amplius nec aliquid eius, sed post ipsum quidam videlicet illius effectus.[26] Virtus quidem illius erit ipsa primi entis essentia, operatio[27] vero vita et intellegentia essentiae primae propria. Haec quidem principii primi praerogativa est, ut circa ipsum pro virtute et actione sit substantia substantialisque actio mox post ipsum in medium afferenda. Forsan vero et Aristoteles ut divisionem atque motum evitaret in primo causam finalem manifestius quam efficientem censuit nominandum.

: LXV :

Quomodo negatur de uno status.

1 Probaturus unum iterum neque stare, propositionem in superioribus probatam repetit asserentem unum in aliquo non manere. Si igitur non manet in aliquo, consequenter neque permanet in eodem. Neque stat igitur, siquidem stare non aliter quam in eodem permanere definiri solet.

2 Concesserit forte quispiam unum neque dicendum mobile neque stabile, ne forte sic intellegatur quoquomodo compositum.

question will be whether the One has produced its power and action through another power or an action which proceed from it, or through its existence. In the first case, you might immediately make clear that this would occur by virtue of an infinite process. In the second case, you will posit that the One is solely accompanied by its existence, whereas it is totally separate from power and action, which would follow far behind. Yet what you had imagined within the One under the form of a power and action will cease to be the One or something belonging to the One, but be something that comes after it, such as one of its effects. Its power will then be the very essence of the first being, its operation, the life and intelligence of the first essence. Such are the prerogatives of the first principle: to have a substance and an activity inherent to its substance, rather than a power and an action that must be placed immediately after it. Surely it was to avoid positing division and motion within the first principle that Aristotle believed that the One should be called "final cause" more explicitly than "efficient cause."[103]

: LXV :

The way in which rest is denied of the One.

To demonstrate that the One is not at rest, Parmenides repeats 1 the proposition that has been demonstrated above and according to which the One is not in anything. If the One is not in anything, then it is not in the same place. Therefore, it is not at rest, since being at rest is usually defined as remaining in the same place [139A–B].

Someone might perhaps concede that the One cannot be said 2 to be in motion nor at rest, lest it be understood to somehow be

Nam et stabile statu stat et mobile motu movetur. Nihil vero prohibere putabit, quominus unum appellemus statum ipsum aut motum. Nos autem opinionem hanc ratione quadam alibi probata respuimus, scilicet unum esse omnibus oppositionibus rebusque invicem quomodolibet oppositis excellentius, ut opposita quaelibet et pariter efficere et in unum conciliare possit. Virtute enim illius quod est ab oppositis segregatum,[28] opposita copulantur. Si enim sit utrumque simul oppositum, compositum erit a superno quodam diversorum conciliatore conflatum. Sin vero oppositorum alterutrum fuerit, oppositum alterum et quae ad ipsum pertinent non efficiat. Oppositorum quidem duorum quod altero est deterius nemo utique dixerit esse ipsum unum universi principium, sed forte quod melius. Verumtamen neque hoc esse potest. Nam et sub ordine quodam cum altero opposito numerabitur et alterum non participabit illius. Oppositum enim non fit per oppositum oppositi particeps. Quod ergo non erit unius ac boni particeps merito nec ullo modo erit unum aut bonum. Denique status ipse, quantumlibet perfectus, et ipse motus, quomodolibet efficax, certa quaedam species est et perfectio definita. Seiuncta enim sunt invicem neque propria alterius perfectio est in altero. Neutrum itaque perfectissimum, neutrum ergo primum. Primum namque, ab omni definita perfectione seiunctum, sub simplici ratione boni perfectiones omnium, tamquam perfectionem pro cunctis unam simul et universam, continet eminenter.

composite. For what is at rest is at rest by virtue of rest, and what is in motion is in motion by virtue of motion. But one will consider that nothing prevents us from calling the One "rest" and "motion." We have refuted elsewhere this opinion with the following proof: the One transcends all oppositions and opposites, so as to have the power to both produce all opposites equally and bring them together into a harmonious unity. For it is through the power of the One, which is separate from opposites, that the opposites are united. Indeed, if the One is both opposites together, it will be a composite produced by a superior principle causing the union of these opposites. Conversely, if it were one of two opposites, it would not produce the other or the things that are related to it. Surely nobody would say that the One, which is the principle of the universe, is the inferior of two opposites, but one might perhaps say that it is the superior of the two. But even this is impossible. For in this case the One will be enumerated under one particular order together with one of the two opposites, while the other opposite will not participate in it. An opposite does not come to be through the opposite participating in its opposite. So it will not participate in the One-and-Good and thus will by no means be the One-and-Good. Finally, rest, inasmuch as it is perfect, and motion, inasmuch as it is an efficient cause of some sort, are each a certain species and a particular perfection. For they are separate from one another and the perfection of one of them is not in the other. Therefore, neither motion nor rest is the most perfect, and thus neither is the first principle. For the first principle, which transcends any particular perfection, eminently contains under the simple rational principle of the Good the perfections of all things, while being the perfection that is simultaneously one and universal for all things.[104]

: LXVI :

Quinque genera entis. Tres negationum gradus.
Decem praedicamenta negata. De eodem
alteroque nonnihil.

1 Quinque genera entis in *Sophiste* tractantur ac nos eadem in *Philebo* et *Timaeo* atque Plotino latius pertractavimus. Hic itaque breviter perstringemus primo quidem, iterum admonentes quod et in superioribus admonuimus: dum Parmenides de uno negat omnia genera et propria entis, totum ens negare de uno, de quo post omnia entis propria manifeste tandem negabit essentiam; dum vero negat quaecumque pertinent ad ens de uno, tamquam illa minus digna, unum universo enti praeponere. Repetam iterum sicut omnis multitudo talium taliumve entium ad unum ens tale reducitur, sic omnia in primis entia talia sive talia ad unum primum simpliciter ens postremo reduci, idque unum ens ab ipso simpliciter uno pendere. Qua igitur ratione hoc unum ens simpliciter est ab uno sortitur essentiam; qua vero procedendo existit ab illo alteritatem nanciscitur atque motum; qua rursus existendo ab illo ad se convertitur et ad illud identitatem accipit atque statum. Per essentiam quidem hoc est secundo quod primo illud existit; per alteritatem vero et ab illo et ipsum intra se ab aliisque distinguitur; per motum quoque progreditur inde, progreditur intra se, progreditur et ad alia operando; per identitatem simile est illi, congruit quoque secum, cum caeteris quoque consentit; per statum denique nec ab illo nec a seipso discedit firmiterque propria retinet neque cum alienis se confundi permittit. Mitto nunc quo-

: LXVI :

The five genera of being, the three levels of negations,
the ten categories denied of the One, and some
considerations on "the same" and "the other."

The five genera of being are treated in the *Sophist*, and we have   1
explored in much detail this doctrine in our commentaries on the
Philebus, the *Timaeus* and Plotinus.[105] So here I shall first briefly
summarize the doctrine, recalling, as we have done before, that by
denying of the One all genera and properties of being, Parmenides
denies of the One the totality of being, and that after denying all
the properties of being, he will finally openly deny essence; by denying of the One all the things that pertain to being, as though
these were inferior to the One, he places the One before universal
being. Secondly, I shall repeat that, just as every multitude of particular beings is brought back to a single one being corresponding
to it, so all the beings that were initially particular are eventually
brought back to the first and absolute one being, and this one being depends on the absolute One. So, inasmuch as this one being
is absolute, it obtains essence from the One; inasmuch as it receives its existence through its procession from the One, it obtains
otherness and motion; inasmuch as by deriving its existence from
the One it turns toward both itself and the One, it obtains sameness and rest. Through essence it is secondarily that which the
One is primarily. Through otherness it is distinguished from the
One, and is distinct from itself internally and from others. Through
motion it proceeds from the One, it proceeds within itself, and it
also proceeds toward others by its activity. Through sameness it is
like the One and is also in harmony with itself as well as in accordance with all others. Finally, through rest it does not depart
from the One or from itself; it firmly retains its own properties

modo essentia dependens ab uno non unum est et unum. Quia vero non unum sortitur infinitatem, sed rursus quia sit unum terminum adipiscitur. Infinitatem quidem habet praecipue penes vitam, terminum vero penes intellectum, rursus per infinitatem praecipue habet motum atque alterum, per terminum vero praecipue statum atque idem. De his profecto in *Philebo* et *Sophiste* latius pertractamus. Post quinque rerum genera quae in primo pro sua dignitate sunt et in sequentibus omnibus pro sua cuiusque natura, in primo emicant multiformes ideae et in sequentibus multae formae.

2   Sed antequam prosequamur quomodo Parmenides hic, postquam negavit de uno statum atque motum, neget idem atque alterum, operae pretium forte fuerit recensere triplicem negationum ordinem a Proclo diligentius observatum. Alia sane negantur de uno quantum sibi competit ad seipsum, atque hic est primus apud Parmenidem negationis gradus. Alia vero quantum sibi pariter et ad alia, hic gradus est secundus. Alia denique quantum spectat ad alia solum, hic gradus tertius. Multitudinem enim et totum figuramque et in aliquo esse motumque et statum de uno negat quantum proprie spectat ad unum. At vero idem et alterum, simile, dissimile, aequale, inaequale, senius, iunius uni aufert et ad se et ad alia. Neque enim sibimet est neque caeteris idem similiter et quae in hac sorte sequuntur. Denique opinabile, scibile, nominabile tollit uni quantum ad alia pertinet. Omnibus enim est hac conditione prorsus incognitum. Cum igitur motus et status ad primum praecipue gradum pertineant, idem vero et alterum potius

and does not let itself be mixed up with alien things. I leave aside for the moment the way in which essence, which depends on the One, is both not-one and one; *qua* not-one it receives infinity and *qua* one it has limit. It possesses infinity especially when essence is in life, and limit especially when it is in the intellect. Moreover, it possesses motion and the attribute "other" especially by way of the infinite; it possesses rest and the attribute "same" especially by way of limit. We treat this doctrine in more detail in our commentaries on the *Philebus* and the *Sophist*.[106] Following the five genera of things, which exist in the first being according to their own dignity and in the things subsequent to it according to the nature proper to each, there shine, within the first being, the multiform Ideas, and, within the realities that follow, the multiple forms.

Before we proceed and explore the way in which Parmenides, 2 after having denied rest and motion, denies the attributes "same" and "other" of the One, it might perhaps be worth reviewing the three orders of negations, as they have been carefully observed by Proclus. Clearly some things are denied of the One itself in relation to itself: this is the first level of negation in the *Parmenides*. Other things are denied in relation to itself and to others alike: this is the second level of negation. Finally, some things are denied only in relation to others: this is the third level of negation. So the attributes "multitude," "whole," "shape," "being in something," "motion" and "rest" are denied of the One properly in relation to the One, whereas the attributes "same" and "other," "like" and "unlike," "equal" and "unequal," "older" and "younger" are denied of the One in relation to itself and to others, because the One is not the same as itself or as the others, and this applies likewise to each of the attributes of that sort that follow. Finally, the attributes "thinkable," "knowable" and "nameable" are denied of the One in relation to others, for the One is utterly unknowable to all things in that condition [of being other than the One]. Since, therefore, "motion" and "rest" mostly concern the first level of negation, while "same"

ad secundum, merito motum statumque priusquam idem alterumve negavit, praesertim quia primum ens per processum declaravit tum se alterum a primo, tum in se alterum aliquid atque alterum, per statum vero suum in uno declaravit identitatem. Prius ergo sunt illa quam ista.

3   Animadverte interim quomodo negat uni praedicamenta: dum enim negat idem aut alterum, demit illi substantiam; dum simile atque dissimile, qualitatem; dum aequale et inaequale, quantitatem; ubi senius aut iunius, tollit 'quando;' passionem vero et actionem sustulit una cum motu; sustulit et 'ubi' locumque, dum in aliquo esse negaret. Habitum quoque et relationem passim aufert, ubi nihil habere probat, cum nullo congruere. Sed ultra praedicamenta decem ens aufert quoque transcendens, cui saltem quinque illa genera ubique conveniunt, manifeste tamen uni negata. Plerique putant praedicamenta decem rebus intelligibilibus, praesertim primis, esse deteriora, nec in illis hanc esse substantiam, quae definitur vicissim opposita capere, multoque minus illic esse speciem atque genus, siquidem minus substantiae sint quam ipsa prius definita substantia, minime omnium accidentia, siquidem exiliora sint[29] speciebus atque generibus. Nihil itaque mirum est praedicamenta negari de primo, si communiter de omnibus sunt negata divinis, neque etiam valde mirum negare de illo species ideales, quales intellectuali etiam et intelligibili monade inferiores existunt. In primis ergo negantur de primo prima ipsa et amplissima entis genera ideis antiquiora ad vitalem essentiam pertinentia. Mitto

and "other" concern the second level, Parmenides was right to deny "motion" and "rest" before denying "same" and "other," especially since through procession the first being manifested itself as both other than the first principle and in itself one thing and another, while through being at rest within the One the first being manifested sameness. Motion and rest precede, therefore, "same" and "other."

Now let us examine the way in which Parmenides denies the categories of the One: by denying "same" and "other," he removes substance from it; by denying "like" and "unlike," quality; by denying "equal" and "unequal," quantity. When he denies that the One is older or younger, he removes the attribute "when"; he removed passivity and action when denying "motion." He also removed "where" and location when he denied that the One is in anything; he also removed disposition and relation by showing that the One does not possess anything, and is not in accordance with anything. Beyond the ten categories, however, he also removes transcendent being, since being always befits at least the first five genera [of being], which are clearly denied of the One. Most Platonists consider that the ten categories are inferior to the intelligible realities, especially the first ones; they consider that intelligible realities do not contain substance, since substance is defined as "being receptive of opposites in succession,"[107] and even less do they contain species and genera, since these are inferior to the substance defined above; they contain no accidents, since accidents are more insubstantial than species and genera. So there is nothing remarkable in denying the categories of the first principle, since they are generally denied of all divine realities; there is nothing surprising in denying the ideal species of the first principle, since these are also inferior to the intellectual and intelligible monad. So Parmenides first denies of the first principle the first and most important genera of being, which precede the Ideas and concern vital essence.[108] I leave

3

nunc, quod Proclus addit, singulos deorum ordines per haec negari de primo tamquam cunctis excelsiore.

4 Denique Parmenides in poemate idem et alterum de uno primoque ente verbis manifestis affirmat. Quae quidem et de eodem affirmabit in suppositione secunda; in hac vero suppositione prima de uno negat, declarans interea super unum ens extare simpliciter unum.

: LXVII :

Unum nec a seipso alterum est nec idem alteri
et ab omnibus conditionibus est absolutum.

1 Quattuor circa idem et alterum conclusiones adducit. Quoniam vero ab evidentioribus est incohandum, merito de uno negat esse vel alterum a seipso vel aliis idem, tamquam manifestiora, priusquam neget vel esse idem sibi, vel ab aliis alterum, quae quidem duo sunt difficiliora probatu. Praeterea quoniam alteritas alienior est ab uno quam identitas, prius argumentatur unum non esse alterum a seipso, tamquam concessu facilius, quam argumentetur unum non esse aliis idem. Probatio vero prima est eiusmodi: si unum esset alterum a seipso, alterum et discrepans ab ipso uno foret, non esset igitur ipsum unum. Secundae vero probationis haec est forma: si unum esset idem alteri, iam esset illud alterum, non igitur erit ulterius ipsum unum, sed alterum erit ab uno, scilicet aliud quiddam praeter ipsum unum.

2 Tu vero hic intellege unum ipsum nullam cum aliis identitatem communionemque habere. Si enim quanto altior causa est, tanto

aside for the moment what Proclus adds, that in this way each order of gods is denied of the first principle because the first principle is superior to all of them.[109]

Finally, Parmenides clearly asserts in his poem the attributes 4 "same" and "other" of the first one being,[110] as he will also do in the second hypothesis. In the first hypothesis, however, he denies these attributes of the first principle, thereby revealing that the absolute One is above the one being.[111]

∴ LXVII ∴

The One is not other than itself, nor the same as another,
and it is separate from all conditions.

Parmenides draws four conclusions regarding the same and the 1 other. Since we must begin with propositions that are more easily understandable to us, Parmenides rightly denies what is more immediately clear — that the One is other than itself or the same as others [139B], before denying that it is the same as itself or other than others, which is more difficult to prove [139C]. In addition, because otherness is more alien to the One than sameness, Parmenides first argues that the One is not other than itself, which is easier to concede, before arguing that the One is not the same as others. The first demonstration is as follows: if the One was other than itself, it would be other than, and different from, "the One," and thus would not be the One. The second proposition goes as follows: if the One was the same as another, then it would be something other; it would cease, therefore, to be the One, and be other than one, i.e. something else than the One.[112]

But here you must bear in mind that the One has no identity 2 or communion with others. If it is true that the higher the cause

remotior est a propriis effectuum suorum conditionibus, altissima certe causa causarum ab omnibus entium omnium proprietatibus est penitus segregata. Itaque cum rebus ullis neque specie neque genere neque ordine congruit, alioquin non solum foret ipsum quod existit, verum etiam speciei vel generis vel ordinis illius foret particeps, neque foret amplius simpliciter unum. Nempe quod participat aliquid non est solum id ipsum quod participatur ab eo, sed praeterea aliquid aliud, alioquin non esset illius particeps, sed illud ipsum prorsus existeret. Ipsum igitur unum nullius est particeps ne forte desinat esse simpliciter unum. Inferiora quidem non participat, ipsius videlicet maiestate prorsus indigna, superius autem aliquid participare non potest. Quid enim superius uno? Profecto quatenus per rerum gradus ad superiorem causam gradatim superioremque conscendimus, eatenus ad magis unum et simplicius pervenimus. Ipsum ergo simpliciter unum est cunctis excelsius.

3 Neque fingere licet ipsum vere unum esse geminum, scilicet hoc et illud, alioquin qua ratione unum est utrumque non different. Distingui tamen necesse est si duo fuerint. Distinguetur igitur hoc ab illo per proprietatem quandam quam praeter ipsum unum habet hoc, et suam similiter habet illud. Utrumque igitur erit mixtum et multiplex et unum quiddam. Neutrum ergo simpliciter unum. Cum igitur ipsum unum sit unicum, singulare, solum, si fingatur alteri cuidam idem evadere, certe fiet idem alicui, quod non vere unum. Si hoc ipsum 'fieri huic idem' est cum hoc aliquo modo congruere, communem ordinem iam subibit fietque cum hoc communis naturae particeps, neque simplex et absolutum amplius erit. Sin autem 'fieri huic idem' est hoc ipsum prorsus eva-

is, the more remote it is from the conditions proper to its own effects, then the highest cause of causes is assuredly totally separate from all the properties of all beings. So the One is in accordance with none of the realities, whether in species, genus, or order, otherwise it would not only exist as "the One," but would also participate in a species, genus, and order, and would cease to be the absolute One. Surely that which participates in something is not only the thing which is participated in by it, but also something else, otherwise it would not participate in this thing, but would be this very thing. So the One does not participate in anything, otherwise it would cease to be the absolute One. Surely it does not participate in inferior realities, since these are unworthy of the majesty of the One. It cannot participate in anything superior, for what is superior to the One? We rise to what is ever more one and simple to the degree that we ascend through the hierarchy of beings toward progressively more elevated causes. Thus the absolute One is superior to all things.[113]

It is impossible to imagine that the One is double, that is, that it is two different things, otherwise, since it is "One," the two elements could not differ. [If we imagine that this is the case, however, since] one must investigate separately the instance where the One would be two things, one thing will be distinguished from the other by virtue of a property that this thing possesses independently from the One, and the same will apply to the other thing. Thus both things will be mixed, multiple and a particular one. So none of them will be the absolute One. Since, therefore, the One is unique, singular and separate, in the case where one imagines that it becomes the same as another, it will assuredly become the same as something that is not really one. Since the fact of "becoming the same as something" consists in being somehow in accordance with that thing, the One will be placed under the same order, and come to participate in the same nature, as this thing, and will cease to be simple and absolute. If, on the other hand, "be-

3

dere, iam illud quod ante asserebatur simpliciter unum, prorsus erit hoc, quod postea ponebatur nec vere nec simpliciter unum. Caetera quidem, quoniam in specie, in genere, in ordine computantur, sic ad identitatem se habere possunt, ut invicem eadem quodammodo esse valeant, neque tamen penitus eadem, ut Socrates cum Platone idem specie, neque prorsus idem, caeteraque similiter. At ipsum unum extra omne consortium segregatum, si praeterea fingatur cuipiam esse idem, cum nequeat externa quapiam conditione vel societate idem fingi, necessario ipsa sua singularitate naturae huic iam erit penitus idem.

: LXVIII :

Unum non est ab aliis alterum.

1 Facile quivis putaverit unum esse et ab aliis alterum et sibi ipsi idem. Communis enim opinio recepisse videtur ad unum pertinere, ut et extra distinctum sit ab aliis et indistinctum sibi sit intus. Verumtamen Parmenides, accuratius ista perpendens, neque alterum neque idem de uno iudicat praedicandum, sive accipias alterum pro ipsa alteritate formali, sive pro alteritatis participe quodam, similiter sive idem pro identitate, sive pro participante susceperis. Cum vero identitas magis ad unum attinere communiter videatur quam alteritas, nimirum, tamquam a faciliori

coming the same as something" is to become that very thing, then what we initially called the absolute One will be the thing that we subsequently postulated as not being the true and absolute One. As to the others, because they are included in a species, a genus and an order, they can be related to sameness in such a way that they can be the same as one another without being completely the same. For instance, Socrates is the same as Plato in species, but is not completely the same, and so on. But if the One, which transcends all associations, is then imagined to be the same as something, since it cannot be imagined to be the same in any outward condition or relation, it will necessarily be the same as the very singularity of its own nature.[114]

: LXVIII :

The One is not other than the others.

Someone could easily believe that the One is other than the others 1
and the same as itself. Indeed, we generally consider, it seems, that it pertains to the One to be outwardly distinct for the others and inwardly indistinct from itself. However, Parmenides, who is very carefully pondering these questions, rules out that the attributes "other" and "same" should be predicated of the One, whether "other" is considered in relation to formal otherness or to something that participates in otherness and, likewise, whether "same" is regarded in relation to sameness or something that participates in it. Since sameness is usually believed to be more akin to the One than otherness, Parmenides begins with the proposition that is easier to demonstrate, and shows that the One is not other than the others, before showing that it is not the same as itself

quodam incipiens, unum non esse ab aliis alterum prius probat
quam non esse sibi ipsi idem. Utrumque tamen inopinabile vulgo.

2   Memento primo quidem quod est ab aliis alterum, aut per alteritatem quam participat esse alterum, aut seipso alterum esse, utpote quod sit alteritas ipsa; deinde vero aliam unius, aliam alteritatis rationem esse. Unum enim absolutum est, alteritas autem
refertur ad alterum. Praeterea unius quidem proprium est unire,
alteritas vero dividere. Quapropter haec non solum alia est ab illo,
sed etiam aliena. Si igitur unum dicatur ab aliis alterum, cum non
qua ratione unum est, sit et alterum, forte tamquam alteritatis
cuiusdam particeps fieri alterum iudicabitur. Itaque alienam admittens alteritatem non erit ultra simpliciter unum. Neque recte
rursum dici potest unum ab aliis alterum ut alteritas ipsa. Haec
enim seipsa est altera, unum vero non seipso, siquidem non qua
ratione unum effici potest alterum, cum alia et aliena ratio unius a
ratione alteritatis existat.

3   Verum dum rationem ipsius unius et ab alteritate dicimus alienam et a generibus entis universoque ente penitus segregatam,
periclitamur interea confiteri unum esse ab his omnibus alterum.
Sed memento alteritatem proprie dici proprietatem quandam divi-
soriam entibus insitam, identitati per conciliationem advenienti
prorsus oppositam. Absit igitur ut per proprietatem entibus desti-
natam et oppositioni subiectam ipsum unum entium principium
concedamus ab entibus segregatum. Quando enim segregatum dicimus tunc incomparabili simplicitate sua ineffabiliter supereminens cogitamus. Aliter enim corpus separatum est a corpore, scilicet per locum, aliter anima a corpore, scilicet per substantiam

[139C]. Both propositions, however, cannot be grasped by ordinary people.

Let us first remember that that which is other than the others 2 is either "other" by participating in otherness, or "other" than itself by virtue of being itself otherness; secondly, that the rational principle of the One is different from that of otherness, for the One is separate, while otherness exists in relation to another. In addition, it pertains to the One to unify, whereas it pertains to otherness to divide. So otherness is not only other than the One, it is also alien to it. Thus if the One is said to be other than others, given that it is not other *qua* One, it might perhaps appear to become other by participating in some otherness, and so by admitting otherness, which is alien to it, it will cease to be the absolute One. One cannot rightly say, either, that the One is other than others as being itself otherness. For otherness is other than itself, whereas the One is not other than itself, since *qua* One it cannot be made other, given that the rational principle of the One is other than, and alien to, that of otherness.

However, when we say that the rational principle of the One is 3 alien to otherness, and totally separate from the genera of being and universal being, we run the risk of admitting that the One is other than all these things. But we must remember that otherness is properly defined as a kind of divisory property, which resides within beings and is the opposite of sameness, which occurs through union. Let us not concede, therefore, that the One, which is the principle of beings, is separate from beings by a property that properly belongs to beings and is subject to opposition. For when we say that the One is separate, we mean that it is ineffably super-eminent by virtue of its incomparable simplicity. Indeed, there are multiple ways to be separate: the body is separate from another body through location, the soul is separated from the body through a separable substance, and it is through essence, or at least through a formal otherness in their rational principle, that

separabilem, aliter intellectus ab anima et plures intellectus invicem et inter se ideae, scilicet per ipsam essentiam[30] vel saltem per formalem rationis alteritatem, ipsum quoque unum aliter, scilicet per simplicissimam eminentiam ipsius propriam nulli convenientem. Alteritas igitur entibus concedatur, in eo autem quod super ens existit vel in nihilo ne nominetur quidem. Quis enim rite dixerit nihilum ab ente alterum esse quasi sit aliquid praeter ipsum? Similiter nemo recte dixerit unum ipsum ente superius per alteritatem, quae entis conditio est, esse ab ente semotum.

: LXIX :

Unum non est sibi ipsi idem.

1 Alia unius, alia identitatis ratio est. Unum enim est absolutum, identitas relativa, nam semper est aliquid alicui idem. Propterea unum tamquam absolutum est ante identitatem utpote relativam. Praeterea si unam hic ceram habeas, ibi vero quattuor, cupiasque hanc illis eandem numero fieri, divides hanc in quattuor. Haec ergo per divisionem atque numerum eadem illis evadet. Si rursum cupias illas ibi ceras his hic ceris alteras numero fieri, quattuor in ceram unam coges. Sic itaque rursus per unionem fit alteritas, quemadmodum modo per multitudinem efficiebatur identitas. Unde concluditur, quod proposui, rationem unitatis et identitatis inter se differre. Si ita se res habet, non potest ipsum unum sibi-

the intellect is separate from the soul, the multiplicity of intellects are separate from one another and the Ideas are separate among themselves, whereas the One is separate through its utterly simple eminence, which properly belongs to nothing else than it. Let us admit, therefore, that otherness resides in beings, but let us not even mention its existence in what is above being or resides in nothing. For who would rightly say that "nothing" is other than "being," as if it were something in addition to nothing? Likewise, nobody could rightly say that the One, which is superior to being, is separate from being through otherness, which is a condition of being.[115]

: LXIX :

The One is not the same as itself.

The rational principle of the One is different from that of same- 1 ness, for the One is absolute, whereas sameness is relative, given that a thing is always the same as something else. Therefore the One *qua* absolute precedes sameness *qua* relative.[116] Let us imagine that we have, on the one hand, one candle and, on the other, four: if we wish the first candle to become the same in number as the other four, we shall divide it into four. So through division the single candle becomes the same in number as the others. Conversely, if we wish this group of four candles to become other in number than the first group of four, we will need to reunite the four candles into one. So again otherness is produced through union, just as before sameness was produced through division into a multitude. Consequently we may conclude, as I supposed, that the rational principle of unity is different from that of sameness. If that is so, the One cannot be the same as itself, otherwise it will

met idem existere, alioquin aut participabit identitatem, per quam sibi fiat idem, alienamque naturam admittens desinet esse simpliciter unum, aut forsan ipsum erit identitas ipsa, ut ex se sibi ipsi sit idem. Esse autem non potest identitas, siquidem alia huius et illius ratio esse deprehenditur. Quod ex eo iterum confirmatur, quoniam identitas cum alteritate et numero commercium habet. Nam in tribus saltem consistit identitas, ad quam necessario requiritur, ut hoc idem sit illi et in conditione quadam idem, sed ipsum unum eiusmodi coniugium subire non potest.

2   Obicit Proclus Parmenidem debuisse multitudinem multitudini potius aequalem fieri aut parem quam eandem.

3   Respondet hic de essentiali numero potius quam accidentali fieri mentionem. Ubi igitur numerus rebus numeratis contingit extrinsecus, aequalitatem rite vel inaequalitatem dici; ubi autem numerus est essentialis et intimus, identitatem dici posse, siquidem identitas sit quaedam in natura communio. Denique unusquisque sequentium ordo novum aliquid secum fert et id quidem deterius, praeter id quod erat in praecedente. Regio subluna mutationem in substantia iam motui caelestium adhibet non permutanti substantiam. Caelum localem circuitum adiungit[31] vitali caelestis animae motui non locali. Anima temporalem discursionem addit intellegentiae non currenti. Intellectus appetitum intellegentiae adhibet enti nondum per se intellegentiam affectanti. Hoc[32] tandem praeter alia genera oppositaque cum identitate subit alteritatem quae in primo non erant, identitate quidem illius unitatem refert, alteritate vero eiusdem eminentiam pro viribus repraesentat.

either participate in sameness, thus becoming the same as itself (and, by admitting an alien nature, it will cease to be the absolute One), or perhaps become sameness, so as to be by itself the same as itself. Yet it cannot be sameness, since the rational principle of the One and that of sameness are different. This is further confirmed by the fact that sameness trades with otherness and number. For sameness consists of at least three elements: for there to be sameness a thing must necessarily be [firstly] "the same," [secondly] "as another," [and thirdly] "according to a particular condition." But the One cannot be subject to linkages of that sort.

Proclus [mentions that some thinkers][117] object that it would 2 have been more appropriate for Parmenides to consider that multitude is "equal" or "matched to" multitude rather than "the same."

Proclus replies that here multitude relates to essential, rather 3 than accidental, number. Thus when number enters into contact with numbered realities from the outside, one can rightly speak of equality or inequality between them; when number is essential and comes from the inside, one can rightly speak of sameness, since sameness is a sort of natural association.[118] Finally, among the realities that derive from the One, each order brings in something new and inferior with itself, in addition to what was brought in by the preceding order. To motion of celestial realities, which does not undergo any change of substance, the sublunar realm adds a change of substance. To vital motion of the celestial soul, which is not spatial, the heavens add circular spatial motion. To intelligence, which remains immobile, the soul adds motion in time. To being, which is not yet in itself attempting intelligence, the intellect adds a striving toward the intelligence. Finally, being undergoes, besides the other genera and opposites, sameness and otherness, which do not exist in the One; through sameness it relates to the unity of the One; through otherness it imitates as much as possible the One's eminence.[119]

: LXX :

Unum nec est simile neque dissimile vel sibi vel cuiquam.

1 Postquam negavit de uno tamquam superiore identitatem atque alteritatem ad essentiam illam intellegibilem pertinentia, negat deinceps quae post illa sequuntur, similitudinem atque dissimilitudinem. Similitudo quidem identitatem sequitur, dissimilitudo autem alteritatem suntque minora. Post haec iterum aequalitatem inaequalitatemque negabit. Illa post similitudinem, haec post dissimilitudinem collocatur. Illa quidem duo ad formales intellegibilis essentiae vires pertinent, haec vero duo ad actiones et quasi mensuras et modos earum virium spectare videntur. Iam vero in mundo intellegibili, ubi vires sunt variae modique multiplices, inveniri quodammodo possunt similitudo, dissimilitudo, aequalitas, inaequalitas quasi generalissima quaedam sequentibus omnibus pro suo cuiusque modo distribuenda. Mox etiam in intellegentia sua emicant eadem ut ideae, idealis quidem similitudo et quae sequuntur. In ipso autem uno haec neque ut genera vel generalissima neque ut ideae formaliter distingui possunt.

2 Formabit vero Parmenides propositiones de hac materia quattuor: unum non est sibi ipsi simile; unum non est alteri simile; unum non est sibi ipsi dissimile; unum alteri cuiquam non est dissimile.

3 Unum non esse sibi aliisve simile ita probat: quicquid alicui simile est necessario identitatis alicuius est particeps. Unum vero identitatis particeps esse non potest. Non est igitur alicui, scilicet vel sibi vel alteri, simile. Profecto unum ipsum identitatis causa est. Haec autem similitudinis est origo, immo etiam aequalitatis ipsius. Nam aequalia dici solent quae quodammodo in quantitate sunt eadem, et similia rursus quae in eadem qualitate conveniunt,

: LXX :

The One is not like or unlike itself or another.

After denying of the One, which is transcendent, sameness and   1
otherness, which pertain to intelligible essence, Parmenides then
denies the attributes that follow them: likeness and unlikeness
[139E–40B]. Likeness follows sameness, unlikeness follows otherness, and they are both inferior. Parmenides is then going to deny
equality and inequality, the former being located after likeness, the
latter after unlikeness.[120] The first two concern the formal forces of
intelligible essence, whereas the last two seem to concern the actions as well as what I would call the measures and modes of these
forces. In fact, in the intelligible world, where the forces are varied
and the modes are multiple, there can be found in some way likeness, unlikeness, equality and inequality, which constitute the most
general genera to be distributed to all the realities that follow, each
according to their own mode. Next, in intelligence too, their same
properties shine as Ideas: the Idea of likeness, and so on. Within
the One, however, these cannot be formally distinguished, whether
as genera or genera of genera, or as Ideas.

Parmenides is going to formulate four propositions on this sub-   2
ject: the One is not like itself; the One is not like another; the
One is not unlike itself; the One is not unlike anything else.

He shows that the One is not like itself or others as follows: 3
anything that is like something necessarily participates in some
sort of sameness. Yet the One cannot participate in sameness.
Thus it is not like anything, whether itself or another [139E–40B].
Surely the One is the cause of sameness. Yet sameness is the origin
of likeness and even of equality.[121] For things are generally called
equal when they are somehow the same in quantity; they are said
to be like, when they share the same quality, that is to say, when

eandem videlicet speciem qualitatis adepta. Unum vero non participare identitatem in superioribus est probatum, quoniam identitas natura quaedam differens est ab uno. Est igitur numerosa. Quapropter si unum hanc admiserit, evadet iam multiplex atque desinet esse simpliciter unum.

4 Post haec unum non esse sibimet aliisve dissimile hac breviter ratione demonstrat: sicut similitudo ab identitate, ita dissimilitudo ab alteritate dependet. Illa namque dissimilia nominantur quae in altera atque altera specie qualitatis existunt. Cum igitur ipsum unum alteritatem ullam, ut supra diximus, tolerare non possit, ne aliena et multiplicia sustinens unum iam esse desinat, merito nec esse dissimile potest.

5 Si quis autem caetera uni dissimilia atque similia esse dixerit, loquetur quidem non admodum proprie, quoniam unum simul cum aliis non potest ad ideam vel genus similitudinis dissimilitudinisve referri. Recte tamen sentiet, si modo iudicaverit caetera esse quidem dissimilia uni quoniam nihil habeant commune cum illo, esse quoque similia quoniam unum quiddam habeant commune invicem ab illo susceptum, qua inquam ratione unitatem illo videlicet largiente participant communique illinc atque illuc desiderio rapiuntur. Neque tamen vicissim illud simile caeteris est dicendum, quoniam similitudinem vel identitatem participare non potest. Imagines quinetiam exemplari similes appellantur neque vicissim. Iam vero quemadmodum ideale exemplar se habet ad formalem seriem suam per multos gradus subinde sequentem, sic ferme ipsum unum bonumque ad omnes entium gradus, tamquam unius bonique participes,[33] se habere videtur. Ob quam sane comparationem Plato in *Republica* ipsum unum universi principium appellavit ideam boni, non quia sit species aliqua vel idea (est enim longe altius atque latius), sed quoniam, ut diximus, idea

they have been given the same species of quality. Yet it has been shown above that the One does not participate in sameness, since the nature of sameness is different from the One, and thus able to be multiplied. So if the One admits sameness within itself, it will then become multiple and will cease to be the absolute One.

Parmenides then briefly shows that the One is not unlike itself 4 and others as follows: unlikeness depends on otherness just as likeness depends on sameness. For things are called unlike when they reside in different species of quality. Therefore, since the One cannot undergo otherness, as we have said (otherwise, if it were undergoing alien and multiple conditions it would cease to be One), it is fair to say that the One cannot be unlike.

But it will be utterly improper to say that others are unlike and 5 like the One, since the One cannot be related to the Idea or the genus of likeness and unlikeness simultaneously with others. It will be correct, however, to decide that others are unlike the One on the grounds that they have nothing in common with it, and that they are also like the One on the grounds that they all possess something that is one, which they have received from the One. In other words, they are like the One because they participate in the One, which dispenses unity, and are all enraptured by their common longing for it. But the reverse is not true: the One cannot be said to be like others, because it cannot participate in likeness or sameness; moreover, images can be said to be like their model, but not the contrary. Just as the ideal Model bears a relation to its own formal series, which derives its existence from it through many levels, so (all things being equal) the One-and-Good appears to be related to all levels of beings, inasmuch as they participate in it. It is assuredly by virtue of this comparison that in the *Republic* Plato called the One, which is the principle of the universe, the "Idea of the Good," not as a species or an Idea (for it is much more eminent and has greater extension than the Ideas) but because, as we

quaelibet in processibus suis quodammodo imitatur universalem omnium ab ipso bono processum.

: LXXI :

Unum nec sibi nec aliis est aequale vel inaequale.

1 In mundo intellegibili, ultra terminum infinitatemque quae alibi declaravimus, identitatem quidem ponunt etiam propter essentiam formarum omnium unam semperque eandem, alteritatem vero etiam propter multiformes ideas, similitudinem quoque quia conformes sunt semperque in habitu simili perseverant, dissimilitudinem vero quoniam ratione inter se sunt differentes proptereaque[34] dissimilia faciunt, aequalitatem insuper, quia semper aequalis virtutis et actionis est modus et quia res singulas intra seipsas et invicem aequalitate proportionis adaequant, inaequalitatem denique quoniam partes, vires, ideae non penitus sunt aequales; sunt enim formales ibi gradus nec aequalia faciunt. Commensurabiles invicem ibi dicuntur generum idearumque gradus, sed haec ad ipsam essentialem intellegibilemque monadem haud similiter commensurabilia iudicantur. Verum in ipso uno unius mundi intellegibilis auctore varietatem eiusmodi collocare non possumus. Ubi si non est terminus et infinitas, consequenter neque sunt vel quae terminum sequuntur, ut idem, simile, aequale, vel quae ad infinitatem spectant, ut alterum, dissimile, inaequale.

2 Parmenides igitur, postquam de uno negavit idem atque simile et alterum atque dissimile, tamquam origines quasdam, consequenter negat aequale et inaequale inde dependens, et quattuor, ut

have said, each Idea somehow imitates in its processions the procession of the universe from the Good.[122]

: LXXI :

The One is not equal or unequal to itself or to the others.

In the intelligible world, besides the two principles limit and infinity that we have mentioned elsewhere, the Platonists also posit sameness, because the essence of all forms is one and always the same; otherness, because the Ideas are multiform; likeness, because Ideas are like and always remain in the same disposition; unlikeness, because the Ideas are different from one another in their rational principle and thus produce things that are unlike one another; equality, because the mode of power and action is always equal and individual things are, both within themselves and in relation to one another, equal in proportion; and finally, inequality, because the parts, forces and Ideas are not at all equal, for there are formal levels in the intelligible world, and the Ideas produce things that are not equal. In the intelligible world, the levels of genera and Ideas are said to be commensurate with one another, but they are not considered to be commensurate with the essential and intelligible monad. But in the One, which is the creator of the intelligible world (which is one), we can locate no variety of this sort. If limit and infinity do not exist in the One, then the things that follow limit (same, like, equal), or those that pertain to infinity (different, unlike, unequal) do not exist in it either.

So after having denied of the One the attributes "same," "like," "other" and "unlike," which are the sources of the attributes that follow, Parmenides consequently denies the attributes "equal" and "unequal," which derive from the former; as he did above, he

supra, propositiones vult intellegi: unum non est sibimet aequale; unum nec aliis est aequale; unum sibi non est inaequale; unum nec aliis inaequale. Negat autem ubique de uno, ut monuimus alibi, sub passionum sensibilium praetextu animales quoque et intellectuales intellegibilesque passiones. Itaque dum audis aequale et inaequale quasi corporeo ritu tractari, intellege incorpoream quoque aequalitatem inaequalitatemque negatam. Inter haec ait aequalia esse quae semel eadem mensura metitur, ut quando pedalis mensura pedem hunc adaequat et illum, inaequalia vero, alia quidem vult esse commensurabilia, alia vero incommensurabilia iudicat. Bipedale quidem lignum ligno pedali est inaequale, sed propterea commensurabile, quoniam mensuram habet cum illo communem. Eadem namque mensura pedalis, quae semel adhibita minus hoc metitur lignum, bis admota metitur et maius. Sed diameter lateri non ita commensurabilis existimatur. Non enim est certa mensura, quae sub certo numero repetita alterum adaequare alteri perpendatur, sed tantum hoc quidem dicitur maiorem mensuram habere, illud vero minorem.

3   Est itaque argumentatio talis: quod alicui est aequale eandem cum illo mensuram habet, quocirca etiam identitatis est particeps. Cum igitur unum identitatem participare non possit, ideoque nec eandem subire mensuram, nimirum nec sibi nec aliis fit aequale.

4   Identitatis vis amplissima est. Dicimus enim aliqua invicem eadem specie, genere, ordine, tempore, qualitate, quantitate, loco, mensura, et denique cunctis. At vero tamquam aequalia invicem comparantur in specie. Quis enim dixerit lineam aequalem superficiei, vel superficiem solido, vel alterationem augmento motuive locali? Sed dicimus potius lineam aequalem vel inaequalem lineae caeteraque similiter. Cum igitur negata sit de uno identitas et alte-

shows this by demonstrating four propositions: the One is not equal to itself; the One is not equal to others; the One is not unequal to itself; the One is not unequal to others [140B–D].[123] As we have suggested elsewhere, each time he appears to deny sensible passions of the One, he really means also to deny the psychic, intellectual and intelligible passions. For this reason, when you hear "equal" and "unequal" being treated like corporeal attributes, you must understand that the incorporeal equality and inequality are also denied. At any rate, Parmenides says that things measured by the same measure applied once are equal (for instance, when a measure in feet makes two feet equal to one another), whereas, among unequal things, some are commensurate, others are incommensurate: a line measuring two feet is unequal to a line measuring one foot, yet it is commensurate with it, since they share the same measure: it is the same measure in feet which, applied once, measures the shorter line and, applied twice, measures the longer one. By contrast, one does not consider the diameter to be commensurate with the side, for there is no fixed measure which, applied a certain number of times, would be considered as making one of them equal to the other, but the latter is only said to have a larger measure than the former.

So the argument goes as follows: that which is equal to something has the same measure as this thing, for which reason it also participates in sameness. Therefore, since the One cannot participate in sameness and thus cannot undergo the same measure, it is not equal to itself or to the others.[124] 3

The power of sameness has the very greatest extension. For we 4 say that things are the same in species, genus, order, time, quality, quantity, place, measure and finally in all things. By contrast, things are equal only in species. For who would say that a line is equal to a surface, or a surface to a solid, or alteration to growth or local motion? Rather we say that a line is equal or unequal to a line, and so on. Thus once sameness and otherness, which have

129

ritas, tamquam amplissima, consequenter, tamquam angustior et inde dependens, aequalitas inaequalitasve negatur. Sin unum ipsum rebus passim multiplicibus ab illo manantibus est incomparabile, quonam pacto est illis aequale vel etiam per inaequalitatem oppositam inaequale? Sed neque aequalitate indiget, cuius ratio est ab illo differens, per quam sibi sit aequale. Habet enim, immo est, ipsum unum aequalitate melius atque praestantius. Neque vero nominamus unum quasi sit aliquid quantum vel ad quantitatem pertinens continuam vel ad numerum, vel quasi sit monas quaedam principium numerorum proportionemve cum illis aliquam habeat, per quas utique conditiones dici possit aequale vel inaequale, sed sub ipso unius nomine singularem simplicitatem penitus individuam eminentissimamque et omnis ad alia comparationis expertem vaticinamur, quae quidem omnibus et singulatim unitatis causa sit et summatim auctor unionis. Quicquid enim est, aut unitas quaedam est aut ex unitatibus quibusdam constat. Id vero munus dumtaxat ab ipso simpliciter uno omnia susceperunt, caeteras vero conditiones quae omnes particulariores posterioresque sunt, ab aliis quoque causis accipere potuerunt.

: LXXII :

Confirmatio superiorum.

1 Alia aequalitatis, alia unius ratio est. Unum enim est absolutum, aequalitas relativa. Aequale enim ad aequale refertur. Praeterea unius natura multitudinem prorsus excludit, aequalitatis includit ternarium saltem. Hoc enim huic in hoc est aequale vel illo. Item unum alicubi quidem unitatem proferens inaequale reddit quod

the most extension, have been denied of the One, equality and
inequality are also consequently denied, because they are less ex-
tensive than the former and derive from them. Yet since the One
cannot be compared with the multiple things that emanate from
it, how can it be equal or even unequal by virtue of its opposite,
inequality? But the One does not need equality, whereby it would
be equal to itself, because the rational principle of equality is different from it. For the One has, or rather is, better than, and superior to, equality and we do not call it "One" because it is a certain
quantity or is related to a continuous quantity or a number, or
because it is the monad, the principle of numbers, or possesses a
certain proportion with these (all conditions whereby it could be
said to be equal or unequal), but because through the very name
of "One" we augur the unitary, utterly undivided, super-eminent
and incomparable simplicity, which is, for all things, the individual
cause of unity and the general creator of union. For every thing
that is, is either a particular unity or is composed of certain unities. This gift can only have been imparted to all things by the
absolute One; the other conditions, which are more particular and
inferior, they could also derive from other causes.[125]

: LXXII :

Confirmation of what has been said above.

The rational principle of equality is different from that of the One,   1
for the One is absolute, whereas equality is relative, since a thing is
equal in relation to something else, which is equal to it. In addition, the nature of the One totally excludes multitude, whereas the
nature of equality implies multitude in at least three ways: one
thing is [firstly] "equal," [secondly] "to another," [thirdly] "in a cer-

prius erat aequale, alicubi vero contra addita unitate reddit aequale quod antea fuerat inaequale. Ubi apparet ipsum unum super aequalitatem inaequalitatemque existere et utramque pariter procreare. Praetermisimus inter haec, si ratio aequalitatis differt ab uno, nimirum et rationem inaequalitatis ab uno differre. Cum igitur aequalitatis natura sit aliquid praeter ipsum bonum, si unum quoquomodo fiat aequale vel sibi vel alteri, alienam iam naturam induet nec erit simpliciter unum. Quicquid enim apposueris uni, mox subducta simplicitate tolles ipsum simpliciter unum reddesque iam unum aliquid atque multiplex.

2   Sin autem unum dixeris sibi vel aliis inaequale, cum per inaequalitatem ab ipso alienam inaequale fiat, similiter esse desinet unum. Profecto quod est inaequale, sive sit maius, plures mensuras habet, sive sit minus, pauciores. Utrobique vero, ut ita dixerim, mensuratur per mensuram quandam seipsam ipsi accommodantem partibusque suis ipsius mensurati partes et particulas contingentem. Quapropter unum, si mensuretur, multitudinem partium iam habebit nec ulterius erit simpliciter unum.

3   Neque fingere licet unum sui ipsius esse mensuram per quam sibi ipsi sit aequale, alioquin penes ipsum erunt rationes duae, et hae quidem inter se oppositae, ratio mensurantis ac ratio mensurati, immo et ipsa mensurae ratio quae etiam alia quam unius ratio est, iamque nec erit simpliciter unum.

4   Sed quisnam dixerit primam causam rebus aequalem, quae propter incomparabilem simplicitatem, eminentiam, potestatem, nullam cum rebus admittit communionem? Alioquin propter eius-

tain condition." Likewise, by bringing forth unity, on the one hand, the One makes unequal what was previously equal, and on the other, once unity has been added, it makes equal what had previously been unequal. In this case, it appears that the One transcends equality and inequality and generates both of them. Meanwhile, we have left aside the fact that if the rational principle of equality differs from the One, then the rational principle of inequality also differs from it. Therefore, given that the nature of equality lies outside the Good, if the One somehow becomes equal to itself or to another, it will adopt a nature that is alien to it, and will cease to be the absolute One. For any addition to the One immediately abolishes it as the absolute One by suppressing its simplicity, and replaces it by something that is one and multiple.[126]

Conversely, if we say that the One is unequal to itself or to others, since it becomes unequal by way of inequality, which is alien to it, it will cease to be One. Assuredly either that which is unequal is greater, and has a greater measurement, or it is smaller, and has a smaller measurement. In both cases, as I said, it is measured by a measure that is in accordance with itself and has contact through its parts with the parts and particles of that which is measured. So if the One is measured, it will have a multitude of parts and will no longer be the absolute One [140B–D].

Let us not imagine that the One is its own measure, on account of which it would be equal to itself; otherwise it will have two rational principles, which will be opposed to one another (the principle of the measuring subject and that of the measured object), as well as the rational principle of measure, which is different from that of the One, and in this case too the One will no longer be the absolute One.[127]

But who would say that the first cause is equal to the realities, since on account of its incomparable simplicity, superiority and power it admits no association with things? Otherwise, if it under-

modi coniugium non fuerit penitus absoluta. Quis iterum inaequalem per inaequalitatem aequalitati vicissim oppositam et circa
subiectum idem se versantem? Alioquin commercium cum rebus
haud prorsus effugerit, immo et patietur oppositum, scilicet melius, ac deteriori erit opposito mancipata.

5   Quonam igitur pacto iam erit mensura rerum, quod ex *Philebo*
et *Theaeteto Legibusque* accepimus? Non erit certe mensura quaedam rebus mensuratis adhibita, alioquin non fuerit absoluta, nec
ita rursus erit in rebus mensura rerum, quemadmodum monas in
numeris numerorum, alioquin pars quaedam multitudinis rerum
futura est imperfectior universo eritque unum quiddam coniugatum cum caeteris quorum quodlibet propter mutuam differentiam est aliquid unum. Si ita se habere impossibile est, ipsum
unum neque erit unaquaedam species idealis in ipso intellegibili
mundo, ne praeterea caeterarum specierum perfectionibus propriis
sit orbatum, neque etiam universus ille mundus; alioquin, ut in
Sophiste probatur, unum si totum aliquid fuerit, iam multiplex et
particeps unius potius quam ipsum unum est futurum.

6   Sit ergo mensura rerum, quoniam rebus singulis gradibusque
rerum ab ipso productis suum cuique distribuit essendi virtutisque
et bene essendi modum singulaque vicissim, quatenus convertuntur et accedunt ad ipsum, eatenus inde proficiunt.

7   Neque vero putandum est Parmenidem tanta moliri ut rem
manifestissime alienam dumtaxat neget uni, aequalitatem scilicet
quantitatis. Negat enim praeterea aequalitatem cum rebus simpli-
citatis, virtutis, excellentiae, causae, inaequalitatemque similiter.
Comparationes enim eiusmodi inter hoc et illud rite fieri solent,
quando in uno quodam eodem congruunt, quod et pariter et magis atque minus utrobique deprehendi possit. Nihil vero idem est

went a union of that kind, it would not be absolutely transcendent. Again, who would say that it is unequal by virtue of inequality, which is the opposite of equality and concerns the same subject? Otherwise, far from avoiding any commerce with things, it will be subject to the better term of the opposition and will be enslaved to the inferior term of the opposition.

How, then, will the One be the measure of things, as we learned from the *Philebus*, the *Theaetetus*, and the *Laws*?[128] It will not, to be sure, be a measure added to things that are being measured, otherwise it would not be separate. Neither will it be the measure of things in things, like the monad of numbers in numbers, otherwise it will be one part among many things, and thus more imperfect than the universe, and it will be some one thing united to all the others, which are each a particular one different from the others.[129] If it is impossible for the One to be so disposed, it will not be any ideal species within the intelligible world (otherwise it would also be orphaned of the perfections proper to all the other species) nor even the universal world itself; otherwise, as demonstrated by the *Sophist*, if [that] one is a whole, it will be multiple and will participate in the One, rather than being the One.[130]

Let us conclude that the One is the measure of things because, after having created all the realities and levels of realities, it distributes to each of them its own mode of being, power and well-being, and in turn each thing proceeds from it, inasmuch as they each turn toward it and reach it.

Let us not think that Parmenides has gone to such a length simply to deny of the One quantitative equality, which is obviously alien to it, since he also denies equality in simplicity, power, excellence, and cause; the same goes for inequality. These comparisons between various things are usually appropriately made between realities that can be unified in one identical unity, which can be apprehended either equally, more, or less. However, there is noth-

in ipso simpliciter uno simul atque rebus, per quod eiusmodi fieri comparatio possit, alioquin coniugabile iam erit et multiplex. Neque vero admittendi sunt quicumque propria rerum munera ipsi uni tribuunt, superlativo quodam gradu stabilissimum appellantes aut velocissimum vel aequalissimum. Cui enim superlativorum fundamenta non competunt, status scilicet, motus, aequalitas, quonammodo superlativa convenient? Est igitur omni superlativo longe superius.

: LXXIII :

Unum neque iunius neque senius neque coaetaneum
vel ad se vel ad alia esse potest.

1 Temporis motusve particeps esse aliquid modis tribus considerare licet. Aut enim actione simul substantiaque mutatur temporaliterve fluit, ut corpus, aut actione tantum, ut anima, aut quasi processu quodam et origine, ut intellectus. Ab his autem omnibus temporis[35] motusve conditionibus Parmenides ipsum unum praedicat absolutum, et interea omnium quae quomodolibet in motu temporeque versantur ipsum asserit esse[36] principium atque finem. Id enim in omnibus negationibus observandum monuimus a principio, ut quaecumque de uno negantur interea intellegantur eminenter ab uno profecta, tamquam incomparabiliter superante. Assumit autem in primis Parmenides quae sint propria eorum quibuscumque tempus quomodolibet competere possit. Tria vero haec sunt: coaetaneum esse aut iunius aut senius, vel aliis vel seipso. Probat vero ab his propriis ipsum unum esse secretum, ut

ing identical that is shared between the absolute One and other things, which would allow such a comparison, otherwise the One would be unifiable and multiple. One must not admit the doctrine of those who attribute to the One the properties of things by naming it by a superlative, such as "the most at rest," "the quickest," or "the most equal." For how could superlatives befit the One, when the principles of these superlatives (rest, motion and equality) do not? Thus it is by far superior to any superlative.[131]

: LXXIII :

The One cannot be younger or older than,
or of equal age with, itself and the others.

One can consider participation in time and motion in three ways: 1 realities undergo a change in both operation and substance, or move in time, like the body; they can undergo a change only in operation, like the soul; or they can undergo a kind of change in procession and origin, like the intellect. Parmenides declares that the One is separated from all the conditions pertaining to time and motion; he also states that the One is the principle and the end of all the things that are related in one way or another to motion and time. For, as we mentioned at the beginning, in all the negations we must consider that all the things that are denied of the One are understood to have eminently proceeded from the One, the One being incomparably superior to them. Parmenides first examines the properties of the things that can relate in some way or other to time. These are triple: "to be of equal age" with, "younger" or "older" than, either others or oneself [140E–41D]. He shows that the One is separated from these properties; in this way, he shows that the One is secluded from any participation in

ab omni temporis motusve participatione secernat, etiam quae in intellectu sublimi fingi possit. Neque vero fuisset operae pretium a corporeo vel etiam animali motu vel tempore ipsum unum absolvere, a quo et intellectus absoluti sunt omnes.

2 In substantia quavis intellectuali prius quidem est secundum originem atque ordinem essentia quam vita, vita quam intellectus, substantia quam virtus, virtus quam operatio. Intellectus ergo quilibet per ipsa priora sui senior est seipso, per posteriora, iunior. Est etiam sibimet coaetaneus. Nam quae ad essentiam proprie pertinent pari quadam origine coniugata sunt invicem, similiter quae ad vitam et caetera quae sequuntur. Est praeterea intellectus ipso intellegibili iunior, senior vero quam anima, coaetanei vero plerique sunt invicem intellectus, similiter animae multae. Ideae similiter universaliores particularioribus seniores sunt. Specialissimae invicem coaetaneae et unaquaeque suis propriis coaetanea. In animabus praeterea vel divinis atque beatis intellegibili mundo fruentibus, circuitus quidam fiunt per species gradatim intimas discurrentes. Hinc et iunior aetas et senior et coaetanea surgit. Quae enim universaliores circuitus agunt seniores sunt animabus quae particularibus periodis pluribus unum illarum circuitum aequare conantur. Coaetaneae sunt quae periodos pares[37] efficiunt. Sunt et seipsis seniores atque iuniores, quatenus tum per universaliores, tum per minus universales formas progrediuntur. Coaetaneae vero sibi quotiens aequales repetunt formas. Omnes tandem eiusmodi motus temporumque modos, sive ad divinas animas, sive ad intellectus et intellegibilia pertinentes, in secunda quidem suppositione de uno ente, ad quod omnes quomodolibet divinae et intellectuales substantiae spectant, affirmabuntur. In prima vero suppositione de ipso simpliciter uno negantur.

time or motion, even the participation that can be imagined in the sublime intellect. It would not have been worthwhile separating off the One from corporeal, or even psychic motion and time, since even intellects transcend these.

In every intellectual substance essence precedes life in origin 2 and in order, life precedes intellect, substance precedes potentiality, and potentiality precedes operation. Thus if one considers the elements that come first, each intellect is older than itself; when one considers the elements that come after, it is younger than itself.[132] It is also of equal age with itself, because its essence's properties are united by virtue of their matching origin, and the same goes for the properties of life, and for all the things subsequent to it. The intellect is also younger than the intelligible object, and older than the soul; most intellects are of equal age, and the same applies to the multitude of souls. Likewise among the Ideas, the more universal are older than the more particular; the most specific are of equal age with each other, and each is of equal age with the things that are proper to it. Within the souls, even those that are divine and enjoy with beatitude the intelligible world, there are circuits which progressively travel through the innermost species, whence the times "younger," "older" and "of equal age" arise: the souls that accomplish the more universal circuits are older than those who need to accomplish several individual circuits to equal one circle of the former; those who accomplish an equal number of circuits are of equal age. They are also older and younger than themselves inasmuch as they proceed through more or less universal forms; they are of equal age with themselves each time they repeat their progression through equal forms. Finally, all these modes of time and motion, whether they concern divine souls, intellects or intelligible realities, will be asserted of the one being (i.e. all the divine and intellectual substances) in the second hypothesis. In the first hypothesis, however, they are denied of the absolute One.[133]

3   Argumentatur autem hunc in modum: quicquid vel coaetaneum est aequalitatem similitudinemque temporis accipit, vel iunius aut senius, inaequalitatem dissimilitudinemque in tempore subit. Probatum est autem in superioribus ipsum unum extra omnem aequalitatem similitudinemque et horum opposita esse. Igitur neque coaetaneum neque iunius aut senius est, vel ad alia vel ad seipsum. Haec quoque argumentatio, ut caeterae, per universaliora procedit. Universalius est enim aequale vel simile simpliciter aut inaequale simpliciter et dissimile esse quam secundum tempus esse tale. Adiunxit autem aequalitati similitudinem, ut aetate invicem compararet, non hominem cani, sed hominem homini, canem cani, specie videlicet similes.

: LXXIV :

Ipsum unum super aeternitatem et tempus et motum est,
nec ulla ratione esse in tempore dici potest.

1   Ipsum unum esse super aeternitatem probatum est quando disputatum fuit esse super statum identitatemque et in nullo manere. Aeternitas autem est ipse in eodem status et mensura quaedam in aeternis stabilibusque permanens. Illic igitur multo magis assertum est ipsum unum super aeterna stabiliaque existere. Item multo magis esse super tempus, tametsi hoc proprie declaratur, ubi super motum et alteritatem necessaria tempori esse monstratur. Igitur ipsum unum neque etiam est ipsum tempus, in quo est necessario motus ipse pariter et alteritas, alioquin si ipsum unum tempus motusve fuerit, sola mutabilia faciet, meliora vero mobilibus causa quaedam excellentior aget. Sed quisnam dixerit universi princi-

The argument goes as follows: a thing is either of equal age and 3
undergoes temporal equality and likeness, or is younger or older
and undergoes temporal inequality and unlikeness. Yet as has been
shown above the One transcends all equality and likeness and
their opposites. It is not, therefore, of equal age with, or younger
and older than, the others or itself [140E–41A]. This argument
also proceeds, like all the others, through more universal properties. For the simple attributes "equal" and "like" and the simple attributes "unequal" and "unlike" are more universal than their temporal equivalents. To the notion of equality Parmenides has added
the notion of likeness, to make sure that one does not compare in
age a man with a dog, but things of the same species — a man with
a man and a dog with a dog.[134]

: LXXIV :

The One is above eternity, time, and motion,
and can by no means be said to be in time.

Parmenides has demonstrated that the One is above eternity when 1
he said that it was above rest and sameness and was not in another. Yet eternity is rest in the same place and a kind of measure
which remains within eternal and stable realities.[135] Hence it is
asserted *a fortiori* that the One transcends eternal and stable realities and likewise, that the One transcends time — although this is
properly clarified when the One is shown to be above motion and
otherness, things that are necessary to time. Thus the One is not
time, either, since time necessarily implies motion and otherness.
Otherwise, if the One is time or motion, it will only produce
changing realities, and a superior cause will produce the things
superior to the ones in motion. But who would say that the prin-

pium esse motum naturaliter imperfectum atque diversum? Moveri enim est ad aliud proficiendo procedere, siquidem motus suapte natura non includens statum aut terminum, tamquam sibi oppositum vagabundus ex se est et erraticus, nondum videlicet absolutus, immo et infinitus infinitate quadam desuper aliunde formabili. Denique si ipsum unum non est ipse motus ipsumve tempus, multo minus mobile et temporale aliquid esse potest.

2   Proinde unum non esse in tempore ita probat: quod est in tempore semper seipso fit senius. Cum vero senius referatur ad iunius, dum seipso senius evadit, simul seipso evadit et iunius. Haec autem ipsi uni competere nequeunt, quemadmodum in superioribus est probatum, igitur nec est in tempore. Propositio argumentationis huius maior, difficilis admodum, expositiones tres[38] admittit, in ea videlicet parte ubi proponit una cum seniore simul effici iunius. Prima quidem expositio est, ut hoc ipsum simul non tam pertineat ad aetatem ipsam, quam ad relationem quandam aetatis illius ad hanc aetatem. Quo enim in tempore fit senius in eodem neque prius, ad seipsum iam senius refertur ut iunius atque vicissim. Expositio vero secunda talis: homo decem annos natus senior est, si comparetur ad novem, in quo quidem novenario ad suum denarium iam refertur, ut iunior, sed in eodem novenario ad octonarium simul refertur, ut senior, atque ita in quolibet anno vel mense vel die vel hora vel momento refertur ad seipsum, per idem simul tempus ut senior atque iunior, quatenus scilicet vel ante vel retro refertur. Tertia expositio Syriani est divinarum animarum accommodata periodis. Ubi enim motus quasi rectus terminum petit a principio discrepantem, illic in proprio aetatis tempore motum pariter consequente, aliud quidem est principium, aliud vero finis. Itaque non potest hic aliquid ita praeteriens fieri seipso

ciple of the universe is motion, since motion is by nature imperfect and diverse? For to be moved consists in proceeding toward another through procession: motion, which does not naturally include rest and limit, which are its opposites, is, in itself, unpredictable and irregular, that is, it is not an absolute principle, but rather infinite by virtue of an infinity that receives its form from another, superior principle. Finally, if the One is neither motion nor time, it can even less be something that is in motion or in time.

So Parmenides shows that the One is not in time as follows: 2 what is in time always becomes older than itself. Since "older" is relative to something younger, during the process of becoming older than itself, it also simultaneously becomes younger than itself [141A–D]. These conditions cannot befit the One, as has been shown above; thus the One is not in time. The major proposition of this demonstration (the part where Parmenides postulates that the One is simultaneously made younger and older [141A5–7]), which is quite difficult to understand, can be interpreted in three different ways: firstly, the very notion of simultaneity does not concern age itself, but a certain relation between two different ages: at the very moment when a thing becomes older, and not before, it is related, *qua* younger, to itself, *qua* older, and conversely. Secondly, a ten-year-old is older when compared to a nine-year-old; within this period of nine years he is compared to his ten years of age as younger, but within this same period of nine years he is at the same time older than his eight years of age, and so in any year, month, day, hour or moment, he is related to himself, through the same period of time, simultaneously as younger or older, depending on whether he is related to the past or the future. The third explanation, that of Syrianus, is related to the circuits of the divine souls: in the case of rectilinear motion accomplished from one point to another, different point, in the time that it takes to accomplish this motion, one point is the starting point, the other is the final point. So what travels this distance in time can

senius simul atque iunius, nisi per relationem quandam a nobis modo descriptam. Sed in circulari motu perpetuo, qui animabus proprie divinis competit, atque inde caelestibus[39] mentibus quoque, metaphorica ratione momentum quodlibet principium pariter est et finis. Quod igitur ita movetur, in quolibet momento senius seipso simul evadit et iunius, senius quidem, quatenus momentum illud ad quod modo discurrendo pervenit, rationem habet ad praecedentem discursionem finis atque termini. Iunius autem, quatenus momentum idem ad discursionem continuata serie consequentem principii rationem habet. Divinae igitur animae in quovis momento seniores seipsis sunt simul atque iuniores. Similem quoque quodammodo aetatis conditionem suspicari licet in circuitu et processibus intellectus excelsi, dum modo quod per fluxum temporalem in anima corporeque peragitur per originem quandam processumque huius ab illo subitum in mentibus expleatur. Nihil vero tale in ipso simpliciter uno fas est confingere.

: LXXV :

Relativorum regula cum confirmatione
quadam superiorum.

1 Tradit interea regulam quandam eorum quae sub diverso nomine tamquam relativa invicem opponuntur, ut iunior refertur ad seniorem, pater ad filium, servus ad dominum. Nempe haec quotiens invicem referuntur, qua tunc conditione alterum accipitur, recipiendum est et alterum, si modo rite relativa haec oppositio fiat. Servus igitur, qua ratione nunc servit, referendus est ad dominum,

only become simultaneously older and younger than itself through a relation such as described above. By contrast, in the case of perpetual circular motion, which is the very motion accomplished by divine souls, and thence by celestial intellects too, any moment (in a metaphorical sense) is simultaneously a beginning and an end. Thus that which is moved in a circle becomes each time simultaneously younger and older than itself; older inasmuch as the movement it accomplishes by rotation is the end and the limit of the preceding rotation; younger inasmuch as this same movement is the beginning of the rotation that immediately follows it. Thus at every moment the divine souls are simultaneously older and younger than themselves.[136] One can postulate the existence of a similar temporal condition in the revolution and the processions accomplished by the superior intellect, except that what occurs in the soul and the body through temporal flux occurs in the intellects through a sudden origin and procession from one mind to the other.[137] But nothing of that sort can be imagined within the absolute One.

: LXXV :

The rule of relative terms confirming
what has been said above.

Meanwhile Parmenides establishes a rule about realities which are   1
different in name[138] and are relative opposites, such as "younger" and "older," father and son, master and slave. Surely opposition can only be relative in the required sense if, whenever a pair of opposites are compared to one another, whatever the condition in which one of them is considered, such must be the condition in which the other is considered. So he who *is* a slave *now* must be

qua ratione in praesentia dominatur. Item servus qui olim serviebat ad dominum qui tunc dominabatur ei. Rursus quandoque serviturus ad dominum, tunc tandem dominaturum, quando aliquis nuper fit alicuius servus, tunc ille fit huius dominus. Quamdiu hic alicuius est servus, tamdiu et ille huius est dominus atque vicissim. Neque rite referre licet futurum servum ad praeteritum dominum vel eum qui mox fit servus ad illum qui iam est dominus. Similia de iuniore et seniore dicta nobis existimato.

: LXXVI :

Cum unum sit supra tempus consequenter conditiones temporis temporaliumque excedit.

1 Postquam negavit ipsum unum esse in tempore ullo, scilicet vel proprio vel metaphorico, per haec consequenter habere negat conditiones necessarias temporalium, et quomodolibet temporalium et quomodocumque eiusmodi conditiones accipiantur, sive ut proprie, sive etiam metaphorice. Tempus ab aeternitate dependens plurimum quidem habet sui, aeternitatis quoque nonnihil. Qua igitur ratione nactum est quandam aeternitatis imaginem dicere solemus in tempore atque temporali est, erat, fuit, erit, fuerit. Simplicia enim haec sunt et praesentiam quandam referunt, sive nunc instantem, sive quae extiterit, sive quae existet. Qua vero conditione tempus ab aeternitate degenerat, nominare in tempore et temporali solemus fit, fiebat, factum fuit, factum erat, fiet, factum erit, factum fuerit. Haec[40] enim ultra praesentiam[41] simplicem

compared to he who *is* a master *now*, and he who *was* a slave in the past must be related to he who *was* a master in the past. Likewise, the slave *will be* the slave of his master whenever his master *will be* his master, and it is precisely when he *becomes* the slave of a person that this person *becomes* his master. He is slave of someone as long as this person is his master, and conversely. By contrast, one cannot properly compare someone who *will be* slave to someone who *has been* master, or someone that *will soon become* slave to someone that *is already* a master. The same goes for the attributes "younger" and "older."

: LXXVI :

Since the One transcends time, it consequently transcends temporal conditions and temporal realities.

After having denied that the One is in time of any kind (whether real or metaphorical), Parmenides consequently denies that the One possesses the conditions necessary to temporal realities — in whatever way you choose to understand the terms "temporal realities" or "conditions," whether in their proper or metaphorical senses. Time, which depends on eternity, consists mostly of time but also retains something of eternity. Hence insofar as time is a kind of image of eternity, we generally say that it is, was, has been, will be, will have been, in time, and in a temporal condition. For these realities are simple and are related to a certain presence,[139] whether present, past, or future. But insofar as time is generated by eternity, we usually say that it becomes, became, has become, had become, will become, will have become, would have become in time and in a temporal condition [141D8–E7].[140] For beyond simple presence, which exists eternally, these realities carry with them

quandolibet existentem fluxum generationemque secum ferunt, quorum nihil ipsi uni tempus exsuperanti contingere potest. De caeteris quidem modo dictis est manifestum, sed de ipso quod praesentiam significat nunc instantem, scilicet est, apud nonnullos erit forte dubium putantes hanc ipsi praesentiam convenire. Tametsi cum haec nihil aliud sit quam momentum fugax inter praeteritum et futurum pertineatque ad tempus, ferme sicut punctum medium ad lineam, merito ipsi uni vel aeternitatem excedenti convenire non potest. Quo vero sensu exponendum sit propheticum illud: 'Qui est, qui erat et qui venturus est omnipotens.' Satis in commentariis in Dionysium exposuimus. Per haec enim declaratur deum omnipotentem esse creatorem omnium quae sunt, quae fuerunt, et quae erunt. Haec ergo, quae temporalia videntur nomina, non temporalem affirmant in deo formam, sed causam auctoritatemque eius super omnes temporis partes et temporalia omnia dominantem.

: LXXVII :

Ipsum unum nec est essentiae particeps nec ipsa
essentia nec ipsum esse, sed longe superius.

1   Interrogat deinde Parmenides numquid alii quidam modi sint essentiae participandae praeter eos qui narrati sunt. Respondetur ei non esse; ipse vero responsionem approbat. Tu igitur cum certo scias Parmenidem aeterna supra temporalia posuisse atque in aeternis veram constituisse essentiam, in temporalibus vero falsam, quae et generari potius quam esse putat, cave suspiceris eum in quaestione sua responsionisque approbatione introducere solas es-

at any given moment flux and generation, none of which can occur in the One, which transcends time. This is clear for the temporal conditions that have just been mentioned; but regarding that which is signified by the "present occurring now," namely "is,"[141] some philosophers might seriously wonder if this presence befits the One. However, since this presence is nothing other than the fleeting moment between past and future, and pertains to time, almost like the point in the middle of a line, it cannot rightly befit the One, which transcends even eternity. It is in this sense that we must interpret the prophetic line: "who is, who was and who is still to come, the Almighty."[142] We have sufficiently explained this in our commentaries on Dionysius: these words mean that God Almighty is the creator of all things that are, have been and will be.[143] In other words, these names, which appear to allude to temporal properties, assert no temporal form of God, but the fact that He is the cause and power that governs and transcends all parts of time and all temporal things.

: LXXVII :

The One does not participate in essence; it is neither essence nor being, but is by far superior to them.

Parmenides then asks whether there are other modes of participat- 1
ing in essence apart from those which have just been described; the reply, which Parmenides agrees with, is that there are not [141E7–10]. Since, therefore, we know as a fact that Parmenides placed eternal realities above temporal ones, and established true essence within eternal realities and false essence within temporal ones (given that, according to him, false essence is generated rather than is), we must not surmise that during this exchange Par-

sentiae participationes in tribus temporum differentiis — praeterito, praesenti, futuro. Praeter enim participationes istas, tamquam falsas apud Platonicos Pythagoreosque, sunt aeternae participationes essentiae verae. Interrogatio igitur illa totius esto primae suppositionis epilogus, quippe cum gradatim enarraverit genera propriaque entis omnia, in quibus varii sunt essentiae participandae modi, atque una cum generum negatione eiusmodi modos de uno iam negaverit omnes, iure tandem in hac quaestionis universae summa ipsum unum esse negat essentiae particeps. Si quis autem pertinacius instet hanc interrogationem ad conditiones temporis pertinere modo narratas, meminisse debet quemadmodum etiam in primo ente motus alteritasque asseritur, ita et tempus suo quodam pacto, ut diximus, collocari, propter processum quendam ex hoc in illud, prius posteriusque, in origine quadam et ordine proferentem, atque talia negari de uno. Sed ad reliqua iam pergamus. Profecto quemadmodum in superioribus admonuimus, ubique ab evidentioribus exordium faciendum. Rite igitur primo negavit uni multitudinem ab ipso extra controversiam alienam, tandem vero per media multa essentiam quoque negavit tamquam uni valde cognatam discretuque difficillimam. Contra vero in suppositione secunda de uno ente tamquam evidentissime cognatam in primis affirmabit essentiam.

2   Parmenides hic in primis ens quidem accipere videtur ut concretum, essentiam ut abstractum, esse autem ut actum entis intimum per essentiam. Sicut enim vivens vivere per vitam habet, ita ens per essentiam formaliter habet esse. Cum ergo negaverit unum

menides only meant the modes of participation in essence according to the three different parts of time, past, present and future.
Indeed, besides these modes of participation, which the Platonists
and the Pythagoreans consider to be false, there are eternal modes
of participation in real essence. In this way, we should consider
that Parmenides' question is the epilogue to the whole first hypothesis. For after having progressively enumerated all the genera
and properties of being, in which there are different modes of participation in essence, and after having denied of the One, together
with the genera of being, all these modes of participation, in the
end he rightly denies that the One participates in essence, and
this last section constitutes a summary of the whole hypothesis
[141E9].[144] However, if someone still insists that this last question
refers to the temporal conditions mentioned above, that person
should keep in mind that just as motion and otherness are said to
exist within the first being, in the same way time is located within
the first being according to its own mode, as we have said, since
there is procession from one principle to the other, before and after, in a certain origin and an order, and that such things are denied of the One. But let us now pass on to what remains. Surely,
as we have suggested above, one must always start from the propositions that are more immediately evident to us. So Parmenides
appropriately first denied of the One "multitude," which is undoubtedly alien to the One, and lastly "essence" through many intermediary propositions, because essence is very much akin to the
One and very difficult to distinguish from it. By contrast, in the
second hypothesis he will first assert essence of the one being, because essence is most clearly cognate with it.

    Here Parmenides appears at first to consider "being" as some-   2
thing concrete, "essence" as something abstract, and "the act of being" as the innermost act of being through essence.[145] For just as
living possesses the act of living through life, so being formally
possesses the act of being through essence. Therefore, since Par-

ullo modo essentiam participare, consequenter de illo ens totum negat atque esse, ens inquam totum, non temporale solummodo, sed aeternum. Inquit enim nec ullo modo essentiam participare nec ullo modo esse.

3   Concedet forte quispiam unum non participare essentiam atque hac conditione de uno negabit ens et esse, sed suspicabitur ne forte ipsum unum ipsa simpliciter essentia prorsus existat, non per quam sit aliquid quod ens nominetur, sed quae sit seipsa. Ideo Parmenides significanter adhibuit unum nullo modo est, adeo ut neque unum sit unum, scilicet cum essentia unum, ne quam secum rationem vel naturam habeat aliam praeter suam. Sicut enim vita cum intellectu non est simpliciter vita, sed quaedam, ita ens cum vita non est simpliciter ens, sed quoddam, scilicet cum differentia quadam per quam est vivens. Similiter unum cum essentia non est simpliciter unum, sed unum quoddam, cum differentia videlicet hac assumptum. Saepe diximus rationem ipsius essentiae rationemque ipsius unius differentem esse. Essentia enim, qua ratione simpliciter est essentia, neque multiplicabilitatem prorsus excludit neque separationem affert. Unum vero, qua simpliciter unum, immultiplicabile est ab omnibusque secretum. Quaprop-ter[42] si essentiae adhibeas unum nihil essentiae detrahes quo minus essentia sit atque perfecta, immo vero perficies. Sin autem uni essentiam admoveas, ut diximus, differentem, propriam ipsius unius eminentiam simplicissimam e medio tolles. Non igitur essentia iuvat unum, videlicet ut inferior, sed unum essentiam potius ut causa finisque perficit. Unum quidem essentiam participare non potest, alioquin non foret simpliciter unum. Essentia vero omnis etiam prima necessario particeps est unius. Prima enim sicut

menides has denied that the One participates in any way in essence, he consequently denies of the One the totality of being and the act of being, and by the totality of being I mean not only temporal being, but also eternal being. For he says that the One by no means participates in essence and by no means is [141E].

One will perhaps agree that the One does not participate in essence, and thus deny being and the act of being of the One, and yet suppose that the One is simple essence — not essence whereby it would be something called being, but essence itself. So Parmenides has deliberately added that the One by no means is, so that the One is not the one, that is, the one that goes with essence, otherwise the One would possess another rational principle or nature besides its own. For just as life that accompanies intellect is not simply life, but a certain life, so being that accompanies life is not simply being, but a certain being, i.e. a being accompanied by a differentia that makes it a living being. Likewise, the one that accompanies essence is not the absolute One, but a certain "one," which also possesses a differentia. We have said several times that the rational principle of essence is different from that of the One. For essence, *qua* simple essence, does not completely exclude multiplicability and does not imply separation. By contrast the One, *qua* absolute One, cannot be multiplied and is hidden from all things. For this reason, if we add the One to essence, we do not remove anything from essence, i.e. essence will not become less essence and less perfect as a result; on the contrary, essence will be better. By contrast, the addition of essence to the One (essence being different from the One, as we have said) will immediately affect the One's simplest eminence. Essence, which is inferior to the One, does not add any perfection to the One; by contrast, the One perfects essence, since it is the cause and end of essence. The One cannot participate in essence, otherwise it would not be the absolute One. But every essence, including the first essence, necessarily participates in the One. For just as the first essence is

maxime est essentia, sic et una quam maxime. Itaque super unum quod in essentia participatum est, est unum imparticipabile[43] super essentiam. Quod quidem evidentibus verbis a Speusippo Platonis nepote dictum testis est Proclus. Ubi etiam addit Speusippum id quoque ex antiquorum opinione confirmavisse, quando dicit eos existimavisse unum esse melius ente entisque principium omni habitudine ad sequentia liberum, sicut et ipsum bonum, ab omni alicuius boni conditione secretum. Appellat autem ibi Speusippus ens primum proprium entium principium, interminabilem duitatem ab uno superiore pendentem. Quid plura? Cur testimonium quaerimus Speusippi, cum in suppositione secunda unum ab ente manifestissime discernatur probeturque, ubi uni adhibetur essentia diciturque esse multitudinem subito compositionemque contingere, per quam cogamur super unum ens ipsum simpliciter unum ponere?

4   Denique ipsum simpliciter unum neque debemus ens appellare, quod est quasi concretum, neque essentiam, quae quasi potentia quaedam ad esse refertur velut actum, neque esse, quod in essentia est ut actus essentiae, neque esse aliquod, quod esse non sit in essentia. Neque enim licet lucere a luce, sapere a sapientia, vivere a vita, esse ab essentia segregare. Sin autem segregaveris esse, non iam esse quidem, sed ipsum unum potius reportabis.

5   Praeterea quaesivimus alibi cum aliud quidem sit ens, aliud vero unum, tamquam ente simplicius atque communius, an haec duo in summo rerum fastigio, quasi paria sint ponenda, an alterum superius altero. Si paria, sequetur ut duo sint principia rerum, quod in

"essence" to the highest degree, so it is also "one" in the highest possible degree. So above the participated one, which resides in essence, there is the unparticipated One, which is beyond essence. This has been clearly stated by Plato's nephew Speusippus, as attested by Proclus. Proclus adds that Speusippus confirmed that his doctrine was also the opinion of the ancients, when he said that the ancients considered that the One was better than being, the principle of being, and was separated from any relation with the other realities, just as the Good is separated from all conditions proper to a particular good. Speusippus calls the first being, which is the proper principle of beings, "indefinite dyad," which depends on the superior One. In short, why should we refer to Speusippus' testimony, since the second hypothesis demonstrates in the clearest terms that the One is distinguished from being (for there essence is added to the one, and it is stated at once that it is multitude and undergoes composition)? Does this not lead us to locate the absolute One above the one being?[146]

Finally, we must not call the absolute One "being," which is   4
practically a concrete term, nor "essence," which is a kind of potentiality related to the act of being *qua* act, nor "the act of being," which is in essence like the act of essence, nor "the act of being something," because the act of being [something] may not be in the essence. For we must not separate the act of being alight from light, the act of knowing from knowledge, the act of living from life, the act of being from essence. If you isolate the act of being from essence, you will no longer reach "the act of being," but the One.

In addition, we have investigated elsewhere the question — given   5
that being and the One are different, as the One is simpler and commoner than being — whether both of them should be placed at the summit of realities as two equal principles, or whether one is prior to the other.[147] If they are equal, there will be two principles for things, which is impossible, as we have shown in our

Theologia refellimus. Quaeretur insuper an invicem coniugata sint an penitus segregata. Si coniugata invicemque permixta, superius aliquid erit utriusque causa et mixtionis effector, ut est in *Philebo* probatum. Si segregata sint, omnino in ente nihil unitatis erit. Itaque vel nihil erit vel multitudo infinities infinita, in qua neque totum sit unum neque pars vel particula usquam sit aliquid unum. Sin autem alterum sit eminentius altero, non licet quidem ens uni praeferre, alioquin nec erit unius particeps, itaque vel nihil vel infinite numerus infinitus, atque unum enti subiectum particeps fiet entis nec erit ultra simpliciter unum. Quamobrem ne inter Scyllam Charibdimque iactemur, ulterius unum enti praeferre debemus. Quod quidem quatenus unitatem unionemque impertit, eatenus suum cuique esse distribuit atque conservat. Propterea quicquid ab unitate passim et unione cadit interim ab essentia labitur.

6   Denique probavimus alibi super formam in materia iacentem, super vitam corpori mixtam, super intellectum infusum animae esse speciem in se subsistentem, vitam in se vigentem, intellectum in seipso micantem, ac iuxta quemlibet multiplicem ordinem ordinis ipsius summum in se subsistens esse, unum, imparticipabile, simplex. Item caput ubique superioris ordinis longius suum ordinem supereminet, quam caput sequentis ordinis suum exsuperet ordinem. Cum igitur in quolibet ente participatum unum inveniamus, merito super ens universum extare vaticinamur imparticipabile unum incomparabiliter simplex et absque proportione et quamlibet et universam essentiam antecellens.

Theology.[148] One will then investigate whether they are united to one another, or totally separate. If they are united and mixed with one another, there will be a superior principle which will be their cause and the author of the mixture, as demonstrated in the *Philebus.*[149] If they are separate, there will be absolutely no unity in being. So there will be either nothing or an infinitely infinite multitude, in which neither the totality will be one, nor will any part or part of part be anywhere a particular one. Conversely, if one of them is superior to the other, being cannot be placed before the One, otherwise it will not participate in the One, for which reason it will either be nothing, or an infinitely infinite number, and the One, as subject to being, will become the one that participates in being and will no longer be the absolute One. So lest we get caught between Charybdis and Scylla, we must locate the One before being. The One provides all realities with their own being and preserves it, inasmuch as it imparts unity and union to them. Thus when the unity and union of realities is affected, their essence is too.

Finally, as we have demonstrated elsewhere, above form-in- 6 matter, above life mixed with body, above intellect infused in soul, there lie the species that subsists by itself, the life that lives by itself, the intellect that shines within itself, and fixed to each multiple order lies the summit of this order, which subsists in itself, is one, unparticipated, and simple. Likewise, the summit of a superior order always transcends its own order to a greater extent than the summit of the next order transcends its own order. So, just as there is a participated one within each being, it is right to divine that above the universal being there is an unparticipated One, incomparably simple, without relation, and transcending all essences, whether particular or universal.

: LXXVIII :

Qua conditione negatur essentia vel esse de uno.
Item quare cognosci vel nominari non possit.

1   Quando Parmenides ipsi uni essentiam et esse tollit tamquam inferiora, non tamen ipsum unum tollit e medio. Ut enim ipsum
unum asseveraret et ipse poema composuit et discipulus eius Zeno
multa disseruit, et hic consequentias deinceps plurimas ob hoc in
primis serie longa contexit ut a deterioribus secernat unum tan-
demque declaret unum ipsum entium esse principium, quo sublato
penitus nihil fore. Alio igitur sensu negatur esse de nihilo tamquam deteriore, aliter autem de uno tamquam superiore, quod
Areopagita noster diligenter observat. Ergo qui unum negat esse
non tamen interim neget existere, sed pro essentia, quoad potest,
intellegat existentiam, ne forsan ente negato labi periclitetur in nihilum. Significanter[44] enim Graeci veteres, ut diximus alibi, quotiens totum penitus volunt e medio tollere, haud sane dicunt non
ens, sciunt enim ente sublato unum forte relinqui, sed inquiunt
μηδέν, id est non unum, quasi dicat ne unum quidem.

2   Postquam igitur Parmenides negavit ens de uno tamquam incomparabiliter altiore, merito negat omne cum ente coniugium.
Ait itaque primum nullum entium est uni aut unius, subdit mox
uni nec esse nomen neque sermonem, item unius nullam esse
cognitionem. Sensus enim cum sensibili, opinio cum opinabili,
scientia cum scibili coniugium habet. Cum igitur sensus, opinio,

: LXXVIII :

Under which condition essence and being are denied of the
One. Likewise, why the One cannot be known or named.

When Parmenides denies essence and being of the One because   1
they are inferior to it, he does not imply that the One does not
exist. Indeed the reason Parmenides wrote his poem and his disciple Zeno held so many discussions was to assert the existence of
the One. In this passage Parmenides first wove together a progressively greater number of consequences in a long series, in order to
separate the One from inferior realities, and in the end he will
declare that the One is the principle of beings, and that absolutely
nothing will exist if the One does not exist. So it is in one sense
that "being" is denied of "nothing," which is inferior to being, and
in another that it is denied of the One, which is superior to being,
as our Areopagite carefully observes.[150] Whenever we deny that
the One is, we should not imply that the One does not exist, but
understand, as much as possible, that "essence" stands for "existence"; otherwise, by denying "being" we would fall into nothingness. As we have said elsewhere, this is clear from the fact that
each time the ancient Greeks wish to suppress absolutely everything they do not say "not-being," knowing that by suppressing
"being" the unity might remain, but *mèden*, "not-one," as if to say
"not even one."

So after having denied being of the One on account of its in-   2
comparable superiority, Parmenides rightly denies any connection
with being. This is why he first says that there is no being *for* it or
of it [142A2], then adds that the One cannot be named or spoken
of, and likewise that it cannot be an object of knowledge [142A3–
4]. For sense perception is related to a sense object, opinion to an
object of opinion, knowledge to an object of knowledge. There-

scientia sint proprietates quaedam quorundam entium habeantque commercium cum obiectis, nimirum sensibile, opinabile, scibile in quodam entium ordine computantur. Quodlibet enim horum est ens eiusmodi atque tale. Ipsum igitur unum, dum propter simplicissimam eminentiam respuit omne cum ente consortium, cognitionem quoque renuit multoque magis nomen a cognitione dependens, sermonem quoque necessario nominibus constitutum.

3   Profecto si scire est rem per causam cognoscere, ipsum unum nullam habens causam scientia cognosci non potest nec insuper intellegentia percipi scientiae duce. Intellegentia enim multiformis est per formamque formas entium intuetur. Non igitur attingit unum. Quod quidem si scientia et intellegentia non percipitur, multo minus facultate quavis inferiore, scilicet imaginaria, opinione, vel sensu. Id quidem Plato in *Epistola ad Syracusanos* asserit dicens ipsum nullo modo doceri dicive posse, sed mentibus ad ipsum unum penitus unitate silentioque, id est consuetae actionis vacatione, conversis lumen unius tandem subito coruscare.

4   Inter haec dum audis unum excedere sensum, opinionem, scientiam, intellegentiam, intellege quattuor haec non humana tantum, sed daemonica etiam et divina. Sensum enim in daemonibus etiam diisque mundanis veteres posuerunt. Hinc Homerus summum inquit Iovem nec a solari quidem sensu posse sentiri. Similiter nec opinione nec scientia nec intellegentia, quantumlibet excelsa, primum cognosci posse putato, sed unitate solum amatoria tandem posse percipi divinitus illustrata.

fore, since sense perception, opinion and knowledge are particular properties of particular beings and have a relation with their objects, assuredly a sense object, an object of opinion and an object of knowledge are included in a particular order of beings: each of these objects is a being of a certain sort and of a certain quality. Thus by rejecting any relation with being on account of its utterly simple eminence, the One also rejects all knowledge, and even more every name, which depends on knowledge, as well as every discourse, which necessarily consists of names.

Surely, given that knowing is to comprehend a thing through its   3
cause, the One, which has no cause, cannot be comprehended by knowledge, nor even be perceived by intelligence, which is the guide of knowledge. For intelligence is multiform and contemplates the forms of beings through its own form. It does not, therefore, reach the One. Now if the One is not perceived by knowledge or intelligence, it is even less perceived by the lower faculties, imagination, opinion or sense perception. This is what Plato asserts in his *Letter to the Syracusans*, when he says that the One can by no means be taught or said, but that it is ultimately by turning our intelligences toward the One, in utter unity and silence, that is, by an emptiness of everyday activities, that at last the light of the One suddenly illuminates us.[151]

Meanwhile, when we hear Parmenides assert that the One tran-   4
scends sense perception, opinion, knowledge and intelligence, we must understand that he not only is denying this of human faculties, but also of demonic and divine ones. For the ancients also placed sense perception within demons and the cosmic gods. Hence Homer says that Almighty Jupiter cannot be perceived even by the perception of the sun.[152] Similarly, we must consider that the first principle cannot be known by opinion, knowledge or intelligence, however excellent these are, but can ultimately only be perceived by erotic unity, when that unity is divinely illuminated.[153]

5   Quaeritur autem, si rerum principium nominari non potest, quomodo appellemus unum. Respondetur per hoc nomen unum non affirmari ipsam primi naturam, sed partim quidem negari circa ipsum multitudinem et compositionem atque commercium, partim vero declarari cuncta ab illo unitatis unionisque munere effici, perfici, conservari. Illud quoque Procli saepe nostri valde placet: per hoc nomen unum non ipsum quidem in se unum, sed intimum hoc quod ex illo nobis inest unum occultumque unius conceptum exprimi. Inest enim cunctis erga primum principium tamquam omnium finem appetitus innatus. Ergo et ante appetitum sensus quidam, ut ita dixerim, illius occultus. Quo quidem naturali sensu sensibus aliis prorsus occulto, grave et leve per rectam lineam locum sibi quasi eligit naturalem respuitve contrarium, radices arborum humorem eligunt ariditate vitata, folia sagaciter umbram fugiunt asciscuntque calorem pariter atque lumen. Hoc itaque sensu appetituque mirabili omnia convertuntur ad primum etiam non cognoscentia primum. Similiter anima etiam ante notitiam manifestam electionemque consilii, naturali sensu inclinationeque per unum inde sibi impressum desiderat ipsum unum. Quo quidem desiderio frequenter admonita unum denique nominat, non tam confidens pronuntiare primum quam enitens desiderium suum circa primum exprimere suumque unum quasi primi illius proferre conceptum. Accedit ad haec quod inter omnia nomina unum vaticinamur esse maxime venerandum, quippe cum sit in omnibus, efficiat, perficiat, conservet omnia, quae divisione vicissim debilitantur et occidunt. Iam vero sicut ad unum, sic ad bonum omnia pariter convertuntur ac divisionem aeque fugiunt atque malum. Eadem enim unius atque boni amplitudo est ea-

But the question arises as to how it is that we call it "the One," 5
given that the principle of things cannot be named. The response
is that to use the term "one," is not to affirm a name for the very
nature of the first principle, but, on the one hand, it is to deny of
the One multitude, composition and relation, and on the other, to
make manifest that all things are created, perfected and preserved
by the gift of unity and union. I also very much agree with the
following doctrine of Proclus, who is often my guide: when we use
the name "one" it is not the One in itself that we express, but our
own innermost one, which proceeds from the One into us, and is
the hidden concept of the One. For in all things there is an innate
striving toward the first principle, which is the end of all things.
So even before this striving there is a hidden sense, so to speak,
that apprehends this principle. It is by virtue of this natural sense,
which is completely hidden from the other senses, that heavy and
light objects on a straight line prefer the place that is natural to
them rather than the place that is contrary to their nature; that the
roots of trees prefer humidity to dryness; that the leaves deliberately avoid shadow and strive for warmth and light. Through this
marvelous sense and striving, therefore, all things turn themselves
toward the first principle, without even knowing it. Likewise, the
soul, even before having any clear knowledge or reasoned choice,
through a natural sense and inclination, strives toward the One
through the intermediary of the one which is imprinted upon it
from above. Apprised over and over by this striving it finally
names it "one," not because it is so bold as to give a name to the
first principle, but because in its desire to express its striving toward it, it utters its own "one" which is like the concept of that first
One. Moreover, among all names we infer that "one" must be the
most venerable, since it is in all things, and since it creates, perfects
and preserves all things, whereas division causes things to weaken
and perish. Furthermore, all things turn themselves toward unity
and goodness and avoid division and evil. For the One and the

demque potestas, neque duae tamen esse naturae possunt, altera quidem unum, altera vero bonum, ne forte duo sint principia rerum, neque bonum ante unum, ne forte bonum careat unione unumque sit inde compositum, neque rursus unum ante bonum, ne quid sit ipso bono melius, ne quid res superius magisque quam bonum appetant.

6   Quaeritur tandem numquid unum ullo modo cognosci possit. Respondetur Parmenidem non putare nullo modo cognosci posse, sed non sensu, non opinione, non scientia. Nam et Plato in *Epistolis* ideam quoque ipsam nedum sensu et opinione, sed etiam nec scientia vult cognosci, quippe cum scientia dividendo, definiendo, demonstrando semper sit adeo multiplex atque mobilis, ut cum ipsa ideae simplicitate stabilitateque non congruat, sed existimat post discussiones eiusmodi ideam ipsam simplici stabilique quodam intellegentiae perspicacioris intuitu percipi posse. Parmenides autem ipsum unum nec etiam intellegentia scientiae duce prorsus attingi, cum haec et multiformis sit et per formas feratur ad entia, sed post intellegentiae serenitatem atque fulgorem coruscare alterum iam ex alto lumen, per quod nostra unitas cum ipso uno mirabiliter uniatur. Quemadmodum vero ideam in *Epistolis* ignotam inquit non conditione materiae ob defectum, sed propter lucis excessum, ita et hic ipsum unum appellat incognitum, non tamquam exile quiddam aut vanum, alioquin non tam longo studio dignum fuerat, sed tamquam universo ente viribusque entia cognoscentibus longe superius.

7   Denique summum deum tandem quoquomodo percipi posse testificatur Plato in *Epistola ad Hermiam* principem atque collegas, dicens si recte philosophando quaeramus deum rerum omnium

Good have the same extension and the same power. The One and the Good cannot, however, be two different natures, otherwise there would be two principles of things; the Good does not precede the One either, otherwise the Good would lack unity and be a composite one, just as the One does not precede the Good, otherwise there would be something better than the Good and things would desire something superior and greater than the Good.[154]

The last question to arise is whether the One can in any way be known.[155] The response is that Parmenides does not think that the One cannot be known in any way, but that it cannot be apprehended by sense perception, opinion or knowledge. Plato too considers in his *Letters* that the Idea not only remains unknown to sense perception and opinion, but also to knowledge, because by using division, definition and demonstration, knowledge is always multiple and in motion, and is not, therefore, in accordance with the Idea's simplicity and rest; but he considers that it is after these ratiocinations that the Idea can be perceived by a kind of simple and motionless sight of a more penetrating intelligence.[156] Parmenides thinks, however, that the One cannot even be reached by intelligence, the guide of knowledge, since intelligence is multiform and transports itself toward beings through forms; rather, beyond the intelligence's serenity and brightness, another light shines from above, whereby our own unity is marvelously united to the One. Just as Plato asserts in the *Letters* that the Idea is not known in a material condition by defect, but because of an excess of light, so here too Parmenides calls the One unknown, not because it is something worthless and without substance, otherwise it would not have been worthy of such a long investigation, but because it is by far superior to universal being and the forces that know beings.

Finally, the supreme God can ultimately be perceived in a way described by Plato in his *Letter* to the prince Hermias and his associates: in this *Letter* Plato states that if we look for God, the Lord of all things, and His Father in the right way, through philo-

6

7

ducem eiusque patrem, nos tandem illum, quantum beatis licet, perspicue cognituros.

: LXXIX :

De firmitate suppositionis primae et
quod unum ente superius.

1   Parmenides in fine primae suppositionis Aristotelem adolescentem sic interrogat: 'an igitur possibile est ista circa ipsum unum ita se habere?' Respondet ille: 'Non, ut mihi videtur.' Tu vero cave suspiceris per eiusmodi quaestionem responsionemque infirmari quaecumque de uno in superioribus gradatim conclusa sunt, quasi minus possibilia sint et quasi quod cogitatur unum ente superius nihil sit aliud praeter nomen, quia videlicet inde sequi putentur absurda. Consequentiae quidem omnes necessario ex antecedentibus sunt adductae. Ipsum quoque simpliciter unum multitudinis expers, quod consequentiarum est omnium fundamentum, est maxime necessarium, si modo in quolibet rerum ordine ad primum est ascendendum, quod et unum sit et ab alienis dissonantibusque penitus absolutum. Itaque super quodlibet unum, quod passim est unum aliquid et quodammodo multiplex, extare oportet ipsum simpliciter unum a multitudine tamquam extranea liberum. Quod et in *Sophiste* probatur, ubi disseritur ens pati unum atque esse unius particeps, videlicet tamquam inferius uno, item illud quod est totum, id est ex multis esse non posse vere unum atque primum. Et hic in sequente suppositione probatur unum illud quod habet cum ente coniugium multitudinem iam subire. Unde compellimur ipsum vere unum super essentiam inda-

sophical inquiry, we shall at last know Him truly, as far as this is possible for the blessed.[157]

: LXXIX :

On the validity of the first hypothesis.
On the superiority of the One over being.

At the end of the first hypothesis Parmenides asks the young Ar- 1 istoteles the following question: "Is it possible, then, that these things hold true of the One?" Aristoteles answers: "I do not think so" [142A7–8]. This exchange does not mean that all the conclusions that have been progressively made above about the One are now made invalid. We should not infer that these consequences are impossible and that what has been conceived as the One superior to being is but a name, on the grounds that absurd consequences would result from that.[158] All the consequences, to be sure, have been necessarily deduced from premises. Moreover, the absolute One, which is simple and devoid of multitude, and the principle of all consequences, is absolutely necessary, given that in every order of things we must ascend to the first principle of that order, which is one and totally separate from contrary and dissonant things. So, above each of these "ones," which are somehow particular and multiple, there must be the absolute One, free from multitude, because multitude is exterior to it. Plato also shows this in the *Sophist*, where he states that being undergoes the One and partakes of the One (since it is inferior to the One), and likewise that what is a whole, i.e. is composed of many, cannot be truly one and first.[159] And in the second hypothesis of the *Parmenides* Parmenides shows that that one which has an affinity with being undergoes multitude; this leads us to find the real One above essence.

gare. Accedit ad haec quod, ut Socrates disputat in *Republica,* ars disserendi est ipsa theologia et, ut ita dixerim, metaphysica, quae quidem, ut ibi describit, per totam progreditur entium latitudinem et unamquamque definit essentiam. Post haec altius ascendit ad ipsum bonum universi entis intellegibilisque principium atque finem ascensumque eiusmodi per omnes negationum modos peragit. Summatim vero, ut ibi saepius repetitur, dialectica vis intellegibilium omnium causam contemplatur, removens ipsam ab omnibus entibus, negationum nulla posthabita. Addit ibi quoque negationes tentans ipsam primam causam super intellectum et intellegibile et veritatem essentiamque existere. Quaerimus igitur ubinam dialectica facultas penes Platonem per omnes negationes gradatim ad primam causam entium intellegibiliumque ascendat: nisi enim in hoc dialogo, certe nusquam. Cum igitur hic dialogus sit ipsa Platonis dialectica, haec vero apud ipsum theologia sit, qui negabit dialogum hunc esse dogmaticum, theologiam quoque dogmaticam esse negaverit. In hoc autem libro non accedit ad primum per negationes in suppositione secunda, ubi gradatim affirmat omnia, nec in tertia rursus, ubi non omnia negat, ubi multa confirmat, in sequentibus autem multo minus. Hic igitur et in suppositione prima officium illud suum dialectica praestat, de uno videlicet intellegibilium principio, id est entis universi causa omnia entis propria negans. Deinceps profecto nusquam[45] infirmaturus quae et ipse Parmenides necessaria ubique serie comprobavit et Aristoteles respondendo frequenter extra controversiam confirmavit, non facile eadem omnia revocaturus in dubium.

2   Quamobrem plerique Platonici putaverunt hanc ultimam suppositionis huius quaestionem responsionemque esse quasi communem quandam conclusionem summatim negativas conclusiones singulas comprehendentem. Singulatim enim quaesitum fuit an ipsum unum possit esse multitudo, an totum, an figuratum, et

In addition, as Socrates says in the *Republic*, dialectic is true theology and, I would say, metaphysics. He shows that it proceeds through the whole extent of beings, defines each essence, then ascends further up to the Good, which is the principle and end of universal being and the intelligible world, and it accomplishes this ascent through all modes of negations. In sum, as I have said several times, dialectic contemplates the cause of all the intelligible objects by separating it from all beings, without leaving aside any negation.[160] He also adds — and here he also uses negations — that the first cause is beyond the intellect, the intelligible, truth and essence.[161] In which dialogue of Plato, then, does dialectical reason progressively ascend through all the negations toward the first cause of beings and intelligible objects? Nowhere else, surely, than in the *Parmenides!* Since, therefore, this dialogue *is* Plato's dialectic, and since Plato considers dialectic to be theology, whoever wishes to deny that this dialogue is dogmatic will at once deny that theology is dogmatic. It is not in the second hypothesis of the *Parmenides*, where it progressively asserts all things of the one, that dialectic reaches the first principle through negations, nor in the third hypothesis, where it denies some things and asserts others,[162] and even less in the following hypotheses. It is here, in the first hypothesis, that dialectic accomplishes its very function, that of denying of the One all the properties of being, because the One is the principle of the intelligible realities and the cause of universal being. Surely then Plato never intended to turn around and invalidate the conclusions which Parmenides everywhere demonstrated through a series of necessary arguments, and which Aristoteles frequently and indisputably confirmed by his responses — surely Plato was never going to call all these in question in some facile way.

Most Platonists have established, therefore, that the last question of the first hypothesis is a general conclusion which summarizes in a word all the negative conclusions.[163] Parmenides asked individual questions to assess whether the One could be a multi- 2

quae sequuntur. Responsum et probatum gradatim non esse possibile. Denique summatim sub una conclusione omnes in iudicium revocantur, an videlicet possibile sit haec esse circa unum, scilicet quod sit multitudo, quod totum, quod figuratum, caeteraque deinceps. Summatim denique respondetur non videri quidem haec possibilia circa unum. Qua quidem responsione praecedentes omnes semel confirmari videntur et merito, cum enim semel simplicem ipsam rei rationem posueris, quicquid insuper adhibueris talem aliquam aut talem naturam pro simplici reportabis: pro vita quandam vitam, pro ideali aequalitate aequalitatem quandam, pro ipso bono quoddam et tale bonum, et aliquod[46] unum pro ipso simpliciter uno. Quapropter ipsum unum nacti non debemus illi conditiones multitudinis vel totius vel figurati vel alias insuper adhibere, ut ita penitus absolutum et simplicissimum communissimumque sit primumque omnium aeque principium. Nam Plato in *Epistola ad Dionysium*, ut exposuimus alibi, graviter eos circa primum errare dicit qui illic quale aliquid investigant. Ex quo patet secundam suppositionem non tractare de primo, nam cum semel unum posuerit, adhibet mox ei ens multiplex, totum, finitum, figuratum, quibus necessario quale quid efficitur. Reliquum est ut de primo in prima suppositione tractetur, quae eiusmodi omnia propulsat ab uno.

3   Syrianus et Proclus diligenter admodum, ut caetera solent, ista rimantur observantesque singula ubique Platonis verba tradunt mysticum hic latere sensum, ubi praesertim dicitur circa ipsum unum. Aliud enim significari volunt ubi legitur de ipso uno, aliud autem ubi legitur circa ipsum unum. De uno siquidem tractare facile possunt ingeniosi sive affirmando sive negando, tametsi tu-

tude, a whole, a shape, and so on, and every time he showed this to be impossible; at the end, the sum of all the conclusions are reexamined in a single conclusion: is it possible that these things hold true for the One, that is, is it possible for the One to be a multitude, a whole, a shape, and so on? — and the final response which summarizes all the [previous] responses is that this does not seem to be possible for the One. This response appears to confirm at once all the previous responses, and rightly so: once we have postulated the simple rational principle of something, then whatever we add to it is a being of a certain quality instead of being simply that thing: a certain life instead of life, a certain equality instead of ideal equality, a certain good of a certain quality instead of the Good, and a certain one instead of the absolute One. So when we reach the One we must not add to it the conditions of multitude, whole, shape, or anything else, otherwise it will not be totally separate, utterly simple and common, and it will not be the first principle of all things. For, as we explained elsewhere, Plato declares in his *Letter to Dionysius* that those who inquire about the quality of the One are making a serious mistake.[164] It appears, therefore, that the second hypothesis does not treat of the first principle: once it postulates the existence of the one, it immediately adds to the one the attributes "being," "multiple," "whole," "limited," "shaped," whereby the one necessarily becomes something with a quality.[165] The only hypothesis that discusses the first principle is the first hypothesis, which removes all these attributes from the One.

Syrianus and Proclus examine very carefully these passages, as they always do; they analyze all Plato's words and establish that a mystical meaning is hidden in each of them, especially when it is a question of the One. For they consider that what is said *in reference to* the One has a different meaning than what is said *about* the One, since intelligent men can easily use assertions or negations *in reference to* the One, although it is safer to use negations. By con-

tius negare licet, sed circa ipsum unum nemo aut ullo modo affirmat quicquam aut exacte negat. Si quis enim circa ipsum medita-
retur, consequeretur iam et attingeret illud, quod quidem contingit
nemini. Merito igitur Plato in *Epistola ad Dionysium* inquit: circa
ipsum regem nihil est tale qualia nobis cognata sunt, sed quod
post ipsum est anima dicit. Ubi sane mysterium quod in superioribus tetigimus latere videtur, animam videlicet quando pronuntiat
unum non ipsum simpliciter unum enuntiare, sed suum quoddam
unum inde sibi insitum edere suumque de illo proferre conceptum,
neque tamen circa ipsum agere, sed de illo. Ipsum namque a nobis
nullo modo dicitur, ut et paulo ante Parmenides ait et in *Epistola
ad Syracusanos* inquit Plato. Mundi quinetiam architectum verbis
exprimi vulgo non posse, testis est Timaeus, multo minus archi-
tecti patrem.

4   Postquam igitur Parmenides affirmationes nobis omnes sustulit
circa unum negationesque vicissim tamquam probabiliores adduxit
in medium tandem, ne quis forte consideret se per eiusmodi negationes ipsum unum exacte consecuturum, Aristotelem his verbis
interrogat: 'An igitur putas esse possibile circa ipsum unum haec
ita se habere?', admonens videlicet eum non ita se prorsus habere,
id est, neque hac quidem negandi ratione nos ipsum penitus assequi. Hinc adolescens redditus accuratior respondit: 'Non ita prorsus, ut mihi videtur.' Iam vero Dionysius Areopagita libri huius
summus astipulator in *Mystica Theologia* longo ordine gradus entium de primo negat, et postquam affirmationes sustulit tamquam
dissonas, negationes quoque tamquam non undique consonas tollit e medio indicitque rationi intellegentiaeque silentium, rationi
quidem quia mobilis, intellegentiae vero quoniam multiformis.
Quo velut in caligine lucem luminum attingamus. Eiusmodi silentium nobis hic imponere Parmenides quoque videtur. Postquam

trast, nobody correctly asserts nor denies anything *about* the One, for if you could engage in contemplation *about* the One, you would pursue and catch it at once, which is never the case.[166] So Plato is right to say in his *Letter to Dionysius* that there is nothing *about* the king itself that is akin to us, but that the soul speaks *about* what is after the king.[167] Here lies the secret mystery mentioned above: the soul, when pronouncing the word "one," does not announce the absolute One, but expresses its own particular one, which derives from the One and is infused in the soul; it formulates its own concept *in reference to* the One, without talking *about* the One, but *in reference* to it. For the One is by no means spoken of by us, as has just been stated by Parmenides and by Plato in his *Letter to the Syracusans*.[168] In addition, the architect of the world cannot be expressed by us through words, as Timaeus bears witness,[169] much less the father of the architect.

So after having removed for us all the assertions about the One, 4 and having finally established that the negations are more probable, Parmenides, who does not wish anyone to believe that he can rightly reach the One through these negations, asks Aristoteles: "Do you think that it is possible for these things to hold true for the One?," putting him on notice that this is not the case; in other words, that even through negations we do not completely attain to the One. Made more cautious by this question, the young man replies: "I do not think so." Indeed, in the *Mystical Theology* Dionysius the Areopagite, who is the most important corroborator of this dialogue, first denies at length the hierarchy of beings of the first principle, and after having suppressed such assertions as inharmonious with the One, he also removes the negations, because they too are not always harmonious with the One, and he enjoins our reason and intelligence to remain silent; reason, because it is in motion; intelligence, because it is multiform, as though it were in darkness that we reach the light of lights.[170] This is the silence Parmenides also appears to impose upon us here. After having

dixit primum neque cognosci neque dici posse ideoque non solum affirmare de illo quicquam prohibet, sed negationes quoque admonet posthabendas. Utrobique enim dicimus sive affirmando sive negando, illud vero dici nullo modo potest. Praeterea quicumque palam negat, interim clam affirmat. Negare enim de primo aliquid est hoc ab illo secernere. Secernere autem hoc ab illo non possumus, nisi prius hoc in seipso firmaverimus[47] atque illud. Si igitur affirmationes tamquam infinitum definientes reprobatae sunt circa primum, negationes quoque tamquam affirmationum participes non sunt penitus approbandae. Quamobrem non iniuria Parmenides admonet non tam negationibus quam silentio tranquillo, divino, amatorio confidendum. Quod quidem Platonici omnes una cum Mercurio et Apollonio Tyaneo proculdubio comprobant et propheta David inquit: 'Laus tibi, o Deus, est silentium.'

5   Si quis autem pertinacius instet per interrogationem responsionemque postremam supra dicta in ambiguitatem trahi, respondebimus multorum Platonicorum consensu non omnia quidem hic reddi dubia. Plurima enim et necessario probata et proculdubio sunt concessa. Sed si quid paradoxon praesertim in calce fuerit, de hoc dumtaxat: adolescentem a simulante et dissimulante sene in dubium provocari, ut hac insinuatione accipiat ansas ad ludum inde sequentem, perinde ac si senex adolescenti dicat: quandoquidem iam dicta suspicionem tibi quandam inferunt et quoniam de ignoto et ineffabili loqui non licet, age hac deinceps occasione quaestionem de uno iterum resumamus loquamurque de uno quodam in posterum quod intellegibile nobis et effabile sit, siquidem nobiscum in ipso entium ordine congruat. Illud vero super essentiam et intellectum atque sermonem super-

said that the first principle cannot be known nor said, he not only forbids us to assert anything of it, but also invites us to reject the negations. For in both cases, whether we use assertions or negations, we say something. Yet the One cannot be expressed in any way. Moreover, when we seem to deny something, we are actually asserting something, for denying something of the first principle consists of separating this thing from the first principle. Yet we cannot separate this thing from the first principle unless we have first asserted the very existence of both this thing and the first principle. Thus while the assertions about the first principle have been rejected on the grounds that they limit the infinite, the negations should not be accepted either, since they participate in the assertions. For this reason, Parmenides rightly invites us to put our confidence not in the negations, but in that tranquil, divine and erotic silence, which all the Neoplatonists, as well as Mercury and Apollonius of Tyana, seem undeniably to approve, as well as the prophet David when he says "Silence is praise to you, God."[171]

If, however, some obstinate interlocutor keeps on questioning 5 what has been said above, on account of the final exchange, we shall respond that most Platonists agree in considering that this final passage does not invalidate all the arguments, because most of these arguments have been shown to be necessary and have been readily admitted. If there were to be a paradox, especially at the end of the *Parmenides,* it would only be the fact that a young man is led to doubt by an elderly man through simulation and dissimulation, and that the young man seizes this opportunity, through Parmenides' allusions, to keep on playing this game in the second hypothesis. It is as if the old man was saying to the young man: "since what has been said so far arouses your suspicion, and given that it is not permitted to speak of the unknown and the ineffable, let us take this opportunity to raise once more the question about unity, and let us talk about a certain one which comes

nis contemplatoribus dimittamus pio quodam silentio venerantes, donec et ipsi, si minus facultate nostra, saltem afflatu divino, quandoque similiter contemplari possimus.

6   Hactenus quidem per has vias, immo vero per haec invia, duces alicubi vel saltem indices habuimus Proclum atque Syrianum. Ultra vero, cum nemo ducat, pergendum iam est nobis duce deo, solo deinceps vaticinio confidendum.

: LXXX :

Secundae suppositionis intentio.

1   Socrates in sexto *De Republica* cum pervenisset ad ipsum bonum universi principium, exclamavit: patrem hunc praesenti contemplationi ignotum prorsus et ineffabilem in praesentia dimittamus, pergamus ad filium. Auditores autem contemplationem quidem filii libentissime receperunt, sperantes interim ut patrem quoque alibi demonstraret. Socrates igitur palam pervenit ad solem ipsius boni filium per imaginem, clam vero progressus est ad intellectum et intellegibile primum, tamquam dei filium per naturam et, ut aiunt Platonici, primo genitum. In quo pater ille summus universum hunc mundum ab aevo condiderit per ideas. Idcirco mundum intellegibilem vocaverunt. De hoc patre et filio Platonem ad Her-

after the One, and which we can understand and talk about, because this one is in accordance with our intellect in the order of beings; however, we should leave the One that is beyond essence, intellect and discourse, to more sublime contemplatives, and venerate it in a pious silence until the day we can contemplate it in the same way—if not by a human faculty, at least by divine inspiration."

Through these paths, or rather these impassable regions, we 6
have hitherto had the guidance, or at least the indications, of Proclus and Syrianus. From this point on, however, since nobody guides us, we must proceed with the guidance of God and then trust solely the power of divine inspiration.[172]

: LXXX :

The purpose of the second hypothesis.

When Socrates reached the Good, principle of the universe, in the 1
sixth book of the *Republic*, he exclaimed: "Let us dismiss for the time being the contemplation of the utterly unknown and ineffable father, and proceed with his son." His audience most readily agreed to contemplate the son, but hoped that Socrates would then go on to describe the father.[173] As such, Socrates appears to have reached the sun, which is the son of the Good, by an image,[174] but in an occult way he reached the first intellect and intelligible, as the son of God by nature, and, as the Platonists say, the firstborn,[175] wherein the eminent father created from eternity the universal world through the Ideas. Thus they called him the intelligible world. We have described what Plato wrote to Hermias on the

miam scripsisse narravimus. De hoc itaque filio, id est intellegibili
mundo, tamquam per intellegentiam cognobili aliquando et effabili
secunda suppositio tractat, agnoscens iam in eo pro sua videlicet
dignitate quaecumque tamquam entis universi propria de primo
propter eminentissimam simplicitatem in prima suppositione negaverat. Tu vero inter haec intellege mundum intellegibilem, non
hunc tantum intellectum, sed omnium quoque sublimium men-
tium coetum apud Platonicos nominari, et si qua praeterea sit,
anima dea. Nam caelestes animas universalesque providentiam
agentes universalem deos nominant ad intellegibilium coetum
quodammodo pertinentes. Ad haec igitur omnia secundae suppositionis affirmationes pertinere memento, intellectusque omnes
eiusmodi propter unitatem uniuscuiusque suam mirabiliter exce-
dentem deos cognominari, totumque summatim de uno ente universo, in quo excellens unitas cum essentia coniugium habet, hic
ubique tractari. Dicitur autem unum ens, ut dicebam, totum intellegibilium intellectuumque genus, praecipue vero intellectus primus cum intellegibili primo, deinceps caetera generis eiusdem.
Merito igitur cum conclusio prima sub hoc unius entis nomine
tangat in primis intellectum summum, conclusio tandem ultima,
scilicet in hac suppositione secunda, sub gradu intellectualium iam
participe temporis universales attingit animas in quibus tempus
est primum, ut continuetur secunda suppositio tertiae de ordine
animarum particularium tractaturae. Verisimile quoque est per
conclusiones medias medios quosdam intellegibilium ordines de-
signari, non tamen singulis singulos quasi depingi.

father and the son.[176] So the second hypothesis is about the Good's son, that is, the intelligible world, which in some way can be known and uttered by intelligence; it asserts the existence, within the intelligible world, and in a manner befitting its rank, of all the things that had been denied of the first principle in the first hypothesis on account of the first principle's utterly eminent simplicity, and which pertain to universal being. One should bear in mind that among the Platonists the intelligible world not only designates the intellect, but also the whole cohort of sublime minds and (if there is one) the goddess soul. For they call gods the celestial and universal souls that exercise universal providence, considering that these somehow belong to the cohort of intelligible objects.[177] One should remember, therefore, that the assertions of the second hypothesis concern all these realities, and that all the intellects are called gods on account of their individual and wonderfully transcendent unity. In sum, in the second hypothesis, everything is asserted of the universal one being, wherein excellent unity is yoked together with being. But, as I said, the term "one being" indicates the whole genus of intelligible objects and intellects, firstly the first intellect, which is coordinate with the first intelligible, then all the others of the same kind. So while the first conclusion reaches under the term "one being" the highest intellect [142B], the last conclusion of the second hypothesis rightly reaches, at the level of the intellects that partake of time, the universal souls, in which time first occurs [151E], so that the second hypothesis announces the third hypothesis, which will be about the level of individual souls.[178] It is also likely that the intermediate orders of intelligible realities are described by the intermediate conclusions. However, not every conclusion describes a specific order.[179]

2   Haec autem Dionysius Areopagita quasi confirmans in libro *De Divinis Nominibus*, quem nuper interpretati sumus, communia apud prophetas dei nomina disputat, ipsam quidem dei naturam nequicquam significare, sed effectus quosdam proprietatesque et dotes ad intellegibilem intellectualemque naturam divinitus procedentes. Itaque nomina haec intellegibilia munera appellationesque intellegibiles frequenter appellat affirmatque de excellentibus creaturis intellectualibusque ordinibus, de creatore vero negat, nisi quatenus ipsum esse horum causam forte significent.

3   Ego vero deinceps suppositionis huius consequentias brevi perstringam. Si enim intellegas qua ratione significationeque singula negata sunt de primo, interim qua de secundo affirmata sint intelleges, quemadmodum et in singulis quae praecesserunt consequentiis pro viribus admonuimus. Praeterea si in hac suppositione varia numina designantur proprietates in medium introductae, etsi communiter cunctis competunt, alio tamen sensu graduque aliis coaptantur, ut ante Syrianum omnes Platonici consenserunt. Idem, status, similitudo, aequalitas in superioribus abundant. Horum opposita in inferioribus quodammodo superant. In mediis se mediocriter habent generatio, tempus, motus, alio sensu primis, alio sequentibus tribuuntur. Neque vero consilium est quot conclusionum capita sunt, numina totidem introducere, ne cum Proclo dicamus etiam in tempore est, fit, erat, fuit, fiebat, erit, fiet, factum fuerit, octo deos existere.

Dionysius the Areopagite confirms this in his treatise *On the* 2 *Divine Names*, which we have recently commented upon,[180] stating that the names of God in use among the prophets by no means describe God's nature, but some effects, properties and qualities that proceed from God into the intelligible and intellectual nature. For this reason he often calls these names intelligible powers and intelligible appellations, and he asserts them of the excellent creatures and intellectual orders, but denies them of the Creator, except insofar, perhaps, as they signify that He is their cause.[181]

In what follows I will briefly summarize [the attributes denied 3 in] the consequences of this hypothesis. For if you understand the reason for which, and signification whereby, these have been denied of the first principle, you will also understand why they have been asserted of the second principle, as we have also tried to point out in our presentation of each of the previous [attributes denied in the] consequences. Moreover, admitting that the properties presented in this hypothesis correspond to different divinities, even if these attributes are in accordance with all the intelligible realities, they each correspond to a different divinity, according to a certain sense and degree, as the Platonists before Syrianus unanimously recognized.[182] Sameness, rest, likeness and equality abound in the superior intelligible realities. Their opposites in some way dominate the inferior intelligible realities; in the intermediate orders generation, time, motion exist in a temperate way, and their sense varies according to whether they are attributed to the first or to the subsequent intelligible realities. However, we do not intend to introduce as many divinities as there are conclusions, lest we say, with Proclus, that even in the temporal realm the attributes "is," "becomes," "was being," "was" "became," "will be," "will become" and "will have become" correspond to eight gods.[183]

: LXXXI :

Quomodo in uno ente alia sit ratio unius,
alia entis sit, totum partes habeat
et multitudinem infinitam.

1   Quando in suppositionis primae principio proponebatur[48] ita 'si
unum est' et reliqua, danda mox erat verbis venia, verba enim intellegentiae suppetere nequeunt. Dicendum forte fuerat 'si unum
existit,' dummodo per existentiam nihil aliud intellegamus quam
merum ipsum unius ipsius actum, perinde ac si diceretur 'si unum,
unum' et reliqua. Merito igitur ita posito, negatur statim multitudo de uno et quaecumque inde sequuntur. Propositio vero prima
in suppositione secunda non adeo simpliciter unum accipit, sed
cum essentia unum. Magna igitur significatione Parmenides hic ita
loquitur: 'Nunc autem non est suppositio nostra, si unum, unum,
sed si unum est,' his verbis admonens dum dicit, 'Nunc autem,'
suppositionem quidem primam de uno simplici tractavisse, secundam vero de uno cum essentia pertractare.

2   Aliam quidem unius, aliam vero essentiae rationem esse et ibi et
hic manifeste testatur ac nos probavimus alibi. Nunc quoque co-
niectura quadam quamvis levi breviter confirmamus. Potest forsitan rei alicuius vel moles vel essentia vel substantia per accumula-
tionem aliquam augeri, dum tamen non augetur unitas ibidem, sed
forte minuitur. Potest et conteri paulatim unitate interim non at-
trita, sed magis forsitan apparente. Potest et res illa quomodolibet
dividi, unitate interim non divisa, sed potius geminata. Cum igitur

: LXXXI :

*How the rational principle of the one is different from
that of being within the one being, and the whole
has parts and an infinite multitude.*

When it was postulated at the beginning of the first hypothesis "if   1
the One is" and so on, it quickly became necessary to beg pardon
for the words used, because words are inadequate for our under-
standing [of the first principle]. One should perhaps have said "if
the One exists," provided that we understand by "existence" nothing else than the pure act of the One, as if we were to say "if the
One, One" and so on. So once the existence of the One is postulated, we immediately deny of the One the multitude and all the
things subsequent to it. But the first proposition of the second
hypothesis does not concern the absolute One, but the one coordinate with essence. So when Parmenides states here with deep
meaning, "but now our hypothesis is not, 'if the One, One,' but 'if
the one is'" [142C2–4], he is reminding us, when using these
words 'but now' [etc.], that he had been discussing the first hypothesis about the absolute One, but now was treating the second
hypothesis about the one coordinate with being.

   That the rational principle of the one is different from that of   2
essence is clearly attested by Parmenides in both hypotheses and
has been demonstrated by us elsewhere. Now let us also briefly
confirm this with the following line of reasoning, even if it is a
trivial one. One could increase the mass, the essence or the substance of a given thing by means of accumulation, without increas-
ing the unity of this thing (in fact, its unity might even decrease).
We could also progressively reduce these without reducing the
unity, which might even appear greater. One can also in some way
divide this thing without dividing its unity, but rather double it.

ratio unius sit alia quam essentiae ac per essentiam sic habeatur esse, sicut per vitam vivere, consequenter si unum proprie loquendo est, per essentiam certe est a se differentem atque ita quodammodo est essentiae particeps sive compos. Similiter essentia particeps est unius, per quod est una. Cum vero utrumque maxime inter se cognatum sit atque fecundum, necessarium est in unam totius formam utrumque coire, de quo inquam toto, tamquam uno quodam supposito atque subsistente, tam unum quam essentia praedicentur[49] ut partes. Quoniam vero pueriliter praedicaretur ens de ente vel unum de uno, Parmenides non inquit praedicari praecipue unum de uno ente aut ens de ente uno, sed unum de ente uno atque ens de uno ente dici. Concluditur ergo sicut de uno super ens existente negatum fuit ab initio totum atque partes, ita nunc de uno ente utrumque probabiliter affirmari. Propterea multitudinem in se habere quam de ipso simpliciter uno negaverat ab initio.

3   Praeterea in quolibet ex quattuor elementis vel liquoribus perfecte mixto quicquid acceperis in se reliqua continet. Similiter et multo magis in uno ente, ubi et unum in primis unificum est et ens unibile. Conditio unius cum entis conditione ita conflatur, ut nusquam alterum re ipsa segregetur ab altero. Nusquam ergo reperies unum scilicet solitarium, sicut in linea, ita continuitas semper cum puncto concurrit, ut quotiens diviseris, totiens occurrat continuitas simul atque punctum. Continuitas quidem repraesentat ens, punctum vero refert unum. Sicut ergo linea, sic ens unum fingi quidem multitudo infinita potest, quamvis non actu vel effectu sit infinita. Quorsum haec? Ut intellegas cuiuslibet intellegibilis divinaeque substantiae naturam hanc esse, ut si mille mil-

Therefore, since the rational principle of the one is different from that of essence, and being occurs through essence (just as living occurs through life), if the one *is* properly speaking, it *is* surely through essence, which is different from itself. In that case, it somehow partakes of essence, or possesses essence. Likewise essence partakes of the one, by virtue of which it is one. But since both are to the highest degree akin and fecund, both must necessarily be united in the unique form of a whole. Of what I call "whole," which is the one postulated and subsistent, both one and essence are predicated as its parts. But since it would be foolish to predicate "being" of being or "one" of the one, Parmenides does not say that the attribute "one" is principally predicated of the one being or "being" of the being one, but that "'one' is asserted of being which is one, and 'being' is asserted of this one which is" [142D1–3]. The conclusion is, therefore, that just as the whole and the parts were first denied of the One above being, in the same way these two predicates are now appropriately asserted of the one being; thus the one being possesses within itself the multitude that had before been denied of the absolute One [142E1–43A2].

Moreover, in any perfect mixture composed of four elements or 3 liquids, each individual element of the mixture contains all the others. The same goes for the one being, and even more so, since the one at once unifies and being is being unified. The condition of the one is in accordance with that of being is such a way that the former is by no means truly separated from the latter. So nowhere can the one be found alone [142D9–E2],[184] just as on a line, continuity is always in accordance with the point, so that whenever one divides the line a continuity and a point simultaneously occur. Continuity represents being, the point corresponds to the one. Accordingly, being, which is one, can be imagined, like a line, as an infinite multitude, even if this multitude is not infinite in act or in effect. Why do I say this? To show that the nature of every intelligible and divine substance is such that if it possesses within

liesve mille quantumlibet differentes in ea suae quaedam partes
sint, seu vires sive rationes aut formae, in unaquaque quodammodo sint et omnes. Atque ita nec ipsi naturae neque contemplatori[50] alicui repugnare innumerabiliter in se invicem ista repetere. Mira siquidem in divinis unio cum mirabili fecunditate
concurrit et in contemplatoris mente progressio libera. Memento
vero unum hoc intellegibile, etsi dicitur essentiae particeps esse,
tamen praestantius et quodammodo superius quam essentia. Similiter etsi unum ens appellatur totum, esse tamen indivisibile.
Item quamvis dicatur habere partes eas interim non discretas,
siquidem sit in qualibet parte totum.

4   Finge momentum, alioquin forte stabile, iam produci vel procedere in motum, item unitatem in duitatem, rursus punctum in
lineam, denique unum in essentiam. Cogita tempus processione
momenti in motum nasci, numerum productione vel processione
unitatis in duitatem, continuum productione puncti in lineam, ens
processione unius in essentiam. Atque sicut in tempore, in numero, in continuo ubique pariter sua illa sunt elementa, sic in ente
ubique unum et essentiam aeque regnare, in ente, inquam, in qualibet scilicet intellectuali divinaque substantia. Inter has quidem
aliae superiores sunt, inferiores aliae. In illis atque istis alia deinceps atque alia munera praevalere memento, sed unum cum essentia in cunctis pariter temperari. Item in ipso intellectu primo et
quovis ferme simili genera cuncta et ideas[51] omnes inesse. Quae
quidem etsi cuncta quodammodo sunt in singulis, alia tamen in
aliis aut aliis praecipue vigent ut identitas, status, alteritas, motus

itself a thousand or a thousand times thousand (as many as one wishes) different parts, whether powers, rational principles or forms, all of them would in some way be in each of them, and that it is contrary to neither nature nor any Contemplator to repeat them infinitely within themselves. It is a wonder that within divine realities union is in accordance with a wonderful fecundity and that within the Contemplator's mind progression is limitless.[185] Let us bear in mind, however, that even if the intelligible one is said to partake of essence [142C4–5], it is better and in some way superior to essence. Likewise, even if the one being is called "whole" [143A], it is nevertheless indivisible. Similarly, even if it is said to have parts [142D], these parts are not separate, since the one being exists as a whole in every part.

Let us imagine that a moment in time, which might be other- 4
wise motionless, was already produced, or was already proceeding, in movement, and let us imagine the same about unity proceeding in the dyad, the point in the line, and finally the one in essence. Let us consider that time is born through the procession of a moment in movement; number, through the production or procession of unity in the dyad; the continuum by the production of a point in the line, and being through the procession of the one in essence. And just as in the case of time, number and continuum the elements that are proper to them are equally present in all their parts, so in being the one and being equally rule in the whole being— and by "in being" I mean in any intellectual and divine essence. Among these essences some are superior, others are inferior. Let us remember that in both the former and the latter some powers prevail, then others, but the one coordinate with essence is present in all of them equally in a tempered way. Similarly, all the genera and all the Ideas are present in the first intellect and in virtually every intellect that is similar to it. Even if all these genera and Ideas are in some way present in every intellect, some thrive more in some than in others, like sameness, rest, otherness, motion, and

atque similia. Unum vero et essentia in quolibet genere, in quavis idea aeque conflantur. Interea memineris Parmenidem saepe sub nomine entis essentiam intellegere. Quae quidem essentia ferme nihil aliud est quam unius productio vel processio quaedam, qua ens interim coalescit. Iam vero entis quasi elementa sunt essentiale unum pariter et essentia una. Quibus sane duobus invicem conflatis divinitus totalis quaedam, ut ita dixerim, forma consurgit, quam et sub ratione concreta ens et sub ratione abstracta entitatem possumus appellare, ut entitas ratio formalis entis intellegatur.

: LXXXII :

In uno ente per binarium et ternarium omnes
numeri continentur. Qui numeri distributionem
entis unius in entia multa praecedunt.

1   Sicut ratio puncti alia est et prior quam continui ratio, sic unius ratio alia priorque est quam essentiae ratio. Itaque et rationem unius seorsum ab essentiae ratione revera contemplari licet et rationem essentiae seorsum ab unius ratione saltem fingere. Quapropter alterum quidem est unum, alterum autem est essentia. In ordine vero entium quicquid alterum est ab aliquo, per alteritatem cogitur esse alterum, sicut calidum per calorem.

2   At cum ratio alteritatis non sit eadem prorsus atque ratio essentiae vel unius, necessarium est in ipso ente non solum duo, scilicet

so on. By contrast, the one and essence together are equally present in every genus and every Idea. Let us remember, too, that Parmenides often understands by the word "being" the notion of essence, which is assuredly nothing else than a production or a procession of the one, from which being emerges by coalescence. Moreover, the one which is essence and the essence which is one constitute, so to speak, elements of being. Surely, it is from the combination of these two elements that what I would call the total form emerges from its divine source, which we can concretely call being and abstractly entity, so that entity may be understood as the formal rational principle of being.[186]

: LXXXII :

All numbers are contained in the one being by virtue of the numbers two and three. These numbers precede the distribution of the one being within the multiple beings.

Just as the rational principle of the point is different from, and   1
superior to, the rational principle of the continuum, so the rational principle of the one is different from, and superior to, the rational principle of essence. Accordingly, we may truly contemplate the rational principle of the one separately from that of essence, and at least imagine the rational principle of essence separately from that of the one. Therefore, the one is not the same as essence. Yet in the order of beings whatever is "other" than something is necessarily "other" by virtue of otherness, just as what is hot is hot by virtue of heat [143B].

However, given that the rational principle of otherness is not at   2
all the same as that of essence or that of the one, there necessarily exist within the one being not only two elements, that is, one and

unum atque essentiam, sed etiam tria, id est alteritatem iam existere. Consurgit et alia ratione ternarius, scilicet ex coniugio essentiae uniusque, coniugio essentiae alteritatisque, coniugio unius
alteritatisque simul. In quolibet vero coniugio cogitamus duo quaedam non quomodolibet existentia, sed sub tertia quadam forma
invicem coniugata. Unde et ambo nominare solemus. Quamobrem
in ente sunt numeri binarius atque ternarius. In binario parium
primo pares omnes. In ternario imparium primo impares similiter
omnes. Sunt omnes differentiae numerorum par, impar, pariter
par, impariter impar, impariter par, pariter impar. Par quidem binarius, impar vero ternarius, pariter par quaternarius. Binarius
enim bis multiplicatus creat illum, sed impariter impar novenarius,
ternarius enim ter multiplicatus hunc efficit. Senarius autem
quando conficitur ex ternario bis multiplicato, tunc impar pariter
nominatur, quando rursus ex binario ter aucto par impariter
nuncupatur.

3   Sed quorsum haec? Nempe ut intellegas per numeros eorumque[52] differentias in primo ente praecipue dominantes disponi in
ordine universi essentiales entium numeros, multitudines specierum, virtutum quoque in specie quavis varietatem, ne forte suspiceris formales entium differentias quibus universus et unus rerum
ordo conficitur vel ex informi materia vel casu quodam inordinato
vel dispersa agentium diversitate contingere. Esse vero numerum
ante entia cum Plotino probavimus atque supra. Et nunc ita breviter comprobamus: in primo ente est ratio unius ratioque essentiae.
Ante hanc essentiam est hoc unum. Binarius ergo simul cum principio essentiae compleri videtur. Ex hac essentiae ratione cum rati-

essence, but also a third one, that is, otherness. On the other hand, there also arises the number three, simultaneously from the union of essence and the one, from that of essence and otherness, and from that of the one and otherness. Yet in each of these unions we consider that the two elements do not exist in some random manner, but are united to one another under a third form. Hence we usually also call them "both" [143D1–2]. So the numbers two and three are within being. In the first binary group of a set of even numbers, all numbers are even; likewise in the first ternary group of a set of odd numbers, all numbers are odd. All the differences of numbers are: even, odd, even multiples of even sets, odd multiples of odd sets, odd multiples of even sets and even multiples of odd sets [143D]. Two is even, three is odd, four is an even multiple of an even set, for two multiplied by two is four; nine is an odd multiple of an odd set because three multiplied by three equals nine. Six is called an even multiple of an odd set when it results from three being multiplied by two, and an odd multiple of an even set when it results from two being multiplied by three.

But what is the point here? Surely to help you understand that ³ it is by virtue of the numbers and their differentiae, which are particularly prevalent in the first being, that the essential numbers of beings, the multitudes of species, and the variety of powers within each species are disposed within the order of the universe; and to prevent you from thinking that the formal differences between beings that compose the universal and unique order of things derive from formless matter, or occur in an inordinate way by chance or through a dispersed diversity of agents. Number precedes the multiplicity of beings, as we have demonstrated with Plotinus and above.[187] Let us presently briefly confirm this as follows: in the first being there are the rational principle of the one and the rational principle of essence. The one precedes essence. The number two seems, therefore, filled with both the principle [i.e. the one] and essence. Therefore, being, or entity, as the form

one unius constat ens vel entitas quasi forma totius. Quae quidem forma post binarium una cum ternario suscipit complementum, deinceps hoc unum ens derivatur iam intus in entia per binarii ternariique virtutem. In quibus sane duobus numeris omnes ante entia numeri concluduntur. Per numeros enim eiusmodi tamquam antecedentes entia velut sequentia discernuntur atque numerantur.

Quomodo in mundo intellegibili dividatur essentia
simul et unum multitudoque finita vel infinita sit.

1 De primo intellectu intellegibilique mundo passim praecipue loquitur, ubi cum primo unoque et universo ente primus et unus universusque numerus oritur. Per hunc essentialem numerum ens unum propagatur intus in entia multa, id est genera et ideas. Ibi et numerus est essentiae particeps[53] et vicissim essentia compos numeri. Quoniam vero indefinita quaedam potentia multiplicabilisque natura et quasi ulterius progressura conditio tum enti tum numero inest, utrumque propterea infinitum quodammodo, id est indefinitum, dici potest. Sed interim quoniam particeps est unius atque termini, censetur utrumque finitum. Finitum praeterea, quoniam certus est numerus idearum absolute inter se formaliterque differentium. Hinc et finitae sunt species divinorum atque naturalium. Infinitum rursus, quoniam intellectus ille divinus

of the whole, is composed of both the rational principle of essence and that of the one. After the number two this form receives the number three as a complement, and then the one being is distributed from within in the beings through the power of the numbers two and three. Surely all the numbers that precede beings are contained in these two numbers. For it is through these numbers, which precede beings, that beings, which come after these numbers, are distinguished and counted.

: LXXXIII :

How essence and the one are together distributed in the intelligible world, and how multitude is limited or infinite.

The second hypothesis is principally about the first intellect and the intelligible world, where the first, unique and universal number comes forth together with the first, unique and universal being. Through this essential number the one being propagates itself from within into the multitude of beings, that is, the genera and the Ideas. There number partakes of essence, and in turn essence possesses number. But since both being and number possess an indefinite potentiality, a nature that tends to multiply itself and a condition that tends to proceed further, both can in some way be said to be infinite, that is indefinite [144A]. Conversely, since they partake of the one and of the limit, they are both considered limited [144E]. They are also limited because there is a certain number of Ideas that differ absolutely and formally from one another. Hence the species of divine and natural things are also limited. Conversely, they are infinite, because the divine intellect eventually

1

unamquamque specialem in se ideam ad singula tandem innumerabilia refert variis illam modis, temporibus, locis participatura.
Sed quoniam multitudo illic actu quidem finita est, quamvis potentia et effectibus infinita, prudenter Parmenides et semel et bis,
postquam dixerat infinita illic esse, mox quasi se corrigens nosque
admonens, subdit illic esse quam plurima.

2   Denique ubi dicit essentiam per numerum in plurima divisam
esse, intellege non sectam in multas ibi substantias, sed unam ibi
communem essentiam in plures ibidem essentiales formas, vires,
modos, propagatam mirabiliter atque derivatam.

3   Qua interim ratione sic, ut diximus, multiplicatur essentia, eadem multiplicatur et unum cum essentia coniugatum. Unaquaeque
igitur idea, sicut unaquaedam essentia vel ratio essentialis existit,
sic est et aliquid certumque unum. Inter haec ubi dicitur unum
non totum quidem inesse singulis, sed divisum, cave suspiceris in
substantia illa penitus individua unum, quod et naturaliter est individuum et instar puncti vel imaginis specularis, cum videtur dividi, geminatur — cave, inquam, suspiceris unum in partes continui
more secari, sed intellege multas ipsi vel universo uni virtutes
inesse. Quae non cunctae quidem simul in qualibet concludantur
idea, sed per ideas passim distribuantur. Denique quemadmodum
illic multiplicatur essentia, ita multiplicatur et unum.

relates each Idea, which is in itself proper to the species, to individual things, which are infinite and are to participate in this Idea according to different modes, times and places. However, because here multitude is limited in act, but infinite in power and effects, Parmenides, after having said that "in this case it is infinite," then prudently states twice, as if to correct himself and draw our attention, that "in this case it is the most numerous possible" [144D–E].

Finally, when he states that essence is numerically divided into   2 the largest number of parts [144B], one should not understand that it has been subdivided into many substances, but that essence, which yonder is one and common to all beings, propagates itself in a wondrous way and is distributed, at the same place, into a large number of essential forms, powers and modes.

However, as we said, the one that is united with essence multi-   3 plies itself in the same way as essence does. Therefore, just as every essence or essential rational principle is one, so every Idea is a certain fixed one. But when Parmenides states that the one is not present within each thing as a whole, but divided [144D], let us not consider that within this substance, which is completely undivided, the one, which also remains undivided by nature, and which, like a point or a mirror reflection, when it seems divided, doubles up—let us not consider, I say, that the one is subdivided into parts in the same way as the continuum, but rather that several powers reside within the one itself or the universal one. These powers are not all simultaneously contained in each Idea, but are distributed through different Ideas. Finally, the one thus multiplies itself in the same way as essence does.

: LXXXIV :

Quomodo in mundo intellegibili partium multitudo
sub gemina totius forma concluditur. Quomodo
terminos mediumque habet atque figuras.

1 Cum ens primum, tamquam ipsi simpliciter uni proximum, maxime unum sit, qualiscumque et quantacumque multitudo sit in eo, ad unam redigitur totius formam. Forma quidem totalis in rebus, quae a diversis causis componuntur solumque aliunde dependent, partes eiusdem rei multas sequi solet. Sed in ente primo, quod ab unico generatur et quodammodo etiam ex se existit, forma totalis est necessario gemina. Prima quidem suam partium multitudinem antecedit, secunda vero sequitur, vel potius comitatur. Illa quidem appellatur superessentialis unitas bonitasque, mundi illius intellegibilis apex, secunda vero pulchritudo, id est contextus quidam et ordo ac series idearum. Sed dum pulchritudinem hic divinam memoro commemorare fas est Franciscum Diacetum dilectissimum complatonicum nostrum de hac ipsa pulchritudine quotidie multa pulcherrimaque scribentem. Quem sane virum ad Platonicam sapientiam natura geniusque formavisse videntur.[54] Ut autem redeamus ad institutum, pulchritudo haec idealis ab illa quam modo diximus unitate, velut a luce, per ideas quasi per radios multos resultat ut splendor. Illa quidem summus est intellegibilis mundi terminus, haec autem terminus eiusdem ultimus. Media vero sunt essentiale unum et essentia una, item finitum et infinitum, rursus substantia, vita, intellectus, praeterea quinque rerum genera, subinde speciales ideae, denique multiformes specierum modi. Cuncta igitur huiusmodi multitudo, etiamsi

: LXXXIV :

How, in the intelligible world, the multitude of parts
is contained in the double form of the whole.
How it possesses limits, a middle, and shapes.

Since the first being, which is the closest to the absolute One, is   1
one to the highest degree, any multitude, whatever its quality and
quantity are, is reduced within the first being to the unique form
of the whole. In things that are composed of different causes and
only depend on another cause, the total form is usually subsequent
to the multiplicity of their parts. By contrast, within the first being, which is generated by a unique principle, but also somehow
exists in itself, the total form is necessarily double. The first precedes the multitude of its parts; the second follows, or rather accompanies, them. The first is called supra-essential Unity and
Goodness and is the summit of the intelligible world; the second
is called beauty, that is, the arrangement, order and series of
Ideas.[188] But as I recall here the existence of this divine beauty, I
must mention Francesco da Diacceto, the most beloved of our
Platonic colleagues, who everyday writes numerous and admirable
things on beauty. Indeed, nature and genius seem to have formed
this man to the apprehension of Plato's wisdom.[189] To return to
our subject, ideal beauty, proceeding from the Unity that we have
just mentioned, as if proceeding from light, through the Ideas as if
through many rays, shines out as the splendor of light.[190] Unity is
the highest limit of the intelligible world, beauty is its ultimate
limit. In between lie the essential one and the unique essence, as
well as limit and infinite, then substance, life, intellect, as well as
the five genera of things, followed by the Ideas proper to species,
and finally the multiform modes of species. This whole multitude,
therefore, even if it can in some way be imagined as infinite, be-

quomodolibet infinita fingatur, evadit interim et finita quatenus intra geminam totius formam hinc et inde concluditur.

2   Inter haec memento cum in natura quavis terminos cogitamus, alterum quidem primum, alterum vero ultimum, eos interim tamquam oppositos ac dissimiles cogitare. Cum vero ultimus tandem proficiscatur a primo primusque ille naturaliter agens debeat ante dissimilia sibi similia procreare, merito inter haec extrema medium collocare debemus. Natura profecto in rebus vel infimis unionis prae caeteris avida vacuum nusquam patitur. Multo minus in ipso rerum superiorum ordine vacuum tolerabit. At vero nisi inter singula evidenter invicem dissimilia inseratur similius aliquid quod mirifica similitudine referat unitatem nescio quid vacui inter gradus universi continget. Quapropter in mundo divino quantalibet multitudo sit, est tamen intus principium atque finis. Si duo haec ibi sunt, igitur est et medium.

3   Paulatim vero deinceps, quemadmodum coepit, de hoc uno ente affirmat quae de ipso simpliciter uno in prima suppositione negaverat. Itaque post partes ac totum multitudinemque et terminos atque medium, consequenter affirmat figuram—rectam et circularem atque mediam[55] caeteraque similiter. Primo quidem in mundo intellegibili sunt figurae, rationes videlicet figurarum, metaphorice vero figura triplex. Recta quidem per quendam aliorum ab aliis ibi processum. Sic ab essentia fecunda procedit vita, ab hac intellegentia. Inter essentiam intellegentiamque vita medium est aeque distans. Pariter enim est hinc quidem essentiae, inde rursus intellegentiae vita conformis. Similiterque de caeteris ibi processibus cogitare licet. Circularem vero figuram agit intellectus ille pri-

comes limited, given that it is contained at both extremities within the double form of the whole.

However, when we consider the limits of any nature (one limit 2 being its first [level], the other its last), we must bear in mind that these limits are opposite and different. But since the last limit ultimately proceeds from the first one, and since the first one, which is an agent by nature, must create the things that are like itself before creating those that are unlike it, we must rightly place a mean between these two extremes. Surely even within the lowest of realities, nature, which longs for union above all things, nowhere allows of emptiness, and will tolerate emptiness within the superior realities even less. But unless someone inserts, among these individual things, which are clearly unlike one another, something more like them, and which represents unity by virtue of an admirable likeness, there will be a sort of emptiness between the levels of the universe.[191] For this reason, in the divine realm any multitude of any quantity whatsoever is in itself both a beginning and an end. If it contains these two elements, it also contains a middle [145A].

Parmenides then progressively asserts of the one being, as he 3 started, all the attributes that he had denied of the absolute One in the first hypothesis. So after having asserted the attributes "parts," "whole," "multitude," "limits," and "middle," he consequently asserts "shape" — "straight," "round," "mixed," and so on [145B]. Literally this means that there are shapes, that is, rational principles of shapes in the intelligible world; metaphorically, it means that there are three shapes: in the intelligible world the straight shape represents the procession of things; for instance, life, which is fecund, proceeds from essence, and intelligence proceeds from life. Life is the mean that is equidistant from essence and intelligence. On each side life conforms equally to essence and intelligence. One may consider that the same goes for all the other processions in the intelligible world. By contrast, the first intellect

mus, dum ad patrem ex quo genitus est convertitur; mediam forte figuram, dum seipsum animadvertit. Illa quidem sui ipsius animadversio, partim quidem ex ipsa sui natura dependet atque ita[56] circulum imitatur, partim quoque pendet ex patre. Itaque ubi ad patrem nondum revertitur adhuc circulum non consummat, sed in se reflexa sinuosum quendam agit motum medium inter rectum atque circularem.

: LXXXV :

Quomodo unum ens in seipso sit et in alio.

1 Unum ens est tum cunctae simul partes suae, tum etiam ipsum totum, id est, ut ita dixerim, forma totalis. Cum igitur cunctae partes sint in toto, sequitur ut unum ens in seipso consistat.

2 Sed alia insuper ratione sequetur ut etiam sit in alio. Nempe neque pars aliqua, neque partes quaedam capiunt ipsum totum, neque partes omnes singulatim sumptae, quod est manifestum, neque simul cunctae, quod breviter est probandum. Mitto in praesentia naturale quodvis totum ex diversis vel contrariis constitutum, cuius ipsa forma totalis ab efficiente idealique causa, potius quam ab elementis suis necessario pendet. Certe forma prima entis illius primi totalis partium quarumlibet viriumque suarum varietatem antecedit, ut radix ramos atque surculos, ut lux radios et splendorem. Pendet autem non ex istis quidem, sed ex ipso dumtaxat simpliciter uno excellenti, videlicet illinc prae partibus suis virtute donata. Quam sane virtutem nec partes quidem cunctae

executes a circular shape when it turns itself toward the father that has generated it, and perhaps a mixed shape, when it becomes conscious of itself. This self-consciousness partly depends on its own very nature, and in that case it imitates the circle, and partly also on the father. For this reason when it does not yet turn back toward the father, it does not yet consummate the complete circle, but as it is turned back on itself, it somehow executes a sort of sinuous movement, which is the mean between the straight and the round.[192]

: LXXXV :

How the one being is in itself and in another than itself.

The one being is both all the parts taken simultaneously and the whole itself, that is, as I have already said, the total form. Therefore, since all the parts are contained in the whole, the one being is consequently in itself [145B–C].   1

On the other hand, it follows that the one being is also in another. Surely a single part, some parts, or all the parts taken individually cannot contain the whole itself, which is obvious, nor all the parts taken simultaneously, which requires a brief demonstration. I leave aside for the moment any whole in nature, which is constituted of different or contrary elements, the total form of which necessarily depends on the efficient and ideal cause rather than on its own elements. Surely the first total form of the first being precedes the variety of its various parts and powers, just as the root precedes the branches and twigs, and light precedes rays and shining. Yet the total form does not depend on these parts and powers, but solely on the simple and excellent One.[193] In other words, it receives from the One its power before receiving its   2

comprehendunt, inde videlicet praecedentes. Quid ergo dicemus? Numquid totalem hanc formam excellentemque virtutem in nullo penitus esse, ut non comprehendatur vel finiatur ab ullo? Certe non ita partibus suis cunctis inest neque rursus id ipsum quod est ex se existit. Cum enim totum hoc varietate sit plenum, a simplicissimo cogitur proficisci, praesertim quia quaelibet in hoc idea finitum quiddam est a caeterisque distinctum. Unde cogitur universum quasi innumerabiliter fore finitum. Qua igitur ratione hoc est totum atque multiforme, necessario consistit in alio, id est in principio procreante[57] simul atque continente.

3   Quamobrem si in uno ente partes suas omnes forte consideres, dum eas in toto videbis, iudicabis ipsum in seipso manere, si modo ipsum totum sit partes cunctae, neque sit aliud ultra partes. Forte enim non est aliud secundum numerum vel materiam, quamvis sit aliud secundum formam atque virtutem atque hac ratione non iam a suis partibus vel sic a seipso, sed ab auctore potius continetur. Quomodo mundus hic intellegibilis in se simul et in alio sit in suppositione prima capite LIII iam est tractatum.

: LXXXVI :

Quomodo unum ens stet semper atque moveatur.

1   In omni composito est unitas atque multitudo. Itaque quamdiu vincit unitas multitudinem ideoque devincit eam, tamdiu permanet compositum insolutum. Quapropter ubi semper vincit atque ita devincit, semper permanet insolubile. Eiusmodi compositum

parts. Surely all the parts do not contain this power; they do not, therefore, precede it [145B–E]. But could we really say that this total form and excellent power reside in absolutely nothing, so that they are contained in, or limited by, nothing? It is true that the total form does not reside in all its parts, and again this total form is not the very principle that exists by itself. For since this whole is filled with variety, it necessarily proceeds from the simplest principle, especially since therein any Idea is something limited and distinct from the rest of the Ideas. Hence the universe is necessarily infinitely limited. Thus for the very reason that it is both whole and multiform, it is necessarily in another, that is, in the principle that simultaneously creates and contains it.

So if one happens to consider all the parts within the one being 3 as if seeing them as a whole, one will consider that the one being is in itself, since the whole is the sum of its parts and is nothing more than its parts. For the one being could not be another according to number or matter, although it is other according to form and power — and for this reason it is no longer contained by its parts or by itself, but rather by its creator. The way in which the intelligible world is both in itself and in another has already been described in Chapter LIII of our commentary on the first hypothesis.

: LXXXVI :

How the one being is always at rest and in movement.

Every composite contains unity and multitude. As such, as long as 1 unity prevails and thus overcomes multitude, the composite remains indissoluble. On this account, where it always prevails and thus overcomes, it always remains indissoluble. The intelligible

est in primis intellegibilis[58] ille mundus, a cuius monade formaque totali sua omnis intro profluit multitudo ideoque inhaeret eidem et ab eadem semper continetur, non solum ut subiecto quodam, sed ut causa. Similis est praeterea compositio in qualibet intellectuali natura. In hac enim omnis[59] multitudo virium formarumque suarum ab ipsa sua monade profluit atque continetur. Sed de his alibi, redeamus ad primum.

2   Intellegibilis[60] ille mundus quodammodo est cunctae suae partes, id est vires atque formae. Dum igitur universa multitudo haec est in forma totali, mundus ille dicitur in seipso esse. Est autem multitudo haec semper in illa velut causa conservante. Est igitur ita mundus ille semper in semetipso. Quapropter in suo quodam eodem semper manet, stat itaque semper.

3   At vero si aliter contempleris nec ultra compares multitudinem illam ad suum illud quod dixi totum, sed totum potius, id est monadem formamque totalem, ad supernum universi principium, videbis mundum eiusmodi non in seipso esse, id est contineri, sed in causa superiore potius esse, tamquam efficiente prorsus et conservante. Hic ergo videbis non tam illum quiescere quam moveri. Quieverint quidem illae partes in suo toto tamquam causa, totum vero non quiescat in semetipso, sed circa superiorem causam moveatur.

4   At quomodo? Nempe qua ratione non tam respicit intus quam vergit ad causam hinc illuc pertransitre videtur, siquidem descendit vicissim atque ascendit. Descendit quidem quatenus inde procedit, ascendit autem quatenus illuc naturali quodam instinctu convertitur. Procedit autem convertiturque semper. Semper ergo movetur.

5   Procedit quidem quatenus inde producitur. Producitur autem non semel tantum, sed etiam quatenus conservatur, id est procul-

world is very much a composite of this sort: its whole multitude flows forth from within, from the monad of the intelligible world and its total form; it is therefore attached to the monad and total form and always contained by them, and they are not only its subject, but also its cause. The same composition can also be found in every intellectual nature, where every multitude constituted of its powers and its forms flows forth from its own monad and is contained by it. But we speak of these realities elsewhere. Let us go back to our initial question.

The intelligible world in some way is the totality of its parts, 2 that is, of its powers and forms. So as long as its universal multitude is in the total form, the intelligible world is said to be in itself. Yet this multitude is always in the total form as in a preserving cause. Thus the intelligible world is always in itself. So it always remains in the same place, which is itself, and accordingly it is always at rest [145E–46A].

On the other hand, if you no longer compare the multitude 3 with what I called its own whole, but rather the whole, that is the monad and the total form, with the superior principle of the universe, you will see that the intelligible world is not — is not contained — in itself, but rather in a superior cause, which creates and preserves it. In this case, you will see that it is not at rest, but in motion [146A]. Let us admit that the parts are at rest within their whole, which is their cause, but that the whole is not at rest in itself, but moves around a superior cause.

But how is that so? Surely it is not so much because it looks 4 within itself, as because it tends toward its cause, that it seems to go from one place to another, since it goes down and up. It goes down inasmuch as it proceeds from its cause, and it goes up inasmuch as it turns toward its cause by a natural instinct. Yet it always proceeds and turns. Thus it is always in motion.

It proceeds from its cause inasmuch as it is produced by it; it is 5 produced not only once, but also to the extent that it is being pre-

dubio semper. Ita vero prius auctor ille suus hunc ex se producit quam hic in seipso sit aliquid, alioquin non secundum totam sui essentiam existeret inde. Videtur ergo quodammodo in essentiam ex nihilo processisse ac nisi producatur procedatque inde, perpetuo statim in nihilum relapsurus. Itaque, ne quando desinat esse, numquam desinet ita moveri.

∶ LXXXVII ∶

Unum ens est sibimet idem atque alterum.
Item caeteris idem atque alterum.

1 Totum necessario refertur ad partem similiterque pars ad totum. Neque sine parte totum est revera totum, neque pars seorsum a toto ulterius existit. Itaque si invicem comparetur utrumque, neque idem neque alterum revera dici potest. Non idem, quia totum maius est parte sua; non alterum quiddam, quia neque totum neque pars seorsum per se subsistit. Subsistere vero seorsum posse putamus, quaecumque inter se altera nominare solemus. Quicquid vero in ordine entium comparatur ad aliquid cuius ipsum neque pars neque totum sit, dici potest aut idem illi esse, aut alterum diversumque ab illo. Quid ergo de uno ente dicemus: quod quidem nec pars sui ipsius est nec totum? Dicemus profecto communiter aut idem sibi esse aut alterum. Dicemus etiam cum Parmenide idem alterumque existere. Idem proculdubio secum ipso

served, which doubtless is always the case. In this way, its creator produces the intelligible world from within itself, before the intelligible world *is* something *in itself*, otherwise it would not receive its existence according to the whole essence of itself. In a certain way, therefore, it seems to have proceeded into essence from nothing. In addition, if it were not produced by its creator and did not proceed from it, it would instantly and eternally fall into nothingness. Therefore, in order to never cease to be, the intelligible world will never cease to be in motion.

: LXXXVII :

The one being is the same as, and different from, itself.
Similarly, it is the same as, and different from, the others.

The whole is necessarily related to the part, just as the part is related to the whole. Without the part the whole is not really a whole, and a part that is separate from the whole is no longer a part. For this reason, if whole and part are compared, they can be said in truth to be neither the same nor different [146A–47B]. They are not the same, because the whole is greater than its part. But they are not different, because neither the whole nor the part can subsist separately by itself. Yet whatever things we usually name as differing among themselves we think can subsist separately too. However, anything in the order of beings that is compared with something of which it is neither a part nor a whole, can be said to be the same as this thing, or different and separate from it. What will we say, then, about the one being? That it is neither a part nor a whole of itself? Surely we will ordinarily say that it is either the same as, or different from, itself. We will even say, together with Parmenides, that it is the same as, and different from,

1

esse. Cum enim unum ens non sit aliud quam ens unum semperque in eodem habitu perseveret, merito sibimet idem est atque
semper idem. Sed alia interim ratione esse alterum a seipso fatebi-
mur. Est enim in seipso, sicut diximus, et in alio. Praeterea stat, ut
probavimus, atque movetur. Eiusmodi vero rationes inter se sunt
oppositae, esse videlicet in se, esse in alio, item stare atque moveri.
Itaque si unum ens rationibus refertum oppositis conferatur ad
semetipsum, nimirum sub hac ratione et illa alterum videbitur atque alterum.

2   Hactenus unum ens comparavimus ad seipsum. Si forte cum
caeteris entibus conferamus, primo quidem occurret ut alterum,
siquidem unum primumque ens et omne valde diversum est a
quolibet ente, quod neque primum est neque adeo vere unum nec
ens universum. Occurret subinde forsan ratione quadam mirabili
quodammodo cum aliis entibus idem, si modo probemus omnimodam alteritatem nec usquam esse nec umquam. Profecto cum
omnia ab ipso simpliciter uno infinita virtute praedito fiant serven-
turque et contineantur atque convertantur, merito regnante in rebus unitate regnat identitas. Omnimoda igitur alteritas nec regnare usquam neque quomodolibet esse potest, cum ubique cogatur
cum quadam identitate misceri. Quamobrem cum nec in ente
primo nec in aliquo pura sit alteritas, merito primum ens a caeteris
penitus alterum prorsusque diversum iudicari non potest. Igitur
quodammodo idem, si non ipsa natura, saltem similitudinis habi-
tudinisque cuiusdam communione, sed haec inter exemplar et
imagines habitudo et qualiscumque communio usque ad generati-

itself [146B]. There is no doubt that it is the same as itself: since the one being is not other than the one being and always remains in the same disposition, it is rightly always the same as itself. On the other hand, we will admit that it is different from itself. For, as we have said, it is both in itself and in another. Moreover, as we have demonstrated, it is at rest and in motion. Yet these rational principles — being in oneself and being in another, as well as being at rest and in motion, are opposed to one other. Therefore, if the one being, which is filled with these opposite rational principles, is related to itself, it will certainly appear at one point under one rational principle, and at another under another rational principle.

So far we have compared the one being with itself. But if we compare it with the other beings, the one being will first appear to be different from them [146D], since the unique, first and whole being is completely different from any particular being, which is neither the first principle, nor, therefore, the truly One, nor the universal being. But then again it might (and surprisingly so) appear to be in some way the same as the other beings [146D–47C] — if we show that otherness nowhere and never exists totally. Surely, since all things are created and preserved by, are contained within, and turn toward, the absolute One, which possesses an infinite power, then it is fair to say that both unity and sameness prevail in all things. So otherness cannot totally prevail anywhere, nor exist in anyway whatsoever, since it is necessarily everywhere mixed with sameness.[194] For this reason, since there is no unmixed otherness in the first being nor in any other being, it is certainly impossible to consider that the first being is completely different and separate from the rest of beings. Thus in some way it is the same as the others, if not by its very nature, at least by virtue of sharing a common aspect and relation. Yet this relation, this sort of association, between the model and its images, goes down as far as the process of generation and the things that are subject to generation,

ones generabiliaque descendit, de quibus in praesentia non tracta-mus. Comparatur enim hic essentia prima non ad generationes, sed ad essentias, scilicet intellectus primus atque divinissimus ad intellectus omnes ubique divinos. Qui tantam ferme cum primo identitatem unionemque putantur habere, quantam cum centro lineae vel stellarum lumina cum lumine solis.

3   Si finxeris omnimodam alteritatem usquam esse, cogeris eam fingere per aliquod tempus esse. Motus enim ac tempus mirificum habent cum alteritate praesertim praevalente coniugium, quemad-modum cum identitate status et aevum. Quapropter dum per ali-quod[61] divisibile tempus illa durabit alteritas, certe per omnes temporis huius partes in eodem erit, scilicet in eodem tenore atque vigore suo, in eodem motu vel tempore vel subiecto. Mixtam igitur secum aliquam habebit identitatem nec omnimoda iam erit alteri-tas, ut fingebas.

4   Saepe Parmenides, ut acrius ingenium adolescentis exerceat, per ambigua et obscura procedit, et frequenter ex dissimilibus locis necnon ex oppositis argumenta deducit. Sic igitur admonitus ad sequentia perge. Quemadmodum primum unum a nullo usquam uno participabile est, ita ens primum a nullo ente, primus intellec-tus ab intellectu nullo, siquidem in quolibet ordine supereminens imparticipabilisque natura participabilem antecedit. Participabilis autem omnia participantia perficit. Quamobrem si unum primum-que ens ad entia conferas, haec illud non participant quidem, sed potius imitantur. Si igitur illud ipsum vel naturale aliquid eius in se non habent, neque etiam primum illum essentialem numerum illi proprium in se possident, sed forte consimilem. Alioquin si

which we do not treat of for the moment. For here the first essence is not compared with the process of generation, but with the essences. In other words, the first and utterly divine intellect is compared with all the other divine intellects. These are considered to have an identity and a unity with the first intellect in nearly the same way as the lines are related to their center and the lights of the stars to the light of the sun.[195]

If we imagined that otherness totally exists somewhere, we would be compelled to imagine that it exists for a certain length of time. For motion and time possess a wondrous link with otherness, especially when otherness prevails, just as rest and eternity are linked to sameness. So as long as otherness lasts for some divisible length of time, it will surely remain in the same place during all the parts of that time, that is to say, it will maintain the same tenor and strength, in the same motion or time or subject. It will possess, therefore, some sameness mixed with itself, and will cease to be this total otherness we imagined [146E]. 3

Parmenides often proceeds through ambiguous and obscure arguments in order to exercise more acutely the young man's mind, and occasionally deduces arguments from different or even opposite propositions. Let us remember this and proceed to the next question. Just as the first One can never be participated in by any other one, so the first being cannot be participated in by any being, nor the first intellect by any intellect, since in each order the super-eminent and imparticipable nature precedes the participable nature, and the participable nature perfects all the things that partake of it. Therefore, if one compares the unique and first being with the other beings, one will see that they do not partake of being, but rather imitate it. If they do not possess within themselves the unique and first being, or anything that naturally pertains to it, they do not possess within themselves the first essential number either, which properly pertains to the first being, but they perhaps possess something that is similar to it. Otherwise, if they pos- 4

numerum ipsum haberent, unum pariter ens ipsum in se comprehenderent. Multo minus conferri invicem illud ad haec vel vicissim ut pars vel totum posse videtur. In superioribus vero probatum est non esse haec invicem prorsus altera. Cum igitur neque ut totum vel pars invicem referantur neque sint penitus altera, sequitur ut sint quodammodo eadem, quemadmodum paulo ante diximus.

: LXXVIII :

Unum ens et ad seipsum et ad alia simile est atque dissimile.

1   In *Philebo* probatur in omnibus post primum esse unum simul atque multitudinem. Igitur in omnibus est idem et alterum, convenientia atque differentia, igitur similitudo simul et dissimilitudo quaedam. Quapropter quodlibet idem mixtum est cum altero atque contra, omne simile cum dissimili quodam atque vicissim, praesertim quoniam ipsius unius[62] regnum omnia quodammodo commiscet in unum. Iam vero eiusmodi mixturae tanta vis est ut utrumque vicissim utrimque sequatur. Sed hac sane distinctione per alteritatem ipsam suapte natura praecipue sequitur ut omnia inter se sint altera proptereaque dissimilia. Contingit insuper communi quadam rerum lege per alteritatem identitas quaedam atque similitudo. Similiter per identitatem propria ratione fit ut omnia

sessed this number, they would also contain the one being in themselves. We can even less compare, it seems, the one being with the other beings as part or as whole. However, we have demonstrated above that the other beings are not completely different from one another. Thus, since they are mutually related to one another neither as whole nor part, nor yet are they completely different from each other, it follows that they are in a certain sense the same as one another, as we have just mentioned above [147A–B].

∴ LXXXVIII ∴

The one being is like and unlike itself and the others.

In the *Philebus* Plato demonstrates that both the one and the many are in all the realities subsequent to the first principle, and so these things all contain the same and the other, similarities and differences, and thus likeness and unlikeness. For this reason, any "same" thing is mixed up with some "other" thing and conversely, and the like is mixed up with the unlike and conversely, especially since the kingship of the One somehow mixes all things up into a unity.[196] Furthermore, the force of this mixture is so powerful that both opposites are in both sides. Surely by virtue of this distinction, which principally occurs through the very nature of otherness, it follows that all things are other and unlike one another. Sameness and likeness, moreover, occur in them through otherness, in accordance with the common law of nature. Similarly, it happens that all things are made the same as, and similar to, one another through sameness, in accordance with its own rational principle. It also happens, meanwhile, that through sameness they

1

invicem sint eadem atque similia. Accidit et interim conditione communi et altera per hanc dissimiliaque videri.

2   Esto igitur alterum hoc ab illo. Certe per eandem[63] similemque alteritatem et eodem ferme similique modo hoc quidem ab illo, illud rursus ab hoc est alterum. Dum igitur eandem quodammodo similemque sortem sustinent, tamquam eadem et similia reputantur. Esto rursus quodammodo idem hoc et illud. Primo quidem logicus quidam argumentabitur oppositam esse identitatem alteritati et opposita facere. Quocirca si ad alteritatis praesentiam contingit[64] similitudo quaedam, similiter identitate praesente dissimilitudinem quoque contingere. Deinde philosophus ita forte probabit: dum naturas duas invicem comparas, intellegens[65] videlicet interea esse duas atque distinctas, si propter communem quandam conditionem easdem similesque dicas, rursus alteras esse dissimilesque cognosces, si modo naturae duae quaedam propriae sint, non una, ac etiamsi proprio[66] quaeque modo identitatem similitudinemque susceperit. Sic enim propter modos eiusmodi differentes interea forsan haec dissimilia videbuntur. Quas ob res, si unum ens ad entia comparatum idem est ad haec et alterum, consequenter simile ad haec est atque dissimile. Per identitatem habebit, primo quidem similitudinem, deinde vero dissimilitudinem, sed per alteritatem in primis dissimilitudinem, sequenti gradu similitudinem. Comparatum quoque ad seipsum, tamquam idem atque alterum, similitudinem ad se dissimilitudinemque subibit.

also seem to be made different and dissimilar, sharing as they do a common condition [147C–48C].

Let us suppose, then, that one thing is other than another. 2 Surely it is through the same and similar otherness, and in almost the same and similar way, that the former is other than the latter and that the latter is in turn other than the former. It is by undergoing the same and similar condition, therefore, that they are considered to be the same as and similar to one another. Again, let us then suppose that one thing is somehow the same as another. Firstly, a logician will argue that sameness is the opposite of otherness and produces things that are opposite. So if likeness occurs in the presence of otherness, similarly unlikeness will also occur in the presence of sameness. Secondly, a philosopher will perhaps prove the following: if, when comparing two natures and realizing that these things are two and distinct, you say that they are the same as one another and similar by virtue of a common condition, you will also recognize that they are other and unlike, so long as they are two individual natures, rather than one, and even if each has received sameness and likeness according to its own proper mode. So they will perhaps seem unlike each other on account of their different modes. For this reason, if in relation to beings the one being is the same as, and different from, the others, it is consequently like and unlike them [148A–C]. By virtue of sameness it will first possess likeness, and then unlikeness, but by virtue of otherness it will first possess unlikeness, and then likeness. Compared to itself, like something both the same and different, it will also experience likeness and unlikeness with respect to itself [148D].

: LXXXIX :

*Quomodo unum ens tangit et tangitur neque tangit neque
tangitur quantum ad se et ad alia pertinet.*

1 Ab ipsa similitudine Parmenides merito venit ad tactum, nomen
hoc in loco latissimum. Quae enim invicem similia sunt libenter
et facile se contingunt, scilicet propinquant sibi, invicem commo-
vent, commoventur, compatiuntur, percipiunt, complectuntur atque fruuntur.[67] Hac utique ratione unum ens, quatenus in seipso
est atque in caeteris entibus, seipsum caeteraque contingit, sed
quoniam tangentis atque tacti est ratio differens, idcirco unum ens
et tangens se simul et tactum a seipso dici potest, quatenus differentes in se rationes admittit. Cum enim non sit primum universi
principium, quodammodo multiplex esse potest. Si vero tangens
et tactum differre inter se considerentur, tamquam essentiae vel
naturae duae, nimirum prima illa unicaque essentia simplex tangere se quasi sit per substantiam differens nullo modo potest.

2 Sed numquid alia quoquomodo tangit? Si consideremus alia,
tamquam in ordine entium enti primo quoquomodo conformia,
proculdubio tangit ea tangiturque ab eis tactu quodam, quemadmodum supra significavimus, metaphorico. Sin autem hinc quidem ipsam unius entis rationem contemplemur in seipsa secretam,
inde vero rationem multitudinis in seipsa inde seiunctam, turbam
fingemus omnino confusam, infinitatem, potentiam multiplicabilem et aliunde formabilem. Quae quidem neque per se sit formale unum necdum participationem formalis unius habeat neque

216

: LXXXIX :

How the one being has, and has not,
contact with itself and with the others.

Parmenides rightly passes from likeness to the attribute "in con- 1
tact," which is here taken in its widest sense. For things that are
alike are readily and easily in contact with one another, that is,
they are close to one another, and together they move and are
moved, undergo, perceive, embrace and enjoy. For this reason the
one being, inasmuch as it is in itself and in all the other beings,
has contact with itself and with the others [148D–E]. But because
there is a difference between the rational principle of that which
touches and the rational principle of that which is touched, the
one being can also be said both to touch itself and to be touched
by itself, inasmuch as it admits within itself different rational principles. For since it is not the first principle of the universe it can in
some way be said to be multiple. But if "touching" and "touched"
are considered as two distinct essences or natures, then the first,
unique and simple essence can in no way have contact with itself
as if it differed [from itself] in substance [148E–49A].

Is the one being really somehow in contact with the others? If 2
we consider that the others are somehow in accordance with the
first being in the order of beings, then, as indicated above, we can
certainly say, by way of a metaphor, that the first being touches the
others and is touched by them. By contrast, if we contemplate, on
the one hand, the rational principle of the one being, hidden in
itself, and, on the other, the rational principle of multitude in itself, apart from the one being, we will then imagine a completely
confused mass, an infinity, a power which undergoes multiplication and formation through another cause. This mass is not formally one in itself; it no longer partakes of the formal one, and

numerum certis unitatibus definitum. Itaque ad unum ens, formam primam formaliter omnia terminantem, nondum attinent, neque tanguntur ab illo neque tangunt.

3   Si punctum ad lineam compares, similiter perquirere poteris tangatne lineam et tangatur, necne, riteque negabis et affirmabis. Negabis quidem tangere simpliciter aut tangi. Non enim proprie tangitur a linea punctum vel a puncto linea, alioquin vel punctum divisibile foret vel linea penitus individua. Sed recte forsitan affirmabis et punctum hoc abs te confictum tangere punctum lineae et vicissim a puncto lineae tangi. Similiter unum ens multitudinem entium neque tangit neque tangitur rursus ab illa, quatenus hoc quidem est iam unum, haec autem simpliciter turba nondum formale unum, sed figmento quodam infinities infinita. Tangit autem tangiturque vicissim, quatenus haec unum aliquid formale iam evasit. Unum enim non aliter tangit vel tangitur quam per unum.

4   Parmenides hic repetit quodammodo, quod ex parte supra dixerat, multitudinem quae non est unum, non participare unum, sed hic adiungit 'quatenus videlicet multitudo est et ab uno penitus aliena.' Quod autem narrat de tangentium tactuumve numero consideranti cuique planum est. Quis enim non viderit, si duo digiti se tangunt, numerum quidem digitorum esse binarium, medium vero tactum esse unum? Si unum digitum adiunxeris tres quidem fore digitos, tactus vero duos. Si digitum addideris alium, quattuor iam digitos esse, tres vero tactus similiterque deinceps.

does not possess any number that is limited by fixed unities. From this point of view, the others no longer reach the one being, which is the first form that limits all beings in terms of form; they are not touched by it and do not touch it.

When comparing the point with the line one can also wonder 3 whether or not the point touches, and is touched by, the line. This question you can answer fittingly in either a negative or a positive sense. You will deny that it simply touches and is touched, for the point is not properly speaking touched by the line, nor the line by the point, otherwise either the point would be divisible, or the line would be utterly indivisible. But you will perhaps be right to assert that this imagined point touches, and is in turn touched by, another point on the line. The same goes for the one being. It does not touch, nor is touched by, the multitude of beings, inasmuch as it is already one, while this multitude is simply a mass and not yet formally one, but is, to use a fictive expression, infinitely infinite. From another point of view, the one being touches, and is touched by, the multitude, inasmuch as this multitude has already become a formal one. For the one touches solely, and is solely touched by, what is one.

Here Parmenides more or less repeats what he has partially said 4 above, that the multitude, which is not one, does not partake of the one, but here he adds "inasmuch as it is multitude and utterly alien to the one" [149C]. As to what he says about the number of touching and touched elements [149A–B], it is very clear to anyone who thinks about it. For who would not see that if two fingers are in contact, the number of fingers is two, but the contact between them is one? If one adds a finger, one will have three fingers, but two points of contact; if one adds one more finger, there will be four fingers, but three points of contact, and so on.

: XC :

Quomodo unum ens sit aequale vel
inaequale sibi vel aliis.

1   Si elementorum moles liquorumque naturae secerni possunt invicem et unaquaeque pura in natura propria reperiri, multo magis
formales ipsae rationes rerum suapte natura simpliciores atque sublimiores inter se discerni possunt, ut et ipsae sincerae maneant in
seipsis et quilibet intellectus verax unamquamque in sua proprietate seorsum ab aliis valeat contemplari, quia videlicet intellectus
ille primus discretas intueatur ab aevo et in ipso intellegibili ratio
alia prorsus aliud sit quam alia.

2   Iam vero si rerum formas in mutua rerum communione contuea-
mur, certe cum Anaxagora omnia quodammodo in omnibus
contuebimur. Si rursum eas per intellegentiam exactissimam in
formalibus suis eminentibusque rationibus, tamquam iam abstrac-
tissimas, inspexerimus, iterum cum Anaxagora intellectum ipsum
esse discretorem omnium confitebimur. Qui autem discretionibus[68] eiusmodi uti nescit non est Platonicus nec umquam utitur
intellectu. Quamobrem Parmenides ad hoc ipsum exercitaturus
ingenui adolescentis ingenium passim per angustissima quaeque
cogit eum vel concedere falsa vel eiusmodi abstractionibus uti, in
quibus, ut ille quoque quem nosti fatetur, non est mendacium.
Praeterea, quemadmodum significavimus ab initio, totam disputationem agit ut logicam exercitationem quandam, sub hac vero

: XC :

*How the one being is equal and unequal
to itself and to the others.*

If the masses of elements and the natures of liquids can be taken   1
separately from one another, and each of them can be found unmixed and in its own nature, then it is even more the case that the
formal rational principles of things can be distinguished from one
another, since they are naturally simpler and more sublime. As a
result, they too remain unmixed in themselves, and any true intellect can contemplate each of them in its own property, separately
from the rest, because the first intellect eternally contemplates
them separately and within the intelligible realm rational principles
are completely different from one another.

However, if we contemplate the forms of things when forms   2
and things are united with one another, surely we will contemplate, as Anaxagoras put it, "all things in everything."[197] But if we
use our acutest intelligence and consider them in their formal and
eminent rational principles, which have reached the highest degree
of abstraction, we shall admit, together with Anaxagoras again,
that the intellect is that which distinguishes all things.[198] The person who does not know how to use these distinctions is not a
Platonist and never makes use of his intellect. It is to train the
noble young man in this method, therefore, that Parmenides leads
him through a series of obstacles and forces him to either admit
what is false, or use these abstractions, wherein, as stated by the
one whom you know, "There is no lie."[199] In addition, as we indicated at the beginning, Parmenides presents the whole discussion
as a logical exercise, but under this dialectical form he often

dialectica forma mystica quoque dogmata frequenter admiscet, non ubique prorsus continuata, sed alicubi sparsa, quatenus admittit exercitatio logica. Ubique vero affectat ardua paradoxaque tentat ita maxime ingenium probaturus.

3   Sed iam pergamus ad reliqua. Alia quidem ratio est ipsius unius, alia aliorum, alia magnitudinis, alia parvitatis, alia aequalitatis. Itaque nec unum nec aliquid aliud praeter unum per ipsam rationem suam maius est vel minus vel aequale. Sed per magnitudinem ipsam naturae suae additam fit maius, per parvitatem vero minus, per aequalitatem evadit aequale. Sed idealis magnitudo vel parvitas vel aequalitas non potest ulla conditione corporea rebus adesse, alioquin multa hic enarrata sequerentur absurda. Si enim parvitas ita subiecto cuidam adsit, certe vel toti prorsus aderit vel parti. Si toti, vel intrinsecus vel extrinsecus. Si igitur intrinsecus, profecto huic aequalis erit; si extrinsecus, erit maior. Id autem est absurdum. Sic enim parvitas auctoritatem sibi aequalitatis et magnitudinis usurparet. Rursus si in parte subiecti ponatur, aut aequalis erit aut maior, atque eadem errata contingent. Continget etiam ut res nulla futura sit maior aut minor, nisi idealis magnitudo vel parvitas auctoritate quadam incorporea possit adesse. Corporea certe conditione non potest. Itaque nullis inerit.

4   Forsan vero nonnulla dici aequalia poterunt dumtaxat propter eiusmodi quandam inaequalitatis absentiam. Animadvertendum est praeterea si hinc quidem rationes magnitudinis vel parvitatis vel aequalitatis proponantur, inde vero rationes caeterorum consi-

adds mystical dogmas, not in every single sentence, but in different passages, as much as is permitted by the logical exercise. But everywhere he feigns difficulties and attempts to lay out paradoxes, in order to test the mind most efficiently.

But let us pass on to what remains. The rational principle of the one differs from that of the others and from that of greatness, smallness and equality. So neither the one nor anything besides the one, is greater, smaller, or equal, by virtue of its own rational principle, but is greater by virtue of greatness, which is added to its own nature; smaller by virtue of smallness, and equal by virtue of equality [149E]. Yet ideal greatness, smallness, and equality cannot be present in things by virtue of any corporeal condition, otherwise many of our conclusions would become absurd. For if smallness was present in a subject in a corporeal way, it would assuredly be present to either the whole of the subject or a part of it. If it is present to the whole of it, it will be either present to it externally or internally. Thus if it is present internally, it will be equal to the whole; if it is present externally, it will be greater than it, which is absurd, for in that case smallness would take up the role of equality and greatness. If, on the other hand, it is located in a part of the subject, it will be either equal to it, or greater than it, and the same errors will follow [150A–B]. It also follows that nothing will be greater or smaller, unless ideal greatness and smallness can be present in a thing according to an incorporeal power. Surely they cannot be so according to a corporeal condition. For this reason they are present in nothing.

However, some things might be said to be equal, solely on account of an absence of inequality [150D]. In addition, one should note that if one postulates, on the one hand, the rational principles of greatness, smallness, and equality, and one considers, on the other, the rational principles of all the other things, then the for-

derentur, nec illas his naturaliter inesse, neque vicissim. Quapropter haec in sinceris rationibus[69] suis considerata dici posse nondum magna vel parva vel aequalia esse, sed postquam ideales illorum rationes ad haec accesserint. Haec nos clam Parmenides admonet, partim quidem artificio quodam logico ingenium adolescentis erudiens, partim vero latentia quaedam passim dogmata serens.

5   Quomodo vero unum ens in seipso sit alibi diximus. Hac igitur ratione seipso maius ac minus dici potest, qua videlicet in eo est comprehendens aliquid et comprehensum. Est quinetiam in alio, id est in causa sua, tamquam effectus eius. Est insuper in aliis, ut causa in effectibus. Sunt et alia in illo, sicut effectus in causa. Haec igitur qua ratione sunt in illo, sunt eo minora virtutis videlicet gradu. Illud quoque qua forte est in istis est quodammodo minus istis, minus inquam compositionis acervo. Haec enim accumulantur ex pluribus atque diversis et quod illius his inest praecipuum in primis est simplex.

6   Attende vero quidnam sibi velit illud 'quicquid est est alicubi vel in aliquo:' hoc quidem non de illo quod ente superius, sed de omni ente dictum puta. Omne vero ens in aliquo est et quodlibet ens per communionem quandam est in quolibet, quandoquidem ens primum est in aliquo et in cunctis. Nam et penes ipsum aliud est in alio. Item ipsum est in causa. Rursus est in entibus ut in imaginibus suis exemplar.

mer are not naturally present in the latter, nor the latter in the former. For this reason, things that are considered in their pure rational principles cannot yet be said to be great, small or equal, but only once the ideal rational principles of greatness, smallness and equality have reached them. Such are the mysteries that Parmenides secretly alludes to, partly by forming the young man's mind to the art of logic, and partly by inserting hidden truths throughout the text.

We have described elsewhere how the one being is in itself. 5
Therefore, since it is in itself both something enveloping and something enveloped, it can be said to be greater and smaller than itself [150E–51A]. In addition, it is in another, that is, in its cause, as the effect of its cause. It is also in the others, as a cause in its effects. The others are also in the one being, as the effects in their cause. Thus, given that the others are in the one being, they are lesser than it [151A–B], that is, lesser in degree of power. The one being too, as it happens to be in the others, is somehow lesser than them, I mean lesser in the compositional mass. For the others are formed by an accumulation of multiple and diverse elements, and the portion of one being peculiar to itself that resides in them is utterly simple.

When Parmenides says that "all that which is, is somewhere or 6
in something" [151A4–5], we should bear in mind that this does not apply to what is superior to being, but to all of being. All being is in something, and each being is in each being by virtue of a sort of sharing, since the first being is in each and all beings. For within it, everything is in everything else. Similarly, the first being is in its cause. Again it is in beings, as the model is in its images.

∶ XCI ∶

Quomodo unum ens sit numero par et plus et minus ad
seipsum atque caetera.

1   A dimensione pergit ad numerum. Nam et saepe divisione continui numerus editur et continua per numeros plerumque metimur.
Quamobrem quod per dimensionem cuipiam est aequale, parem
quoque partium habet numerum. Quod vero maius, plurem, quod
autem minus, pauciorem. Unum igitur ens, quatenus totum sibi
toti est aequale, universa videlicet virtute sua, par quoque sibi est
virtutum numero variarum. Si quae praeterea sunt illic praestan-
tiores ideae, illae profecto, tamquam auctoritate maiores, numero
quoque plures et ad facienda plura virtutes habent. Minores autem
ideae pauciores et ad pauciora vires habent. Itaque unum ens et
par et plus et minus dicitur ad seipsum.

2   Similiter et ad universum. Intellegibilis enim ille mundus universo huic operi suo quodammodo videtur aequalis, quatenus
unum hoc opus cum uno artifice congruit. Apparet quoque par
numero, si Timaeo credimus dicenti quot ideas architectus inspicit
intellectus, totidem in mundo formas effingit, quot rursus archety-
pus ille mundus viventia in se intellegibilia continet,[70] totidem hic
sensibilia complectitur animalia. Praeterea quatenus ille mundus
hoc est mundo potestate maior, eatenus et plus virtutum numero
iudicatur. Denique quemadmodum ille hoc mundo acervo et accu-
mulatione minor est, sic et numero quodammodo[71] superatur ab

: XCI :

How the one being is equal, superior, and inferior
in number in relation to itself and to the others.

From dimension Parmenides passes to number, for number is of- 1
ten produced by the division of the continuum, and we generally
measure continua with numbers. So, what is equal to something
in dimension also possesses an equal number of parts, while what
is greater, possesses a greater number of parts, and what is smaller,
a smaller number of parts. The one being, therefore, inasmuch as
it is a whole that is equal to the whole that it forms itself, that is,
in its universal power, is also equal to itself, that is, in the number
of its various powers. In addition, if there exist superior Ideas in
the intelligible world, since they are surely greater in their ascen-
dency, they possess powers that are greater in number and capable
of producing a greater number of things. Conversely, the inferior
Ideas possess powers that are fewer in number and capable of producing a smaller number of things. So the one being is said to be
equal, greater and less than itself [151B–D].

The same goes for the universe: the intelligible world appears to 2
be in some way equal to the universe, which is its creation, inasmuch as the unity of the creation is in accordance with the unity
of the creator. It also appears to be equal in number, if one is to
believe Timaeus when he says that the intellect architect shapes as
many forms in the world as he contemplates Ideas, and again, that
the archetypical world embraces as many sensible animate things
down here as it contains within itself intelligible living beings.[200]
In addition, the intelligible world is considered superior in regard
to the number of its powers inasmuch as it is greater in power
than the sensible world. Finally, just as the intelligible world is
smaller in mass and cumulative size than the sensible world, so it

isto. Numerus enim accidentium quorumlibet mundanorum et quolibet momento innumerabiliter contingentium excedit numerum idearum idealiumque virtutum.

: XCII :

Quomodo unum ens dicatur senius et iunius
atque coaetaneum ad seipsum atque caetera.

1 Parmenides a numero non iniuria descendit in tempus. Ubi enim primus numerus oritur, ibi motus nascitur atque tempus, siquidem in ente primo simul cum certo formarum viriumque et actuum numero motus quidam emicat per quem aliud prodit ex alio. Emicat simul et tempus, per quod aliud alio origine quadam prius est atque posterius. Iam vero motus et tempus necessario est in ipso ente primo et in quolibet ente, siquidem essentia est quasi quidam processus ab uno. Ubi sane unum in essentiam quasi signum in lineam produci videtur, essentia rursus velut linea in superficiem prodit in esse, item esse in vitam velut superficies in profundum, vita pergit in mentem ceu profundum absolvitur in formam atque figuram. Mens denique sui quadam animadversione reflectitur, sicut figura primi profundi prima consummatur volviturque in orbem. Sed ut summatim revertamur ad institutum, necessarius quoque motus[72] est in ente necessariumque tempus, si modo illic tamquam elementa quaedam sunt infinitudo, motus, alteritas, si qua rursus est ibi motus ipsius temporisque idea.

2 Semper vero memento motum tempusque in intellectu intelligibilique sub forma quadam aeternitatis implicitum prorsus et

is also somehow numerically surpassed by it. For the number of accidents in the world and that of contingents, which occur in any numbers at any time, are greater than the number of Ideas and of ideal powers.

: XCII :

How the one being is said to be older, younger, and equal in age, in relation to itself and the others.

From number Parmenides rightly descends to time [151E–52E]. 1
For motion and time rise at the same place as the first number, since there springs up within the first being, at the same time as a certain number of forms, powers and acts, a kind of motion whereby one thing proceeds from another, and at the same time there also springs up time, whereby things are younger and older in origin than others. In addition, motion and time are necessarily in every being, including the first being, since essence is a sort of procession from the one. Surely where the one appears to proceed in essence like a mark on a line, essence in turn proceeds into being like a line on a surface. Likewise, being proceeds into life like surface proceeds into a solid, and life proceeds into mind in the same way as solids are resolved into form and shape. Finally, intelligence turns toward itself through its awareness of itself, just as the first shape of the first solid is achieved and moved around to form a circle.[201] In sum, to return to our subject, both motion and time necessarily exist in being, provided that infinity, motion, and otherness exist in being like elements of being, and provided that there is an Idea of motion and time yonder.

One should always remember that motion and time, which in 2
the intellect and the intelligible are enveloped, enfolded and shel-

involutum atque subitum, mox in animam emicare ibique per cur-
ricula quaedam iam explicari latius et evolvi. Motumque eiusmodi
in anima quidem actionem esse, in corpore vero iam evadere passionem. Memento rursus, quemadmodum admonuimus ab initio,
Parmenidem hic ultra naturam intellectualem, animalem iam assumere animamque divinam.

3 Ubi vero definit esse quasi quandam participationem essentiae
una cum praesenti tempore, primo quidem adverte confirmari,
quod dici plerumque solet, ipsum esse actum essentiae, ferme sicut
lucere lucis et calere[73] caloris est actus. Deinde praesens id tempus
esse latissimum, ut non solum sit in corpore, sed etiam in anima et
intellectu vel summo. Similiter quod hic dicitur 'erat' et 'erit,' praeteritum atque futurum, sed in unoquoque pro natura dignitateque
sua. De motu quidem temporeque huiusmodi multa in prima suppositione tractavimus. Quapropter hic breviter percurremus.

4 Probaturi sumus unum ens, praesertim ubi consideratur in
anima vel divina, quantum ad seipsum spectat et alia, quodammodo nominari posse senius et iunius atque, ut ita dixerim,
coaetaneum. Sed quomodo id dicatur ad seipsum? Qualiscumque
fluxus vel processus sit in eo vel penes intellectum vel penes animam divinam, est certe perpetuus. Dum igitur ipsam in longum
productionem consideramus, gradatim senius appellamus. Senius
inquam fieri, quantum spectat ad procedendum, senius quoque
iam esse, quantum pertinet ad praesens aliquid 'nunc' acceptum.
Cum vero perpetuo id contingat semper fieri esseque, senius iudicatur, sed, cum senius, necessario referatur ad iunius, interim iudicatur et iunius. Quia vero, dum ipsum totum summatim compara-

tered beneath a certain form of eternity, subsequently spring forth in the soul, and there they unfurl and unroll very widely in circular motions. This motion is an action in the soul, but in the body it becomes a passion. One should also remember, as we have said at the beginning, that here Parmenides goes beyond the intellectual nature and is already taking up the animal and divine soul.

When Parmenides defines being as "a participation in essence in conjunction with time present" [151E7-8], one should first note that this confirms what is usually said in the following form: the act of being itself is the act of essence, in almost the same way as being luminous is assuredly the act of light, and being hot is that of heat; secondly, that this present time unfolds in the most extended way, so that it is not only present in the body, but also in the soul and the intellect, even the highest intellect. The same goes for what is here called "was" and "will be" [151E9-10], the past and the future, but in every being according to its own nature and dignity. We have abundantly treated of motion and time in the first hypothesis; therefore, we will briefly approach the question here. 3

Our purpose is to demonstrate that the one being, especially when it is considered to be in the soul, even the divine soul, can somehow be called older, younger and even equal in age, so to speak, in relation to itself and to the others. But how could this be said in relation to the one being itself? Surely any flux or procession in the one being, whether within the intellect or the divine soul, is perpetual. When considering this procession in its duration, therefore, we call the one being progressively older: I mean that it becomes older in relation to the processing time, and it is already older in relation to something present that is conceived of as "now." Since it eternally pertains to the one being to always become and be, it is considered older, but since, inasmuch as it is older, it is necessarily related to something younger, it is also from time to time considered to be younger. From another point of view, since, when the whole is wholly compared with the whole 4

tur ad seipsum totum, neque maiorem neque minorem seipso tandem habet aetatem, merito sibimet aetate iudicatur aequale.

5   Post haec dum comparat unum ad multa, declarat multipliciter hoc unum ens quo de agitur non esse ipsum simpliciter unum, quia confirmat quod etiam supra dixerat, partes multitudinemque habere et fieri atque esse factum, igitur et a quodam superiore pendere. Comparat autem hic ipsum ad multitudinem entium, non tam externorum quam intimorum, quod quidem planius patefacit ubi partes eius in comparatione commemorat, partes inquam, scilicet vires eius et formas et actus.

6   Recordare quod etiam supra diximus in mente vel anima divina unitatem, ut ita loquar, totalem esse geminam. Quarum prima quidem internam multitudinem antecedit, secunda vero sequitur. Illa igitur multis antiquior, haec autem multis iunior iudicatur. Sic igitur unum ad multa ut antiquius existimatur et iunius. Sed dum ad multitudinem idearum intimam comparatur, videtur quodammodo ad externas etiam conferri formas, tamquam imagines idearum. Unum quidem ibi multitudinem antecedens, iam latius explicatam quam in genere quodam numeri, simul cum hac multitudine collocatur paucissimumque in gradu sui primo numerum habet intimum. Merito iudicatur antiquius, praesertim quoniam explicatae multitudinis est origo. Unum vero ibidem resultans ex multitudine, id est splendor idearum universusque decor, non iniuria iunius multitudine nominatur, praesertim quoniam, post singulorum genituram, ipsum denique completur ex cunctis. Sed interim instar puncti quod et primum et ultimum est ad partes lineae comparatum, et tamen est in qualibet parte lineae, nimirum illud unum intellegibile non solum hinc quidem[74] primum est, inde vero ultimum idearum, sed etiam ideam quamlibet prorsus occupat. Quodlibet enim multorum necessario unum aliquid est et unius primi virtute refertum et ad ultimum unum conspirare vide-

formed by itself, it is ultimately not superior or inferior in age to itself, it is rightly considered to have the same age as itself.

Secondly, when comparing the one with the others, Parmenides 5 states in several ways that the one in question is not the absolute One, because he confirms what he had also said above: the one being possesses parts and multitude, becomes and is created, and thus depends on a higher principle. But here he does not so much compare it with the multitude of beings that are exterior to it, as with those inside it, something he makes very clear by recalling that the parts are parts of the one [153C]; in other words, the parts that constitute the powers, forms and acts of the one.

Let us bear in mind, as we have also mentioned above, that 6 within the divine mind or soul the total unity, so to speak, is double. The first precedes internal multitude, the second follows it. The first is considered older than the many, the other, younger than the many. In this way, therefore, the one is considered older and younger than the others. But while it is compared with the internal multitude of Ideas, it also appears to be compared with external forms, which are the images of the Ideas. In that case, the one, while preceding multitude (which is already unfolded more widely than in any genus of number), accompanies this multitude and possesses, at its first level, the smallest and innermost number. It is therefore considered older, especially since it is the origin of the unfolding of multitude. But the one, which at the same place springs forth from multitude as the splendor of Ideas and universal beauty, is rightly called younger than the multitude, especially since, after having generated all the individual things, it is eventually filled with all of them. However, just as the point, which is both first and last in relation to the parts of the line, is nevertheless in each part of the line, so the intelligible one is not only the first and the last of the Ideas, but it is also fully present in each Idea. For every element among the many is necessarily a certain one, is filled with the power of the first one, and appears to act in

tur. Dum igitur unum multitudinem ibi sibi prorsus adaequat, multitudini coaetaneum esse censetur.

7   Comparare quoque licet intellectualem illum animalemve mundum, praecipue in se unum, ad universam mundi sensibilis multitudinem. Sic unum illud hac multitudine est antiquius, tamquam huius opifex et exemplar. Est et iunius, quoniam cum hic perpetuo fluat quotidieque iam fluxerit, aeternus interim ille mundus, huic quasi superstes, ferme succedit ut iunior. Similiter dum in se consistit mundum quotidie quasi renasciturum antecedere putatur ut senior. Sed quoniam quatenus agit ille, eatenus hic inde pendet, aequalem agere videntur[75] aetatem.

: XCIII :

Quomodo distinguatur[76] senius iuniusve fieri rursumque
senius iuniusve esse. Ac de uno ente conclusio.

1   Inter haec animadverte quemadmodum Parmenides inter[77] dogmata quaedam saepe divulsa cautum reddat adolescentem ad respondendum et sagacem ad distinguendum. Dum igitur de seniore iunioreque mystice disputat, distinctionem eiusmodi logicam ab adolescente desiderare videtur: agat hodie Socrates annos aetatis decem, impleat hodie Plato annos quinque, quaeratur quanto senior Socrates sit Platone. Respondebit arithmetra quinario, per numeros enim respondere solet. Respondebit geometra duplo, nam proportiones considerat in mensuris. Uterque vera loquitur. Proce-

harmony with the last one. Therefore, since yonder the one makes multitude equal to itself, it is considered to have the same age as multitude.

We may also compare the intellectual or the psychic world, 7 which are individually one in themselves, with the universal multitude of the sensible world. In this way, the one is older than the multitude, as its artisan and model. It is also younger, because, as the sensible world perpetually flows and each day has already flowed, the intelligible world, which is eternal, succeeds the multitude, so to speak, almost as if it survived it, as younger. Similarly, while it remains within itself, it is considered to precede, and to be older than, the sensible world, which must be reborn each day. But because the sensible world depends on the activity of the intelligible world, inasmuch as the intelligible world creates the sensible world, they appear to have the same age.

: XCIII :

How to distinguish between becoming older and younger and being older and younger. Conclusion on the one being.

Let us notice the way in which Parmenides presents teachings that 1 are often violently dissociated from each other, thereby encouraging his young pupil to be prudent with answers and expert in distinctions. Thus while discussing in a mystical way the attributes "older" and "younger," he wishes, it seems, the young man to establish the following logical distinction: let us suppose that today Socrates is ten years old and that Plato is five. Let us ask how much older Socrates is than Plato. An arithmetician will answer: by five years, for he is used to answer in numbers; a geometrician will answer: twice as much, since he considers the relations be-

dant aetate deinceps quinquennio saltem, donec Socrates quidem quindecim agat annos, Plato vero decem. Quaeratur iterum quanto aetatis spatio differant. Respondebit arithmetra sicut prius quinario, atque ita Socratem semel quidem seniorem Platone fuisse, hunc vero iuniorem illo, sed deinceps numquam alterum altero seniorem evasisse vel iuniorem, siquidem quamdiu vivunt pari quodam inter se numero differant. Respondebit interea geometra forsitan una cum musico, Socratem iamdiu Platonis annos superavisse duplo, proportio namque inter decem et quinque dupla, hodie vero non tanto spatio superare, sed minore. Nempe inter quindecim ac decem proportio sequi altera. Ergo quindecim minore sui parte decem superat quam decem excedat quinque. Superat enim decem quinque dimidia sui parte, quindecim vero excedit decem tertia parte sui similiterque deinceps minor apparebit in dies excessus Socratis ad Platonem adeo ut qui quondam longo intervallo senior erat, minore gradatim intervallo senior videatur. Itaque comparatus ad alterum, quodammodo iuvenescere, alter vero ad hunc quasi senescere dici possit. Denique concludetur etsi fieri quidem iunior seniorve videtur, numquam tamen alterum altero seniorem vel iuniorem quam semel existerit esse.

2   Inter haec ubi hoc ipsum de quo tractat manifeste nominat unum ens, caetera vero entia, confirmatur quod diximus hic non de ipso simpliciter uno, sed de uno ente tractari.

3   Summatim vero concluditur unum ens, sive in intellectu intellegibilique sive in anima quadam divina consideratum, motum tempusque aliquod temporisque differentias quasdam in se habere, unde quodammodo fieri dici possit, id est in se latius propagari,

tween measures. Both answers are correct. If Socrates and Plato then grow older by at least five years, until Socrates is fifteen years old, and Plato is ten, and one asks again how many years separate them, the arithmetician will answer as before: five years. In this case, we say that initially Socrates was older than Plato and Plato younger than Socrates, but they subsequently ceased to become older or younger than each other, since, as long as they remain alive, they remain separated by the same number of years. By contrast, the geometrician will perhaps reply, together with the musician, that while Socrates in times past was twice Plato's age, since ten is the double of five, today Socrates exceeds Plato's age by a lesser proportion: for surely the ratio between fifteen and ten is different. Thus the number fifteen exceeds the number ten by a portion of itself that is smaller than that by which ten exceeds five: ten exceeds five by half of itself; fifteen exceeds ten by a third of itself; similarly, Socrates' superiority in age in relation to Plato will progressively appear smaller, so that Socrates, who was at a certain time older by a great length of time, seems older by a progressively smaller length of time. For this reason, one can say that Socrates becomes younger in relation to Plato, and that Plato becomes older in relation to Socrates. Finally, we shall conclude that even if one seems to become younger or older than the other, one is never older or younger in relation to the other by a greater number of years than by that which he was so initially.

In addition, the fact that Parmenides clearly calls the one of the 2 second hypothesis "one being," and the others "beings," confirms what we said: the second hypothesis is not about the absolute One, but about the one being.

In sum, the one being, whether in the intellect and the intelli- 3 gible or in a divine soul, possesses within itself motion, time and temporal differences. As a result, it can somehow be said to become, that is, to propagate itself very widely within itself, and to

atque aliter et aliter conformari vel agere, tametsi eiusmodi transmutatio manifestius explicatur in anima.

4   Cum igitur ens eiusmodi nonnullum habeat cum quolibet intellectu coniugium, merito cognosci nominarique potest perque suas
imagines sensu saltem sagaciore[78] sentiri.

: XCIV :

Summa vel epilogus suppositionis secundae.
De distinctionibus divinorum.

1   Ad tertiam suppositionem mihi iam properanti succurrit operae
pretium fore prius summam secundae suppositionis quandam iterum ab initio facere, seu mavis[79] epilogum. Trinitatem, quam
saepe diximus principiorum ordinibus nullis connumerabilem esse,
Platonici putant ipsum bonum, ipsum intellectum, mundi animam. Bonum quidem saepe patrem nominant, intellectum vero
filium, animam mundi spiritum—'spiritus intus alit.' Si trinitatis
huius eandem volunt esse substantiam, quasi Christiani sunt Ca-
tholici; si tres substantias, ferme sunt Arriani.

2   Ipsum intellectum primum mundum vocant intellegibilem, atque inter illum mundumque sensibilem multos deorum, id est sublimium intellectuum, ordines communiter esse putant. Ego vero
esse multos arbitror, quemadmodum in *Theologia* probavi. Si forte
quomodo distinguantur apud Syrianum atque Proclum te taedet
legere, quod et me certe narrare piget, saltem in praesentia ita pingui Minerva distingue. Dii supermundani, seu mavis angeli, iidem

conform and act in different ways, even if such a transmutation unfolds in a more manifest way in the soul.

Therefore, since this being possesses some link with every intel- 4 lect, it can rightly be known and named, and through its images it can be perceived by sense perception, or at least by the keener senses [155D–E].

: XCIV :

Summary or epilogue of the second hypothesis.
Regarding the distinctions of divine realities.

As I hasten to comment on the third hypothesis, it occurs to me 1 that it would be worthwhile first to make a summary, or if you prefer, an epilogue of the second hypothesis, starting from the beginning. The Platonists think that the Good, the intellect and the world soul form a trinity — which, as we have often said, cannot be numbered in accord with any orders of principles. Indeed, the Platonists often call the Good the father, the intellect the son and the world soul the spirit. "The spirit nourishes within."[202] If they wish the Trinity to be of one and the same substance, they are almost Catholic Christians; if they consider that it is formed of three substances, they are almost Arians.

They call the first intellect the intelligible world, and they usu- 2 ally consider that between the intelligible and the sensible worlds there are several orders of gods, that is, of sublime intellects. I myself think that there are several orders, as I have demonstrated in the *Platonic Theology*.[203] If you find it tedious to read the way in which these orders are distinguished in Syrianus and Proclus, as it is certainly tedious for me to relate it, let us presently at least establish "with our own dull wits"[204] the following distinctions. Among

namque sunt, alii quidem propinquiores sunt intellegibili[80] mundo, alii vero sensibili mundo quam proximi, sed alii medii. Illos Syrianus et Proclus vocant intellegibiles, hos intellectuales, medios autem intellegibiles intellectualesque simul. Nos certe superiores potius et inferiores et medios communiter nominamus, sed supramundanos omnes. Mundanos quoque ternario alios quidem superiores, alios autem inferiores, alios vero medios numeramus. In ordine primo sphaerarum ampliorum animae sunt, in medio stellarum animae, in ultimo invisibilia in sphaeris numina collocantur. Reliquas autem et ultra mundanorum et mundanorum distinctiones in praesentia praetermitto, praesertim quales Syrianus et Proclus introduxerunt.

3   Parmenidem totidem ad unguem deorum ordines introducere, quot propositiones in prima secundaque suppositione ponit, hi quidem probare conantur. Sed hanc ego curiositatem, ut alibi dixi, non probo rursus, neque talem divinorum ordinum distinctionem, qualem ipsi laboriose potius quam utiliter persequuntur. Placuit vero nunc, ut modo dicebam, pingui Minerva distinguere. Placet et Parmenidem interdum ipso unius nomine aliter atque aliter uti. Item varios nonnumquam ordines tangere divinorum, quatenus quae deinceps tractat ad hunc ordinem magis pertinent quam ad illum, quamvis ad omnes interea quoquomodo pertineant.

4   Hac itaque ratione cunctae quidem suppositionis secundae propositiones de divinis disserunt intellectibus, qua videlicet ratione sunt dii. Dii vero sunt qua in essentiis suis superessentiale unum habent, ut alibi diximus. Quatenus ergo de uno ente hic agit ubique, eatenus et de superis agit, et quotiens mutari placet nominis huius, id est unius entis, significatum atque usum, totidem attingi

the hypercosmic gods, or if you prefer, the angels (they are the same), some are closer to the intelligible world, others are as close as possible to the sensible world, others are in the middle. Syrianus and Proclus call the first ones intelligible, the second, intellectual, the third, both intelligible and intellectual.[205] I would rather call all of them superior, inferior and intermediary gods, but all are hypercosmic. Among the cosmic gods, there are also three orders: the superior, the inferior, and the intermediate. In the first order, there are the souls of the greater spheres; in the middle, the souls of the stars; in the last, the invisible divinities contained within the spheres.[206] I leave aside for the moment the other distinctions among the hypercosmic and cosmic gods, especially such as they have been established by Syrianus and Proclus.[207]

These philosophers attempt to demonstrate that Parmenides 3 introduces as many orders of gods as there are propositions in the first and second hypotheses.[208] But, as I have said elsewhere, I do not approve of such inquisitiveness, and I reject this distinction, which they pursue in a manner that is more laborious than useful. However, as I just said, I have so far considered it appropriate to establish some distinctions "with our own dull wits."[209] Parmenides also considers it appropriate to use the name "one" with different meanings. Likewise, he often mentions various orders of divine beings, inasmuch as the attributes that he subsequently treats of concern one specific order rather than another — even if these attributes somehow concern all the orders.

All the propositions of the second hypothesis concern, there- 4 fore, the divine intellects, precisely because they are gods. But they are gods inasmuch as they possess the super-essential One within their essences, as we have said elsewhere.[210] So to the extent that Parmenides treats of the one being in the second hypothesis, to that extent he also treats of the superior intellects. And he considers it proper to mention the divine orders as often as he considers

placeat ordines divinorum. Sed non debes interea cum clausulis singulis deos singulos computare.

: XCV :

Summae huius vel epilogi distinctiones. De uno ente, multitudine, numero infinito ordinibusque deorum.

1 Inter ipsa suppositionis secundae principia mundum in primis attingit intellegibilem, consequenter autem et deos omnes ultra mundanos.[81] In quibus duo quidem palam praecipua ponit, unum scilicet atque ens, tertium vero clam innuit, potentiam scilicet utriusque mediam. Quae quidem est mutua quaedam unius ad ens habitudo, per quam et unum est entis et ens unius, per quam superessentialis haec unitas, quae etiam dicitur existentia, producit essentiam sibi coniunctam, per quam et haec inde producitur convertiturque ad unitatem et cum illa conectitur. Est autem potentia haec quasi motus efficax processusque unitatis in essentiam, siquidem ex ipso simpliciter uno nullo medio procedit hoc unum mox essentiam coniugem habiturum. Hoc unum per potentiam sibi naturaliter intimam progreditur in essentiam, quemadmodum essentia per intimam vitam procedit in mentem. Profecto qualis inter essentiam intellectumque vita est, talis inter unum et essentiam est potentia. Hinc itaque non solum sunt in rebus potentiae quaedam, quae sequuntur essentias, sed etiam sunt in diis, ut Platonice loquar, occultae quaedam mirificaeque potentiae, quae eorum essentias antecedunt, continuatae penitus cum unitatibus deitatibusque suis. Per has ergo dii facere posse putantur essentias, quae quidem per vires ullas posteriores essentiis fieri numquam pos-

it appropriate to modify the sense of the name "one being." But one should not derive individual gods from each little clause.

: XCV :

Distinctions in this summary or epilogue. On the one being, multitude, infinite number, and the orders of gods.

Among the principles mentioned in the second hypothesis, Par- 1
menides first reaches the intelligible world, and consequently all the hypercosmic gods,[211] where he explicitly locates two principles, the one and being, and occultly alludes to a third principle, an intermediary power, a certain relation between the one and being, whereby the one belongs to being and being to the one.[212] It is through this intermediate power that super-essential Unity, which is also called existence, produces the essence united to it, and that essence is produced by unity, turns itself toward it, and is united to it. This power is an efficient motion of some sort, and a procession of unity in essence, since the one that is about to unite itself with essence proceeds from the absolute One without intermediary. This one proceeds into essence by virtue of a power that is naturally contained within its innermost part, just as essence proceeds into mind by virtue of life, which is contained within its innermost part. Certainly that power is the mean between the one and essence, just as life is the mean between essence and intellect. As a result, there not only exist in things powers that follow essences, but in the gods too (to speak like the Platonists) there lie occult and wonderful powers, which precede their essences and are tightly united with their unities and deities. So, according to the Platonists, the gods can produce essences by virtue of these powers, which can never and by no force become posterior to the es-

sunt. Procedit autem Parmenides ordine communiora passim minus communibus anteponens. Multitudinem quidem introducit in primis partibus communiorem atque priorem. Partes enim omnes multitudo sunt. Non omnis multitudo partes, sed cognata. Mox totum constituit ex partibus, ad partes interim relativum. Hinc venit ad infinitum. Omne quidem infinitum est quodammodo totum neque contra. Post multitudinem infinitam descendit ad numerum infinitum, siquidem amplior est multitudo quam numerus, omnis numerus multitudo neque vicissim, multitudo enim partium in continuo nondum revera numerus appellatur nisi fuerit quandoque discreta. Verus namque numerus est non multitudino quaelibet, sed discreta.

2   Hinc occasionem accipiunt Syrianici ad gradus propositionum ampliores deinceps angustioresque interea similes deorum gradus introducentes, et quoniam intellegibilia ab intellectualibus ut superiora ab inferioribus discernunt alicubi per substantias, nimirum hoc ipsum quod dicitur totum multitudinemque quasi continuam intellegibili substantiae tribuunt, intellectuali vero discretam. Nos autem una cum his prima quidem, illa magis ad superiores deos, sequentia vero, haec magis ad sequentes pertinere putamus, sed quodammodo etiam ad utrosque. Nam[82] intellegibile ab intellectuali non tam substantia quam ratione discernimus. Quamobrem in quolibet intellectu divino, seu primo sive sequente, intellegibilem essentialemque naturam intellectuali eiusdem virtuti praeponimus multitudinemque partium, vel virium vel formarum, utrobique locamus. Sed quoniam eiusmodi multitudo in ipso intellegibili gradu mirabiliter est implicita aliaque penitus insunt aliis et in quolibet totum mirabili conexione comprehenditur ideoque multi-

sences.[213] Parmenides proceeds in order by placing the commonest properties before those that are less common. He first introduces the attribute "multitude," because it is more common than, and superior to, the attribute "parts." For all parts constitute a multitude, while every multitude does not constitute parts, but has a kinship with parts. Parmenides then establishes from the existence of parts that of the whole, which is however relative to its parts. Thence he mentions the infinite: every infinite is a whole of some sort, but not the reverse. After the infinite multitude he goes down to the infinite number, since multitude is more extended than number. Every number is a multitude, but not the reverse, for a multitude of parts on a continuum cannot be really called a number yet, unless it has been at some point separated. For real number is not any multitude at all, but a multitude that is separate.[214]

In this way, the disciples of Syrianus take the fact that the propositions of the *Parmenides* vary in their degree of extension as an opportunity to introduce similar degrees of gods; and because they elsewhere distinguish in substance the intelligible from the intellectual realities, considering the former superior to the latter, they indeed attribute the terms "whole" and "continuous multitude" to the intelligible substance,[215] and "separate multitude" to the intellectual substance.[216] We agree that the first propositions concern more the superior gods and the following propositions, the following gods, but they also in some way concern both orders of gods. For we do not distinguish the intelligible order from the intellectual in substance, but according to reason.[217] Thus in every divine intellect (whether the first intellect or any intellect subsequent to it) we place its intelligible and essential nature before its intellectual power, and we place on both sides the multitude of its parts, whether these are forces or forms. Given that this multitude is wondrously enveloped at the intelligible level, that some beings exist in others, and the whole of beings is within each of them by virtue of a wondrous union, and that for this reason, this multi-

tudo haec quasi continuata videtur, merito multitudinem eiusmodi Syrianicis concedimus nondum numerum appellare. Quoniam vero multitudo iam dicta in gradu intellectuali per intellegentiam cuncta discriminantem iam latius et particularius explicatur discernunturque ab aliis alia, ut aliud sine alio cerni possit, concedimus hic numerum manifestiorem originem iam habere. Hinc efficitur ut numerosa passim in universo[83] formarum distinctio referatur ad mentem, ad ipsos scilicet intellegentiae radios sincere singula discernentes, hinc et visibile lumen tamquam intellegentiae ipsius imago passim confusa distinguit. Iam vero ipsum intellegibile per modum essentiae, substantiae, naturae, lucis, motoris sese habet. In ipso igitur cuncta per modum naturae coniugata sunt. Cognata enim sunt invicem omnia naturaliter. Exacta vero discretio per intellegentiam advenit tamquam oculum radiosum, hoc iam ab illo quamvis cognatum exactissime secernentem. Quapropter Anaxagoras discretionem intellectui tribuit, eidem videlicet explicatum numerum concessurus. Sit igitur multitudo rerum et in praecedente intellegibili et in intellectu suo mox sequente, sed ibi quidem sicut in centro circuli lineae vel in centrali solis luce radii, hic autem quemadmodum in circumferentia sphaerae lineae vel in solis ambitu radii. Hinc efficitur ut actus intellegentiae cuiuslibet proprius sit quasi discretio quaedam, intellectusque plures frequenter penes intellegibile congrediantur in unum.

3   Sed quaeritur inter haec quomodo infinita ibi sit multitudo. Etsi in superioribus id iam diximus, tamen iterum declarabimus:

tude seems to be continuous, so to speak—for these reasons we rightly admit, together with the disciples of Syrianus, that a multitude of this sort is not yet designated as "number."[218] However, because at the intellectual level this multitude unfolds in a more extended and individual way by virtue of intelligence, which distinguishes all things, and because beings are distinguished from one another, so that they can be discerned as separate from one another, we admit that number has a more manifest origin at this level. As a result, on the one hand the quantitative distinction of forms in the universe is always related to mind, that is, to the rays of intelligence which distinguish individual things in their unmixed purity; on the other hand, visible light, which is the image of intelligence, always distinguishes things when they are mixed. In addition, the intelligible is disposed according to the modes of essence, substance, nature, light and mover. So at the intelligible level all things are joined according to the mode of nature, because all are akin by nature. But the precise distinction between things occurs through intelligence, which, like a radiating eye, separates with the greatest precision things from one another despite their kinship. For this reason, Anaxagoras attributes the power of distinction to the intellect, and he would concede, therefore, that number also unfolds at the intellectual level. Let the multitude of things, therefore, exist in both the intelligible, which comes first, and its intellect, which comes immediately after it, but in the former they will be like the lines within the center of a circle, or the rays within the light at the center of the sun; in the latter, they will be like the lines in the circumference of a sphere, or the rays around the sun. Consequently, the proper act of any intelligence is a sort of distinction, and within the intelligible world several intellects are often joined into one.

Another question concerns the way in which multitude is infinite in the intelligible world.[219] Even if we have already mentioned it above, we will nevertheless state it once more: at the in-

non quantitate vel numero ibi ponitur infinitum. Nam et quantitas non est ibi et numero in species iam redacto ad mensuramque pertinenti infinitudo repugnat, atque in divinis tamquam ipsi uni propinquis infinita turba quae diversissima est ab uno regnare non potest. Illic enim multitudo prorsus cohibetur ab uno. Illic ergo infinitudo significat universitatem omnia comprehendentem nec ab alia universitate comprehensam, et quae per intellegibilia usque adeo iam processit, ut nec ipsa possit ultra procedere nec ab aliquo possit ultra procedi. Iam vero multitudo illa congruit infinitati primae, sicut unio vel terminatio in multitudine termino respondet primo. Sicut igitur infinitudo prima non dicitur infinita numero, sed potentia, non solum forte multiplicabili, sed forte etiam, ut vult Syrianus, multiplicativa atque progressiva, ita multitudo intellegibilis, quae est multitudo prima, et intellectualis multitudo illius quasi coniunx dicitur infinita, tum quia multitudo, qua ratione multitudo est, necdum definita est, immo et infinitati respondet, tum etiam quia haec tamquam prima primam praecipue refert infinitatem, tum denique quoniam per potentiam entium omnium genitricem una cum alteritate explicat in se universam multitudinem unitatum entiumque intellegibilium usque ad minima intellegibilia. Qua ratione intellegibilia sunt tam particularia quam universalia, quatenus illic explicari possunt.

4   Itaque cum sit multitudo non quaedam, sed universa primaque nec ab ulla multitudine comprehendatur, sed comprehendat omnes, merito dicitur infinita, atque sicut primum unum primus est terminus, ita multitudo prima post infinitatem primum dicitur infinitum, infinitum inquam praecipue nobis, quoniam natura, virtus, amplitudo eius nedum a nostro, sed nec ab ullo intellectu

telligible level one does not postulate the existence of the infinite in quantity or number, because quantity does not exist there, and infinity rejects number, since number concerns species and pertains to measure. Moreover, there cannot be in divine things, which are proximate to the one, an infinite mass that would be totally different from the one: at this level multitude is completely enveloped by the one. So here the term "infinite" designates the universality which envelops all things, rather than a universality which is enveloped by another universality — the universality which has proceeded so far through the intelligible realities that it cannot proceed or be proceeded any further. Moreover, this multitude is in accordance with the first infinity, just as union or limitation within the multitude corresponds to the first limit. Therefore, just as the first infinity is not called infinite in number, but in power (this power is not only multiple but perhaps also, according to Syrianus, multiplicative and progressive),[220] so the intelligible multitude, which is the first multitude, and the intellectual multitude, which is united to it, are called infinite, because (1) multitude, *qua* multitude, is not yet bounded, but is rather related to infinity; (2) multitude, *qua* first, is related above all to the first infinity; and (3) finally, through its power of generating all beings, and together with otherness, it unfolds within itself the universal multitude of unities and of intelligible beings, all the way down to the lowest intelligible objects. So the intelligible beings are both individual and universal, to the extent that they can unfold in the intelligible world.

For this reason, since this multitude is not particular but universal and first, and since it is not enveloped by any multitude, but envelops them all, it can rightly be said to be infinite; just as the first One is the first limit, so the first multitude that comes after infinity is called the first infinite — I call it infinite mostly from our perspective, because its nature, power and extension cannot yet be completely apprehended by any individual intellect, not to men-

4

particulari penitus comprehendi potest. Hinc et in ultimis accidit ut totum numeri processum comprehendere nequeamus ab ipsa illius infinitate perpetuo superati. Denique rectius de infinito loquemur, si dixerimus ibi multitudinem infinitam potius quam multitudine infinitum.

5   Esse vero in divina mente efficaciam numerosam et suos illinc cuique naturae numeros destinatos declarat rerum naturalium dispositio mira perpetuaque in rebus admodum mutabilibus observatio numerorum. Quapropter et magi solares lunaresve numeros observantes eosque rebus his applicantes et illis, illinc ad has et illas saepe solares lunaresve dotes attrahunt et res invicem ita compatientes mirabili potestate conciliant. Scribit Proclus veteres sacerdotes numeris quibusdam ineffabilem vim habentibus ad praecipua sacrorum opera perficienda frequenter uti consuevisse, sed haec ille viderit. Plato certe periodos animarum atque civitatum suis expleri numeris asserit et universum mundi circuitum perfecto numero contineri, Pythagoramque[84] secutus duo ponit principia numerorum, paternum scilicet et maternum, unitatem videlicet atque duitatem, quasi terminum et infinitum. Primum vero numerum vult esse ternarium ex termino infinitoque mixtum et unitatem quidem referre ipsum simpliciter unum, duitatem vero essentiam, trinitatem quoque ens et intellegibile primum. In unitate praeterea duitateque cunctos per virtutes numeros contineri. Illinc igitur omnes numeros explicari, per duitatem quidem pares, per unitatem vero duitati praesidentem impares. Per hos itaque numeros in sequentibus omnia disponuntur, per pares quidem praecipue processus divisiones compositionesque solubiles, per im-

tion our own intellect. Hence even in the lowest degrees of reality we cannot comprehend in its totality the procession of number, because we are eternally surpassed by its infinity. Finally, we will speak more correctly of the infinite if we say that in the intelligible world the infinite is an infinite multitude rather than infinite in multitude.

There is a numerical efficacy in the divine mind and each num- 5 ber, proceeding from there, is destined to a particular nature, as manifested by the wondrous disposition of things within nature and the perpetual observation of numbers within highly change-able things. For this reason, the Magi, who observe the solar or lunar numbers and apply them to various things, often draw down the solar and lunar properties into them, and by a marvelous power they harmonize these things, which are thus in sympathy with one another. Proclus writes that the ancient priests used to employ certain numbers that possessed an ineffable power, in or-der to accomplish the most important operations of sacred rites — but this is Proclus' opinion.[221] Certainly Plato states that the cycles of the souls and of political communities are filled with their own numbers, and the universal, circular motion of the world is con-tained in a perfect number;[222] following Pythagoras he postulates two principles for the numbers, the paternal and the maternal, that is, the unity and the dyad, as the limit and the infinite,[223] the first number being the number three, which is formed by a mix-ture of limit and infinite. According to him, unity is related to the absolute One, the dyad to essence, and the trinity to the first be-ing and intelligible.[224] Moreover, all numbers are virtually con-tained in the unity and the dyad. Therefore, all the numbers un-fold from there, the even numbers through the dyad, the odd numbers through unity, which presides over the dyad. So all things are arranged by virtue of numbers in the following degrees: by virtue of even numbers, the processions, divisions and separable

pares autem simpliciora quaedam munera praestantioraque et insolubilia passim et collectiones in unum.

6 Verum ad distinctiones supermundanorum ordinum breviter redeamus. Etsi quaecumque in hac suppositione connumerantur et ad omnes et ad caput eorum intellectum primum quodammodo pertinent, alia tamen aliis magis propria sunt, ut diximus. Stare quidem in se sibique idem esse, simile, aequale, contiguum, et similia, item, ab aliis alterum et dissimile illis et inaequale, neque tangere illa neque tangi caeteraque id genus, superioribus magis propria sunt, opposita vero inferioribus potius tribuuntur. Inter haec adverte, ubi dicitur deorum aliquis idem aliis esse et simile et aequale, si tunc ad sensibilia comparetur, apte admodum exponi posse: ipsum deum quibuscumque adest adesse, quantum ad se spectat, totum eundemque et similem et aequalem, modoque eodem et simili et aequali, quamvis caetera nec eodem modo neque similiter neque aequaliter illinc accipiant.

7 Ultimum vero intellectualium ordinem Parmenides potissimum designare videtur, ubi dicit 'tangit alia tangiturque vicissim.' Huic simile est illud in *Republica* deam Necessitatem mundi sphaeras tangere genibus, Parcas[85] quoque manibus. Item illud in *Cratylo* Proserpinam una cum Plutone inferiores profecto deos naturam mobilem attractare. Qui enim sensibili mundo deisque mundanis proximi sunt videntur iam a communiori ad particulariorem distinctioremque providentiam declinare et e proximo iam quasi quodam affectu corporalia tangere. Sed interim unusquisque deorum neque seipsum tangit neque alia. Non seipsum, ubi enim individuum caput habet, ibi non opus est contactu. Non alia, quo-

compositions; by virtue of odd numbers, the simpler, superior and inseparable powers and the gatherings into unity.[225]

But let us briefly return to the distinctions between the hyper- 6
cosmic orders. Even if all the attributes enumerated in this hypothesis concern all the intellects as well as the first intellect, which is at their summit, some attributes pertain more to certain orders than others, as we have said. The attributes "at rest," "in relation to oneself," "same," "like," "equal," "in contact" and so forth, as well as, in relation to the others, the attributes "other," "unlike," "unequal," "not touching or being touched," and all the rest, rather pertain to the superior orders, while their opposites are rather attributed to the inferior orders. Moreover, one should note that when it is said that one god is the same as, like, or equal to the others, if this god is then compared with the sensible realities, one can appropriately say that in the things in which he is present this god is present as a whole, as the same, like and equal in relation to himself, and in a way that is same, like and equal to himself, whereas the others do not receive from him anything in a way that would be the same, like and equal.

Parmenides appears specifically to designate the last intellectual 7
order when he says that "the one touches the others and is touched by them" [148E3–4], which echoes the following passage of the *Republic*: the goddess Necessity touches the world's spheres on her knees, the Fates with their hands,[226] as well as the following passage in the *Cratylus*: Proserpine and Pluto, who are surely inferior gods, attract the nature that is in motion.[227] For the gods that are very close to the sensible world and to the cosmic gods seem to pass from the more general to the more individual and distinct providence, and gradually, by a sort of influence, touch the corporeals.[228] However, each of these gods has no contact with himself or with the others. Not with himself, because he does not need any contact where he possesses an indivisible summit; nor with the others, because despite arranging all things individually, he

niam dum dispensat singula, numquam e suo statu et puritate
declinat. Tangit interea et seipsum, quatenus plures in se partes
habet atque hae vicissim se tangentes totum quoque contingunt.
Tangit et alia, quatenus proxime et efficaciter ea tractans quoddam
quasi vestigium suum operi videtur imprimere.

8   Tandem vero Parmenides, ubi ad motum et tempus aetatemque
descendit, deos iam intellectuales ad animales deos mundanosque
traducit sequentemque de anima disputationem opportune admodum anticipare videtur.

: XCVI :

*Tertia suppositio. Intentio suppositionis. Quomodo
anima ens dicatur atque non ens, de motu et
tempore in anima. Item de quodam eius
aeterno. Rursus quomodo commutatione
quadam sui ipsius omnia repraesentet.*

1   Tertia suppositio de anima tractans non quamlibet animam introducit in primis, sed divinam prorsus omnem. Divinam inquam,
non deam per substantiam, sed expressam quandam similitudinem
cum diis habentem. Huius vero tres sunt ordines. Primum quidem
tenent sphaerarum ampliorum animae, secundum vero stellarum
animae, tertium numinum invisibilium animae universalem providentiam in sphaeris agentium. De his omnibus disserit suppositio
tertia, mundanos deos introducens in tres ordines distributos. Si

never departs from his state of rest and purity. By contrast, he is in contact with himself to the extent that he possesses within himself a large number of parts, which are in contact with one another and are also in contact with the whole.[229] He is also in contact with the others, inasmuch as by drawing them very close to himself in an efficient way, he appears to imprint upon his creation a trace of himself.

Finally, when Parmenides descends to motion, time and age, he passes from the intellectual gods to the psychic and cosmic gods, and appears to anticipate opportunely the discussion about the soul that follows in the third hypothesis. 8

: XCVI :

Third hypothesis. The purpose of the hypothesis. The way
in which the soul is called being and not-being. On
motion and time within the soul. On a certain
eternal thing belonging to it. Again, how by a
kind of change of itself it represents all things.

The third hypothesis, which is about the soul, does not initially concern every particular soul, but all the souls that are utterly divine, and by "divine" I do not mean a soul that is a goddess in substance, but the soul that possesses, by reproduction, a certain likeness with the gods. Of this type there are three orders. The first order is occupied by the souls of the greater spheres; the second, by the souls of the stars; and the third, by the souls of the invisible divinities which exercise divine providence within the spheres.[230] The third hypothesis concerns all these and describes the cosmic gods, which are divided into three orders. If perchance 1

quid forte aliter alicubi de intentione suppositionis huius dixerim, aliorum fuerit; haec autem sit interpretatio nostra: apte admodum suppositio haec inter[86] quinque media distribuitur animae, quae inter quinque rerum gradus, quemadmodum in *Theologia* probamus, tenet medium et corpori accommodata est ubique, quinario scilicet ex quattuor elementorum proprietatibus conflato et caelesti quadam insuper virtute referto. Id autem caelestibus quoque animabus competere Platonici putant. Praeterea quemadmodum anima componitur ex oppositis, ut probavimus in *Timaeo*, ita suppositio tertia tractans animam ex affirmationibus negationibusque miscetur et opportune admodum ab initio statim descendit in tempus. Ubi enim proprie loquimur, primum motum tempusque in anima collocamus.

2   Confestim quoque dicitur hoc unum, quod intellegitur anima et iam unum animale factum, non solum esse, sed etiam non esse. In quolibet enim fluxu per prius atque posterius procedente non esse cum esse miscetur. Propterea dictum est iamdiu hoc unum, de quo hic agitur, quodammodo sub ente locandum quasi temporale aliquid sub aeterno.

3   Profecto sicut unum, quando procedit in ens, cadit in non unum, sic ens purum processu quodam extra se suo labitur in non ens, id est in ens aliquod deinceps quodammodo mixtum cum non ente, et quemadmodum hactenus in ente primo, id est intellectuali, fuit aliqua, ut ita dixerim, prioritas naturalis, per quam origine quadam et ordine extitit aliquid penes ipsum prius aliquidve posterius, sic in ente secundo, id est animali, distantia iam et divisione crescente, prioritas, ut ita loquar,[87] accidit temporalis posterioritasque consimilis. Item sicut ubi prioritas est natu-

I have elsewhere said anything else about the purpose of this hypothesis, then it will have been the opinion of others than myself.[231] Let our interpretation be as follows: the third hypothesis, which holds the middle rank among the five hypotheses,[232] is very appropriately attributed to the soul, which, as we show in the *Theology*, occupies the middle rank among the five levels of realities and is always linked to the body, since the number five results from the conflation of the properties of the four elements and is also filled with some celestial power.[233] According to the Platonists, it is also in agreement with the celestial souls. Furthermore, just as the soul is composed of opposites, as we have shown in [the commentary on] the *Timaeus*,[234] so the third hypothesis, which is about the soul, mingles negations and assertions. In addition, this hypothesis, appropriately, descends to time from its outset [155E], for properly speaking, we put the first motion and time within the soul.

At the outset too the one of the third hypothesis, which is understood to be soul and to have now become the one at the level of the soul, is said to be and not to be [155E]. Indeed, in any flux, which proceeds through past and future times, not-being is mixed up with being. In this way, Parmenides has long been saying that the one in question must in some way be placed under being, since the temporal should be placed under the eternal.

Certainly, just as the one, when it processes into being, falls into the not-one, so pure being, when it processes outside itself, lapses into not-being, that is, into a particular being that is then somehow mixed with not-being; just as there was so far within the first being, — that is, the intellectual being — a sort of natural anteriority, so to speak, whereby a thing within being was prior or posterior in origin and in order, so within the second being — that is, the being at the level of the soul — where there is an increase in distance and division, anteriority, as I call it, becomes temporal, and the same goes for posteriority. Likewise, just as in the cases

rae, illic gradus quidam sunt in ordine et in quo gradu iam est ibi primum aliquod nondum pariter est secundum, e vestigio videlicet successurum, sic ubi est prioritas temporalis, ibi iam multoque distinctius, in quo tempore prius aliquid est nondum est pariter, si quid ibidem est, posterius proventurum.

4 Commutatio vero successioque per prius atque posterius in anima etiam fit divina atque, ut communis Platonicorum schola consentit, etiam in ratione intellectuque ipsius temporalis aliqua fit discursio, quamvis velox, siquidem motus atque tempus naturaliter primoque competit animae, igitur et omni animae et omnibus animae cuiusque virtutibus. Propterea si quis in intellectu animae actus est subitus, quantum congruit cum intellectu puro, interea tamen comitatur illum ibidem discursio temporalis, sicut coruscationem quandam ventus atque caligo.

5 Efficitur autem transmutatio quaedam penes animam vel divinam in infima[88] eius potentia vegetali, quatenus rationes[89] seminales alias aliae vigent potius atque regnant, aliisque temporibus aliae explicantur in opus. Fit etiam in sensuali sive imaginali potius eiusdem parte, nunc has, tunc illas praecipue rerum imagines affectante. Agitur et in ipsa rationali potentia rationes formasque rerum naturalium aliis temporum curriculis alias potius evolvente. Efficitur tandem et in eius mente ideas et spectacula divinorum vario quodam et successorio, quamvis celerrimo, intuitu contuente.

6 Commutationes eiusmodi, dum in anima nostra contingunt, non adeo videntur ad essentiam pertinere. Non enim adeo uniformes continuaeque aguntur nec affectu vel actione tam efficaci nec formae, vires actionesque animae tam proximae sunt essentiae nostrae quam intimae sunt divinarum essentiis animarum. Quas ob res hic ausus est Parmenides, dum sublimes animas sic intus

where anteriority is natural, degrees are arranged in order and in any given degree what is first is not yet second (that is, about to occur immediately), even so, in the cases where anteriority is temporal (and in that case it is much more distinct), in any given time, that which is first will not yet spring forth as second (if one admits that it is in the same place).

Change and succession through past and future times also occur in the divine soul and, as the whole school of Platonists agree, even in the soul's reason and intellect there occurs a temporal yet swift movement back and forth, since motion and time befit naturally and firstly the soul, and thus every soul and all the powers of each soul. For this reason, if there is any instantaneous act within the soul's intellect, to the degree that it is in accordance with pure intellect, there is nevertheless in the same place a temporal movement to accompany it, just as wind and thunder accompany lightning.

But a kind of transmutation occurs within the soul, even the divine soul, in its lowest vegetative power, insofar as some seminal reasons thrive and prevail at different times, while at other times other seminal reasons are unfolded into activity. It also occurs in the sensitive or rather imaginative part of the soul, since this part seizes upon different images at different times. It also occurs within the rational power of the soul, which unfolds different rational principles and forms of natural things in different temporal cycles. Finally, it also occurs in the soul's mind, which contemplates the Ideas and spectacles of divine beings with a sight that, though very swift, is still varied and consecutive.

While these changes occur within our soul, they do not really concern the soul's essence. For they do not really occur in a uniform and continuous way, by virtue of an affect or action; and the forms, forces and actions of the soul are not so proximate to our essence as they are intimately involved in the essences of divine souls. For these reasons, when Parmenides saw that the sublime

permutari videret, confiteri permutationes eiusmodi ad ipsum earum esse quodammodo et ad ipsam essentiam pertinere, perinde ac si Proteus ille formas tanta potestate commutet, ut alter deinceps evasisse videatur et alter et interire iugiter atque renasci.

7 Interea tamen sublimes animae, quoniam non solum animalem intellectualemque vim habent, sed etiam divinum aliquid et individuum penitus et aeternum et forsan aeternitate superius, idcirco quomodocumque mutentur, si comparentur ad illud. Neque moventur passionesve subeunt temporales neque quietem ullam, oppositam motui quasi necessariam,[90] quandoque resumunt. Dum igitur temporales mobilesque passiones ratione superius assignata de divinis animis affirmantur, hac interim ratione quam modo dicebam aeque negantur. Caelestis enim anima ita ferme se habet ut sphaera caelestis. In sphaera vero centrum quidem individuum est atque stabile, dum circa ipsum universus ambitus mobilis est et multiplex. In anima ergo simile quiddam centrum est similisque circuitus.

8 Forte vero potissimum Parmenidis studium fuit imitatoriam animae naturam quasi quendam universi minimum nobis ante oculos ponere. Cum enim sit media rerum et motionis universae principium, facile admodum atque acriter imitatur omnes varietatemque actionum omnium ipsa multiplicis sui motus diversitate refert. Super animam quidem mundus extat intelligibilis, infra vero mundus iste sensibilis, et ille faciem suam habet et iste suam, ille plures semper habet, iste plures semper agit. Inter hos autem anima media, tamquam elementum elementorum medium vel qualitas media qualitatum, extremis se utrimque conformat, immo, tamquam strenuus quidam minimus, omnes utriusque facies in se prorsus effigiat.

souls undergo change inwardly in this way, he dared to claim that these changes somehow concern the souls' very being and essence [156A], just as if Proteus changed forms with such a power that he would each time become different and continuously die and be reborn.[235]

Meanwhile, because they not only possess a psychic and intellectual force, but also something that is divine, completely undivided, and eternal — and perhaps superior to eternity — the sublime souls somehow undergo change when they are compared to this divine part of themselves. They undergo no motion or temporal passion, nor rest, which is necessarily opposed to motion, whenever they regain their initial place. Therefore, whereas temporal and moving passions are asserted of divine souls for the reason referred to above, conversely, they are equally denied of them for the reason just mentioned. For the celestial soul is disposed in almost the same way as the celestial sphere. In the sphere the center is undivided and immobile, while the universal revolution around the center itself is in movement and multiple. Thus a similar center and a similar revolution reside in the soul.

But perhaps Parmenides' main purpose was to place before our eyes the imitative nature of the soul, which is like the microcosm of the universe. For since the soul stands at the middle rank of nature, and is the principle of universal motion, it very easily and readily imitates all things, and refers the variety of all actions to the very diversity of its own motion, which is multiple. Above the soul there is the intelligible world, and underneath it there is the sensible world, and each of these two worlds possesses its own configuration. The former always possesses more things, the latter always engages in more activity. In the middle, the soul, as the median element among the elements, or the median quality among qualities, conforms to the extremes on both sides, or rather, as an active microcosm, it fashions within itself all the configurations of both worlds.

7

8

9   Si enim cameleon superficie et speculare corpus similiter superficie obiectum quodlibet figura, colore motuque repraesentat,
multo magis anima non tam exterius quam interius imitans utriusque mundi vultus penetralibus suis obiectos naturaliterque infusos
in se prorsus effingit, ut pro varia variorum imitatione potenter
effecta nimirum ipsa interim anima, si modo introspici possit, altera vicissim et altera fieri videatur, praesertim si vegetalis ipsius
natura cernatur, cuius virtus et actio quaelibet non imago quaedam est, sed qualitas potius naturalis et natura quaedam et ipsa
natura. Itaque dum alios temporibus aliis in se vultus effigiesque
promit, naturam suam protinus variare videtur. Actus quoque
formasque superiorum virium Plotinus adeo essentiales existimat,
ut si anima deinceps per varias sui vires formasque agat, quae omnes ipsa sunt anima, dici possit anima nunc quidem eiusmodi,
tunc autem illius modi se prorsus habere, et aliam nonnumquam
habere vitam atque naturam, ut non mireris si Parmenides fieri
animam dicat atque perire.

10   Sed tu interim intellexeris non ipsam quidem animae essentiam
speciemque primam, sed vultum et effigiem et habitum permutari,
non animam quidem aliunde compulsam vel quomodolibet agita-
tam, sed ipsam suapte natura sua sponte seipsam iugiter transfor-
mantem. Non enim dicunt mutatum Protea formis, sed mutantem
Protea formas, sicut et artificiosus minimus facies, figuras, perso-
nas, ipse varias induit, ipse pariter exuit.

11   Non igitur horrere debes quando audis divinas animas, id est
caelestes, augeri, minui, rare fieri, condensari, nasci, perire, si memineris interim et haec metaphorica quadam accipi ratione et
motiones ipsas, quae in corporibus praesertim inferioribus et

Indeed, if it is true that a chameleon and likewise a transparent 9
body both represent an object's figure, color and motion on their
surface, it is even truer that the soul, which does not imitate objects so much outwardly as inwardly, fashions within itself the
faces of both worlds, which are both produced in the soul's innermost part and naturally infused within it, so that rather than imi-
tating various things in an efficient way, the soul, if it can look into
itself, appears to become one thing and then another, especially
regarding its vegetative nature, the power and action of which is
not an image, but a natural quality, a nature, and nature itself. For
this reason, as it takes on different appearances and images in different times, it appears to modify its own nature. Plotinus reckons
that the acts and the forms of superior forces pertain to essence,[236]
so that if the soul then acts through various forces and forms, all
of which *are* the soul itself, it can be said to be disposed in one
way at one time, and in another at another time, and sometimes to
take on another life and nature, so that one should not be sur-
prised when Parmenides says that the soul comes into existence
and ceases to exist [156A9].

However, you should understand that what is changed is by no 10
means the very essence and the first species of the soul, but its appearance, image and disposition, and that the soul is by no means
pushed or somehow agitated by something else, but that it continuously transforms itself by virtue of its own nature and will.
Indeed, they do not say that Proteus is changed by his forms, but
that Proteus changes his forms, just as the microcosm-artisan
himself takes on and likewise takes off various appearances, figures
and persons.

You should not be repelled, therefore, to hear that the divine, 11
i.e. the celestial, souls increase, diminish, become rarefied and con-
densed, and that they come into existence and cease to exist
[155E–56B], if one remembers that these expressions are to be
understood metaphorically: these motions, which, when in bodies,

aliunde fiunt et passiones quaedam sunt, easdem in animabus praesertim illis et ex seipsis effici et actiones existere animasque ipsas eiusmodi vicissitudine perpetuo quasi perfici. Certe perpetuo delectari ac tam futura quam praeterita figura et varietate gaudere, quemadmodum et caelum ab illis sic interea revolutum perpetua revolutionum configurationumque varietate perficitur quiescitque in motu, ac dum videtur desinere, iterum exorditur; praetereundo revertitur; pereundo renascitur. Hinc et materia per se in primis habet ut omnes rerum omnium formas admittens vicissimque amittens iterumque recipiens singulis habitibus aeque gaudeat videaturque fieri semper atque perire et crescere iterumque decrescere, dum instar animae caelestis atque caeli semper permanet eadem.

: XCVII :

Qua ratione caelestis anima circa mentem
stabilem moveatur agatque circuitum.
Quot sint motus animae. Quot
motus et quies in tempore, et de
medio inter motus.

1 Divina mens, quemadmodum in *Theologia Timaeoque* probavimus, omnes omnium formas unico stabilique semper actu concipit paritque intus et inspicit. Probavimus ibidem divinam animam illinc formis cunctis gravidam proficisci et tamquam illius aemulam si-

especially inferior ones, are created by something else and are passions, are within the souls, especially the divine souls, produced by the souls themselves and are actions, and the souls are themselves perpetually perfected by these changes. Certainly they are perpetually filled with delight and rejoice in past and future figure and variety, just as the heaven, which is moved this way by the celestial souls, is perfected by the perpetual variety of revolutions and configurations; it is at rest when in motion; when it seems to stop, it starts again; by going too far, it turns back again; by ceasing to exist, it is born again. Hence matter too is in itself primarily disposed in such a way that as it receives all the forms of all things and as it rejects them, then takes them up again, it equally enjoys every disposition, and it appears always to come into existence and perish, grow and then diminish, yet always remains the same, like the celestial soul and the heaven.

: XCVII :

The way in which the celestial soul is moved and accomplishes circular motion around the mind, which remains motionless. The number of motions in the soul. How many kinds of motion and rest there are in time, and on the mean between motions.

As we have shown in our *Theology* and in our commentary on the 1 *Timaeus*,[237] the divine mind conceives, brings forth from within itself, and contemplates all the forms of all things in an act that remains unique and motionless. There we have also shown that the divine soul, which is pregnant with all these forms, proceeds from the mind and, seeking to emulate the mind, as it were, strives to

milem quoque conceptum et partum et intuitum affectare, sed et magis in se quasi divisam esse et minus interim efficacem. Itaque cum nequeat mentis instar semel consequi totum, eniti saltem successione[91] quadam temporis actibus in seipsa multiplicibus assequi. Quapropter modo formas viresque alias edit, modo alias, actionesque progressu multiplicat seminalesque proles gradatim explicat multiformes. Hinc[92] Boetianum illud: 'Mentemque profundam circuit et simili convertit imagine caelum.'

2   Esse vero necessarium illi circuitum hinc breviter confirmamus, siquidem primus est in anima praesertim caelesti motus primumque tempus est. Utique motus ibi totus atque sempiternus, si per formas incedit assidue ipsaeque speciales[93] rerum formae certo sunt numero definitae. Omnes denique praeterit, unde cogatur sistere pedem, nisi regrediatur ad easdem iterumque resumat. Cum vero quiescere nesciat tamquam natura studioque mobilis nimirum, agit tam voluntate quam necessitate circuitum. Simili quadam necessitate caelum quoque revolvitur, quemadmodum in *Theologia* probavimus et Plotino.

3   In caelo quidem luna duodecim revolutionibus unam solis ac sol duodecim quoque suis ferme similiter unam Iovis adaequat, unde apparet quantum amica est Phoebe Phoebi tantum esse Phoebum Iovis amicum. Sed de hoc in libro *De Sole et Lumine* et in libro *De Vita*. Similiter inter caelestes animas suprema quidem anima unica et universa formarum actionumque revolutione conficit quod sequentes illic animae pluribus et subinde pluribus ambagibus agunt.

accomplish the same acts of conception, birth and contemplation, except that the soul is in itself more divided and less efficient. For this reason, since the soul cannot attain all the things at once like the mind does, it seeks to reach them at least in a temporal succession, through the multitude of acts that reside within itself. Thus it produces different forms and powers at different times; it progressively multiplies the number of actions and gradually unfolds its seminal and multiform progeny. Hence Boethius' words: "The soul circles around the mind, which is the innermost part of being, and turns round the heaven in its image."[238]

Let us briefly confirm here that circular motion necessarily exists in the soul, since first motion and first time reside in the soul, especially the celestial one. To be sure, motion is total and eternal yonder, since it proceeds through the forms in a continuous way and the specific forms of things are themselves defined by a certain number. Finally, the soul goes through them all and, as a result, is necessarily at rest, except when it turns back to these same forms, and takes up the same journey [through the forms] a second time. However, since it cannot be at rest, given that it is moving by nature and with effort, it accomplishes a circular motion both by will and necessity. The heaven also accomplishes its revolution by virtue of the same necessity, as we have shown in our *Theology* and our Plotinus commentary.[239]

In heaven twelve revolutions of the moon equals one revolution of the sun, and so twelve revolutions of the sun almost equals one revolution of Jupiter. It appears, therefore, that Phoebus is Jupiter's friend, as much as Phoebe is the friend of Phoebus. We explore this question in our treatise *On the Sun and Light* and in the *De vita*.[240] Likewise among celestial souls the most sublime soul accomplishes in a unique and universal revolution composed of forms and actions what the following souls accomplish in progressively greater number of revolutions.

4 Verum ut ad paradoxa Parmenidis revertamur: quonam modo fit anima? Quomodo perit? Profecto dum certam hanc formarum et rationum actionumque habitudinem induit, tunc anima fieri, id est eiusmodi habitudo effici dicitur. Dum vero hanc exuit, tunc quoque perire, id est desinere iam ita se habere, atque ita perpetuo ferme phoenicis instar ex se et in seipsam, sed certe multo praestantius, interit atque renascitur.

5 Quomodo rursus anima rare fit? Quomodo condensatur? Condensare quidem sese videtur, quatenus in unum varia colligit vel agendo vel contuendo, rare facere vero, quando unum in multa distinguit et explicat. Auget quoque seipsam anima, dum conspicit et in seipsa expedit ampliora; comminuit vero, ubi angustiora parit atque discernit. Ita maior minorve videtur evadere. Aequalis autem effici, quatenus interdum tractat aequalia seque ipsam tunc quasi librare putatur.

6 Sed dicti iam motus ad substantiam et quantitatem quodammodo pertinere videntur. Quidnam igitur alteratio est in anima praecipue spectans ad qualitatem? Affectus forte varius tum ad haec intentior, tunc ad illa. Affectus enim varius affectionem variat, affectio qualitatem.

7 Suntne et locales quidam in anima motus? Sunt profecto. Omnes enim motus sunt in motu primo, per virtutem videlicet et exemplar. Ascendit igitur ad causas anima, descendit iterum ad effectus, ad dexteram movetur atque sinistram coniugia pensitans, ante procedit retroque recedit, posterioribus videlicet priora compensans. Denique movetur in rectum, aliud semper ex alio sumens. In obliquum quoque se contuens, in circulum denique tum

To return to Parmenides' paradoxes, in what way does the soul   4
come into existence and cease to exist [156B]? Assuredly, when it
takes on a certain disposition made of forms, rational principles
and actions, it is said to come into existence, i.e. to be in a certain
disposition; and when it strips this disposition off, it is said to
cease to exist, i.e. to cease to be in that disposition, and so it perpetually perishes and is reborn from itself and within itself, like
the phoenix, as it were, but in a way that is assuredly far superior.

Now in what way is the soul rarefied and in what way does it   5
become dense [156B]? It appears to become dense inasmuch as it
gathers different things into a unity by either acting on or contem-
plating them; it appears to be rarefied when it divides and unfolds
unity into many. The soul is also increased when it comprehends
and releases within itself things that are greater; it is diminished,
when it generates and distinguishes things that are smaller. In this
way, it appears to become greater and smaller [156B]. It seems to
be equalized, inasmuch as, at times, it treats things that are equal,
and at that moment it is thought to be balancing itself [156B].

But the motions that we have just mentioned seem to somehow   6
concern substance and quantity. In what way, therefore, does alteration in the soul principally concern quality? Perhaps the soul's
emotion might vary, being at times more intense toward certain
things than others. For emotion varies when it alters the soul's
habitual attitudes, and attitudes alters quality.

Are there also spatial motions in the soul? Certainly. For all   7
motions are within the first motion, by virtue of being their power
and their model. Thus the soul moves upward to its causes, then
downward to its effects; it is moved to the right and the left when
it contemplates realities that are joined to one another; it moves
forward and backward when it establishes a balance between past
and future things. Finally, it is moved in a straight line when it
takes one thing from another thing; it is moved obliquely when it

ubi revolutiones a formis ad formas easdem denique refert, tum
etiam quando a causis ad effectus progressa ad causas iterato regre-
ditur, tum denique dum ipsa ad parentes suos unde processit
affectu prorsus et contemplatione convertitur. Frequenter vero in
motibus enarrandis activo quodam verbo Parmenides utitur, scilicet μεταβάλλειν, quo significat animam non aliunde mutatam,
sed mutare seipsam atque migrare ex statu in motum atque contra,
a motu rursus opposito in oppositum. Inter omnia haec opposita
aeternum quiddam individuumque servare in quo neutrum patiatur oppositorum.

8   Sed quoniam mentionem individui fecimus, operae pretium est
a physicis nonnihil assumere. Probant in continuo punctum quodlibet per dividuum quiddam a puncto distare, ne si forte ponatur
punctum puncto quam proximum, confiteri cogamur ex individuis dividuum continuumque componi, confiteri rursus individuum fore dividuum. Si enim punctum tangat punctum, quaeretur numquid punctum puncto penitus inseratur, an potius per sua
quaedam extrema foris vicissim se contingant. Si detur primum,
nullum inde continuum componetur; si concedatur secundum,
utrumque punctum dividuum[94] iam evadet.

9   Post haec argumentantur motum quoque corporum tamquam
in continuo factum conditionem continui necessario sequi, ut quodlibet similiter in motu momentum per aliquem motum discrepet a
momento, ne alioquin eadem in motu quae et in continuo absurda
sequantur. Cum vero tempus sit passio quaedam motus, idem de
omnibus temporis momentis argumentantur.

10   Mox etiam asserunt motum nullum in momento individuo peragi. Cum enim motus sit processio quaedam ab alio semper in

contemplates itself, and finally it is moved in a circle when it eventually brings the revolutions, which started from the forms, back to the forms again; when, having proceeded from the causes to the effects, it returns to the causes again; finally, when it turns itself through emotion and contemplation to the parents from which it proceeded. In many passages, Parmenides uses an active verb, *metaballein*, to express the motions of the soul, whereby he means that the soul is not altered by something else, but alters itself, passes from rest to motion and conversely, and again from one motion to its opposite. Among all these opposite motions, there remains something eternal and undivided, in which the soul undergoes none of the opposite motions [156C–57B].

But since we have mentioned the undivided, it is worth drawing   8 upon the doctrine of the natural philosophers.[241] According to them, any point on a continuum is distant from another point by something that is divisible, so that if a point happens to be placed as close as possible to another point, we are not compelled to admit that the divisible and the continuous are composed of indivisible points, and then to admit [the contradiction] that the indivisible would be divisible. For if a point touches another point, the question will be whether one point is superimposed on the other, or if the points are in contact with one another externally, through their extremities. In the first case, the continuum will cease to be composed; in the second, both points will become divisible.

Secondly, the natural philosophers argue that corporeal motion,   9 which occurs on a continuum, also necessarily follows the condition of the continuum, so that any moment in motion is likewise distinct from another moment by some motion. In this way, one avoids the same absurdities as those that we mentioned regarding the continuum. Since time is a passion of motion,[242] they reason that the same goes for all the moments in time.

Thirdly, the natural philosophers assert that no motion is ac-   10 complished in an indivisible moment. Indeed, since motion is a

aliud in continuo certo peracta, non fore motum nisi per aliquod temporis intervallum certum aliquod spatium transeatur. Finge vero motum in momento fieri super spatium forte pedale. Potest quidem hoc motu posito motus alius velocior inveniri. Quod ergo celerius ibidem motum fuerit, profecto citius idem spatium praeteribit. Si citius ergo momentum illud quod modo fictum fuerat individuum dividetur. Summatim vero quod ita movebitur per continuum prius quidem partem continui priorem tanget, deinde vero sequentem. Unde statim tempus sive momentum illud in quo moveri concessum fuerat dividetur. Hinc ergo concludunt motus corporum omnes in tempore quodam dividuo peragi. Cum vero quies sit opposita motui et circa idem fiat atque similiter et in qua mora fit motus agi possit quies atque vicissim pariter, colligunt quietem non in momento, sed in tempore fieri.

11   Argumentantur praeterea inter omnes oppositos invicem motus medium aliquod esse in quo mobile motum neutrum perpetiatur, alioquin nisi medium fuerit ullum fore ut et oppositi motus sint motus unus et aliquid simul totum oppositis quibusdam motibus agitetur. Quod vero medium inter hos motus inseritur, physici forte tempus aliquod esse putant, cum forte sit quies et quies tempore peragatur ac si momentum dumtaxat individuum interceperit, verebuntur, ut arbitror, ne propterea cogantur momentum momentis esse quam proximum.

12   Parmenides autem non de motibus corporum, sed animae loquitur, qui non omnino legibus similibus astringuntur. Quid enim prohibet, sicut anima constat ex individuis, ita motum tempusque animae ex individuis quoque componi atque haec in anima simi-

procession that is always accomplished from one point to another on a certain continuum, motion will only occur if a certain space is traversed in a certain interval of time. Let us imagine a motion that is longer, say, than the length of a foot occurring in a [single] moment. Once this motion is posited, one can assuredly find another, swifter motion. Thus that which at the same place has been moved more swiftly, will indeed traverse the same space more swiftly. In this case, the moment that we had just imagined to be undivided will be divided. In sum, what will be moved on a continuum will first touch one part of the continuum, then another. As a result, the time or the moment in which we have admitted that it will be moved, will immediately be divisible. The natural philosophers conclude, therefore, that all corporeal motions are accomplished in a time that is divisible. But since rest is opposed to motion, pertains to the same body and in the same way, and can occur in the interval when there is no motion, and conversely, they also conclude that rest does not occur in a moment, but in time.

Moreover, they reason that between all opposite motions there is a mean during which a moving thing undergoes no motion; otherwise, if there was no mean, opposite motions would be one single motion, and every whole would be simultaneously agitated by opposite motions. According to the natural philosophers, this mean, which is inserted between these motions, is perhaps a certain interval of time, since it is perhaps a form of rest, and rest is accomplished in time; and if this mean were merely to interrupt an indivisible moment, then they will be afraid, I think, of being forced to admit that this moment is continuous with another moment.[243]

However, Parmenides does not speak about corporeal motions, but the motions of the soul, which are bound by laws that are somewhat different. For what prevents the soul's motion and time from being composed of indivisible parts, just as the soul itself is composed of indivisible parts, and these parts from being in the

273

liora esse numeris quam mensuris? Medium quoque hic positum inter motus invicem et inter motum atque statum esse penitus individuum, praesertim quia neque motus illi tales in anima sunt quales sunt in corpore neque hoc individuum subitumque tam temporale momentum est quam aeternum ac forte sublimius, siquidem caelestis anima per unitatem suam, essentiae suae apicem, secundum individuum semper idem firmumque momentum ipso simpliciter uno fruitur, atque in hoc gradu ferme sic est super omnes oppositorum passiones, quemadmodum ipsum unum super opposita mirabiliter extat. Gradum eiusmodi, ut in superioribus quoque significavi, Parmenides appellat inter opposita medium, quoniam et neutrum oppositorum sit et quasi centrum sit et cardo quo quaelibet inter opposita vicissitudines aeque regantur. Recipit vero Parmenides quod physici probant motum et quietem in tempore quodam semper absolvi, et quod contraria patitur non eodem in tempore, sed alio atque alio perpeti.

: XCVIII :

Summa suppositionis tertiae vel epilogus. De uno, multitudine,
ente, non ente, motu, statu, momento, tempore, oppositione.
Motus ad motum atque statum.

1 Reliquum est ut suppositionis huius contextum breviter perstringamus. Unum ens non est simpliciter unum, sed unum aliquid et unum atque multa. Igitur est unum et non unum. Qua enim rati-

soul more like numbers than measures?²⁴⁴ In this case, the mean
—both between motions and between motion and rest—is also
completely indivisible, especially since the motions that occur in
the soul are different from the motions that occur in the body, and
this indivisible and sudden moment is not temporal, but eternal,
and perhaps more sublime, since the celestial soul enjoys union
with the absolute One through its unity, which is the summit of
its essence, in an undivided, always identical and stable moment,
and at this level it transcends all the passions pertaining to opposites, in the same way, as it were, that the One wonderfully transcends the opposites. As I have also indicated above, Parmenides
calls this level the mean between opposites, because it is none of
the opposites and is like the center and the pivot whereby all the
alternations between opposite motions are equally governed. Yet
he concedes what the natural philosophers demonstrate, i.e. that
motion and rest are always achieved in a certain time, and that
which undergoes these opposite states, does not do so at the same
time, but in different times.

<h2 style="text-align:center">: XCVIII :</h2>

Summary or epilogue of the third hypothesis. On the one,
multitude, being, not-being, motion, rest, moment, time,
and opposition. Motion in relation to motion and rest.

It remains to summarize briefly the structure of the third hypoth-   1
esis. The one being is not the absolute One, but some particular
one, and one and many. Thus it is both one and not-one. For it is
not one for the same reason as it is many. Likewise, since the psy-

one multa est, non eadem est et unum. Item cum illud unum post intellectualem gradum in animali gradu fluxum subeat atque tempus, iam non solum esse, sed etiam non esse dici potest. Si ita se habet, participat essentiam et non participat. Si ita, contingit etiam ut quando accipit essentiam, fiat quidem, quando vero amittit eam, pereat, cumque haec opposita eodem in tempore sustinere non possit, sequitur ut id quidem in alio tempore, illud autem in alio patiatur. Quam enim nunc formarum actionumque dispositionem habitudinemque in seipso profert paulo post non edit prorsus eandem simillimamve, sed variam, ut aliud quodammodo nunc existat, aliud rursus postea sit futurum.

2   In quibusdam sane configurationibus actionibusque suis ad unitatem, terminum, identitatem, statum, simplicitatem unamque multis communem formam vehementius sese conferens, quasi deponere multitudinem iam videtur atque desinere quidem esse multa, incipere autem esse unum; saepe vero vicissim, quando videlicet ad opposita eorum quae dicta sunt acrius se convertens distrahi videtur in multa ac desinere esse unum quale prius erat fierique iam multa. Ibi quidem congregari, hic autem disgregari videtur.

3   Fit saepe sibimet dissimile, quando videlicet priorem variat habitudinem. Redit et simile, quando iamdiu dimissam quandoque recipit habitudinem.

4   Fit maius seipso, quando concipit ampliora; quando autem angustiora, fit minus; aequale vero, cum circumspicit et parit aequalia. Itaque crescere, decrescere, aequari videtur.

chic one, which comes immediately after the intellectual one, undergoes flux and time, it cannot only be said to be, but also not to be. In this case, it does and does not participate in essence. Then it is also the case that when it receives essence, it comes to be, and when it is deprived of essence, it ceases to be, and since it cannot undergo these opposite states at the same time, it follows that it undergoes the state of being at one time and the state of not being at another. For the disposition and propensity of forms and actions that the psychic one produces within itself in the present time, are not the same as, nor like, those which it produces in the time that immediately follows, but are different, so that it is one thing in the present time, and it will then be another thing in the time that comes afterward.

Certainly, in some of its configurations and actions, when the psychic one relates itself with all its force to unity, limit, sameness, rest, simplicity and the unique form common to the many, it appears to abandon multitude, to cease to be many, and to start to be one; conversely when it turns itself with great keenness toward the states that are opposed to those mentioned above (which occurs frequently), it appears to be divided into many, to cease to be the one that it was before, and to become many. Yonder, it seems to be united; here, to be divided. 2

It often becomes unlike itself, when it alters the way it was initially disposed. It also becomes like itself again, when it regains the disposition that it had abandoned during that time. 3

It becomes greater than itself, when it conceives greater things; but when it conceives smaller things, it becomes smaller than itself; it becomes equal to itself when it contemplates and generates things that are equal. For this reason, it appears to increase, decrease and be equal. 4

5   Hactenus oppositos inter se motus vicissim subisse videtur. Ubique vero temporibus aliis alios[95] subire putatur atque inter quaelibet hic opposita medium semper est aliquid eminentius admodum oppositis nullis obnoxium.

6   Sed quidnam sibi vult Parmenides, ubi ait hoc ens animale de quo iampridem loquimur, divinam scilicet animam, ex statu in motum vicissimque pertransize? Opinor equidem animam hanc in statu quidem esse potius iudicandam quam in motu, dum aeterna intellegibiliaque et rationes statui cognatiores attentius inspicit, ardentius affectat, efficacius exprimit; magis autem in motu versari quando se potius ad opposita transfert. Haec autem alterius temporum vicibus efficit, sed inter vices eiusmodi medium est, ut diximus, non solum momentum quiddam quasi temporis individuum—ne opposti habitus fiant habitus unus, neve anima simul habitibus afficiatur oppositis—sed etiam et multo magis medium est divinum, ut ita loquar, momentum quale diximus aeternitate superius, ita ut quemadmodum in illo quasi temporali momento, ita et in hoc multoque verius nullum patiatur oppositorum.

7   Recte quidem Parmenides ait nullum tempus esse in quo aliquid neque moveatur neque quiescat. In omni enim tempore, id est intervallo temporali, oportet rem temporalem vel moveri vel quietem agere motui prorsus oppositam. Est tamen aliquid penitus individuum sive circa tempus sive in aevo sive superius, in quo res aliqua praesertim divina neque proprie moveatur neque[96] quietem oppositam motui subeat. Inter haec in momento mutationem quidem subitam ex opposito in oppositum effici iudicat; motum

So far the psychic one seems to have undergone opposite mo-   5
tions. However, it is considered always to undergo these different
motions at different times, and there is always a mean between
these opposites, which is superior to them and is subject to none
of them.

But what does Parmenides mean when he says that the being of   6
the soul, which we have been talking about for a long time now,
and which is the divine soul, passes from rest to motion and conversely [156C]? I myself think that this soul should be considered
at rest rather than in motion, when it contemplates with great attention the eternal and intelligible realities, as well as the rational
principles that are more kindred to rest, desires them with great
ardor, and imitates them with great efficiency. One should consider that it is in motion, when it turns itself toward the opposite
realities. It accomplishes these motions by passing from one moment in time to another, but in this transition from one condition
to another there is, as we have said, a mean, not only a sort of
undivided temporal moment (which prevents opposite dispositions from becoming one single disposition, or the soul from being
simultaneously affected by opposite dispositions), but also, and
even more so, a divine mean, so to speak, the kind of moment that
we said was superior to eternity; and just as in the case of temporal moment, the soul does not undergo any opposite in this divine
and much more real moment.

Parmenides rightly says that there is no time during which a   7
thing is neither in motion nor at rest [156C]. For in all time, that
is, in any interval of time, the thing-in-time must be either in motion or at rest, which is the opposite of motion. However, there
exists something that is completely undivided and pertains either
to time, or to eternity or above it, in which a thing, especially
when it is divine, does not properly undergo any motion nor its
opposite, rest. Parmenides considers that this sudden change from
one condition to its opposite is accomplished in that moment, but

vero proprium et tempori et intervallo prorsus addictum peragi
momento non putat. Quod praeterea movetur non potest, qua ratione movetur, eadem interim et quiescere neque vicissim. Haec
igitur aliis temporibus agit atque dum quiescit qua ratione quiescit
nititur ad quietem. Dum movetur similiter contendit ad motum,
quare neque dum stat se mutat erga motum neque dum movetur
se mutat in statum. Mutatione tamen opus est aliqua per quam ex
alio migretur in aliud, quae quidem necessario in momento fit
utriusque medio. Quod sane medium est inter opposita necessarium ne forte contra eorum naturam continuentur[97] in unum. Si
qui forte physici medium hoc velint esse dividuum, nihil ad Parmenidem qui non corporeos hic vult intellegi motus, sed animales,
concluditque in hoc quasi signo inter statum motumque medio
animam neque moveri, motus enim exigit intervallum, neque quietem huic motui oppositam, quae et longa futura sit, peragere.

8 In ipso quinetiam individuo praesertim aeterno, immo vero in
ipso divino, unum etiam animale neque dicendum est non esse sive
non ens, existit enim ibi super fluxum, neque proprie ens vel esse,
existit enim illic super essentiam penes ipsum simpliciter unum,
neque statum adhuc in eo gradu subit aut motum, nec identitatem
nec alteritatem, haec enim non sunt penes ipsum unum, subit autem haec in gradu quodam secundo vel tertio. Concludit denique
in ipso etiam individuo quod circa tempus est nullum oppositorum motuum effici. Non enim momento motus efficiuntur. Et
si qui sint ibi motus forsan oppositi, simul ibi motus agentur.
Concluditur clam interea, quod saepe iam diximus, unum quod
etiam in anima divina secundum seipsum acceptum super essen-

he does not think that what is accomplished in that moment is properly speaking a motion bound to time and space. Moreover, what is in motion cannot be at rest, for the very reason that it is in motion, and conversely. Thus the soul accomplishes these motions at different times, and when it is at rest, because it is at rest, it tends toward rest; likewise, when it is in motion, it tends toward motion, because when it is at rest, it does not mutate into motion, and when it is in motion, it does not mutate into rest. There must be a change, however, whereby it passes from one condition to another. This necessarily occurs during the instant that is the mean between the two conditions. This mean is necessarily the mean between two opposites, otherwise these opposites would be united into one, which would be against their nature. Some natural philosophers might wish this mean to be divisible, but Parmenides does not wish it to be so, since he does not mean corporeal motions here, but the soul's motions, and concludes that in the mean between rest and motion, which is a sort of point, the soul does not undergo any motion (for motion requires an interval of time), nor rest, which is the opposite of motion and will also occur in a long duration of time.

Furthermore, during this undivided moment which is especially 8 eternal, or rather during this divine moment, the psychic one should not be called "act of not-being" or "not-being" (for at that level it is above flux), nor should it be properly called "being" or "act of being" (for yonder it is above essence, within the absolute One). At that level it does not yet undergo rest, motion, sameness, or otherness (for these genera are not in the One), but does so at the second and third levels. Finally, Parmenides concludes that in this undivided moment which pertains to time, no opposite motions are accomplished. For motions are not accomplished in an undivided moment. And even if there are opposite motions in that moment, they are accomplished simultaneously. Meanwhile, one secretly concludes, as we have said many times, that the one,

tiam est, non solum oppositas motiones, sed nec opposita in
seipso prorsus ulla suscipere.

: XCIX :

Suppositio quarta. Quartae[98] *suppositionis intentio.*
Totum ante partes, totum post partes,
res divinae, res naturales, relatio
partium ad totum.

1 Tres, ut alibi diximus, praecedentes suppositiones unum ipsum
potius quam alia contemplatae illud ad se in primis, deinde ad
caetera quoque comparaverunt. Sequentes vero in quinario, duae
contra considerantes alia magis quam unum, haec ipsa triplici
comparant ratione. Nempe quodlibet horum partim quidem ad
ipsum unum, partim vero ad seipsum, partim etiam ad alia confe-
runt. Quarta igitur quam nunc aggredimur suppositio tripliciter
considerat alia. Nam cum primo existere posuerit unum ens sub
ipso simpliciter uno, hoc enim ab initio repetit, mox alia probat
non esse vel hoc ipsum simpliciter unum vel ens unum illi proximum, sed unum inde participare. Sic igitur ad unum alia refert.
Refert et horum quodlibet ad seipsum, ubi disputat naturaliter
esse multiplex, habere partes, esse totum aliquid atque unum caeteraque deinceps. Refert invicem et ad alia quando disserit hoc illi
simile vel dissimile caeteraque similiter.

which is understood to be in itself above essence, even when it is in the soul, does not undergo within itself opposite motions, nor opposite conditions.

: XCIX :

Fourth hypothesis. The purpose of the fourth hypothesis. The whole that precedes the parts, the whole that follows the parts, the divine realities, the natural realities, the relation of the parts with their whole.

As we have said elsewhere, the first three hypotheses, which con- 1
cerned the one rather than the others, first examined the one in relation to itself, then in relation to the others. Now the following hypotheses are five in number. The first two consider the others rather than the one, and examine their relation to the one in three ways: they consider every "other" partly in relation to the one, partly in relation to itself, and partly in relation to the rest of the others. So the fourth hypothesis, which we will now interpret, considers the others in three ways: it first postulates that the one being is subordinated to the absolute One (for the fourth hypothesis restates what has been said at the beginning) [157B8–9], and then shows that the others are not the absolute One, nor the one being that is closest to it, but the one that partakes of them [157C1–2]. Such is the way, therefore, that the fourth hypothesis compares the others with the one. It also compares every "other" with itself, when it states that by nature it is multiple, has parts, is a certain whole, one, and so on [157C–58C]. It then relates each "other" to the rest of the others when it states that it is like or unlike another, and so on [158D–59B].

2   Operae pretium fuerit reminisci quod alibi quoque diximus, hanc suppositionem quartam sub hoc nomine alia res speciesque naturales considerare, quae animas proximo quodam gradu sequuntur. Praeterea quemadmodum alibi declaravimus, intellectuales omnes rationalesque substantiae quorum in numero sunt et animae nostrae, quoniam ab aeterno principio, immo et ab ipso aevo maximeque uno proficiscuntur, tantum inde muneris habent ut aeterna quaedam in ipsis unitas eminenter multitudinem motumque exsuperet et origine quapiam antecedat. Sic igitur ab ipsa earum unitate sua intus profluit virium multitudo. Unde et ad se et ad causam convertuntur et a materia separatae sunt vel separabiles iudicantur. Simile quiddam divinitatis donum in naturalibus quoque formae substantiales speciesque, praecipue in hoc uno, saltem imitari videntur, quod substantialis specialisque forma multiplicium proprietatum suarum est origo, ut species ignis, lucem, calorem, siccitatem, acumen, levitatem, mobilitatem secum attulit, sed in hoc inde labitur, quemadmodum in *Theologia* nostra probavimus, quod esse suum existentiamque non quidem in essentia sua possident, sicut substantiae superiores habent, sed in composito comparant. Quapropter si compositionem eiusmodi cogitamus quatenus unum esse, ut ita dicam, totale ex forma simul materiaque consurgit, hoc totum ex partibus, hoc unum ex multitudine dicimus dependere, unifico scilicet superioris causae munere. Hac igitur ratione etiam quae videntur simplicia corpora componuntur et quod uniforme continuum multarum partium continuatione componitur et quod ex elementis mixtum ex multitudine quo-

It would be worth remembering, as we have also said elsewhere,   2
that the fourth hypothesis uses the term "others" to designate the
natural things and species, which come after the souls, at the next
level. In addition, as we have declared elsewhere, all the intellectual
and rational substances, including the human souls, proceed from
an eternal principle, or rather from a principle that is eternity itself
and "one" to the highest degree; so they receive a gift from this
principle and, as a result, possess within themselves a certain eternal unity, which eminently transcends multitude and motion, and
precedes them in origin. In this way, the multitude of forces flows
forth inwardly from the very unity proper to each substance. As a
result, they turn themselves toward both themselves and their
cause, and they are separate (or understood as separable) from
matter. It is a similar gift from the divinity that the substantial
forms and species within natural realities (especially at the level of
the one of the fourth hypothesis) seek at least to emulate, given
that the substantial and specific form of each reality is the origin
of its many properties (the species of fire, for instance, brings
along light, heat, dryness, sharpness, lightness, quickness), but
subsequently falls into this world, as we have shown in the *Theology*.[245] These substantial forms and species do not possess their
own being and existence within their essence, as the superior substances do, but receive them in the composite [that they form].
For this reason, when we consider a composition where a total being one, so to speak, emerges from the combination of form and
matter, we say that this whole depends on its parts, that this one
depends on multitude, that is to say, on the unifying power of its
superior cause. So even the bodies that seem simple are composed,
and what seems uniform and continuous is composed of the continuity of many parts, and what results from the mixture of elements is ultimately achieved, from the multitude that somehow

dammodo praecedente in unam denique formam totius absolvitur. Has itaque formas, haec continua, haec mixta, similiaque suppositio quarta considerat, in quibus totum ex partibus, unum dependet ex multitudine, sublimioris videlicet causae munere ac primi tandem principii potestate.

3 Proinde ars ubi ex pluribus perfecte suum opus absolvit unam quandam praeter plura figuram et formam vimque conficit, multo magis natura, tamquam unitatis divinae perpetuum instrumentum, ubi expedit motoris intentionem, unum aliquid praeter multa conflat ex multis, ut generationis terminus cum motoris unitate consentiat, utque sit opus unius artificis unum, ut denique unius operis una sit actio.

4 Summatim vero cum opera naturalia referimus ad ipsum simpliciter unum, extra controversiam opus eiusmodi iudicamus, cum aliud quiddam sit quam ipsum unum, iam esse non unum, id est esse multiplex aliquid atque numerosum, et quoniam dependet ab uno potenter in omnibus operante, unius particeps evasisse ideoque esse unum, non quidem divulsum vel imperfecte congestum, sed unum ex partibus per ipsius unius imperium ex perfecta partium conflatione progenitum.

5 Eiusmodi partes ad totum eiusmodi referuntur neque totum est, nisi constet ex partibus, neque vere sunt partes, nisi partes totius existant. Cum vero totum dicimus, aut novam quandam formam praeter numerum partium intelligimus, aut solum partium, sed hunc quidem universum, numerum cogitamus. Si prima totum ratione recipimus atque ad hoc ipsum unum partes comparamus ut partes, cum Parmenide consentimus; sin autem ratione

precedes it, in the unique form of the whole. So the fourth hypothesis considers these forms, some of which are continuous, some mixed, and so on; in these forms the whole depends on its parts and the one depends on its multitude, that is, on the gift of a more sublime cause and ultimately on the power of the supreme first principle.

As a result, when art perfectly achieves its work by unifying   3 multiple elements, it produces a certain figure, form and force which is one and transcends these multiple elements. It is even more the case that when nature, which is the eternal instrument of divine unity, executes the intention of the mover, it gathers multiple parts into a certain one that transcends these multiple parts; as a result, the limit of generation is in accordance with the unity of the mover; the work of the artisan who is one, is one; and finally the action of the work, which is one, is one.

In sum, when we compare natural creations with the absolute   4 One, we undoubtedly consider that given that a creation in nature is something other than the One, it is at once not-one, that is, it is something multiple and numerous, and because it depends on the One, which operates powerfully in all things, it partakes of the One and thus is one — not a one that is divided or imperfectly formed, but a one which results from parts, and which is generated from the perfect conflation of parts by virtue of the sovereignty of the One.

These parts are compared with their whole, and there is no   5 whole without parts and no real parts without a whole. By "whole" we either consider a new form beyond the number of parts, or we only envisage the number of parts (which is, however, universal).[246] If we take the term "whole" in the first sense, and compare the parts *qua* parts with the one that constitutes this whole, we agree with Parmenides. If, however, we take the term "whole" in

secunda, a Parmenide longius aberramus, quotiens partem aliquam ad eiusmodi totum referre conamur. Esto igitur eiusmodi totum quattuor partium numerus, accipio primam, quaero numquid pars haec prima dicenda sit pars totius, id est universae turbae. Si dicenda sit, sequetur ut sit pars uniuscuiusque quod connumeratur in turba. Non enim ad aliud hanc referre licet ut partem praeter quam ad ista quattuor, si semel concessum fuerit nihil omnino praeter partium turbam esse totum. Sequetur igitur quod modo dicebam, ut pars quaelibet accepta, si modo totius turbae sit pars, uniuscuiusque pars existat. Erit igitur pars quaelibet et sui ipsius pars et partis uniuscuiusque pars, quod est prorsus absurdum. Ut igitur et declinemus a falso et referre partem ad totum revera possimus, confitendum est praeter quattuor partium multitudinem formam unam totalemque existere, cuius quidem unius, quod cunctis pariter est commune, multa penes ipsum quaelibet partes esse dicantur. Usque adeo vero in rebus non discretis necessaria est haec praeter partes forma totius, ut Platonici in numeris quoque necessariam arbitrentur, putantes videlicet in ternario ultra particulares unitates eius ipsam speciem trinitatis existere, unitatis participem generalis. In caeteris quoque similiter. Non solum vero totum quodlibet unius esse particeps asserit, sed etiam partes singulas esse compotes unitatis, tum quia unitatis in toto communis sunt participes, tum etiam quia pars quaelibet et a qualibet distincta est differensque a toto. Itaque pars quaelibet rite dicitur unaquaeque, id est unum quiddam, in sua quadam proprietate ab alio differens. Quae quidem differentia ad unitatem necessario pertinet.

the second sense, we contradict Parmenides whenever we try to compare a part with such a whole. Let us suppose, for instance, that the whole is a number of four parts: if we take the first part, should this first part be said to be part of the whole, that is, of the total multitude? If so, it will consequently be a part of each element that composes the multitude. For it is impossible to relate this part, as a part, to something other than the four parts, since we have established that the whole is nothing else than the multitude of parts. So the consequence will be, as I just said, that any given part, if it is a part of the whole that constitutes the multitude, is part of each element of this whole. Each part will then be both a part of itself and part of each part, which is completely absurd. So, in order to avoid this error and to be able to relate the part to the whole truly, we must say that beyond the multitude of four parts there is a form which is one and total. Of this one, which is equally common to all, the multiple things that are within this one are said to be the parts. As a result, in the things that are not separate, there must be, beyond the parts, the form of the whole, just as the Platonists also consider necessary in the case of numbers — when they think, for example that in the number three there is, beyond the particular unities, the very species of this trinity, which partakes of the general unity.[247] The same goes for all the other numbers. But Parmenides not only says that each whole partakes of the one, but also that each part possesses a unity, both because they all partake of the unity within the whole and because each part is both distinct from the others and different from the whole. So each part is rightly called "each" [158A1–3], that is, a certain one, and differs from the rest by virtue of its own property. This difference necessarily pertains to unity.

: C :

De multitudine quomodo se habeat ad unum, de infinito et
termino entium elementis, de caeteris inter se oppositis.

1   Si fingas multitudinem prorsus unius expertem,[99] ut saepe probavimus, et tota multitudo infinita erit et pars quaelibet partisque
particula per infinitum erit pariter infinita. Sed numquid ita multitudinem licet fingere? Licet forte Parmenidi exactissima ratione consideranti rationem ipsam unius atque multitudinis esse
diversam, siquidem ad unius rationem necessario sequitur unio,
terminus, status, identitas, aequalitas, similitudo; ad ipsam vero
multitudinis rationem consequuntur opposita, divisio, infinitudo,
motus, alteritas, inaequalitas, dissimilitudo caeteraque id genus.
Quando vero multitudinem seorsum ab uno considerat, non multitudinem hanc vel illam, non multitudinem unitatum aliarumve
rerum quoquomodo certarum, non multitudinem hoc modo vel
illo se habentem, sed ipsam simpliciter multitudinem ac forte potentiam indefinite multiplicabilem et quomodolibet aliunde[100] formabilem, semper indifferenter se habentem ad suscipiendam multitudinem hanc aut illam modosque terminosque multiplices per
has formas motionesque vel illas. Parmenides ergo dum incertam
et quomodolibet vagabundam turbam auguratur et per seipsam
procul ab uno diversam unius nondum participem, merito infinite
prospicit infinitam, sed quoniam sub uno est efficaciter formare et
terminare potenter,[101] vaticinatur eandem[102] mox inde formas et
terminos subituram atque ita iam compositum quiddam effici ex
infinito terminoque commixtum. Qualia sunt quidem omnia prae-

: C :

How multitude relates to the one; on infinity and
limit as elements of beings; on all the others
which are opposed to one another.

As we have shown several times, if one imagines a multitude that   1
is completely deprived of unity, then the whole multitude will be
infinite and any part and particle of a part will equally be infinitely
infinite [158B–C]. But can we really imagine a multitude of that
kind? Parmenides might do, since he takes into account with the
most exacting logic that the rational principle of the one and that
of multitude are distinct. Indeed, union, limit, rest, sameness,
equality, likeness necessarily follow upon the rational principle of
the one, while their opposites, division, infinity, motion, otherness,
inequality, unlikeness, and so on follow upon the rational principle of multitude. When he considers multitude separately from
the one, he does not consider any particular multitude, nor any
multitude of unities or of other, particular things, nor any multitude that is in any particular disposition, but multitude as such,
and perhaps also the potentiality toward indefinite multiplication,
which receives its forms from another principle, and always accepts
indifferently various multitudes and multiple modes and limits
through various forms and motions. So when Parmenides sup-
poses the existence of an indeterminate and somehow wandering
multitude, which in itself is completely distinct from the one, and
does not yet partake of the one, he rightly presumes that it is infinitely infinite [158C]; however, because the acts of forming with
efficiency and limiting with power are under the one, he divines
that this infinitely infinite multitude will then receive forms and
limits from the one, and thus become a composite resulting from
the combination of infinity and limit [158C–D]. Such is the nature

ter primum; sed in rebus naturalibus quas nunc ad primum comparat, infinitudo praecipue praevalet et conditiones infinitudinem consequentes.

2   Hinc efficitur ut omnia naturalia in hoc saltem inter se conveniant, quod singula ex infinito terminoque conflantur. Conveniunt inquam per ipsum simul utriusque coniugium. Hoc enim coniugium est in cunctis. Interea vero quoniam haec duo invicem sunt opposita, eandem sustinent passionem, sive infinitatem spectes, sive terminum, sed quoniam duo haec inter se opposita sunt, merito diversitatem rebus afferunt, per quam unaquaeque et intra seipsam dissimilitudinem quandam patitur, partim quidem infinitatis ad terminum, partim etiam eorum quae consequuntur ad ista, et invicem res quaelibet ab aliis sit quoque diversa, quandoquidem etiam in se coniugium sustinet diversorum. Hinc enim et discordiae deinceps oriuntur et alia aliter utriusque participant.

3   Summatim vero ex isto infinitatis terminique coniugio, quae prima sunt entium elementa, caetera quoque oppositorum coniugia passim accidunt. Coniugia inquam in dissidendo, identitas, alteritas, similitudo, dissimilitudo, status, motus, aequalitas, inaequalitas, paritas, imparitas caeteraque deinceps. Horum quidem oppositorum alia infinitatem, alia terminum comitantur. Eiusmodi vero coniugia diversorum habent concordiamque discordem, discordiamve concordem, qualem canit Empedocles, quoniam unum quidem ipsum non sunt, sed interim sunt sub uno unumque participant.

of all things besides the first principle. However, infinity, as well as the conditions following upon infinity, are particularly prevalent in the natural realities, which he compares here with the first principle.[248]

As a result, all natural realities are at least in accordance with one another in the fact that each of them results from the combination of infinity and limit. They are in accordance, I say, by virtue of the union of these two principles taken simultaneously. For this union exists in all things. However, because these principles are opposites, they undergo the same passion, whether infinity or limit; but because these two principles are opposed to one another, they rightly bring diversity to things, whereby each thing within itself undergoes some unlikeness—in part that of infinity in relation to limit and in part too that of the things that are consequent upon those two principles—and in turn each thing is also distinct from the others, given that it also undergoes in itself a union of different things. For it is from this union of opposites that discords then arise and that natural realities each partake of these two principles in a different way.

In sum, from this union of infinity and limit, which are the first elements of beings, there also occur all the other unions of opposites. By "unions in disagreement," I mean [the opposition between] sameness and otherness, likeness and unlikeness, rest and motion, equality and inequality, even and odd, and so on.[249] Among these opposites some are associated with infinity, others with limit. These unions of distinct things also possess a discordant concord, or a concordant discord, as celebrated in Empedocles' poem,[250] because they are not the One itself, but they are under the One and partake of the One.

: CI :

Suppositio quinta. Quintae suppositionis intentio.
De uno, de aliis ab uno, utrum unum cum
his conveniat. De omniformi ente,
de informi materia.

1 Principio memoria repetendum est quod inter principia diximus: de uno ente atque de materia potissimum in suppositione quinta tractari, atque dum ad unum ens hic alia comparantur, hoc nomine alia materiam primam significari, quae quamvis unica sit tamen quasi sit plura non solum aliud, sed etiam alia nominatur, quoniam potentia formabilis est ad omnia. Locus interea suus artificio logico concedendus ut unum et alia pro arbitrio tractet, dummodo per haec argumentationum doceat consequentias. Itaque si forte hic tangat ipsum etiam simpliciter unum et alia cuncta summatim, verum fuerit quod in praesentia dicitur ipsum unum cum caeteris in nullo penitus convenire tamquam utrisque communi, alioquin non esset primum, simplicissimum, absolutum. Fuerit quoque verum ipsum unum nullas partes habere neque caeteris vel per totum vel per partes inesse. Caetera deinde, quemadmodum in praesentia digeruntur pro eruditione, ad logicam consequantur. Sub his lateat quoque mysterium quo intellegamus materiam primam ad unum ens et ad seipsam et ad caetera comparari.

2 Unum ens hic in primis accipe mundum intellegibilem, formam primam, uniformem et omniformem. Ad hunc materiam compara prorsus informem. Duo haec, etsi in hoc saltem forte conveniunt, quod utrumque suo quodam pacto participat ipsum simpliciter

: CI :

Fifth hypothesis. The purpose of the fifth hypothesis.
On the one and others that come from the one,
whether the one is in accordance with them. On
the omniform being, and on formless matter.

We must first recall what we said at the beginning: the fifth hy- 1
pothesis concerns particularly the one being and matter; when the
others are compared with the one being, the term "others" refers to
prime matter. Despite being one, prime matter is called both
"other" and "others" as if it were multiple, given its potentiality to
form all things.[251] But we also need to give the art of logic the
place it deserves, and let it use the terms "one" and "the others" as
it sees fit, since these are used to teach us the consequences of the
arguments. So, even if Parmenides mentioned here the absolute
One and all the others as a whole, what is presently being said
would hold true: the One is not in accordance with the others in
anything that would be common to both of them, otherwise the
One would not be the first, simplest and absolute principle [159B–
C]. It would also be true to say that the One has no parts and is
not in the others as a whole or as parts [159C]. All the other
propositions, which are presently set out for the sake of teaching,
would be the logical consequences of this conclusion;[252] behind
these propositions there could also be a mystery, which secretly
states that prime matter is to be compared with the one being in
relation to both itself and the others.[253]

Here the one being must primarily be understood as the intel- 2
ligible world, the uniform and omniform prime form, and it must
be compared with totally formless matter.[254] Even if both are in
accordance with one another, at least in the fact that each partakes

unum, non tamen in hoc conveniunt, tamquam communi quodam utrisque communicabili (extat enim supereminens absolutum), etsi forte convenire videntur quatenus utraque per unitatem
suam dependent ab ipso simpliciter uno ipsumque pro viribus
repraesentant.

3   Sed dimisso principii illius charactere utrisque, ut ita dixerim,
peregrino, utrumque sub ipsa sua proprietate considera: illud quidem penitus omniforme, hoc autem prorsus informe; omnino inter se videbis opposita atque tam diversa, ut neque quicquam illius
sit in isto, neque aliquid istius sit in illo, neque ambo rursus in
communi aliquo ente intellegibili formali conveniant. De illo quidem formae omnes formaliaque omnia simpliciter affirmantur. De
hoc autem eiusmodi cuncta rite negantur.

4   Ubi vero Parmenides inquit non esse quicquam praeter unum
et alia, si per unum, ut admonebam, mundum illum divinum acci-
pis omniformem, per alia vero mundum quoque materialem, certe
non est in ullo entium ordine aliud praeter ista. Sin autem per alia
informem materiam subintellegis, non est aliquid praeter ista, in
quo videlicet haec invicem in aliqua forma conveniant.

5   Praeterea quod dicitur unum non habere partes, si de uno ente
id dictum velis, dicito sicut ipsum simpliciter unum nullas simpliciter habet partes, ita nec ens unum essentiales partes habere, per
quas videlicet revera dici possit essentias in se plures habere, vel
essentiam in variis ideis segregabilem a seipsa. Summatim vero
negatur partes habere ut hinc intellegas intellegibilem mundum,
quando velut artifex et exemplar materiam formare censetur, neque se totum materiae mancipare neque quicquam naturae suae
communicare materiae, sed imagines potius atque umbras. Con-

in its own way in the absolute One, they are not in accordance in anything that would be common and communicable between them (for the One is super-eminent and absolute). They might, however, appear to be in accordance inasmuch as they both depend through their own unity on the absolute One and are each according to its ability an image of the One.

But let us leave aside the character of this principle, which is 3 alien, so to speak, to these two realities, and let us consider both the intelligible world and matter according to their own properties, the former completely omniform, the latter completely formless. You will see that they are completely opposed to one another and so distinct that nothing of the former is in the latter and nothing of the latter is in the former, and that the two have no intelligible formal being in common. Of the former all forms and formal qualities are openly asserted; of the latter all these are rightly denied [159D–60B].

But when Parmenides asserts that there is nothing beside the 4 one and the others [159B] — if, as I just suggested, one understands by "one" the divine, omniform world, and by "others" the material world — then Parmenides surely means that there is nothing else in any order of beings beside them. But if by "others" one understands formless matter, Parmenides means that there is nothing beside the intelligible world and the material world in which those others could harmonize in some form.

In addition, when it is said that the one has no parts [159C], if 5 you wish this to apply to the one being, say that just as the absolute One has simply no parts, so the one being has no essential parts whereby it could truly be said to have several essences within itself, or one essence that could divide itself into different Ideas. In sum, it is denied that the one has parts so that we understand that the intelligible world, when it is thought to form matter like an artisan and his model, does not totally subject itself to matter, and does not communicate anything of its own nature to matter, but

clude igitur, ubi dicitur alia, nec esse unum neque aliquid in se unum habere, materiam neque formale unum esse neque ipsius formalis unius speciem in se ullam naturaliter possidere.

: CII :

Confirmatio superiorum, et quomodo materia
formales in se conditiones nullas habeat.
Item unde sit vel formetur vel moveatur.

1   Sed haec iterum resumentes ad reliqua subinde pergamus. Si hinc quidem ipsum unum in ipsa sua eminentissima simplicitate consideremus, inde vero materiam in ipso mero primoque sui ipsius gradu solum inde (id est ab uno) pendentem, videbimus hanc aliquid illius habere vel ab illo. Utrumque enim et unicum est et simplex. De utroque negantur omnia,[103] quamvis de illo quidem per excessum, de hac autem per defectum. Inter utraque tamquam summum atque infimum omnia coercentur. Sin autem iterum contemplemur unum quodammodo ex sua illa eminentia simplicitateque descendere fierique protinus omniforme, quod unum ens Platonici nominant, iterumque ad hoc materiam conferamus, proculdubio deprehendemus hanc velut prorsus informem nihil in se omniformis illius habere neque inde ipso primo sui gradu pendere, si modo ipsius simpliciter unius imperium amplius quam potestas unius entis esse debet. Si quo vero pacto materia nondum formas

rather some images and shadows. So one should conclude that when it is said that the others are not one and do not possess any unity within themselves [159D], it means that matter is not a formal unity, and does not naturally possess within itself any species of this formal one.

: CII :

Confirmation of what has been said. How matter possesses no formal conditions within itself. Similarly, whence matter exists, is formed, and is moved.

Let us take up these questions one more time, and then pass on to the rest. If we consider, on the hand, the One in its most eminent simplicity and, on the other, matter, which in its pure and first degree solely depends on the One, we will see that it possesses something of, or from, the One. For both the One and matter are unique and simple. All things are denied of both of them, although they are denied of the One by excess, and of matter by defect.[255] All things are contained between these two extremes, which are the highest and the lowest limits of the universe. However, if we now consider that the One is leaving its eminence and simplicity and becoming at once omniform, which the Platonists call the one being, and if we now compare matter to this one being, we undoubtedly discover that matter, which is completely formless, does not possess anything of the omniform one within itself; at its first level it does not depend on it, since the sovereignty of the absolute One must extend further than the power of the one being. But if matter, which does not yet undergo forms, must in any way depend on the one being, surely it is not as being,

1

subiens ex uno ente pendet, certe, ut alibi diximus, non inde qua ratione illud est ens, sed qua unum potius pendere videtur.

2   Materia igitur non est aliquid unum formale, neque igitur formalia multa neque totum aliquod est, siquidem totum est forma quaedam. Neque partes totius habet neque pars formalis est alicuius totius quod sit formale, quandoquidem nihil intus formale naturaliter habet. Mitto quod Plotinus ait hanc nullius compositi revera partem fieri, sed imaginum ubique subiectum forte quasi speculum neque numerum proprium in se habet ullum, siquidem numerus in formali discretione consistit.

3   Praeterea cum similitudo dissimilitudoque ad formas qualitatesque pertineat, materia nondum formata nec uni enti nec ulli similis vel dissimilis iudicatur nec aequalis iterum nec inaequalis, si nondum acceperit quantitatem a se videlicet differentem, nec eadem neque diversa, siquidem identitas et alteritas formales quaedam ipsius unius entis differentiae sunt, quas materia nondum subiit nisi prius inde formata. Quapropter neque stat adhuc neque movetur, quippe cum status et motus formales sint proprietates entis et materia naturaliter utrisque[104] carens ad oppositos utriusque actus sit indifferens. Si nullum adhuc[105] ipsa motum habet, merito neque de non esse ad esse movetur neque vicissim. Quare neque nascitur neque perit. Nullum denique oppositorum vel simul naturaliter habet vel vicissim, non quidem simul, opposita enim in re prorsus individua et infima, quae illa conciliare non possit, simul coire non possunt, neque vicissim naturaliter habet opposita, siquidem et immutabilis est in se et formales in primo sui gradu conditiones et differentias non admittit neque numeros insuper vel differentias numerales, quippe cum haec omnia sint formalia.

but as one, that it appears to depend on it, as we have said else-where.

So matter is not a something that is formally one, and thus it is 2 neither a formal multiplicity nor a whole something, since a whole is a certain form. It has no parts of a whole and is not a formal part of a formal whole, since it does not possess within itself any-thing that is naturally formal. I need hardly mention that Plotinus says that matter does not truly become the part of any composite, but is everywhere the receptacle of images, like a mirror, perhaps, and it does not possess within itself any proper number, since number consists in formal distinction.[256]

In addition, since likeness and unlikeness pertain to forms and 3 qualities, matter, which has not yet been formed, is considered not to be like or unlike the one being or any being, nor equal or un-equal, since it has not yet received quantity, which is different from itself, nor the same or the other, since sameness and otherness are formal differences which pertain to the one being, and which mat-ter does not undergo before it has been formed by the one being. For this reason, matter is not yet at rest nor in motion, since rest and motion are formal properties of being; so matter, which is by nature devoid of both rest and motion, is indifferent toward the opposite acts of rest and motion. Since it is not yet in motion, it is fair to say that it does not move from not-being to being and con-versely. So it does not come to be or cease to be. Finally, it does not naturally possess any of the opposites, whether taken together at once or one after the other. It does not possess them together at once, for opposites cannot be united in a reality that is completely undivided and at the lowest level, and that cannot bring together these opposites; it does not naturally possess opposites taken one by one, since matter is immutable in itself; at its first level it ad-mits no formal conditions and differences, and besides it admits no numbers or numeric differences, since all these are formal [159D–60B].

4　　Materia denique sua quidem natura, si qua modo natura dicenda est, nec unitatem habet neque formam neque motum, sed ab ipso simpliciter uno mox inde procedens[106] sortita est unitatem, deinde vero ab uno ente formas, tertio tandem ab anima motus. Si vero mens prima et anima mundi ad ipsam materiae unitatem existentiamque conducunt, non tamen ut mens vel anima, sed ut unum quiddam ipsiusque quod unum est simpliciter instrumentum. Putant vero materiam ut informem produci ab uno, derivatam scilicet per infinitatem quae in mundo intelligibili vel etiam animali proportionalis est materiae. Dicitur etiam unum ex infinitate materiam derivare. Haec vero ex opinione scholae Platonicorum communioris dicta fuerint.

: CIII :

Sexta suppositio. Sextae suppositionis intentio, et quomodo
Parmenides poeticus. Item de ente atque non ente.

1　Parmenides non philosophus tantum, sed etiam poeta divinus, carminibus philosophica mysteria cecinit atque in hoc dialogo agit quoque poetam. Novenarium enim quasi poeta colit numerum Musis, ut dicitur, consecratum. Per novem sane suppositiones quasi per novem Musas scientiae duces ad veritatem Apollinemque nos ducit. Dum enim ad ipsum provehit simpliciter unum, ad Apollinem promovere videtur. Quo nomine Pythagorici sui solent ipsum simpliciter unum mystice designare, quippe cum Apollo, ut Platonici quoque cum Platone docent, absolutorem significat simplicem a multitudine segregatum. Interea ut exactius poetam agat

Finally, by its own nature (if one is to speak of "nature") matter 4
has no unity, no form, no motion, but in its procession from the
absolute One it directly receives unity, then forms from the one
being, and thirdly and finally, it receives motion from the soul. But
if the prime mind and the world soul infuse unity and existence
into matter, they do not, however, do so as mind or soul, but as a
certain one and as the instrument of the absolute One. Some
think that matter, being formless, is created by the One, that matter is derived from the One by virtue of infinity, which in the intelligible or even the psychic world is proportional to matter. It is
also said that the One derives matter from infinity. But let these
words be said in accordance with the opinion of the most common
Platonic school.[257]

: CIII :

*Sixth hypothesis. Purpose of the sixth hypothesis. In what
way Parmenides is poetic. On being and not-being.*

Parmenides was not only a philosopher, but also a divine poet, 1
who sang of philosophical mysteries in his poems. He also acts as
a poet in this dialogue. For it is as a poet that he celebrates the
number nine, which is traditionally consecrated to the Muses.
Surely it is by way of nine hypotheses, as if they were the nine
Muses who are guides to knowledge, that he leads us to truth and
Apollo. For as he moves toward the absolute One, he seems to
move toward Apollo. It is by this name "Apollo" that his Pythagorean colleagues often designate mystically the absolute One, since
Apollo, as the Platonists and Plato also teach us, means the simple
Separator devoid of multitude.[258] In addition, he acts in a more
precise way as a poet when he uses words in different senses; for

nominum sensus variat, hoc nomen unum alibi aliter introducens, ac passim varia sentit in caeteris plerumque. Simili quadam ratione versutus fingit etiam nonnumquam, ut poeta. Non enim sola quae sunt asserit, sed etiam quae non sunt saepe confingit, illa quinetiam quae esse non possunt. Poetica sane licentia frequenter aggreditur paradoxa. Alia frequenter aliorum nominibus occulit. Delectatur saepe metaphoris, quibus aliena significanter ad alia transfert. Quisnam praeter poetam individuae naturae figuram dederit, aeternae motum? Poeta solus animadversionem sui sphaeram vocitat. Itaque ferme omnis verborum facies poscit allegoriam. Quas ob res Plato in *Theaeteto* nos monuit opportune ut caveremus ne forte in hoc dialogo sua nos arte deluderet, dum et res et ipsa verba aliter quam ipse sentiat et loquatur accipiamus. Verum quidnam dialectico cum poeta commercii? Certe quam plurimum. Utrique enim atque soli circa suos, ut aiunt, conceptus et propria machinamenta versantur, habentur utrique divini et habent nescio quid furoris.

2   Sed ad institutum iam pergamus. Hactenus quinque suppositiones, si unum sit, peregit, deinceps vero quattuor, si unum non sit, adiunget. In superioribus igitur nomen hoc unum quasi poeta multifariam introducens, primo quidem disseruit, si unum super ens existit, ipsum nullum entium prorsus existere idque munus in eo coluit ut venerandum. Satius enim luci est extra colores existere quam inesse coloribus. Deinde, si unum est in ente, ipsum esse essentia cuncta probavit. Tertio, si unum non solum in ente, sed etiam sub ente sit, omnia esse pariter atque non esse. Quarto et

instance, he uses the term "one" in different senses throughout the dialogue, and often the meaning of words varies in different passages. For the same reason, Parmenides acts as a poet whenever he has recourse to wit and imagination, for he not only asserts the existence of the things that are, but also often imagines the existence of those that are not, and even those that cannot be. Surely it is by poetic license that he often introduces paradoxes, and repeatedly disguises one thing under the name of another. He often delights in metaphors, when he uses the names of certain things to allude to others. Who, besides a poet, would attribute "shape" to undivided nature, and "motion" to eternal nature? Only a poet calls self-consciousness a sphere.[259] So nearly every verbal surface requires an allegorical interpretation. For this reason, Plato has appropriately warned us in the *Theaetetus* lest we be deceived in this dialogue by Parmenides' art and interpret the words differently from Parmenides' very intention.[260] But what dealings do a poet and a dialectician have in common? Clearly almost everything. For both are alone in using their own concepts, so to speak, and their own devices; both are considered divine and both possess a form of madness.[261]

But let us return to our subject. So far Parmenides has consid- 2 ered in the first five hypotheses that the one is; he will now consider in the four following hypotheses what happens if we postulate that the one is not. Therefore, when he introduced in the first hypotheses the word "one," and gave it several different meanings, in the manner of a poet, he first asserted that if the One beyond being is, then it is none of the beings, and he celebrated this venerable power within the One, for it is better for light to be beyond colors than within colors. He then demonstrated that if there is a one coordinate with being, then it is all things by essence. Thirdly, if the one is not only coordinate with, but also inferior to, being, then all things both are and are not.[262] In the fourth and the fifth hypotheses he compared the others to the one — the One that

quinto caetera comparavit ad unum et quod superens et quod in ente consistit, praecipue vero ad unum quod in ente.

3   Post haec, quasi licere omnia poetis existimans, non solum fingit non esse unum, quod quidem necessario[107] esse putat, sed etiam postquam non esse finxit, quaeritat quidnam accidat uni, perinde ac si ei quod non est, aliquid possit accidere. Sed interea nihil temptat inepte. Praeterea cum non ignoret opposita versari circa idem, in hac suppositione sexta pariter atque septima et octava et nona ficturus non esse unum, non repetit illud simpliciter unum ad quod non pertinet esse, cum longe sit praestantius quam essentia, sed unum post hoc potius ad quod iam attinet esse, de quo probabilius oppositum, id est non esse, licet fingere.

4   Hic igitur atque deinceps praecipue quaeritur, si non sit illud unum quod est in entibus, id est intellectualibus divinisque substantiis, quidnam inde contingat, neque vero ausus est, ut dixi, primum unum e medio tollere. Licentius enim potuit secundum unum tamquam aliunde profectum et idcirco per se nequaquam existens fingere, quoquomodo non esse, atque hoc quomodolibet non existente nonnihil inferius introducere quod interim a primo dependeat. Ineptissimum vero fuisset vel negare primum, quod est ipsa necessitas existendi, vel illo utcumque negato ulterius aliquid somniare. Sic ergo negavit ut figmentum suum, hyperbolicum quidem, foret non ineptum.

is beyond being and, above all, the one that is coordinate with being.

The following hypotheses are characterized by poetic license, for Parmenides not only imagines that the one does not exist (even though he considers that the One necessarily exists), but after having imagined that the One does not exist, he examines what results for the one, as if something could result for something that does not exist [160B]. Yet Parmenides is not being facetious when he makes these propositions. In addition, since he is aware that opposites concern the same term, and in order to be able to postulate that the one does not exist in the sixth, seventh, eighth and ninth hypotheses, he does not use the absolute One, which does not concern being, since it is by far superior to essence, but he rather chooses the one that comes after the absolute One, which is reached by being, and about which someone could more plausibly imagine an opposite, i.e. not-being.   3

Therefore, in this hypothesis and those that follow, Parmenides examines specifically what the consequences are if the one that is in beings, that is, the intellectual and divine substances, does not exist. However, as I have said, Parmenides does not dare remove the first One completely from consideration. For he might have taken greater license in imagining that the second one, which proceeds from another and thus does not exist by itself, does not exist somehow, and, having postulated that this one does not exist, he could introduce some inferior principle which would still depend on the first principle. But it would have been utterly foolish to deny the existence of the first principle, which is the necessary condition of existence itself, or, after having indeed denied its existence, to dream up some principle beyond that One. So that is why he denied the existence of the one being, so that his thought experiment, which was, to be sure, hyperbolical, would not turn out to be foolish as well.   4

5   Fingit denique in hac suppositione sexta unum ens, id est naturam intellectualem, ita non esse ut partim quidem sit, partim vero
non sit. In septima vero licentius finget omnino non esse, quid
utrimque sequatur absurdi facile deprehensurus.

: CIV :

Quomodo unum, dum dicitur non ens, possit etiam
quodammodo ut ens intellegi, et quomodo non
ens eiusmodi cognoscatur et de anima.

1   Logicus in propositione subiectum ponit et praedicatum. In hac
enim propositione 'unum non est,' quasi subiectum quidem est
'unum,' praedicatum vero 'non est,' ac si resolvatur in non ens,
quasi dicatur unum est non ens. Compone igitur propositionem
aliam eiusmodi: 'non unum non est,' haec utique videtur illi contraria, primo quidem quia subiectum ibi est ipsum unum, hic vero
non unum, quae sunt contraria vel contradictoria invicem, deinde
quia sensus earum inter se repugnant. Prima enim unum quodammodo e medio tollit; secunda omnino reducit in medium.
Conferamus iterum non propositiones quidem totas invicem, sed
subiecta, id est 'unum' ad 'non unum,' certe subiectum hoc oppositum est illius. Dum enim dicimus 'unum,' nondum ipsum ex universa rerum natura sustulimus, dum vero 'non unum,' iam deie-
cimus. Igitur in subiecto propositionis primae unum nondum

Finally, in this sixth hypothesis he imagines that the one being, 5
that is, the intellectual nature, does not exist in such a way that it
partly exists and partly does not; in the seventh hypothesis, he will
imagine with more audacity that the one is absolutely not. This
will allow him to apprehend easily the absurd consequences that
result in both cases.[263]

: CIV :

*How the one, when it is said not to be, can also
be in some way understood as being, and how
this not-being can be known; on the soul.*

In each proposition the logician postulates a subject and a predi- 1
cate: in the proposition "the one is not," the subject is "the one"
and the predicate is "is not." "Is-not" translates into not-being, as
though the proposition means "the one is not-being." Then compose another proposition like this: "not-one is not": this proposition seems entirely contrary to the preceding one, firstly because in
the first case the subject is the one, in the second, the not-one, and
these are contrary or contradictory [160B]; secondly, because these
propositions have opposite meanings: the first proposition in some
way removes the one from consideration; the second brings it back
in. Again, if we compare the subjects of these propositions, i.e. the
one and the not-one, rather than the propositions as a whole, we
can surely see that these subjects are opposed to one another:
when we say "one" we have not yet removed it from universal nature, but when we say "not-one" we have already removed it. Thus
in the subject of the first proposition, the one has not yet been

ablatum est neque ut indefinitum prorsus excogitatur, sed tamquam ratio quaedam differens a non ente, quandoquidem nondum illi non ens adiunximus, et quando subdimus, tamquam aliud addimus, immo ipsum unum potius tamquam aliud introducimus. Similiter quando dicimus 'si magnitudo non est,' ipsam magnitudinem velut aliud quam unum et aliud quam non ens proferimus, et utrobique, dum sub conditione pronuntiamus dicendo 'si unum non est,' 'si magnitudo non est,' declaramus aliud esse unum vel magnitudinem quam non ens. Affirmare igitur hic nonnihil forte videbimur, aliquid interim cognoscendo, ipsam scilicet per se rationem ipsius unius, tamquam differens aliquid ab aliis atque non ente. Ipsa igitur unius ratio in se proprium aliquid est et excogitabile quiddam ab aliis et a non ente distinctum. Prius enim secundum se est ipsa unius ratio quam addatur sibi ratio essendi vel non essendi vel ratio quaevis alia, ac dum illi non esse subiungimus, interim intellegimus quid sit ipsum in se de quo non ens praedicamus et quo differat a non ente vel aliis. Cum igitur dum dicimus 'si unum non est,' certo quid loquamur intellegamus, videmur interea scientiam quandam ipsius unius et ipsius non entis et nunc positae conditionis habere. Quamobrem si unum hoc pacto non est, ut etiam quodammodo sit certamque sui nobis offerat rationem, nimirum et aliqua eius scientia est.

2   Operae pretium fuerit animadvertere, si ipsum simpliciter unum quandoque fiat unum ens, statim intellegibile intellectumque simul evadere. Rursum si hoc unum ens intellegibile intellectuale declinet etiam quodammodo in non ens, dum ita motum tempusque primum subit, in animam transformari. Hac ergo commuta-

suppressed and is considered as a rational principle that differs from not-being, rather than as an indefinite one, since not-being has not yet been added to it; when we apply not-being to it, we add not-being as something that is other than the one, or rather we introduce the one as something that is other. Likewise when we say "if greatness is not" [160C], we speak of greatness itself, as something other than the one and other than not-being; in both cases, when we thus formulate the propositions "if the one is not," or "if greatness is not," we state that the one, or greatness, is other than not-being. Thus here we will appear to be asserting something, but at the same time we know another thing: i.e., that the very rational principle of the one is something different from others and from not-being. So the rational principle of the one is something proper in itself, something that can be conceived of as distinct from others and from not-being. Indeed, the very rational principle of the one exists in itself, before having the rational principle of being, that of not-being, or any other rational principle added to it; when we add not-being to the one, we understand the way in which the nature of that about which we predicate not-being differs from not-being and from other things. Thus, since we clearly understand what we mean when we say "if the one is not," we also possess, it seems, some kind of knowledge of the one, of not-being and of the condition that has just been postulated. For this reason, if the one is not, in such a way that it also *is* in another way, and provides us with a certain rational principle of itself, then there is a knowledge of this one [160C–E].

It would be worth noting that whenever the absolute One becomes the one being, it becomes at once the intelligible and the intellect. Likewise, if this intelligible and intellectual one being also falls in some way into not-being, and thus undergoes prime motion and time, it transforms itself into the soul. So it is through

2

tione, dum pro intellectu et intellegibili summo iam sublato regnat anima, omnia post hac in universo mobilia fore, stabilia sub anima nusquam, siquidem anima, per motum naturaliter agens, efficit ubique mobilia. Sed de hoc si opportunum fuerit in sequentibus. Si rursus unum ens in non ens omnino mutetur, iam anima pereunte, deinceps mobilia insuper cessatura, sed similiter de hoc in posterum. Satis vero in praesentia fuerit reminisci Parmenidem in hac suppositione sexta, dum multas unius quodammodo entis et quodammodo non entis conditiones prosequitur, conditiones animae prosequi. Quomodo[108] vero anima non ens in seipsa cum ente permisceat in suppositione tertia satis aperuisse videmur. Ibi quidem aeternam et temporalem animae partem pariter introduxit, hic autem potius declinat ad temporalem, sed in hac quoque parte, ubi ad non ens propter fluxum degenerare[109] videtur, probat interim omnes ferme entis conditiones habere. Tanta est primi motus et temporis excellentia atque oppositorum in anima tantum permixta natura! In hac ergo suppositione quod maxime convenit animae oppositis opposita miscet motumque prosequitur et partim quidem affirmat, partim vero negat, quemadmodum fecit in tertia.

this mutation, whereby the soul governs in lieu of the supreme intellect and the intelligible, which have been suppressed, that all the things that come after the soul in the universe will be in motion (as there are no things at rest at the level of the soul), since the soul, which acts naturally through motion, always creates things in motion. But let us talk of this in what follows, if time permits. Again, if the one being completely transforms itself into not-being, then the soul will cease to exist and things in motion will also cease to exist—but we will also talk about this later. Let it suffice for the moment to remember that when Parmenides examines in the sixth hypothesis the many conditions of the one that in one way is being and in another not-being, he is describing the conditions that are proper to the soul. The way in which the soul mixes not-being and being within itself we have sufficiently explained, it seems, in our interpretation of the third hypothesis. However, there Parmenides had introduced both the eternal and the temporal parts of the soul alike, while here he rather descends into the temporal part. But in this part too, where the soul seems to degenerate into not-being because of the flux it undergoes, he shows that the soul possesses almost all the conditions of being. So great is the excellence of the first motion and first time, so mixed within the soul is the nature of opposites! Thus in this hypothesis, which concerns above all the soul, he mixes opposites together with opposites, he tries to describe motion, and he uses both assertions and negations, just as he had done in the third hypothesis.

: CV :

Quomodo unum, quod dicitur non ens, sit natura
animae; qua ratione mobilis est, de hoc non
ente est scientia; huic competunt alteritas et
multitudo et signa indicativa.

1 Dum in hac suppositione similiterque in caeteris latentia passim
mysteria investigas, disce interim artificium sagacissimum, quo et
consequentiae mirabiliter contexuntur et quodlibet non ex cogna-
tis solum, sed ex oppositis confirmatur. Exactissime singula discernuntur, cuncta feliciter inveniuntur in singulis, ut quasi quodlibet
ex quolibet, quod Anaxagoras promiserat, reportetur. Esto igitur
ubique sollers atque sagax. Esto logicus pariter atque philosophus.
Sic admonitus ad reliqua perge.

2 De hoc animali non ente veritas quaedam est in ipsa universali
natura rationibusque formalibus. Convenit huic et alteritas etiam
(ita non enti, ita scilicet fluitanti), per quam hoc et aliud sit quam
caetera, et alia sit motus temporisque conditio in hoc, alia sit in
aliis.

3 Platonici quotiens esse et ens pronuntiant, nisi aliud addiderint,
stabile intellegunt et aeternum. Hic igitur, dum de natura vel actu
animae mobili ens negatur et esse, intellege non quodlibet ens aut
esse negatum, sed aeternum. Quamvis autem hac ratione non
conveniat ei ens et esse verum, id est aeternum, esse tamen et ens
competit temporale cum quodam non esse et non ente permix-

: CV :

*How the one, which is said to be not-being, is the soul's
nature; its principle of motion; that there is knowledge
of this not-being; otherness, multitude, and
indicative signs that pertain to it.*[264]

As we explore the hidden mysteries in this hypothesis and all the　1
others, we should also learn the way in which the consequences of
each proposition are admirably interwoven, and the existence of
every being is not only confirmed by the existence of the elements
that are akin to it, but also by that of its opposites. This is
achieved through an art that is utterly brilliant. Each reality is
distinguished with the greatest precision, and all realities are felici-
tously found in each of them, so that one may despoil, as Anaxagoras predicted: "anything from anything else."[265] Be always cun-
ning and wise; be both a logician and a philosopher. With this
advice in mind, let us proceed.

Regarding the soul's not-being we can find some truth within　2
the very nature of the universe and its formal rational principles.[266]
Otherness is also consistent with soul (and so with not-being, i.e.
its state of flux); by this otherness it is something other than everything else, and the condition of motion and time is one thing in
this one and something else in other things [160B–D].

Whenever the Platonists mention the terms "act of being" and　3
"being," they mean something that is stable and eternal (unless
they add something else to it). So here, when being and the act of
being are negated of the soul's moving nature and act [160B–C],
we should understand that what is negated is eternal being rather
than any indeterminate being or act of being. However, whereas
on this account the true, or eternal, being and act of being do not
befit the soul, on the other hand the temporal act of being and

tum. Nam in hac ipsa temporali mobilique affectione duo quaedam consideramus, mobilitatem scilicet ipsam et stabilem insuper vigorem, quo regitur, perpetuumque tenorem. Quantum ad stabilitatem eiusmodi permixtam motui pertinet, ens similiterque non ens dici potest; quantum vero spectat ad fluxum, non ens potius appellatur, neque[110] potest ei ens et esse eadem ipsa fluxus ipsius ratione competere. Hac tamen ratione dici multiplex rite potest. Est enim unum multa et multitudo quaedam una. Appellare et hac ratione licet hoc aliquid unum, et quandam multitudinem huius quoque et huic esse fluxum, et cum non quaelibet de hoc uno negentur, sed ens dumtaxat, et hoc quidem aeternum atque verum, nihil prohibet interim huic alia multa competere, alioquin neque diceretur vel cogitaretur ut unum vel ut multiplex vel ut mobile, neque loqui de ipso possemus.

: CVI :

Circa hoc unum non ens existunt dissimilitudo, similitudo, inaequalitas, aequalitas, magnitudo, parvitas, essentia quodammodo, et de anima.

1   Hanc mobilitatem in anima vere dicimus esse ab aliis admodum differentem, ab aliis quidem quae stabilia sunt omnino, quia statui motus opponitur, ab aliis quoque mobilibus, quoniam anima per se mobilis, alia aliunde moventur. Recte itaque iudicamus eam aliis esse dissimilem per dissimilitudinem, scilicet mobilitati eiusmodi

being, which are mingled with some act of not-being and not-being, do. For in the soul's temporal and mobile disposition we consider the two following elements: the energy for both mobility and stability, by which it is governed, as well as its perpetual continuity of action. As far as concerns the soul's stability, which is mixed with motion, being and not-being alike can be asserted of it; but when we consider its flux, the soul is rather called "not-being," nor can being and the act of being befit the soul on the same principle as flux does. Conversely, for the same reason the soul can rightly be said to be multiple, for the one [within the soul] is multiple and any multitude is one, and for this reason it may also be called "this something that is one," and we can attribute a certain multitude "of it" and a flux "to it" [160E]. And since not everything is denied of the [soul's] one, but only eternal and true being, nothing prevents it from having many other attributes, otherwise it would not be said or thought of as one, multiple or in motion, and we could not talk about it [161A].

: CVI :

Unlikeness, likeness, inequality, equality, greatness, smallness, and essence in a certain sense exist in respect of this one not-being. On the soul.

It is true to say that the mobility in the soul is completely different   1
from other entities—from other entities that are completely at rest, because motion is opposed to rest, and from others that are in motion, because the soul is in motion in itself, while others are moved by another. For this reason, we rightly consider that the soul is unlike the others by virtue of unlikeness, which pertains to this kind of mobility. However, by virtue of the same

competentem. Qua vero ratione distinguitur a caeteris eadem proprietate sibimet congruit estque simile, alioquin sua ipsa proprietate careret.

2   Post haec negat aequalitatem et merito. Mobilitas enim animae non est aequalis aequalitate vera, id est aequalitate stabili penitus et aeterna. Non est aequalis aliis, scilicet substantiis prorsus aeternis, quae revera iudicantur aequales, semper videlicet aequabiliter se habentes, alioquin si ipsa mobilitas animae veram haberet aequalitatem, vere esset veramque similitudinem possideret. Neque rursus aequalis est omnino caeteris temporalibus, cum natura sit admodum excellentior. Cum igitur qua ratione mobilitas differens iudicatur, eadem sit etiam inaequalis, nimirum propter inaequalitatem cum maior dicitur, tum vero minor, et quoniam maius atque minus, propter oppositionem valde distantia, medium quiddam, id est aequalitatem quandam, exigunt, merito et mobilis ipsa conditio, dum a minori crescit in maius vel vicissim, in aliquam aequalitatem interim videtur incidere—non inquam aequalitatem veram, scilicet permanentem, sed fluentem et cum fluxu quodam vel parte fluxus pariter comparabilem. Quapropter uni huic animali (ita non enti, id est fluenti) competit inaequalitas, aequalitas, parvitas, magnitudo, similitudo, dissimilitudo, alteritas.

3   Competit eidem Quodammodo et essentia, et merito. Quae enim dicebamus entis ipsius differentiae quaedam existimantur. Praeterea quando de uno hoc mobili non ens praedicamus et reliqua superius enarrata, verum cogitamus et loquimur. Si verum, igitur id quod est. Verum enim et ens invicem convertuntur. Unum itaque hoc vere est non ens atque est hoc ipsum verum in universali natura formalibusque rationibus, scilicet unum hoc non

property that distinguishes it from the others, it is in accordance with, and like, itself, otherwise it would lack its very own property [161A–C].

Parmenides then denies equality of the one, and rightly so, 2 [161C], for the soul's mobility is not equal, that is, it does not come about by virtue of true equality, which is completely at rest and eternal. It is not equal to the others that are eternal substances, which are truly considered equal, given that they are always equally disposed — otherwise, if the very mobility of the soul possessed true equality, it would truly be and would possess true likeness. Nor again is it equal to the rest of the temporal substances, since by nature it is far superior to them. Therefore, for the very reason mobility is considered its differentia, it is also considered unequal, and assuredly by virtue of inequality it is said to be greater or smaller. And since "greater" and "smaller," as opposites set apart from one another, require a mean, that is, an equality, it is right that this condition of mobility, as it increases from being smaller to being greater or conversely, at some point seems to fall into equality — and I do not mean true, permanent, equality, but that which is flowing, and is comparable to some flux or part of flux alike [161D–E]. For this reason, inequality, equality, smallness, greatness, likeness, unlikeness and otherness pertain to the one at the level of the soul, which is not-being in the sense that it is flowing.

Essence also pertains in a certain sense to this same one, and 3 rightly so, [161E], for the things we mentioned are considered as differentiae with respect to being. In addition, when we assert not-being and the other attributes mentioned above of this one in motion, we think and talk about something that is true, and if it is true, it is something that is, for truth and being are [metaphysically] convertible [161E–62A].²⁶⁷ For this reason, this one is really not-being, and is this very truth within universal nature and its formal rational principles. In other words, this one is a nonexistent

esse ens, scilicet non esse ens perfectum. Unum igitur hoc ita est non ens ut sit quodammodo alicuius essentiae particeps, alioquin, si auferas hoc ipsum verum, hoc ipsum esse, quo dicitur esse non ens, falsum certe loquemur, quando unum non esse dixerimus. Veridica igitur confirmatio quando praedicatur non ens de hoc uno est ipsum esse, scilicet ut sit non ens. Ratio enim confirmativa entis est non esse non ens, ratio vero confirmativa non entis est esse non ens. Vinculum ergo per quod cum uno non ens subnectitur est quoddam esse. Si hoc sit integrum esse, non conectet unum cum non ente, sed cum ente perfecto. Sin autem nullo modo sit, conectet praedicabitve nihil. Est ergo quoddam esse remissum per quod de uno non ens praedicare licet.

4   Hoc interim ens quod non entis est particeps, et rursus hoc non ens quod entis est compos est ipsa natura, ut diximus, animae, penes quam status motui motusque statui commiscetur atque hoc ipsum quod in ea est unum mobile, partim quidem propter fluxum non ens appellatur, partim vero propter tenorem quendam in motu vicissim similiter restitutum ens recte vocatur.

: CVII :

Circa hoc unum non ens existunt esse atque
non esse, motus, alteratio, interitus atque
horum opposita, et de anima.

1   In motu[111] animae, qualem descripsimus alibi, praeteritum et futurum invicem opponuntur ut simul esse non possint. Praesens quoque nec amplius praeteritum habet necdum futurum. In eius-

being, the perfection of its being is not to exist [162A]. So this one is not-being in such a way that it participates in some way in essence; otherwise, if one removes this very truth, this very act of being whereby it is said to be not-being, it would be false when we said that the one is not. That we can predicate not-being of this one is truly confirmed by its very act of being, that is, the fact that it *is* not-being. For the reason that confirms the existence of being is *not to be* not-being, while the reason that confirms the existence of not-being *is to be* not-being. So the link that connects not-being with the one is a certain act of being. If this act of being is unmixed, it will not link the one with not-being, but with perfect being; if it does not exist at all, it will connect and predicate nothing. There exists, therefore, a kind of remission of the act of being whereby it is possible to predicate not-being of the one.

This being which partakes of not-being, and again this not-being, which is in possession of being, constitute the very nature of the soul, as we said, where rest is mixed with motion and motion with rest, and that which in the soul is the one in motion, is partly called not-being because it is in flux, and partly — and rightly — called being because of a certain continuity it maintains when in motion [161E–62B].

4

: CVII :

The acts of being and not-being, motion, alteration,
dissolution, and their opposites exist in respect
of this one not-being. On the soul.

In the soul's motion, as we have described elsewhere, past and future times are opposed to one another, so that they cannot exist simultaneously. In addition, present time no longer possesses past

1

modi motu temporeque varios, ut supra diximus, habitus anima in seipsa commutat. Qui sane habitus simul omnes esse non possunt, et cum hic quidem est praesens, iste iam est praeteritus, ille futurus. Hac igitur ratione anima vicissim est atque non est quodammodo mutatione perpetua atque necesse est hoc unum mobile, si est atque non est, successione quadam duo haec perpeti ideoque moveri.

2   Videtur etiam alia ratione moveri non posse, siquidem mutari non possit. Hoc enim unum mobile, qua ratione fluitans, non est in ipso entium ordine constitutum. Haec enim omnia stabilia sunt. Nequit igitur ex ente in ens aliquod permutari, ex aeterno videlicet in aeternum. Non igitur hoc pacto mutatur neque hac conditione movetur.

3   Non solum vero eiusmodi motus quasi rectus de hoc uno negatur, sed etiam circularis. Circularis namque perfectus, qualis puro competit intellectui, in ipsa identitate versatur. Ipsa vero identitas, ad ens perfectum et stabile pertinens, fluxui huic animali non convenit, neque rursus huic competit alteratio, tanta ut ab ipsa natura sua et proprietate discedat. Per rationes quidem superiores moveri videtur, per sequentes vero quiescere, et utrumque suo quodam pacto verum. Denique qua ratione permanet scilicet in natura sua, eadem nec alteratur ab ipsa. Qua vero habitus quosdam vicissim commutando movetur, eadem alteratur in habitu; atque ita priores quidem habitus exuens, posteriores autem induens, occidere videtur atque renasci, sed rursum proprietatem sibi naturalem nec nuper accipiens nec aliquando deserens, neque fit umquam neque perit.

time nor yet future time. During motion and time like this the soul changes within itself, as we have said, from one disposition to another. These dispositions cannot exist simultaneously: one is in the present, another is already in the past, and a third one is in the future. For this reason the soul both is and is not in alternation, in perpetual change, as it were, and if this one in motion is and is not, it must necessarily undergo these two conditions successively, and is thus in motion [162B–C].

By yet another line of reasoning, it appears that it cannot be in motion, since it cannot be changed. For this one in motion, because it is in flux, does not belong to the order of beings, for all beings are at rest. Thus it cannot exchange one being for another, that is to say, it cannot be changed from one eternal being to another eternal being. From this point of view, therefore, it does not undergo any alteration and in this condition it is not in motion [162C–D].

Not only is straight motion denied of this one, but also circular motion. For perfect circular motion such as that which pertains to pure intellect concerns sameness. Yet sameness, which concerns being that is perfect and at rest, does not befit the soul's flux; and alteration does not befit it either, since it would result in the soul being separate from its own nature and property. By virtue of the first reasons, it appears to be in motion, but by virtue of the second reasons, it appears to be at rest [162D–E], and both propositions are true in their own way. Finally, for the reason that it remains within its nature, it is not changed by it, whereas for the reason that it is in motion by passing from one disposition to another, the soul's disposition undergoes alteration. In this way, by stripping off past dispositions and putting on future dispositions, it appears to perish and be reborn. Conversely, by never receiving nor abandoning its own natural property [motion], the soul never comes to be or ceases to be [163A–B].

4 Si quis autem ubi fingitur unum ens partim quidem esse, partim vero non esse, intellexerit post figmentum reliquum fore ens non animale quemadmodum nos, immo sensibile, exponat non mutari neque perire neque nasci, quia videlicet materia in rebus etiam sensibilibus est sempiterna, reliqua nos imitatus interpretetur. Nos autem interpretationem iam expositam magis consentaneam arbitrati sumus.

: CVIII :

Suppositio septima. Septimae suppositionis intentio. De gradibus unius et entis atque non entis. Quomodo negantur omnia de uno atque de non ente.

1 Quando ipsum simpliciter unum vaticinamur, infinitum prorsus auguramur quasi negando scilicet non multiplex, non compositum, non circumscriptum, non coniugatum. Quando vero unum ens asserimus, iam ipsum unum sub ipsa essentiae forma comprehendimus definitum, sed mera illa quidem et penitus universa. Quando rursus unum ens in essentia non[112] quodammodo mobili, sed per se mobili cogitamus, iam ens habemus quodammodo cum non ente permixtum pro intellectu puro deinceps intellectualem animam reportantes. Quando praeterea unum in conditione quadam ab altero mobili reputamus, iam minimum quiddam entis cum quam plurimo non ente referimus. Quando denique motum omnem mixturamque penitus auferimus, tunc omnino non ens somniare videmur, idque forte geminum, aut quolibet ente

If anyone, when hypothesizing that the one being partly is and 4
partly is not, understood that once the hypothesis was laid aside,
there would remain a being that is not a psychic being like ourselves, but a sensible being, that person would explain that a sensible being does not undergo change and does not cease to be or
come to be, given that even in sense objects matter is eternal, and
one would interpret the rest in the same way as we did. We think,
however, that the interpretation presented above is more appropriate.

: CVIII :

Seventh hypothesis. Purpose of the seventh hypothesis.
On the degrees of the one, being, and not-being. How
all things are denied of the one and of not-being.

When by prophetic insight we glimpse the absolute One, we di- 1
vine that it is infinite by saying that it is not multiple, not composite, not circumscribed, not united to anything. But when we assert
the existence of the one being, we understand that the one is already delimited under the form of essence—yet this form is pure
and universal. Again, when we conceive the one being within essence (essence being in motion in itself, rather than in an indeterminate way), we obtain a being that is already mixed with not-
being and we no longer get the pure intellect, but the intellectual
soul. In addition, when we consider the one which is in a certain
condition and is moved by the action of another principle of motion, we already allude to a one that is composed of being to the
lowest degree and of not-being to the highest degree. Finally, when
we remove motion and mixture altogether we appear to imagine
something that is totally not-being. This not-being might be of

deterius et insuper uno privatum, id est nihilum, aut ente quantumlibet excelso superius, id est ipsum simpliciter unum.

2   Quamobrem in suppositione septima unum ens non solum in animam per se mobilem degeneratum excogitamus, nec solum in fluxum ab alio dependentem praecipitatum, sed in ipsum omnino non ens denique resolutum, proprie forsan in nihilum iam prolapsum, metaphorice vero in ipsum simpliciter unum, ut ita dixerim, restitutum.

3   Hoc ipsum tractare videtur suppositio septima, quatenus de hoc simpliciter non ente omnia entium propria negat, quae quidem et de nihilo per defectum et de ipso simpliciter uno per excessum rite negantur. Posset forsitan hic et aliquis unum, quod nullo modo est, informem quoque materiam intellegere, quae quidem ita nullo modo est, ut essentiam formalem per se nullam habeat, participatione vero unius existit unum. Sed de his si oportuerit in sequentibus.

4   Parmenides vero non solum in his quattuor suppositionibus, sed etiam in praecedentibus frequenter argumentatur opposita circa idem. Ego quidem singula ferme pro viribus accommodare studeo et probabilia facere, saltem ne ubi fingit temere fingere videatur. Tu vero interim disce in materia qualibet et utrimque argumenta captare et utrobique distinguere sensus, ne impossibilia cogaris admittere. In his vero suppositionibus quattuor affert opposita circa idem, non solum ut te reddat argumentando versatilem, sed etiam ut deprehendas quot absurda contradictoriaque propter fictam unius absentiam contingere compellantur.

two kinds: it is either inferior to all being, deprived, what is more, of the one, i.e. nothing, or it is superior to being, be it ever so sublime, i.e. the absolute One.

For this reason, in the seventh hypothesis we consider that the one being has not only descended into the soul that is in motion in itself; it has not only fallen into a flux that depends on another, but it also eventually ends up in absolute not-being [163C]; properly speaking, this means that it might perhaps have already lapsed into nothingness; metaphorically it means that it has been brought back, so to speak, to the absolute One.

This is the one that the seventh hypothesis appears to be about, inasmuch as it negates of absolute not-being all the properties of beings; these are rightly negated of nothingness by defect and of the absolute One by excess. Someone might also understand that here the one which is absolutely not is formless matter: formless matter is absolutely not, as it possesses no formal essence within itself, but is one through partaking of the One. But of this we shall talk in what follows, if appropriate.

Parmenides frequently makes contradictory statements, not only in these four hypotheses, but also in the preceding ones. I myself try to the best of my ability to make almost each statement fit and to advance probable interpretations, if for no other reason than to prevent Parmenides from appearing to make rash hypotheses. But you must learn in the meantime how to grasp the arguments pro and contra in any subject, and to distinguish the meaning of both sides of an argument, lest you be forced to concede that propositions which are impossible hold true. In these four hypotheses Parmenides ascribes opposite attributes to the same object, not only to teach you skill in argument, but also to make you realize how many absurdities and contradictions must result from hypothesizing that the one is not.

: CIX :

Octava suppositio. Octavae suppositionis intentio.
Si mens auferatur supersitque anima, haec
erit mendax et versabitur circa umbras.

1   Octava suppositio comparat invicem alia, qualia videlicet futura
sint, si unum ens ita fingatur non esse ut partim quidem sit, partim vero non sit, id est si tollatur e medio intellegibilis intellectualisque omnis substantia pura, quae solum atque simpliciter est.
Subinde vero pro illa regnet anima, in qua, ut diximus, unum ens
propter fluxum cum non ente miscetur.

2   Nunc quidem anima per intellegibilem substantiam illustrata
atque roborata vere cognoscit et formas efficit naturales; tunc autem ab intellectu deserta imaginaretur, falso et pro naturalibus
formis simulacra quaedam et umbras effingeret, et imaginamenta
velut somnia prorsus inania secum ipsa confingeret, quae quidem
nullam substantiam formalemque distinctionem et unitatem habitura sint, si quando foras ex anima prosilierint. Praeterea cum in
anima, quam conditione iam posita deseruerit intellegibilis[113] illa
substantia prorsus unita, deinceps degeneraverit unitas adeo ut in
ipsa anima multitudo superatura sit unitatem, multo magis in his
quae confingentur vel effingentur ab anima, turba quaelibet unitatem penitus absorbebit, ut nihil in his agat ulterius unitas, nisi
forsan unitate utcumque multiplicata turba contingat. In qua tamen turba unitas penitus superata iam nihil agendo quae dispersa sunt conglutinare non possit, at perinde se habeat atque si

: CIX :

Eighth hypothesis. Purpose of the eighth hypothesis.
If mind is subtracted and soul remains, soul will
be untruthful and will concern itself with shadows.

The eighth hypothesis compares the others in relation to one an- 1
other: it examines what their nature will be if the one being is
hypothesized as not existing, in the sense of partly being and
partly not being [163C], that is, if the whole pure intelligible and
intellectual substance, which is unique and simple, is removed
from discussion. Thereupon the soul will rule in lieu of the intellect; there, as we have said, the one being, which undergoes flux, is
mixed with not-being.

Sometimes, when it is illuminated and strengthened by the 2
intelligible substance, the soul truly knows and creates natural
forms; but if we may imagine it abandoned by the intellect, there
would be other times when the soul's imagination would produce
false images; when it would create, instead of natural forms, simulacra and shadows, and fabricate images from itself, which (if they
ever sprung forth from the soul) would be vain dreams, as it were,
without substance, formal distinction or unity. In addition, given
that when the soul is in the condition postulated above it will have
been abandoned by the intelligible substance which is highly unified, the soul's unity would be so weakened that multitude would
be becoming superior to unity; within the things that are created
or fabricated by the soul, the mass will even more totally absorb
unity, so that unity has no longer any power—unless, perhaps,
this mass is constituted by the multiplication, in whatever way, of
its unity. In the latter case, however, unity, which is completely
surpassed [by multitude] and has absolutely no power, is unable to
stick together the things that have been scattered; it is disposed

nusquam adsit. Forte vero non solum non aget in his quicquam
unitas, sed nulla quidem erit. Cum enim iampridem in anima,
quemadmodum supposuimus, destituta ad summum ferme degeneraverit unitas, verisimile videtur in machinamentis animae penitus defecturam.

3   Sed numquid unitate iam perdita fingere liceat multitudinem?
Fingere forte licet semel atque subito, siquidem aliud sit multitudo
quam unitas et aliud divisio sit quam unio et alteritas quam identitas et fluxus aliud sit quam status, sed non licet in eo figmento
perseverare parumper, siquidem multitudo sit unitatis repetitio vel
processio quaedam. Probabile quoque est sicut in ascendendo per
ipsos rerum gradus ultra multitudinem extat unitas, sic deinceps
descendendo per gradus infra unitatem multitudinem contra su-
besse, saltem quoquomodo confictam. Inanium sane umbratilium-
que rerum magis propria est turba quam unitas.

4   Proinde si Parmenides finxisset unum nullo modo esse, non
posset[114] deinceps ulla ratione confingere alia quaelibet esse, cum
ab uno cuncta necessario pendeant. Cum vero finxerit esse quodammodo atque non esse, licuit ei concedere alia quomodolibet
esse, sed multo minus esse quam unum. Praeterea sublato forsan
intellectu puro excogitare licet animam esse vivam et imaginantem
atque sentientem, falso tamen, omnis enim cognitio vera a prima
cognitione intellectuali dependet. Qua per concessionem adempta
nulla restat imaginatio vera, nullus sensus alicubi verax. Quid igitur erit reliqui? Sensus et imaginatio mendax, sensibilia falsa ap-
parebuntque forte quemadmodum speculares quaedam imagines
aut umbrae, quae quidem non tam sint quam existere videantur,
vel potius quicquid sint, non erunt haec extra conceptus animae,

exactly as if it were in no place at all. But perhaps this unity will not only do nothing in these realities; it will *be* nothing; for since, as we have postulated, unity has completely lost its power in the soul, which has been deprived of unity in nearly the highest degree, it is likely that it will be totally absent from the soul's workings.

Yet is it possible to imagine a multitude without unity? Perhaps   3 it is possible to imagine it once and for a brief moment, since multitude and unity are two different things, like division and union, otherness and sameness, flux and rest, but this figment cannot hold true for very long, since multitude is the repetition of unity, or a procession from unity. It is also probable that just as by ascending through the degrees of being unity is beyond multitude because it transcends it, in the same way when descending through the degrees of things this multitude (at least the multitude that we imagined) is, by contrast, beyond unity because it is below it. Surely mass pertains more than unity to vain and shadowy things.

Consequently, if Parmenides had hypothesized that the one is   4 absolutely not, he could not imagine that the others would exist in any way, since all things necessarily depend on the one. But since he hypothesized that the one somehow is and is not, he could concede that the others exist in some way (but much less so than the one). In addition, without the existence of pure intellect one could conceive that the soul lives, imagines and perceives, but it would do so falsely, since every true cognition depends on the first intellectual cognition. Once we concede that intellectual cognition does not exist, no true imagination, no reliable sense perception remains anywhere. What will then remain? There will remain mendacious sense perception and imagination, false sense objects, and these will perhaps appear as if they were mirror reflections or shadows, which do not so much exist as appear to exist, or rather, whatever they are, they will not exist outside the soul's conceiving,

sed animae ipsius machinamenta quaedam et haec quidem falsa. Haec enim Parmenides appellat apparitiones, phantasmata, somnia. Quae si foras forte processerint, vaniora futura sint quam exiles umbrae, quae quidem vix appareant statimque cum apparuerint evanescant. Summatim vero dementes et somniantes et quibus oculi patiuntur imagines saepe quae concipiunt intus opinantur se extra percipere. Similiter forsan afficietur anima demens mente iam ut finximus ex universo sublata.

: CX :

Si sustuleris unum, res ipsae desinent, umbratiles erunt turbae innumerabiliter infinitae, contingent opposita circa idem. Imaginatio ambigua semper erit mendax.

1 Primo quidem finguntur alia quodammodo esse, post haec esse diversa, tertio vero a quonam haec diversa sint exquiritur. Non quidem ab ipso vere uno, non enim comparari possunt ad ipsum vere unum, id est ens unum verum, postquam finximus id non esse. Quinetiam nec ad unam animam facile comparari, nisi enim fuerit intellectus unus non erit anima quaedam una, inde enim unio ad animam transferri debet. Comparabuntur igitur turbae quaelibet invicem. Sed quales turbae? Primo quidem umbratiles, deinde innumerabiles, praeterea turba quaelibet erit infinite penitus infinita, neque tam erit quam sic occurret imaginanti. Sed quomodo inter se different? Non ita quidem ut turba haec sit

but will be some workings of the soul itself, and they will be false. These Parmenides calls apparitions, phantasms, and dreams [164D]. If they perchance proceed outside the soul, they will be emptier than empty shadows, which are hardly visible and disappear as soon as they appear. In sum, those who are under the influence of madness, dreams, or hallucinations, often believe that they perceive as visible objects what they conceive in their imagination. The soul will perhaps be similarly affected by madness if we imagine that the mind is completely absent from the universe.

: CX :

If we suppose that the one is not, things themselves will cease to exist, there will be shadowy, innumerably infinite masses, and opposites will occur in respect of the same thing. Imagination, always ambiguous, will be untruthful.

We hypothesize, firstly, that others exist in some way, then that they are different, and thirdly, we examine what they are different from [164B–C]. They are not different from the true one, for they cannot be compared with the true one, that is, the true one being, since *ex hypothesi* the true one being does not exist. Neither can it easily be compared with the psychic one: if the intellectual one does not exist, there will be no psychic one, for unity is transferred into the soul from the intellect. As a result, random masses will be compared with one another. But what is the nature of these masses? Firstly, they are like shadows; secondly, they are innumerable [164B]. In addition, every mass will be infinitely infinite, and it will appear to exist more in the imagination than in reality. But in what way do others differ from one another? Not in the sense

1

unum aliud, illa vero sit aliud unum, postquam semel hinc ipsum unum est ablatum. Probavimus saepe alibi multitudinem quamlibet si unius fuerit expers, non solum totam innumerabilem esse, sed partem etiam particulamque deinceps infinite perceptam innumerabilem pariter esse futuram. Nam si nusquam unum aliquid individuumque reperiatur, innumerabiliter licebit in multa partiri. Haec atque talia semel uno sublato consequenter eveniunt. Quam vero stultum est ista concedere, tam nefarium est et unitatem adimere singulis et ipsum unum universo negare.

2   Quaelibet praeterea turba imaginantibus momento succurret ut unum, neque deinde se praestabit unum; occurret ut numerus neque numerus inde succedet, quippe cum desit et unitas et modus ipse numero necessaria. Apparebit ut minimum simul atque maximum, ut minimum quidem in portione selecta, ut vero maximum atque quam plurimum in portiunculis illinc emergentibus immo subito confluentibus. Videbuntur turbae quaedam quibusdam turbis aequales, siquidem turba quaelibet tum minor, tum maior appareat, et interea forsan aequalis, nec ulla tamen aequalitas, si desit unitas aequalitatis origo.

3   Dum plures occurrunt acervi, videbitur alter extra terminos alterius esse et ambo invicem esse confines. Nullus tamen intus terminos mediumve habebit. Quicquid enim acceperis ut principium, cum sit perpetuo multiplex, in principium aliud resolvetur similiter et in finem semper alium, quicquid obvium erit ut finis. Quod vero aeque distans inter haec medium cogitatur, cum perpetuo sit in plurima divisibile, semper erit in medium aliud referendum.

that each mass would be a different unity, since the one has hypothetically been abolished. We have often demonstrated elsewhere that if a multitude is without unity, it will not only be innumerable as a whole, but part of it, and part of part of it, and so on ad infinitum, will also be perceived as innumerable. For if there is nothing that is one and undivided to be found anywhere, it will be possible to divide things infinitely into many. Such are the consequences that result when someone postulates that the one is not. It is as wrong to remove unity from the many and deny the existence of the one in the universe as it is foolish to admit that these consequences are true.

In addition, any mass will immediately appear to the imagination to be one, without subsequently acting as one [164D]. It will appear to be a number, without ever becoming a number [164D], since both unity and measure, which are necessary to number, do not exist. It will appear both the smallest and the greatest [164E]: the smallest in any given portion, the greatest and most numerous in the smaller portions that emerge from it and immediately converge. Some masses will appear equal to other masses [165A], since each mass will appear smaller at times and greater at others; and in some intermediate stage it might appear to be equal; there is, however, no [real] equality, since unity, which is the origin of equality, does not exist.

In the case of several masses, one of the masses will seem to exist outside the limits of another, and both will appear to be the limits of one another. However, neither will possess within itself limits or a middle. For whatever is considered as a beginning, given that it is also eternally multiple, will likewise end up in another beginning, and whatever presents itself as an end will always end up in another end. But what is considered to be a middle, equally distant between these two masses, given that it is perpetually divisible in more and more parts, will have to be related to another middle, and so on *ad infinitum* [165A–B].

4 Quicquid imaginatione diviseris ubi unum individuumque defuerit, succurret ibi semper iterum dividendum et primo quidem apparebit unum, mox autem et infinitum. Eadem igitur ut unum et ut multa, item ut finita iterumque infinita imaginantibus vel quomodolibet sentientibus apparebunt, atque dum summatim turbae occurrent ut unum, in hoc uno similes vel eaedem apparebunt, dum vero succurrent ut varietate plenae, dissimiles.

5 Videbuntur et invicem contiguae turbae, nec erunt alicubi certa contiguitate confines, siquidem quae in eis videntur extrema semper ultra resolvuntur in aliud. Itaque videbuntur etiam fore seorsum. Apparebunt moveri etiam atque non moveri. Moveri quidem, quia semper de alio imaginando pertransitur in aliud. Iterum non moveri, siquidem infinito non patet locus alius in quem transeat. Putabis eiusmodi turbas oriri atque perire, dum videris adeo divisibiles atque dispersas. Suspicaberis interim sempiternas, dum in ipso infinito neque principium inveneris[115] neque finem et virtutem iudicaveris[116] infinitam. In haec itaque similiaque paradoxa, immo deliramenta, praecipitabere si quo pacto unum ex universo deieceris.

: CXI :

Suppositio nona. Nonae suppositionis intentio.

1 Nona tandem suppositio docet si nullo modo in rebus et in universo sit ens unum, non modo intellectum e medio tolli, sed etiam animam, quae partim in entibus computatur, et hac sublata, non

In the absence of the one and the indivisible, everything you   4
divide in the imagination will always appear to need division one
more time, and it will initially appear to be one, then to be infinite.
The same things, therefore, will appear to the imagination or even
sense perception to be one and many, and likewise limited and
then unlimited. When the masses taken together are seen as one,
they will appear within this one to be like, or the same as, each
other, whereas when they occur in their variety, they will appear
unlike each other [165C–D].

The masses will also appear to be in contact with one another,   5
and in other cases not to be connected to one another by any particular contact, since their so-called extremities always extend further into something else. Thus they will also appear to be separate.
They will also appear to be in motion and not in motion. In motion, because by always imagining something else, one moves into
another place; not in motion, since one cannot postulate *ad infinitum* the existence of another place into which to move. You will
think that these masses come and cease to be, when seeing them
so divisible and dispersed. But you will also conjecture that they
are eternal, given that you don't find any beginning or end in the
infinite, and you will conclude that their power is infinite. Such
are some of the paradoxes, or rather delusions, that you will be
plunged into if you cast out the one from the universe [165D–E].

: CXI :

Ninth hypothesis. Purpose of the ninth hypothesis.

Finally, the ninth hypothesis teaches us that if the one being does   1
not at all exist in things and in the universe, then not only is the
intellect abolished, but also the soul, which is in part counted

solum sensibilia cuncta disperdi, verumetiam umbratilia et sensus imaginationesque perire, neque superfore ullam umbratilium multitudinem, postquam defuerit unum multitudini necessarium, neque materiam ipsam nudam, quae seorsum a formis subsistere nequit, nec apparere praeterea quicquam, vel ut multa vel ut unum. Non quidem apparere, neque enim est apparitura res ulla, nec imaginatio superest vel sensus cui apparere quomodolibet quicquam possit; atque si qua fingatur imaginatio superfore (quam in capite superiore sub intellegentiae nomine Parmenides occuluisse videtur), non poterit illa rite perseveranterque imaginari multitudinem sine uno. Ubi vero nos cogitari multitudinem sine uno licere diximus, licentius et ipsi finxisse videmur. Immo vero quod nullo modo est et nullo modo unum neque cogitari rite potest neque fingi. Nam quicquid et quomodocumque finxeris ipsum saltem figmentum penes te conceptum est aliquid ens et unum, et ipse ad hoc effingendum alicunde motus ab ente quopiam atque uno atque ipse ens et unum.

2   Post haec eiusmodi affertur totius libri conclusio. Si ipsum simpliciter unum, a quo est ens unum et ex quo tandem est ubique quodlibet unum, ex universo tollatur, nihil penitus usquam erit. Huic autem universae conclusioni subnectuntur et aliae per universum dialogum enarratae partim quidem utrimque per opposita vera secundum significata varia, partim etiam adductae ut et ingenium audientis exercitetur utrimque, ut saepe iam diximus, et interim certius deprehendatur quot impossibilia consequantur, si ipsum unum auferatur omnibus necessarium tamquam effector omnium et servator et finis.

among beings; that in the absence of soul, not only do all the sense objects disappear, but the shadows, sense perceptions and imaginations also perish, and no multitude of shadows will remain in the absence of the one, the existence of which is necessary to multitude; not even bare matter will exist, since it cannot subsist apart from the forms [165E]; nothing else will appear either as one or as many — indeed, not even appear [166A], for there will be no appearance, no imagination, no sense perception left, things which are necessary for appearance to take place. And even if one hypothesizes that imagination (which Parmenides seems to have disguised under the name of intelligence in the previous chapter) remains, it will not be able to imagine correctly and in a sustained way a multitude without the one. But when we said that we can conceive a multitude without the one, we seemed to have exceeded the limits of hypothesis. To be more precise, what is absolutely not and absolutely not-one cannot be correctly conceived of nor hypothesized. For whatever one hypothesizes in whatever way, even the figment that is conceived within one's soul is at least itself a being and a "one"; and the very motion employed in hypothesizing this figment derives from a being and a "one" and is itself a being and a "one."

Following these conclusions, the conclusion of the whole dialogue is presented as follows [166C]. If the absolute One, from which the one being derives, as well as every single "one" in the world, is removed from the universe, there will be absolutely nothing anywhere. To this universal conclusion we must add the other conclusions established throughout the whole dialogue, which are partly expounded pro and contra by using true opposites in different senses, and are partly expounded to exercise the pupil's mind in pro and contra arguments, as we have already said several times, and to comprehend with more certainty how many impossible consequences would result if the One, which is necessary to all things as the creator, preserver and end of all things, did not exist.

Note on the Text

༃

TEXT OF THE COMMENTARY

The text of the commentary proper is based on the *editio princeps* printed in Florence in 1496. Ficino's corrigenda from the 1496 edition have also been incorporated. Typographical errors have been corrected without comment; the spelling has been regularized (with the *u/v* and *e/ae* distinctions), abbreviations and diacritics have been silently expanded, fusions such as *siquis* and *siquid* have been disaggregated, and the punctuation has been modernized. Spelling of names has been regularized according to modern use. The subdivision in chapters and paragraphs is based on that of the 1496 edition; however, the editor has adopted a continuous chapter numbering, and has supplied the division in paragraphs in instances where there is no paragraphing in the 1496 edition (chapters 1–36). The text in the three editions of Ficino's *Opera omnia* (1541, 1576, and 1641) has been dismissed as too corrupt to be of any value, although some of the emendations of the 1576 edition have been adopted.

Notes to the Text

※೭※

SIGLA AND ABBREVIATIONS

E	*Commentaria in Platonem*, Florence, 1496
Ec	Ficino's corrigenda in E
corr.	The editor's emendations
add.	The editor's additions
del.	The editor's deletions
e Bas.	The editor's emendations or additions based on Ficino's *Opera Omnia*, Basel, 1576
e Proclo	The editor's emendations or additions based on Proclus's *Parmenides Commentary*

1. mutaturi Ec: imitaturi E

2. *This passage does not make sense, because Ficino does not recognize that there is a lacuna in Proclus'* Parmenides *commentary (see Proclus,* In Parmenidem *VI, 1060. 8–11, p. 28 Steel). The lacuna, which is present in both Greek and Latin manuscripts, has been filled as follows by Steel:* τῆς γὰρ δευτέρας δεικνύσης ⟨ὡς εἰ ἔστι τὸ ἕν, ἔσται πᾶσα ἡ τοῦ νοῦ τάχις, ἡ ἕκτη δείκνυσιν ὡς εἰ μὴ ἔστι, μόνον ἔσται τὸ αἰσθητὸν καὶ τῶν γνώσεων αἴσθησις· τῆς δὲ τρίτης δεικνύσης⟩ ὡς . . . ; *it reads as follows in Dillon's translation (p. 416): "the second shows ⟨that if the One exists, then the realm of Intellect exists, the sixth shows that, if it does not exist, then only sense perception and perceptibles exists; where the third⟩ shows that . . ."*

3. affirmans Ec: affirmaus E

4. impartibile Ec: inpatibile E

5. principiumque corr. e Bas: principiumquam E

6. oppositionales Ec: oppositi naturales E

7. ideoque Ec: ideaque E

8. praesertim quia Ec: praesertimque E

9. quinque suppositiones Ec: quinque suppositionem E

10. inde *Ec*: in se *E*

11. intellegibilemque *Ec*: intellectualemque *E*

12. pleno *Ec*: plene *E*

13. convenit *Ec*: convetit *E*

14. episcopus *Ec*: episopus *E*

15. ferme *Ec*: forme *E*

16. entia *Ec*: entiam *E*

17. duitatem *corr.*: divinitatem *E*

18. primam *Ec*: primum *E*

19. nec *Ec*: haec *E*

20. supereminens *Ec*: supereminentes *E*

21. ut totum *corr.*: totum ut *E*

22. producit *Ec*: producitur *E*

23. possint *corr.*: possit *E*

24. sunt *Ec*: sub *E*

25. fit *Ec*: sit *E*

26. effectus *Ec*: affectus *E*

27. operatio *Ec*: operatur *E*

28. segregatum *Ec*: segregatis *E*

29. sint *corr.*: fint *E*

30. essentiam *corr.*: essentiae *E*

31. adiungit *corr. e Bas.*: adiungint *E*

32. hoc *corr. e Proclo In Parm.* VII, 1188.29 (τὸ δὲ ἓν ὂν): hec *E*

33. participes *corr.*: particeps *E*

34. proptereaque *corr.*: propterea et *E*

35. temporis *Ec*: tempori *E*

36. esse *Ec*: etiam *E*

37. pares *Ec*: partes *E*

38. tres *corr. e Bas.*: tris E

39. caelestibus *corr.*: caelis E

40. haec *corr. e Bas.*: nec E

41. praesentiam *Ec*: praesertim E

42. quapropter *Ec*: quia propter E

43. imparticipabile *Ec*: impartibile E

44. significanter *corr. e Bas.*: significantem E

45. nusquam *Ec*: numquam E

46. aliquod *Ec*: aliquid E

47. firmaverimus *Ec*: formaverimus E

48. proponebatur *Ec*: proponebat E

49. praedicentur *Ec*: praedicantur E

50. contemplatori *Ec*: contemplari E

51. et quovis ferme simili genera cuncta et ideas *Ec*: et quovis ferme genera cuncta similiter et ideas E

52. eorumque *Ec*: eorum E

53. particeps *corr. e Bas.*: participes E

54. videntur *Ec*: videtur E

55. mediam *corr. e Bas.*: media E

56. ita *add. Ec*

57. procreante *Ec*: procredente E

58. intellegibilis *Ec*: intellectualis E

59. omnis *corr. e Bas.*: omni E

60. intellegibilis *Ec*: intellectualis E

61. aliquod *corr.*: aliquid E

62. unius *add. Ec*

63. eandem *corr.*: eadem E

64. contingit *Ec*: confugit E

65. intellegens *Ec*: intelleges E

66. proprio *Ec*: propria *E*

67. percipiunt, complectuntur atque fruuntur *Ec*: percipiuntur atque fruuntur *E*

68. discretionibus *corr.*: discretiones *E*

69. rationibus *corr.*: orationibus *E*

70. continet *corr. e Bas.*: continent *E*

71. quodammodo *corr. e Bas.*: quodam quodammodo *E*

72. motus *corr. e Bas.*: notus *E*

73. calere *Ec*: calore *E*

74. hinc quidem *Ec*: hinc quid *E*

75. agere videntur *Ec*: agere videtur *E*

76. distinguatur *Ec*: distinguitur *E*

77. inter *Ec*: intre *E*

78. sagaciore *corr.*: sagaciora *E*

79. mavis *corr. e Bas.*: maius *E*

80. intellegibili *Ec*: intellectuali *E*

81. ultra mundanos *Ec*: vel tramundanos *E*

82. nam *Ec*: natura *E*

83. universo *Ec*: numeroso *E*

84. Pythagoramque *Ec*: Pythagoricamque *E*

85. Parcas *Ec*: pareas *E*

86. inter *add. Ec*

87. loquar *corr. e Bas.*: loquor *E*

88. infima *corr.*: infimia *E*

89. aliae *del. post* rationes

90. necessariam *Ec*: natura *E*

91. a *del. post* saltem

92. hinc *corr.*: hic *E*

93. speciales *Ec*: specales *E*

94. dividuum *Ec*: diviuum *E*

95. alios *add. Ec*

96. neque *add. Ec*

97. continuentur *Ec*: continentur *E*

98. quartae *corr.*: quarta *E*

99. expertem *Ec*: expartem *E*

100. aliunde *Ec*: alium *E*

101. potenter *corr.*: potente *E*

102. eandem *Ec*: eadem *E*

103. omnia *corr.*: omniam *E*

104. utrisque *corr.*: utriusque *E*

105. adhuc *Ec*: ad hoc *E*

106. procedens *Ec*: praecedens *E*

107. necessario *Ec*: numero *E*

108. quomodo *Ec*: quodammodo *E*

109. degenerare *Ec*: degenare *E*

110. neque *Ec*: nam *E*

111. motu *corr.*: motum *E*

112. non *add.*

113. intellegibilis *Ec*: intellectualis *E*

114. posset *corr. e Bas.*: posse *E*

115. inveneris *corr. e Bas.*: inveneri *E*

116. iudicaveris *corr. e Bas.*: iudicaveri *E*

Notes to the Translation

꙰১৩৯

ABBREVIATIONS

Allen (*In Philebum*)   Marsilio Ficino, *The Philebus Commentary*, ed. and
                        tr. Michael J. B. Allen (Berkeley: University of
                        California Press, 1975; repr. Tempe: Arizona
                        Center of Medieval and Renaissance Studies,
                        2000).

Allen (*In Sophistam*) Michael J. B. Allen, *Icastes: Marsilio Ficino's
                        Interpretation of Plato's Sophist. Five Studies and a
                        Critical Edition with Translation* (Berkeley:
                        University of California Press, 1989).

Dillon   Proclus, *Commentary on Plato's Parmenides*, tr. Glenn
                        R. Morrow and John M. Dillon (Princeton:
                        Princeton University Press, 1987).

Dodds   Proclus, *The Elements of Theology*, ed. and tr. E. R.
                        Dodds (Oxford: Clarendon, 1963; repr. 2000).

Hankins-Allen   Marsilio Ficino, *Platonic Theology*, ed. James
                        Hankins and tr. Michael J. B. Allen, 6 vols.
                        (Cambridge, MA: Harvard University Press,
                        2001–2006).

Henry-Hadot   Marius Victorinus, *Traités théologiques sur la Trinité*,
                        ed. Paul Henry and tr. Pierre Hadot, 2 vols.
                        (Paris: Editions du Cerf, 1960).

Kaske-Clark   Marsilio Ficino, *Three Books on Life*, ed. and tr.
                        Carol V. Kaske and John R. Clark (Binghamton,
                        NY: Renaissance Society of America, 1989).

Laurens   Marsilio Ficino, *Commentaire sur le Banquet de
                        Platon, de l'Amour*, ed. and tr. Pierre Laurens
                        (Paris: Belles Lettres, 2002).

Matton	Francesco Diaceto, *De Pulchro Libri III*, ed. Sylvain Matton (Pisa: Scuola Normale Superiore di Pisa, 1986).
Moerbeke	Proclus, *Commentaire sur le Parménide de Platon, traduction de Guillaume de Moerbeke*, ed. Carlos Steel, 2 vols. (Louvain: Presses Universitaires de Louvain-Brill, 1982–1985).
Op.	Marsilio Ficino, *Opera quae hactenus extitere et quae in lucem nunc primum prodiere omnia* (Basel: Heinrich Petri, 1576; repr. Turin: Bottega d'Erasmo, 1959 and 1962; Paris: Phénix Editions, 2000).
Saffrey-Westerink	Proclus, *Théologie Platonicienne*, ed. and tr. Henri D. Saffrey and Leendert G. Westerink, 6 vols. (Paris: Belles Lettres, 1968–1997).
Steel	*Procli in Platonis Parmenidem Commentaria*, ed. Carlos Steel, 3 vols. (Oxford: Clarendon, 2007–2009).
Westerink	Leendert G. Westerink, *The Greek Commentaries on Plato's Phaedo*, 2 vols. (Amsterdam: North-Holland, 1976–1977).

1. See Proclus, *Elements of Theology* prop. 135. These divine unities are Proclus' henads, unities between the One and the Ideas.

2. See Proclus, *In Parmenidem* 6.1048.9–27 (ed. Steel, pp. 13–14).

3. See Proclus, *In Parmenidem* 6.1050.

4. See Proclus, *In Parmenidem* 6.1050–51.

5. See Proclus, *In Parmenidem* 6.1050–51.

6. See Proclus, *In Parmenidem* 6.1056.3–1057.4 (ed. Steel, pp. 24–25).

7. See Proclus, *Platonic Theology* 2.4; *In Parmenidem* 6.1064.17–1065.11 (ed. Steel, pp. 33–34) and 7.515.4–14 (ed. Steel, p. 334), who rejects Origen the Platonist's thesis according to which the One of the first hypothesis is a mere name and without substance. Here Ficino alludes to Pico's thesis according to which the *Parmenides* is a logical exercise.

8. Allusion to the fact that Proclus' interpretation of the final hypotheses is lost. What follows is a close paraphrase of Proclus, *In Parmenidem* 6.1058–60. Plutarch of Athens is the master of Proclus' master Syrianus, not the second-century biographer and Platonist Plutarch of Chaeronea.

9. Plato, *Phaedo* 96a–99d; *Timaeus* 46d–e.

10. This passage, which establishes a distinction within the first five principles of reality (those that are exterior to things and those that are immanent in them), corresponds to Proclus, *In Parmenidem* 6.1059.15–17 (ed. Steel, p. 27), which reads in translation (tr. Dillon, p. 415): "having surveyed in these five hypotheses these principles, both those external to things and those immanent in them" (*tas archas tautas tas te exô tôn pragmatôn kai tas en autois ousas; principia hec extra res et ea que in ipsis entia* Moerbeke). There seems, therefore, to be a lacuna in Ficino's text: *haec principia, <et quae extra entia sunt> et quae in eis vel circa ea sunt.* Given that Ficino adopts in the passage above Proclus' distinction between external and immanent principles, there is no reason to assume that he deliberately modifies the meaning of the text.

11. The whole passage is omitted in the manuscripts of Proclus' *Parmenides* commentary (probably because of *homoeoteleuton*) as well as in Moerbeke's translation.

12. See Proclus, *In Parmenidem* 6.1062.17–26 (ed. Steel, pp. 31–32).

13. According to Syrianus and Proclus, each characteristic denied or asserted of the One (for instance "whole," "part," "shape," and so on) corresponds to a distinct class of gods (for instance, intelligible, intellectual, supra-cosmic, and so on). In this way, by denying these characteristics of the One, the first hypothesis indicates that the first principle transcends all the divine orders and their attributes; by asserting these characteristics of the one being, the second hypothesis describes the whole hierarchy of the gods and souls that are created by the One and compose the universe. See Proclus, *In Parmenidem* 4.1062.

14. Although this passage clearly paraphrases Proclus, it differs from what Proclus says at 6.1063.4–6 (ed. Steel, p. 32), which reads in translation as follows (tr. Dillon, p. 418): the third hypothesis is "not about all Soul pure and simple, but such as has proceeded forth from the divine

soul" (*tèn ge mèn tritèn ouch haplôs einai peri pasès psychès, all'hosè meta tèn theian proelèluthe*; in Moerbeke's translation: *tertiam uero non simpliciter esse de omni anima, sed quecumque post diuinam processit*). The same interpretation is found in chap. LXXX. In the third hypothesis, Ficino explicitly rejects Proclus' interpretation.

15. I.e. (according to Proclus), the second rather than the third hypothesis; see Proclus, *In Parmenidem* 6.1063.5–9.

16. See Proclus, *In Parmenidem* 6.1063.4–10 (ed. Steel, p. 31). Ficino's interpretation, according to which the Platonists distinguish between a goddess soul and the divine souls, does not exactly correspond with what Proclus says; see n. 3. Proclus establishes a distinction between the whole divine soul, introduced in the second hypothesis by the attribute "time" (*Parmenides* 151e–55c), and the souls that derive from it, introduced in the third hypothesis. The same interpretation is found in chap. LXXX. In the third hypothesis, Ficino explicitly rejects Proclus' interpretation.

17. See Proclus, *In Parmenidem* 6.1063.14–1064.10 (ed. Steel, pp. 32–33).

18. See Proclus, *Platonic Theology* 1.12 (ed. Saffrey-Westerink, pp. 57.22–58.3).

19. Plato, *Sophist* 245a–e.

20. See Proclus, *In Parmenidem* 6.1065.12–20 (ed. Steel, p. 34). Like Proclus, Ficino considers that *Sophist* 242c–45e does not refute Parmenides' doctrine but anticipates and confirms the thesis of the supremacy of the One over being expounded in the *Parmenides*. See also Proclus, *Platonic Theology* 1.4 (ed. Saffrey-Westerink, p. 18.13–24). The essential link between the *Sophist* and the *Parmenides* is a fundamental point in Proclus' metaphysics, especially in the context of his refutation of Origen the Platonist's thesis that the *Parmenides* is not theological but logical. Ficino reuses Proclus' arguments against Origen to counter (in a different context) Pico's *De ente et uno*.

21. See Proclus, *In Parmenidem* 6.1065–66, where the One is defined as "existing" (*hyphestôs*), in opposition to Origen's thesis according to which the One is "without subsistence" (*anypostaton*). With *existente vel subsistente* Ficino uses scholastic terminology to refer to Proclus' ideas.

22. This doctrine is mentioned by Proclus, *In Parmenidem* 6.1066.13–21 (ed. Steel, pp. 35–36).

23. See Proclus, *In Parmenidem* 6.1069.18–1070.12 (ed. Steel, pp. 39–40).

24. See Proclus, *In Parmenidem* 6.1070.1–12 (ed. Steel, pp. 39–40), which distinguishes the intelligible object in individual intellects from the intelligible object pure and simple. Ficino is aware that Proclus' position contradicts that of Plotinus, who maintained that the intelligible objects always reside within the intellects (*Enneads* 5.5). He seeks to establish a compromise between the two, by adopting Proclus' doctrine up to the ultimate degree of the hierarchy and Plotinus' doctrine regarding the first intellect.

25. The image of the watchtower is a Neoplatonic topos deriving from Plato's *Republic* 4.445c4 and *Statesman* 272e5; see Proclus, *Platonic Theology* 1.3 (ed. Saffrey-Westerink, p. 16.1) and 1.7 (ed. Saffrey-Westerink, p. 31.1). It was further developed in the Christian mystical tradition; see P. Courcelle, "La vision cosmique de St Benoît," *Revue des Etudes Augustiniennes* 13 (1967): 97–117.

26. The use of the images of the line and point to elucidate the relationship between unity and multiplicity, which ultimately derives from Pythagoras, is used by Plato (*Republic* 509d and 549d) and Aristotle (*De anima* 3.427a), then by the Neoplatonists, in particular Plotinus.

27. See Proclus, *In Parmenidem* 6.1071–72. The need for the presence of divine love in rising to the One beyond all possibility of intellection is, however, an Augustinian theme which Ficino discusses frequently in his works. For analysis, see Kristeller, *Il pensiero filosofico di Marsilio Ficino*, 246–310; and Hankins, *Humanism and Platonism*, 2: 335–38.

28. See Proclus, *In Parmenidem* 6.1074.

29. An allusion to (pseudo) Dionysius the Areopagite's negative theology; see the Introduction, pp. xii–xiii, and n. 85, both in Vol. 1.

30. This oxymoron, which is used to describe the relation that matter has with the first principle, is frequently used by Proclus; see *Platonic Theology* 1.12 (ed. Saffrey-Westerink, p. 57.20 and note ad. loc., p. 144), then by Christian philosophers.

31. See Proclus, *In Parmenidem* 6.1075–77.

32. I.e., unity has greater extension than being.

33. Plato, *Sophist* 245a–c.

34. Ficino, *De Christiana religione* 17 (*Op.*, pp. 21–22).

35. See Proclus, *In Parmenidem* 6.1078–83.

36. See Plotinus, *Enneads* 5.3.33–44, who considers that the second hypostasis is an internal multiplicity constituted by the triple act of being, life, and intellect. The identification of intellect and intelligible is objected to by Proclus, who prefers to postulate the existence of several intelligible triads, the first one containing everything in a unified and indistinct mode, the second in a distinct way (see, e.g., *Platonic Theology* 4.32 and 3.20 and 25).

37. Plato, *Sophist* 245a.

38. See Proclus, *In Parmenidem* 6.1089–92.

39. Plato, *Sophist* 249a–c.

40. See Proclus, *Platonic Theology* 4.28 (ed. Saffrey-Westerink, pp. 80–83).

41. See Ficino, *In Sophistam* 31 (ed. Allen, p. 249).

42. See Proclus, *Platonic Theology* 1.10 (ed. Saffrey-Westerink, p. 42) and *In Parmenidem* 6.1085.11–1086.7 (ed. Steel, pp. 57–58).

43. See Proclus, *In Parmenidem* 6.1088–89.

44. Plato, *Letters* 2.313a. Note the scholastic terminology *quale vel quale quid* rendering the Greek *poion*.

45. See Proclus, *In Parmenidem* 6.1088–89.

46. See Proclus, *In Parmenidem* 6.1089–90.

47. Allusion to Nicholas, the twelfth-century Byzantine bishop of Methone, who wrote a refutation of Proclus' *Elements of Theology* in defense of Christian orthodoxy. Ficino's autograph annotations, now in Paris, Bibliothèque Nationale de France, MS Par. gr. 1256, have been edited by J. Monfasani, "Marsilio Ficino and the Plato-Aristotle Controversy. Ap-

pendix 3: Marsilio Ficino's Autograph Annotations in Nicholaus Methonensis' Refutation of Proclus' Elements of Theology," in Allen and Rees, *Marsilio Ficino*, 200–201.

48. Plato, *Republic* 6.509c.

49. Plato, *Phaedo* 99c.

50. See Proclus, *In Parmenidem* 6.1097.

51. *Una totius forma* is a scholastic expression used here to characterize the intelligible world.

52. Here Ficino combines Plotinus' doctrine, which defines the intelligible substance as composed of the five genera of being in the *Sophist* and of life and intellect (*Enneads* 5.9.10), and Proclus' definition of the first mixed, which is composed of limit and infinity, essence, life, and intellect (*Platonic Theology* 3.9–10).

53. See Proclus, *In Parmenidem* 6.1098.

54. See Proclus, *In Parmenidem* 6.1099.

55. See *Op.*, pp. 1771–79; 1784–87; 1787–94.

56. An allusion to Plotinus' criticism of Aristotle's categories as genera of being; see *Enneads* 6.1–2 (on the rejection of unity and multitude as genera of being, see *Enneads* 6.2.3, 9, and 17) and 6.6.

57. I.e., because we would need to identify the cause of this second multitude, and so on *ad infinitum*.

58. See Proclus, *In Parmenidem* 6.1101.

59. Following a trend initiated by Iamblichus, Proclus elaborates within Plotinus's second hypostasis (being and intellect) a subordinate triad, being-life-intellect, the first and second hypostases being separated by a further series of divine unities, the henads. See *Elements of Theology* props. 101–3 and note ad loc. (ed. Dodds, pp. 252–53), and *Platonic Theology* 3.6 (ed. Saffrey-Westerink, pp. 22.12–23.10). The triad itself derives from Plotinus' interpretation of *Sophist* 248e, where life and intellect are said to be characters of being (*Enneads* 1.6.7 and 5.4.2). Plotinus thus considers that being, life, and intellect are three aspects of the same reality. In *En-*

neads 5.9.8, however, Plotinus establishes a distinction between ontology, where intellect and being are the same, and human logic, which tends to separate being from intellect and considers being superior to intellect. In his commentary on the passage of Plotinus, *ad Enn.* 5.9.8 (*Op.*, p. 1771), Ficino acknowledges the precedence of being over intellect in "some natural order," but underlines that this is not the case for the first principle. See also (pseudo) Dionysius the Areopagite, *On Divine Names* 5.3, and Ficino's commentary ad loc. (*Op.*, p. 1091–92).

60. Following a well-known Proclean principle; see Proclus, *In Parmenidem* 6.1099.

61. Plotinus, *Enneads* 6.2.7. 9, 17, and 35.

62. Plotinus, *Enneads* 6.2.8.11.

63. Following Plotinus' interpretation, which ultimately derives from *Sophist* 248e. See *Enneads* 1.6.7; 5.4.2; 5.6.6. The question is further explored by Proclus, *Elements of Theology* prop. 103, who considers that being, life, and intellect are *both* three aspects of the same reality (being) *and* three successive stages in the unfolding of the universe from the One.

64. Plotinus, *Enneads* 6.6.8.17–18.

65. Ficino here follows Proclus, *In Parmenidem* 6.1107.8–16 (ed. Steel, p. 87) and 1106.2–24 (ed. Steel, pp. 85–86). Proclus does not identify who these "more ancient Platonists" (i.e., Platonists before Proclus) are, and Ficino's "opinion of the more ancient Platonists," below, conflates two distinct sets of opinions related by Proclus. Some modern commentators infer from similarities of language that Proclus means to refer to Iamblichus and Porphyry.

66. The expression "abstractions of abstracts" has no equivalent in Proclus. Ficino may well be attacking the use of scholastic neologisms in -*itas* (already ridiculed by Valla), especially in the context of his refutation of Pico's *De ente et uno* 5 (equivalence between Neoplatonic negations and scholastic abstractions).

67. This refers to the Plotinian and post-Plotinian principle (generally applied to the intelligible world, or to the triad being-life-intellect) that

all things are in all things, but each after its own fashion, whereby one can account for differences and oppositions in the universe without threatening its fundamental unity. See Proclus, *Elements of Theology*, props. 1–3 and notes ad loc. (ed. Dodds, p. 254). Here Ficino assumes that the ancient interpreters reasoned as follows: the triad *essentialitas-vitalitas-intellectualitas* is considered to befit the One because it consists of three aspects of one single entity, whereas the triad *essentia-vita-intellectus*, which consists of three distinct elements, cannot befit God's unity. As he notes above, Ficino himself regards the triad *essentia-vita-intellectus* as three aspects of a single reality, being.

68. The equivalence between the Neoplatonic triad being-life-intellect and the Christian triad *sapientia, veritas,* and *virtus* derives from Augustine, *De fide et symbolo* 2.

69. The "later Platonists" are Proclus and Syrianus.

70. Plato, *Letters* 2.313a3–4.

71. See Proclus, *In Parmenidem* 6.1107.16–1108.15 (ed. Steel, pp. 87–89) and 1109.4–16 (ed. Steel, p. 90).

72. See Proclus, *In Parmenidem* 6.1110.24–1111.15 (ed. Steel, pp. 91–93).

73. See Proclus, *In Parmenidem* 6.1111–12.

74. Plato, *Laws* 4.715e–16a.

75. See Proclus, *In Parmenidem* 6.1113–15.

76. An allusion to Aesop's proverb, immortalized by Horace in *Ars Poetica* 139.

77. Ficino, *In Philebum* 2.1–4 (ed. Allen, pp. 385–425).

78. Prior to all that is composed of limit and infinite Proclus posits the limit and the infinite, as principles immediately after the One. See Proclus, *In Parmenidem* 6.1119–23. See also *Elements of Theology* prop. 90 and *Platonic Theology* 3.8–9.

79. Plotinus (*Enneads* 2.4.5 and 6.7.17) considers limit and infinite as two moments in the process of the emergence of being from the One (the

first is the appearance of unlimited intelligible matter; the second is matter's turning back to its source), whereas Proclus considers limit and infinite as two elements distinct from, and superior to, being.

80. Here Ficino actually uses Proclus' interpretation of *Philebus* to refute . . . Proclus. In his *Platonic Theology* 3.9 (ed. Saffrey-Westerink, p. 36.10–19), Proclus underlines the fact that in the *Philebus* Socrates says that God "has revealed" (in the existential sense of giving existence) the limit and the infinite [23c9–10], but "has made" the mixture (= being) [26e6–8], which he sees as an indication that the limit and the infinite, revealed by God, are two principles separate from being, which is created by God. By contrast, Ficino sees the use of the verbs "reveal" and "create" as evidence that being (created by God) is a principle in itself, while the elements limit and infinite (revealed by God) cannot exist in themselves and are not therefore separate principles. See also Ficino, *In Philebum* 2.4 (ed. Allen, p. 417), where Ficino introduces another distinction between God's *ostensio* or *creatio*, the intellect's *effectio*, and the soul's *generatio*, depending on the nature of the creating principle.

81. See Proclus, *In Parmenidem* 6.1126.

82. See Proclus, *In Parmenidem* 6.1129.

83. See Proclus, *In Parmenidem* 6.1127–28, referring to *Phaedrus* 247c–d.

84. See Plotinus, *Enneads* 2.2.1, and Ficino's commentary ad loc. (*Op.*, pp. 1604–8).

85. Parmenides, fgmt 8.43–44. On the interpretation of this passage and the equivalence between the one of Parmenides' poem and the one of the second hypothesis of the *Parmenides*, see Proclus, *In Parmenidem* 6.1129–30.

86. See Proclus, *In Parmenidem* 6.1130–31.

87. Parmenides, fgmt 8.29; see Proclus, *In Parmenidem* 7.1134.

88. See Proclus, *In Parmenidem* 7.1134–35.

89. Proclus, *In Parmenidem* 7.1140–41.

90. Proclus, *In Parmenidem* 7.1142.

91. Following the principle that what is in itself has one element that encompasses itself and one element that is encompassed by itself. See Proclus, *In Parmenidem* 7.1145–46. Separated substances in scholastic language often refers to the Christian angels.

92. See Proclus, *In Parmenidem* 7.1148.

93. See Proclus, *In Parmenidem* 7.1149.

94. Parmenides, fgmt 8.4 and 26; see Proclus, *In Parmenidem* 7.1152.

95. Parmenides, fgmt 3 and fgmt 8.34–36.

96. Parmenides, fgmt 8.41.

97. Ficino, *Platonic Theology* 5.13.7 (ed. Hankins-Allen, 2: 82–83).

98. Proclus, *In Parmenidem* 7.1154.

99. Proclus, *In Parmenidem* 7.1155.

100. Allusion to the circuits that the soul accomplishes cyclically, as described by Plato's *Phaedrus* and linked to the doctrine of transmigration; see Ficino, *Platonic Theology* 12.3.2 and 12.3.5 (ed. Hankins-Allen, 4: 35–37); 18.8.6 (ibid. 6: 128–29).

101. The notion of oblique motion, intermediary between straight and circular motion (which is absent from the *Parmenides*), derives from the Neoplatonist (pseudo) Dionysius the Areopagite (possibly via Thomas Aquinas; see, e.g., *De veritate* 8.15.3), paraphrased by Ficino in *In Philebum* 26 (ed. Allen, pp. 240–41).

102. See Proclus, *In Parmenidem* 7.1165.

103. See Proclus, *In Parmenidem* 7.1167–69, with a Neoplatonic reinterpretation of Aristotle's "final cause," as in chap. XLVII (Vol. 1).

104. See Proclus, *In Parmenidem* 7.1171–72.

105. *Sophist* 256a. See Ficino, *In Philebum* 2.2 (ed. Allen, pp. 402–7); *In Timaeum* 28 (*Op.*, pp. 1451–53); *In Plotinum, ad Enn.*6.1–3 (*Op.*, pp. 1771–79). The Neoplatonists (Iamblichus, Porphyry, Plotinus, Proclus), who sought to appropriate Aristotle within a Pythagorean-Platonic framework, tried to demonstrate that (1) Aristotle's ten categories ultimately derive from a Pythagorean doctrine developed by Archytas, and (2) while

Aristotle's categories describe the sensible world, the five "more universal" genera of being described by Melissus in the *Sophist* are more appropriate to describe the intelligible realm. Ficino gives a good account of this tradition in his *In Sophistam* 34 (ed. Allen, pp. 255–59).

106. Ficino, *In Philebum* 2.3 (ed. Allen, pp. 408–15); *In Sophistam* 30–31 (ed. Allen, pp. 246–49).

107. See Aristotle's definition in *Categories* 5.4a10–11, quoted in the same context by Proclus, *In Parmenidem* 7.1192.

108. See Proclus, *In Parmenidem* 7.1192.

109. See Proclus, *In Parmenidem* 7.1193–95.

110. Parmenides, fgmt 8.29.

111. See Proclus, *In Parmenidem* 7.1175–77.

112. See Proclus, *In Parmenidem* 7.1177–78.

113. See Proclus, *In Parmenidem* 7.1179–80.

114. See Proclus, *In Parmenidem* 7.1180–81.

115. See Proclus, *In Parmenidem* 7.1182–85.

116. See Proclus, *In Parmenidem* 7.1187.13–29 (ed. Steel, pp. 198–99).

117. Ficino's Latin condenses Proclus's sentence; see the passage cited in the next note.

118. See Proclus, *In Parmenidem* 7.1187.30–1188.14 (ed. Steel, p. 199).

119. See Proclus, *In Parmenidem* 7.1188.24–1189.2 (ed. Steel, p. 200).

120. See Proclus, *In Parmenidem* 7.1198.2–9 (ed. Steel, p. 213), following the Pythagorean table of opposites (which lists ten pairs of opposite attributes) as set out by Aristotle in *Metaphysics* 1.3.986a22 ff.

121. According to the Pythagorean table of opposites, sameness, likeness, and equality belong to the same series. See Proclus, *In Parmenidem* 7.1198.

122. See Proclus, *In Parmenidem* 7.1199–1200, with reference to Plato, *Republic* 6.7.502c–21c.

123. See Proclus, *In Parmenidem* 7.1198.9–21 (ed. Steel, pp. 213–14).

124. See Proclus, *In Parmenidem* 7.1206.

125. See Proclus, *In Parmenidem* 7.1207, with reference to Aristotle's doctrine of motion in *Physics* 7.4.

126. See Proclus, *In Parmenidem* 7.1208.29–1209.2 (ed. Steel, pp. 229–30).

127. See Proclus, *In Parmenidem* 7.1208.21–29 (ed. Steel, p. 229) and 1209.4–11 (ed. Steel, p. 230); Proclus' text contains a lacuna, which is correctly emended by Ficino.

128. Plato, *Philebus* 66a–c, *Theaetetus* 176c, and *Laws* 716c. See Proclus, *In Parmenidem* 7.1209.29–1210.18 (ed. Steel, pp. 231–32).

129. Proclus, *In Parmenidem* 7.1209.11–20 (ed. Steel, pp. 230–31).

130. Plato, *Sophist* 244e; see Proclus, *In Parmenidem* 7.1209.20–29 (ed. Steel, p. 231).

131. See Proclus, *In Parmenidem* 7.1211.18–1212.4 (ed. Steel, pp. 233–34).

132. The notion that the intellects could participate in time contradicts the doctrine of Proclus, who considers that the intellect is in motion but not in time (see *In Parmenidem* 7.1213). However, as is made clear in chap. LXXIV and in chap. XIII of his commentary on the second hypothesis, Ficino stresses that in the intelligible world this form of "time" (*aetas*, i.e., the Idea of time) is not yet unfolded (it will only unfold in the soul) and is enveloped in eternity; in chaps. LXXIII and LXXVI Ficino stresses that "time" in the intellect is a metaphor that refers to a nontemporal, instantaneous process. In this way, he is closer to Plotinus, who considers that eternity (what Ficino considers as the Idea of time before it unfolds at the level of soul) is the life of real being (i.e., the intelligible world), while time, which is the image of eternity, is the life of the soul when seeking to imitate intelligible eternity (*Enneads* 3.7.11–13). See also Ficino, *In Plotinum, ad Enn.* 3.7 (*Op.*, p. 1712).

133. See Proclus, *In Parmenidem* 7.1217–18, where Proclus only relates the attributes "motion" and "time" to the souls and not to the intellects or the intelligible substances. As will become clear in chaps. LXXIII and LXXVI, Ficino considers these attributes to exist metaphorically in the intellects, i.e., they constitute the only way for humans to describe the nontemporal, instantaneous process that occurs within the intellects.

134. See Proclus, *In Parmenidem* 7.1221.

135. Reference to Proclus' definition of eternity as the measure of things eternal; see *Elements of Theology* prop. 54.

136. See Proclus, *In Parmenidem* 7.1225.30–1228.18, who rejects the first two interpretations.

137. As in chap. LXXIII, Ficino allows the existence within the intellect of a sort of instantaneous temporality (equivalent to the Neoplatonic concept of *exaiphnès*, in opposition to discontinuous temporality, *kairos*). As is made clear in chap. LXXVI, the concept of time in the intellect is to be taken metaphorically, as the only way for the human mind to grasp a nontemporal, instantaneous process.

138. See Proclus, *In Parmenidem* 7.1228.23–1229.6 (ed. Steel, p. 258). Proclus distinguishes between heteronymous terms such as son and father, which are different in name and form, and synonymous terms, such as like and equal, which are different in name but identical in form.

139. I.e., the presence of their model, eternity.

140. Theological interpretation of *Parmenides* 141d8–e7. See Proclus, *In Parmenidem* 7.1229.

141. See the expression "time now present" (*to nun paron*) in *Parmenides* 141e3.

142. Revelation 1:8.

143. See (pseudo) Dionysius the Areopagite, *On Divine Names* 10.10.1–3, and Ficino's commentary ad loc. (*Op.*, pp. 1116–18).

144. See Proclus, *In Parmenidem* 7.1240.5–1241.6 (ed. Steel, pp. 275–76).

145. Reference to the scholastic distinction between abstract and concrete being used by Ficino in his commentaries on Plotinus (*Op.*, p. 1764), *Philebus* (ed. Allen, p. 405) and *Sophist* 34 (ed. Allen, pp. 255–57).

146. See Proclus, *In Parmenidem* 7.500.27–501.15 (ed. Steel, p. 288–91). This passage, as well as all subsequent passages from Proclus' *Parmenides* commentary, are only preserved in William of Moerbeke's Latin translation.

147. The demonstration that follows is largely paraphrasing Proclus, *In Parmenidem* 7.500.1–27 (ed. Steel, pp. 286–89).

148. Ficino, *Platonic Theology* 2.2 (ed. Hankins-Allen, 1: 96–106).

149. Plato, *Philebus* 23e9–d1.

150. (Pseudo) Dionysius the Areopagite, *On Divine Names* 4.19–21. This principle is actually mentioned by Proclus, *In Parmenidem* 7.503.18–504.7 (ed. Steel, pp. 298–99).

151. Plato, *Letter* 7.342a–44b.

152. Homer, *Iliad* 14.344–45.

153. See Proclus, *In Parmenidem* 7.506.19–28 (ed. Steel, pp. 304–7). See also n. 27 above.

154. See Proclus, *In Parmenidem* 7.509.10–24 (ed. Steel, pp. 314–17).

155. See Proclus, *In Parmenidem* 7.514.9–35 (ed. Steel, pp. 330–33).

156. Plato, *Letter* 7.343a–44c.

157. Plato, *Letter* 6.323d.

158. See Proclus, *In Parmenidem* 7.515.4–30 (ed. Steel, pp. 334–37). The reference is to *Parmenides* 142a6–8, a passage that led some philosophers, such as Origen the Platonist, to infer that the One of the first hypothesis is without substance and that the first principle is the one being described in the second hypothesis.

159. Plato, *Sophist* 245a–b.

160. Plato, *Republic* 7.533b–34d. See Proclus, *In Parmenidem* 7.515.21–24 (ed. Steel, pp. 336–37).

161. Plato, *Republic* 6.509b.

162. See Proclus, *In Parmenidem* 7.515.26 (ed. Steel, pp. 336–37). Here Ficino's text (*ubi non omnia negat, ubi multa confirmat*) modifies Moerbeke's translation (*neque per tertiam, in qua omnia abnegatiue*).

163. See Proclus, *In Parmenidem* 7.516.33–517.21 (ed. Steel, pp. 340–43), which might be the opinion of Iamblichus.

164. Plato, *Letter* 1.313a.

165. *Quale quid* is a scholastic expression.

166. See Proclus, *In Parmenidem* 7.518.21–28 (ed. Steel, pp. 346–47).

167. Plato, *Letter* 2.312e–13a.

168. Plato, *Letter* 7.342b.

169. Plato, *Timaeus* 29b–c.

170. See (pseudo) Dionysius the Areopagite, *Mystical Theology* 3–5, which draws upon Proclus, *In Parmenidem* 7.519.8–521.25 (ed. Steel, pp. 348–55).

171. "Mercury" here is Hermes Trismegistus. Ficino refers to Philostratus, *Life of Apollonius of Tyana* 1.1; *Corpus Hermeticum* 1.30, 10.5, and 13.2 and 6; and Psalm 65:1. On the doctrine, see Proclus, *In Parmenidem* 7.519.8–521.25 (ed. Steel, pp. 348–55) and *Platonic Theology* 2.11 (ed. Saffrey-Westerink, p. 109).

172. An allusion to the fact that Proclus' commentary (preserved in the Greek original up to 141e and in William of Moerbeke's Latin translation up to 142a) breaks off at the end of the first hypothesis. While Ficino could not rely on Proclus' commentary for the other hypotheses of the *Parmenides*, he could have a fair idea of Proclus' interpretation by reading the latter's *Platonic Theology*.

173. Plato, *Republic* 6.506d8–e7.

174. Plato, *Republic* 6.508c.

175. Orphic term applied by Proclus to the third triad of intelligible gods, which is associated with *Parmenides* 142d9–43a3. See Proclus, *Platonic Theology* 3.26 (ed. Saffrey-Westerink, p. 91.11).

176. Plato, *Letter* 6.323d4, and Ficino's commentary ad loc. (*Op.*, p. 1533–34). See Plotinus, *Enneads* 5.1.8.1–27, which is the first Neoplatonic text that associates the first three hypotheses of the *Parmenides* with the "three kings" mentioned in Plato's *Letter* 2, the "father of the cause" in *Letter* 6, the good in *Republic* 6, and the intellect in the *Timaeus*, and develops the doctrine of the first three hypostases (One, intellect, and soul) of the universe.

177. This is not exactly what Proclus says. According to Proclus, the whole divine soul is introduced in the second hypothesis (on the grounds that the second hypothesis states that the one partakes of "time," which is the property of souls and not of intellectual beings), while the third hypothesis concerns the souls that derive from the divine soul. See Proclus, *Platonic Theology* 1.11 (ed. Saffrey-Westerink, p. 49.17–21); *In Parmenidem* 6.1063.4–1064.10 (ed. Steel, pp. 32–33) and 7.1217.11–22 (ed. Steel, p. 241). The same interpretation is found in chap. LII.

178. See n. 162 above.

179. Here Ficino departs from Proclus' interpretation, according to which each conclusion of the *Parmenides* corresponds to an intelligible order.

180. See the Introduction, pp. xv and xx (Vol. 1), for Ficino's commentary on (pseudo) Dionysius the Areopagite.

181. (Pseudo) Dionysius the Areopagite, *On Divine Names* 1.8 and 5.2.

182. See Proclus, *Platonic Theology* 1.11 (ed. Saffrey-Westerink, pp. 49.6–52.10), where Proclus demonstrates that his predecessors Plotinus, Porphyry, and Iamblichus considered the existence of different orders at the level of being.

183. See the interpretation of *Parmenides* 141d8–e5 by Proclus, *In Parmenidem* 7.1233–39.

184. See Plotinus, *Enneads* 2.7.6–24; Proclus, *Platonic Theology* 3.4 (ed. Saffrey-Westerink, p. 15.4–14).

185. This interpretation corresponds to a Plotinian vision of reality, where every intelligible being is both part and whole; see Plotinus, *Enneads* 5.8.4.

186. The expression *forma totalis,* which has no equivalent in Proclus, describes the emergence of the intellect and being from the One in order to stress the nonidentity of the whole (= the One) and its elements (= intellect and being). *Forma totalis* echoes the expressions *forma totius* and *principium formale* in medieval mereology; see Thomas Aquinas, *De ente et essentia* 2.13; *Summa contra Gentiles* 2.72; *In Aristotelis Metaphysicam* 7.17.27; and *Summa theologiae* 1.76.8. The notions of whole-before-parts, wholes-

of-parts, and wholes-in-the-parts derive from Proclus, *Elements of Theology* props. 67–69, and notes ad loc. (ed. Dodds, pp. 236–37). See also Plotinus, *Enneads* 5.4. On Ficino's distinction between *ens*, *essentia*, and *entitas*, see *In Plotinum, ad Enn.* 5.5 (*Op.*, p. 1764); *In Sophistam* 34 (ed. Allen, pp. 255–57); *In Philebum* 2.2 (ed. Allen, p. 405).

187. See Plotinus, *Enneads* 5.4.2 and 6.6.9 and 15, and Ficino's interpretation ad. loc. (*Op.*, pp. 1784–87).

188. On goodness and beauty as principles that structure and limit the intelligible world, see Ficino, *Platonic Theology* 12.3, echoing Plotinus, *Enneads* 5.5.12; Proclus, *Platonic Theology* 3.28 (ed. Saffrey-Westerink, pp. 101.5–2.5). Ficino's notion of a double intelligible *forma totalis* enables him to describe both God's transcendence (as One and Good) and immanence (as beauty).

189. See Francesco di Zanobi Cattani da Diacceto (1466–1522), Ficino's disciple, later a professor at the Florentine Studio. His major philosophical work is the *De pulchro* in three books, written in 1499; in reference to Ficino's remarks, see 1.9 (ed. Matton, p. 74). Ficino's evocation of Diacceto stands in marked contrast to his mention of Pico in chap. XLIX.

190. For this image, see Ficino, *De amore* 2.3 (ed. Laurens, pp. 27 and 31).

191. Application of Proclus' law of continuity, which justifies the existence of mean terms between two opposites; in scholastic philosophy the mean term is often called a *tertium quid*. See *Elements of Theology* props. 28–29 and notes ad loc. (ed. Dodds, pp. 216–17).

192. See (pseudo) Dionysius the Areopagite, *On Divine Names* 4.8, also cited by Ficino, *In Philebum* 26 (ed. Allen, pp. 240–41). The allegorical meaning here is obvious.

193. The language here is inconsistent, but given what is said in the rest of the paragraph, Ficino probably means the absolute One (*simpliciter unum*).

194. See Plotinus, *Enneads* 6.2.8.32–37.

195. The use of these two images to describe the relation between a transcendent principle and the lower levels of reality derives from Plotinus.

The image of the sun and its rays (*Enneads* 1.7.1; 5.3.12; 5.5.8; 5.6.4; 6.8.18 and 6.9.9) underlines the movement of procession-emanation of the principle toward the realities, while that of the center, the circle, and the rays (*Enneads* 1.7.1; 5.1.11; 6.5.5; 6.8.18; 6.9.8) compares the unity of the principle with the progressive multiplicity of the realities that proceed from it.

196. Plato, *Philebus* 16c–e.

197. See Anaxagoras 59b3.

198. See Anaxagoras 59b3. See also Ficino, *In Plotinum, ad Enn.* 5.8 (*Op.*, p. 1768).

199. Here Ficino refers to a scholastic maxim (*Astrahentium non est mendacium*) which derives from Aristotle, *Physics* 2.193b35. See Thomas Aquinas, *Summa theologiae* 1.7.3.1. This implies that the method of abstraction is only a preparation for the apprehension of divine mysteries.

200. Plato, *Timaeus* 28a–29b.

201. The geometrical shaping of the number from the point to the line, then to the surface, then to the solid is a Pythagorean topos referred to by Aristotle (e.g., *De caelo* 1.1.268a7; *De anima* 1.2.404b21; *Topics* 4.141b5–22; *Metaphysics* 3.4.1001b26–1002b11). Ficino's source is likely to be Proclus, *In Rem Publicam* 2 (ed. Kroll, pp. 51–52), which describes the procession of numbers from the indivisible intellects to the solids.

202. A famous verse of Vergil's *Aeneid* (6.726–27), which was associated by Neoplatonic commentators with the *Timaeus'* world soul (see Macrobius, *Dream of Scipio* 1.14.14). This interpretation was later adopted by the Church fathers, who further identified the world soul with the Holy Ghost.

203. See Ficino, *Platonic Theology* 16.1.9–15 (ed. Hankins-Allen, pp. 234–43).

204. *Pingui* (or *crassa*) *Minerva*, "with a dull Minerva," a well-known phrase in ancient and medieval literature, which denotes that one is using one's own limited gifts; see Cicero, *De amicitia* 5.19, and Horace, *Satires* 2.2.3.

205. See Proclus, *Platonic Theology* 2.10 (ed. Saffrey-Westerink, p. 42.12–20); *In Parmenidem* 7.1191.10–1201.21.

206. See Ficino, *Platonic Theology* 4.1, where he establishes three levels of rational souls: the world soul, the souls of the spheres, and the souls of the living creatures contained within the individual spheres.

207. An allusion to "the Ruling and Liberated Gods" between the hyper-cosmic and the cosmic gods, the four classes of cosmic gods mentioned in Proclus, *Platonic Theology* 6, as well as the cosmic gods, universal souls, and "higher beings" (angels, demons, and heroes) mentioned in Proclus, *In Parmenidem* 7.1201.22–1239.21.

208. See chap. LI; this is an allusion to Syrianus' interpretation of the *Parmenides*, which is based on the notion that each characteristic denied or asserted of the One represents a distinct class of gods.

209. Literally "with a dull Minerva." See n. 204 above.

210. In chap. LIII, on the first hypothesis. See Proclus, *In Parmenidem* 5.1009.1–12.

211. See Proclus, *In Parmenidem* 7.1191.10–1201.12 and *Platonic Theology* 6.14. These gods correspond to Proclus' hypercosmic gods, whose existence is derived from the attributes "like" and "unlike" asserted of the one being.

212. See Proclus, *Platonic Theology* 3.24.

213. See Proclus, *Platonic Theology* 3.24 (ed. Saffrey-Westerink, p. 86.6–9).

214. See Proclus, *Platonic Theology* 4.28.

215. See Proclus, *Platonic Theology* 3.25–26.

216. See Proclus, *Platonic Theology* 4.28–30.

217. The distinction between the reality of the divine world and the way human reason can actually describe it is typical of Plotinus. In *Platonic Theology* 1.10 (ed. Saffrey-Westerink, p. 42.2–20), Proclus distinguishes Plotinus' interpretation of Parmenides' second hypothesis (attributed to the degree of being) from that of Syrianus, who attributed to each characteristic asserted of the one a class of gods.

218. See Proclus, *Platonic Theology* 3.26 and 4.28.

219. See Proclus, *Platonic Theology* 3.26 (ed. Saffrey-Westerink, pp. 91.25–92.28).

220. See Proclus, *Platonic Theology* 3.8 (ed. Saffrey-Westerink, p. 32).

221. See Proclus, *Platonic Theology* 4.34 (ed. Saffrey-Westerink, p. 101.1–4). Allusion to the theory of magic numbers, which are seen as the archetypes of the planets and can thus carry the influences of these planets; see Ficino, *De vita* 3.9–10 and 17.

222. I.e., the perfect number, which embraces the unique and total motion of the universe. See Plato, *Republic* 8.546b–e, and the Neoplatonic interpretation of this passage by Proclus, *Platonic Theology* 4.29 (ed. Saffrey-Westerink, p. 87.5–19); *In Rem Publicam* 2 (ed. Kroll, pp. 16.3–22.19). On Ficino's interpretation, see Michael J. B. Allen, *Nuptial Arithmetic: Marsilio Ficino's Commentary on the Fatal Number in Book VIII of Plato's Republic* (Berkeley, 1994).

223. See Proclus, *Platonic Theology* 4.28 (ed. Saffrey-Westerink, p. 81.14–16).

224. Allusion to the Pythagorean triadic division of the first number adopted by Proclus, *Platonic Theology* 4.31 (ed. Saffrey-Westerink, p. 92.2–5), which Ficino also mentions in his *De numero fatali* 6.46–47 and 8.79–80 and compares with the Trinity (8.22–23).

225. See Proclus, *Platonic Theology* 4.29 (ed. Saffrey-Westerink, pp. 84.22–85.16).

226. Plato, *Republic* 10.617–18. See Proclus, *Platonic Theology* 6.24 (ed. Saffrey-Westerink, p. 110.20–22); Ficino, *Platonic Theology* 17.3 (ed. Hankins-Allen, 6: 28–44).

227. Plato, *Cratylus* 404d. See Proclus, *Platonic Theology* 6.24 (ed. Saffrey-Westerink, p. 110.21–25).

228. See Proclus, *Platonic Theology* 6.24 (ed. Saffrey-Westerink, p. 111.3–6).

229. See Proclus, *Platonic Theology* 6.24 (ed. Saffrey-Westerink, p. 111.11–15).

230. See Ficino, *Platonic Theology* 4.1 (ed. Hankins-Allen, 1: 248–96).

231. See chaps. LII and LXXX. Here Ficino explicitly rejects what he understands to be Proclus' distinction between the goddess soul and the divine souls. According to Proclus, the divine soul is comprised in the second hypothesis (on the grounds that the second hypothesis states that the one partakes of time, which is the property of souls, and not of intellectual beings), while the third hypothesis concerns the souls that derive from the divine soul. See Proclus, *Platonic Theology* 1.11 (ed. Saffrey-Westerink, p. 49.17–21); *In Parmenidem* 6.1063.4–1064.10 (ed. Steel, pp. 32–33) and 7.1217.11–22 (ed. Steel, p. 241). In chaps. LII and LXXX, Ficino interprets Proclus' distinction to be between the goddess soul, object of the final part of the second hypothesis, and the divine soul, object of the third hypothesis.

232. That is, the first five hypotheses, which bring about real conclusions about the five elements, in opposition to the last four hypotheses, which demonstrate through reductions *ad absurdum* that the One must exist.

233. See Ficino, *Platonic Theology* 3.2. The *anima* and *corpus mundi* are linked by the world spirit, which is the quintessence, traditionally associated with the *aether* mentioned in Plato's *Timaeus* and the pseudo-Platonic *Epinomis* as well as Aristotle's *De caelo*, and in late antiquity with the Neoplatonic vehicle of the soul. For Ficino this fifth essence is an ethereal body associated with the *spiritus mundi* and the stuff planets and stars are made of. See Ficino, *In Timaeum* 27 (*Op.*, pp. 1451–52) and *De vita* 3.1 and 3.

234. Ficino, *In Timaeum* 27 (*Op.*, pp. 1451–52).

235. The image of Proteus as an ever-changing prophetic god is a classical topos (see Homer, Vergil, Ovid) that acquires specific meaning in the Renaissance, when it becomes associated with the mutability of the soul and its magic and prophetic powers. Here Ficino alludes to the Orphic *Hymn of Proteus* (Hymn 25) as in *Platonic Theology* 4.2.5 (ed. Hankins-Allen, 1: 302–3).

236. See Plotinus, *Enneads* 4.1–2.

237. See Ficino, *Platonic Theology* 4.2.5 (ed. Hankins-Allen, 1: 300–305) and *In Timaeum* 15–16 (*Op.*, p. 1444). On the circular motion of the universe and mind, see Plotinus, *Enneads* 2.2.1–2.

238. Boethius, *Consolatio philosophiae* 3.9.16–17.

239. Ficino, *Platonic Theology* 4.2 and *In Plotinum, ad Enn.* 2.2 (*Op.*, pp. 1604–8).

240. Phoebe is the Moon, Phoebus is the Sun. See Ficino, *De sole* 8 and *De vita* 3.6.

241. See Aristotle, *Physics* 6.1–4.10–14 and 8.1.

242. See Aristotle, *Physics* 8.1.

243. Which would result in admitting that the rest required for opposite motion is in fact an indivisible moment in a motion, a contradiction.

244. Aristotle considers that motion and time are divisible. Ficino's argument is that Aristotle's definition of motion concerns bodies rather than souls, whereas at the level of soul, motion and time are indivisible.

245. In natural objects essence differs from and precedes existence; see Ficino, *Platonic Theology* 5.7 (ed. Hankins-Allen, 2: 36–41).

246. On the distinction between the whole as sum of its parts, the whole before the parts, and the whole as implicit in each of its parts, see Proclus, *Elements of Theology* props. 67–69.

247. See Plotinus, *Enneads* 6.6.5–6.

248. Here Ficino interprets the *Parmenides* through the *Philebus*, which establishes the existence of a mixture composed of limit and infinity in all beings.

249. Following the Pythagorean table of opposites; see Proclus, *In Parmenidem* 7.1198.2–11.

250. The doctrine of *concordia discors* refers to the idea that the conflicts between the four elements in nature paradoxically create an overall harmony in the world. The Latin expression was coined by Horace (*Epistles* 1.12.19–20) to describe Empedocles' theory according to which the world is governed by love and strife, sympathies and antipathies.

251. "Prime matter" refers to Plotinus' "intelligible matter," the infinity and receptacle of forms in the intelligible world, to be distinguished from matter in the sensible world. See *Enneads* 2.4.15.

252. I.e., the proposition at *Parmenides* 159d–60b, which denies what had been asserted of the others in the fourth hypothesis (the others are not one in any sense, are not many, etc.) and, if taken literally, contradicts some basic Neoplatonic tenets.

253. In other words, the fifth hypothesis could secretly concern the relation between the first being (i.e., the limit, which gives forms) and the intelligible matter (i.e., infinity, which receives forms) within the intelligible world, rather than the sensible matter. See Plotinus, *Enneads* 2.4. Proclus rejects this doctrine, considering that limit and infinity in the intelligible world are related to one another as substance to potency rather than as form and matter; see Proclus, *Platonic Theology* 3.9.

254. In other words, the hypothesis considers the relation between the one being and sensible, formless matter, even if there is a possibility for it to secretly consider the relation between the one being and intelligible matter. As the last degree in the universe, sensible matter is nothing except one.

255. On the distinction between negations by excess and by defect, see Proclus, *In Parmenidem* 6.1075–77 and (pseudo) Dionysius the Areopagite, *On Divine Names* 7.2 and 11.1.

256. See Plotinus, *Enneads* 3.6.7–8 and 13–14. Matter, like a mirror, remains unaffected by that which is reflected on it.

257. See Plotinus' and Proclus' doctrines of sensible matter. Plotinus maintains that sensible matter, as the last stage of emanation from the One-and-Good, is pure indeterminacy and evil, although it is created by the first principle (*Enneads* 2.4.1.8–14). This paradoxical consequence leads his followers to reject this doctrine. Thus Proclus, drawing upon *Philebus* 23c–30e, maintains that the first principle is immediately followed by two principles, limit and infinity, which are present at every level of reality. At the lowest level form and matter are distinguished into two separate elements, the former under the series of limit and the latter under the series of infinity. So matter is both indeterminate and good, since it stems directly from the One. See Proclus, *Platonic Theology* 3.9–10 and *In Parmenidem* 6.1119–20.

258. The same allusion is found in Proclus' *Platonic Theology* 4.1.16 (ed. Saffrey-Westerink, p. 270). Ficino alludes to a Pythagorean and Neoplatonic tradition according to which the appellation "Apollôn" derives from the Greek terms *haploun*, meaning "simple," and *apo-* or *a-pollôn*, "cut off from the many"; as such it symbolizes the One. Although this tradition is already present in Plotinus (*Enneads* 5.5.6.27–28), here Ficino is clearly drawing upon Proclus, *Platonic Theology* 6.12 (ed. Saffrey-Westerink, pp. 58.1–61.2), where Apollo is identified with the sun, truth, and the One-and-Good.

259. Parmenides, fgmt 8.43–44. According to a certain tradition described by Proclus (*In Parmenidem* 6.1129–30), Parmenides' mention of a sphere refers to the intellect's turning back upon itself. On the shapelessness of the intelligible world, see chap. LXI, 3–4.

260. Plato, *Theaetetus* 184a.

261. Here Ficino passes from a Proclean reading of Parmenides' "paradoxical" statements (in the present context, the hypothesis that the one is not) as maieutic in character to an interpretation that underlines the poetic and mystical aspects of divinely inspired philosophy.

262. On the triple modality of the One (superior to, coordinate with, and inferior to being) associated with the first three hypotheses, see Proclus, *In Parmenidem* 6.1039–40.

263. On the two modalities of not-being (absolutely or partially), see Proclus, *In Parmenidem* 6.1039.

264. *Signa indicativa* is a scholastic expression that refers to the manifest and visible signs of hidden things, in opposition to the "telling signs," which are the natural accompaniments of the thing signified. Here Ficino refers to the hidden mysteries that lie behind Parmenides' paradoxes.

265. See Anaxagoras 59b6 and b1.

266. See chap. CVI above: at the level of the soul, not-being truly is not; it is therefore true and perfect not-being within nature.

267. A traditional scholastic expression referring to the doctrine of transcendentals that Ficino had refuted (mostly to oppose Pico), in the context of the supreme One, in the discourses proving the superiority of the One over being.

Bibliography

༜ৡ༜

Allen, Michael J. B. "Ficino's Theory of the Five Substances and the Neo-platonists' *Parmenides*." *Journal of Medieval and Renaissance Studies* 12 (1982): 19–44. Reprinted in Allen's *Plato's Third Eye: Studies in Marsilio Ficino's Metaphysics and Its Sources*, no. VIII. Aldershot: Variorum, 1995.

——. *Icastes: Marsilio Ficino's Interpretation of Plato's* Sophist. *Five Studies and a Critical Edition with Translation*. Berkeley: University of California Press, 1989.

——. "Marsilio Ficino on Plato, the Neoplatonists and the Christian Doctrine of the Trinity." *Renaissance Quarterly* 37 (1984): 555–84.

——. *The Platonism of Marsilio Ficino: A Study of his Phaedrus Commentary, Its Sources and Genesis*. Berkeley: University of California Press, 1984.

——. "The Second Ficino-Pico Controversy." In *Marsilio Ficino e il ritorno di Platone, Studi e Documenti* 2: 418–55. Edited by Gian Carlo Garfagn-ini. Florence: Olschki, 1986. Reprinted in *Plato's Third Eye*, no. X.

—— and Valerie Rees, eds. *Marsilio Ficino: His Theology, His Philosophy, His Legacy*. London: E. J. Brill, 2002.

Beierwaltes, Werner. *Denken des Einen. Studien zur neuplatonischen Philoso-phie und ihrer Wirkungsgeschichte*. Frankfurt: Klostermann, 1985. Italian translation: *Pensare l'Uno. Studi sulla filosofia neoplatonica e sulla storia dei suoi influssi*. Translated by Maria Luisa Gatti. Milan: Vita e Pensiero, 1992.

——. "L'interpretazione ficiniana del *Parmenide* platonico." In *Il Par-menide di Platone e la sua tradizione. Atti del III Colloquio internazionale del Centro di Ricerca sul Neoplatonismo, Università degli studi di Catania, 31 maggio–2 giugno 2001*, 389–410. Edited by Maria Barbanti and Fran-cesco Romano. Catania: CUECM, 2002.

Dodds, E. R. "The *Parmenides* of Plato and the Origin of the Neopla-tonic 'One.'" *Classical Quarterly* 22 (1928): 129–42.

Étienne, A. "Marsile Ficin, lecteur et interprète du *Parménide* à la Renais-sance." In *Images de Platon et lectures de ses oeuvres: les interprétations de*

Platon à travers les siècles, 153–85. Edited by Ada Neschke-Hentschke. Louvain: Peeters, 1997.

Gersh, Stephen, and M. J. F. M. Hoenen, eds. *The Platonic Tradition in the Middle Ages: A Doxographic Approach.* Berlin: Walter de Gruyter, 2002.

Hankins, James. *Humanism and Platonism in the Italian Renaissance.* 2 vols. Rome: Edizioni di Storia e Letteratura, 2004–2008.

——. *Plato in the Italian Renaissance.* 2 vols. Leiden: E. J. Brill, 1990.

Klibansky, Raymond. "Plato's *Parmenides* in the Middle Ages and the Renaissance." *Medieval and Renaissance Studies* 1 (1943): 281–330. Reprinted in *The Continuity of the Platonic Tradition during the Middle Ages.* Millwood, NY: Kraus, 1982.

Kristeller, Paul Oskar. *Marsilio Ficino and His Works after Five Hundred Years.* Florence: Olschki, 1987.

——. *The Philosophy of Marsilio Ficino.* Translated by Virginia Conant. New York: Columbia University Press, 1943. Original Italian version: *Il pensiero filosofico di Marsilio Ficino.* Florence: Sansoni, 1953; revised edition Florence: Le Lettere, 1988.

Lazzarin, Francesca. "L'*Argumentum in Parmenidem* di Marsilio Ficino." *Accademia* 6 (2004): 7–34.

——. "Note sull'interpretazione ficiniana del *Parmenide* di Platone." *Accademia* 5 (2003): 17–37.

Malmsheimer, Arne. *Platons* Parmenides *und Marsilio Ficinos* Parmenides-Kommentar. Ein kritischer Vergleich. Amsterdam: B. R. Gruner, 2001.

Saffrey, Henri Dominique. "La philosophie néoplatonicienne, fruit de l'exégèse du *Parménide.*" *Revue de Théologie et de Philosophie* 116 (1984): 1–12.

Vanhaelen, Maude. "The Pico-Ficino Controversy: New Evidence in Ficino's Commentary on Plato's *Parmenides.*" *Rinascimento* n.s. 49 (2009): 301–39.

Vasoli, Cesare. *Quasi sit Deus. Studi su Marsilio Ficino.* Lecce: Conte, 1999.

Index

꙳ᱬꙶ

Note: Works are listed by author and title, so that the entries for works follow the main entry for the author; e.g., the entry for Plotinus is followed by the entry for Plotinus, *Enneads*. References are to volume and page number.

about, and One, 2:171–73

absolute Good, 1:173, 1:203, 1:205, 1:217, 1:219, 2:61

absolute goodness, 1:235

absolute knowledge, and absolute truth, 1:119–23

absolute One, 1:193n156, 1:203, 2:31–35, 2:67; Apollo as, 2:303; conversion of all things toward, 2:209; distinguished from henads, 2:25; existence of, 2:11–13; in first hypothesis, 2:15, 2:23, 2:25, 2:33, 2:183; and matter, 2:303; name of, 2:173; necessity of, 2:339; negations about, 2:185, 2:199, 2:327; perception of, 2:25, 2:27, 2:325; as principle of universe, 1:225–29, 2:17, 2:299; separated from properties of being, 2:71, 2:75, 2:77, 2:79, 2:81, 2:83, 2:85, 2:89, 2:93, 2:115, 2:117, 2:121, 2:125, 2:133, 2:137, 2:139, 2:167, 2:171; superior to all things, 2:113, 2:283, 2:287, 2:295, 2:297; superior to being, 2:15, 2:105, 2:111, 2:153,

2:155, 2:157, 2:233, 2:237, 2:243, 2:275, 2:311; union with, 2:275

absolute truth, and absolute knowledge, 1:119–23

absolute Unity, as first principle, 2:33

abstract appellations, about God, 2:61

abstractions of abstracts, 1:xxxiii–xxxiv, 2:59–63, 2:61n66

Academy, Plato's (Athens), 1:xi

accidental qualities, 1:61

accidents, 2:71, 2:109, 2:229; Ideas of, 1:61

action, 1:39, 1:49, 1:67, 1:69, 1:95, 1:97, 1:107, 1:127, 1:131, 1:209–11; denied of One, 2:91; as one of four elements, 2:91; proceeds from power, 2:99

act of being, 2:3, 2:23, 2:83, 2:151–53, 2:231, 2:281, 2:315, 2:317, 2:321

actualized intelligence, 1:215

actus directus/actus reflexus, 1:xxxi–xxxii, 1:113n60, 1:113n62, 1:119n68. See also *consequenter;*

deuterôs; per consequentiam; per reflexionem

Adeimantus (character), 1:39

age: denied of One, 2:137–41, 2:143; example of, 2:235–37; and One, 2:143; and one being, 2:229–39; and third hypothesis, 2:255

Aglaophemus, 1:xiv

agriculture, 1:65

Albert the Great, 1:xii

Albert the Great, *Summa de bono 1.1.10*, 1:xxxiv n84

Albinus (Alcinous), 1:ix

Alexandria, Neoplatonists in, 1:x

Al-Kindi, 1:53n8

Allen, Michael J. B., 1:xxix

alteration: denied of the One, 2:93–95; denied and asserted of the soul, 2:269, 2:321–23; use of term, 2:93–95. *See also* change

Amelius, 1:ix, 1:173

Ammonius Saccas, 1:173, 1:173n131

analysis, 1:35n2, 1:139, 1:147, 1:193

Anaxagoras, 2:221, 2:247, 2:315; *59b3*, 2:221n197–2:221n198; *59b6*, 2:315n265

angels, 1:xii, 1:xxvi, 1:123, 1:231, 2:87n91, 2:239–41

anteriority, 2:257–59

Antiphon (character), 1:39

apex: in the expression *apex mentis*, 1:xviii n35; to render *akrotès*, 1:187n150; unity as summit, 2:25, 2:197

Apollo, 2:303n258; as absolute One, 2:303. *See also* Phoebus

Apollonius of Tyana, 2:175, 2:303

Aquinas, Thomas, 1:xii–xiii, 1:xxxii, 1:119n68

Aquinas, Thomas, *De ente et essentia 2.13*, 1:xxxvi n91, 2:189n186

Aquinas, Thomas, *De Malo 3.12.10*, 1:xxxii n79

Aquinas, Thomas, *De veritate: 8.12*, 1:217n179; *8.15.3*, 2:95n101

Aquinas, Thomas, *In Aristotelis Metaphysicam 7.17.27*, 1:xxxvi n91, 2:189n186

Aquinas, Thomas, *Summa contra Gentiles 2.72*, 1:xxxvi n91, 2:189n186

Aquinas, Thomas, *Summa theologiae: 1.5.1.3*, 1:xxxiii n81, 1:213n173, 1:215n177; *1.5–6*, 1:211n172; *1.6.1*, 1:219n180; *1.6.2*, 1:205n165; *1.6.28*, 1:xxxiv n84; *1.7.3.1*, 1:xxii n48, 2:221n199; *1.14.5*, 1:113n61; *1.14.6*, 1:121n69; *1.76.8*, 2:189n186; *1.86.1*, 1:xxxii n79, 1:117n66; *3.63.3*, 1:121n71; *76.8*, 1:xxxvi n91

Arians, 2:239

Aristoteles (character), 1:vii

Aristotle, 1:75n30; compared with Plato, 1:xi, 1:xiii, 1:xvi, 1:xxi–xxii, 1:xxiii–xxiv, 1:35n4, 1:173n132, 1:223–25, 1:235; on dialectic, 1:35n4; and doctrine of categories, 2:105n105, 2:109n107; on motion and time, 2:275n244; Neoplatonists' interpretation of, 1:xi–xii, 1:205n165, 1:223–25, 2:101,

Aristotle (continued)
2:105n105; on the One/Good
and Being, 1:213n174, 1:223–25,
1:235, 1:205n165, 2:101; Pico's interpretation of, 1:xx–xxv, 1:xxix,
1:173n132, 1:179n143, 1:205n165,
1:207n167, 1:225n184, 1:225n185,
1:235; refuted by Plotinus,
2:53n56; refuted by Proclus,
1:127n77, 1:133n81; Third Man
argument, 1:87n42; Valla's use
of, 1:xxxiv
Aristotle, Categories 5.4a10–11,
2:109n107
Aristotle, De anima: 1.2.404b21,
2:229n201; 3.427a, 2:25n26
Aristotle, De caelo, 2:257n233;
1.1.268a7, 2:229n201
Aristotle, Metaphysics: 1.2.404b21,
2:229n201, 1.3.986a22, 2:123n120;
1.9.990b17, 1:87n42; 3.4.1001b26–
1002b11, 2:229n201; 6.1056b33,
1:179n143; 10.3.1054a20,
1:179n143; 12.5.1071a, 1:127n77;
12.7.1072b13, 1:205n165
Aristotle, Nicomachean Ethics
1.1.1094a3, 1:205n165
Aristotle, Physics: 2.193b35, 1:xxii
n48, 2:221n199; 6.1–4,
2:271n241; 7.4, 2:131n125; 8.1,
2:271n241, 2:271n242
Aristotle, Topics: 1.1.101a–b, 1:xxii
n47, 1:35n4; 4.141b5–22,
2:229n201; 7.14.136a37–b13, 1:xxii
n47; 7.14.136a–b, 1:35n4
art: forms in, 1:49; and nature,
2:287

artificial objects, lacking Ideas, 1:63
artisan, image of, 2:29, 2:235,
2:263, 2:287, 2:297
ascent: to first intellect, 2:23–25;
of soul, 1:xvii–xviii, 1:xli–xlv,
1:203n162
assertions: in hypotheses, 2:15–19,
2:29, 2:41–43, 2:179, 2:257,
2:313; about One, 2:27, 2:59–63,
2:171–75; about one being,
2:199–201
association between things, does
not imply existence of single
common Idea, 1:87
astrology, 1:xli–xlv
astronomy, 2:267
Athena, 1:65
Augustine, against demons, 1:xli
Augustine, De Civitate Dei 8.30,
1:3n5
Augustine, De fide et symbolo 2,
2:61n68
Augustine, De Trinitate 15.13,
1:121n70

Bacchelli, Franco, 1:xxiii
Balbi, Pietro, 1:xiv n20
Barbaro, Ermolao, 1:xxiii
to be, as name for first principle,
1:207–9
beautiful, Idea of, 1:173
beauty, intelligible, 2:197, 2:233;
and light, 2:197; as plenum of
forms (formosa), 1:195; in relation to the Good and being,
1:197; residing in ideal species,
1:151; and ugly objects, 1:69

becoming, 1:189; and essence, 1:189
becoming older/younger, and being older/younger, 2:235–39
"becoming the same as something," 2:113–15
beginning: asserted of One, 2:63, 2:85; denied of One, 2:65–69
being: concrete and abstract, 1:207n167, 2:151, 2:155, 2:189; defined, 2:231; degrees of, 1:221, 2:325–27; denied of "nothing," 2:159; denied of One, 2:159–67; and desirable, 1:213; and first principle, 1:205n163; and Good, 1:xxii–xxxiii, 1:211n172, 1:213, 1:215–25; and matter, 2:301; multiple modalities of, 1:221; and not-being, 2:257, 2:303–13, 2:321–25; and number, 2:49–63; and One, 1:169–71, 1:193, 2:149–57; as one of four elements, 2:91; opposite of, 1:41; rational principle of, 1:41, 1:217; in Sophist, 1:xxix–xxx; and soul, 2:275–83; "universal or all being is one," 1:39–41; use of term, 2:151–53, 2:189, 2:315; and well-being, 1:213n175; as whole, multiple, and one, 1:169. See also first being; not-being; one being
"being in something," 2:99
beings, 1:85; relation to Ideas, 1:51
"being to the highest degree," 1:219
Benivieni, Girolamo, 1:xxiii
Bessarion, Cardinal, 1:xiii, 1:xiii n16, 1:xxi

Bessarion, Cardinal, *In calumniatorem Platonis*, 1:xiii n16
Bible: *Acts 17:34*, 1:xii; *Psalm 65:1*, 2:175n171; *Revelation 1:8*, 2:149n142
Boccaccio, Giovanni, 1:xl
bodies, and corporeal forms, 1:53
body, as whole or part, 1:77. *See also* mirror reflection
body as a whole, Idea of, 1:61, 1:67
Boethius, Anicius Manlius Severinus, 1:129, 2:267
Boethius, Anicius Manlius Severinus, *Consolatio philosophiae*: *3.9.16–17*, 2:267n238; *4.6.12*, 1:129n78
Book of XXXIV Philosophers, 1:3n5
"both," 2:191
Brisson, Luc, 1:ix n5
bronze-working, 1:65
Bruni, Leonardo, 1:xl
Bussanich, John, 1:xxv
Byzantine scholars, and *Parmenides*, 1:xii

candle, image of, 2:119
Catholics, 2:239
cause, and paradigm, 1:59. *See also* divine cause, all things pertain to; efficient cause/causes; final cause
celestial souls, 2:179, 2:257, 2:261, 2:263; motion and, 2:265–67, 2:275
celestial sphere, 2:261
Cephalus (character), 1:39
Ceres, 1:65

certainty, and intelligence, 1:215–17

Chaldaean Oracles, 1:viii–ix

chameleon, image of, 2:263

change: as characteristic of particulars, 1:59; soul and, 2:259–61, 2:263–65

Charybdis and Scylla, 2:157

choosing, not simply to be but to be well and good, 1:209–13

Christian mysticism, 1:xii, 1:xviii, 1:xx, 1:xxxiv–xxxv; Ficino and, xxvi, 1:xx, 1:xxviii

Christian ritual, 1:xl

Christian Trinity, 1:xxxviii, 2:47, 2:55, 2:57, 2:239, 2:251

Cicero, De amicitia 5.19, 2:239n204

circle, 2:201; and conversion, 2:79–81; image of, 2:3, 2:25, 2:85, 2:229, 2:247

circuit, of soul, 2:93n100, 2:139, 2:143–45

circular motion: denied of One, 2:97–101; and intellect, 2:201; and intelligence, 2:79–81, 2:229; perpetual, 2:145; and soul, 2:93, 2:265–75, 2:323

circular shape, 2:201

cognition, 1:55, 1:209–11. See also divine cognition

cold, Idea of, 1:117

"coming to be in something," 2:97–99

communicability, 1:135

communicable providence, 1:107–11

comparison, method of, 1:175–79; between equal things, 2:135–37; between sun and Good, 1:169

comparisons, about God, 1:xxxiv–xxxv, 1:175–79, 2:59–63, 2:125

composite, 2:103, 2:203–5; and forms, 2:285–87; multitude as, 2:291

conclusions: negative and assertive, 2:17, 2:21, 2:41–43, 2:49, 2:167, 2:169, 2:171; and orders of gods, 2:17, 2:41, 2:179–81, 2:339; true and absurd, 2:7, 2:257n232

concordia discors, 2:293n250

concrete appellations, about God, 2:61

condition, and material forms, 1:85

cone, as geometric shape, 2:75

consequent, more universal than premise, 2:51

consequenter, 1:xxxii

contact: in eighth hypothesis, 2:337; and one being, 2:85, 2:217–19, 2:253–55

contemplation: of the Good, 1:201; in relation to intellect and Ideas, 1:49, 1:55, 1:139; of truth, 1:x, 1:xvi, 1:xxii–xxiii, 1:xl, 1:5

contemplative sciences, Ideas of, 1:65

continuum: of corporeal motion, 2:271–73; as image, 2:187–89, 2:195; and number, 2:227, 2:245

contradictions, 2:39–41, 2:327

contradictories, related to same subject, 2:45–47

conversion, 1:105, 1:157, 1:179; and circle, 2:79–81; denied of One, 2:81; One and, 2:89; power of, 2:87–89

Corbinelli, Antonio, 1:xv
corporeal forms, and bodies, 1:53
corporeal qualities, as components
    of corporeal world, 1:53
Corpus Dionysiacum, 1:xii n13
Corpus Hermeticum: 1.30, 2:175n171;
    10.5, 2:175n171; *13.2*, 2:175n171
correspondences, 1:xli, 1:xliii
cosmic gods, 2:161, 2:241,
    2:241n207, 2:253, 2:255
Council of Lateran (649), 1:xii n13
curiositas (inquisitiveness), 1:xxvi,
    1:xxvi n61
cylinder, as geometric shape, 2:75

Damascius, 1:ix–x, 1:173
Dante Alighieri, *Divine Comedy*,
    1:xxxix
David, prophet, 2:175
definition, 1:35, 1:35n2, 1:143–47,
    1:89
degrees: of being, 1:221, 1:223n182,
    2:7, 2:331; of essence, 1:211, 1:221;
    of gods, 2:245; of "more or
    less," 1:xxxii, 1:213, 1:217; varia-
    tion of, 1:221n181
demons, 1:xlii–xliii, 1:65, 1:85; gov-
    ern men, 1:119, 1:231; lunar, 1:99;
    and sense perception, 2:161
demonstration, 1:35, 1:35n2, 1:143–
    47
density, and soul, 2:269
desirable: and being, 1:213; and
    Good, 1:213, 1:217, 1:219,
    1:221n181, 2:59; as highest
    Good, 1:167
desire, 1:209–11; for the One/

Good, 1:xx, 1:xxxv, 1:179, 1:203–
    5, 1:211–13, 1:215–17, 1:221–25,
    2:27, 2:63, 2:69, 2:81, 2:83, 2:163
deuterôs, 1:xxxii
Diacceto, Francesco da, 2:197; *De
    pulchro*, 2:197n189
dialectic: 1:vii, 1:35n2, 1:151,
    1:193n155, 2:169, 2:221–23; com-
    parison of Plato with Aristotle
    on, 1:xxii, 1:35n4; Ficino on,
    1:xxii, 1:xxvi; and ideal species,
    1:147; Plato's use of method,
    1:vii–viii, 1:xxii; Plato's use
    of term, 1:35; and poetry,
    1:xxxviii–xli, 2:305; Proclus on,
    1:x; stages of, 1:xxi, 1:139n90,
    1:141, 1:143–47; and theology,
    1:xxvi, 1:157–63, 2:169, 2:221; as
    training, 1:71, 1:111, 2:221
dialectica/dialektikè, 1:xxii, 1:35
dialectical exercise, 1:149–51
dialectical rules, for hypothesizing
    being or not-being, 1:151–57
differentiae, 2:39, 2:191, 2:319
dimension, 1:191, 1:195; as compo-
    nent of corporeal world, 1:53;
    principle of, 2:69; related to
    equal and unequal, 2:45, 2:227
Dionysius the Areopagite, 1:xii,
    1:xii n11; 1:xii n13, 1:xv, 1:xvii,
    1:xx, 1:xxiii, 1:xli, 1:137, 1:137n85,
    1:163, 1:209, 2:17, 2:23, 2:29,
    2:29n29, 2:57, 2:59, 2:95n101,
    2:149, 2:181. See also *Corpus Di-
    onysiacum*
Dionysius the Areopagite, *Celestial
    Hierarchy*, 1:xii

Dionysius the Areopagite, *Mystical Theology*, 2:173; *3–5*, 2:173n170

Dionysius the Areopagite, *On Divine Names*: 1:xii, 2:181; *1.5–6*, 1:209n169; *1.8*, 2:181n181; *4.8*, 2:201n192; *4.19–21*, 2:159n150; *5.2*, 2:181n181; *5.3*, 2:57n59; *7.2*, 2:299n255; *10.10.1–3*, 2:149n143; *11.1*, 2:299n255

discourses: embedded in *Commentary on Parmenides*, 1:xxiv–xxv; first discourse, 1:179–87; second discourse, 1:187–91; third discourse, 1:191–99; fourth discourse, 1:201–5; fifth discourse, 1:207–9; sixth discourse, 1:209–13; seventh discourse, 1:215–25

dispositions, and rational principle of being, 1:213

dissolution, and soul, 2:321–25

distinction, and intelligence, 2:247

divine cause, all things pertain to, 1:67–69

divine cognition, 1:133–37

divine gaze, 1:113, 1:133, 1:201

divine intellect, 2:211, 2:241, 2:245

divine knowledge, 1:123–37

divine light, 1:201

divine madness (*mania, furor*), 1:xxxix, 2:305

divine mastership, 1:133–37

divine matters, cannot be known like scientific knowledge, 1:113

divine names: invocation of, 1:xliv–xlv; as *sunthemata* of the gods, 1:75n33

divine orders, number of, 2:17

divine providence, 1:123–33; all things pertain to, 1:67–69

divine realities, 2:283–93

divine sense perception, 1:131

divine soul, 2:19n16, 2:255, 2:257n231; and change, 2:263–65; and mind, 2:265–75

divine species, 1:89–91

division, 1:35, 1:35n2, 1:79–83, 1:129, 1:145–47, 1:193, 1:225; method of, 2:85

Dodds, E. R., 1:ix

doubt, 1:67–69

dyad, 1:xliv, 1:165–67; "having parts" as, 2:65; related to essence, 2:251

each (term), 2:289

Eckhardt, Meister, 1:xxxvii

efficient cause/causes, 1:xi n9, 1:63, 1:65, 1:73, 1:109, 1:127, 1:131, 1:133, 1:183, 1:223n183, 2:15, 2:31, 2:53, 2:101, 2:201

efficient force, 1:101–3

efficient powers, 1:97, 2:17

"Eleatic Stranger" (character in *Sophist*), 1:xxix, 1:159n109, 1:173n130. *See also* Melissus (disciple of Parmenides)

emotion, and soul, 2:93, 2:95, 2:269–71

Empedocles, 2:293

end: asserted of One, 2:63, 2:85, 2:137, 2:153, 2:163, 2:169, 2:339; denied of One, 2:65–69

ens, essentia, and *entitas,* 1:209n168

entity, and being, 2:189, 2:191

equal and unequal, 2:123, 2:127–37; and matter, 2:301; and not-being, 2:317–21; and one being, 2:221–25

equality, 2:181; Idea of, 1:79–83; implies multitude, 2:131–33; and one being, 2:223–25; and soul, 2:269

essence, 1:167, 1:169, 1:209–11; denied of One, 2:43, 2:159–67; and desire for good, 1:211–13; differs formally from life and intellect, 1:221; distinguished from generation, 1:189; distributed in intelligible world, 2:193–95; does not admit of more or less, 1:221; and first principle, 1:229–35; and the Good, 1:215; is both not-one and one, 2:107; is not common to all things, 1:189; as name for first principle, 1:207–9; and not-being, 2:317–21; and One, 1:185–87, 2:149–57; and one being, 2:183–89, 2:325; as one of four elements, 2:91; participation in, 2:149–57; possesses number, 2:193; precedes life, 2:139; as procession from One, 2:229; rational principle of, 2:189, 2:191; relation to unity, 2:3; separate from greatness, number, time, and quality, 1:217; and soul, 2:259–61; and unity, 1:203; use of term, 2:151–53. See also first essence

essentiality, 1:xxxiii–xxxiv, 2:61

eternity, 2:141, 2:147. See also time

evil, 1:201, 1:215; as dispersion, 1:203; divine knowledge of, 1:133–35

evils lack Ideas, 1:65–67

exaiphnès, 2:145n137

ex se, 1:47

Ficino, Marsilio: and Christian mysticism, 1:xx, 1:xxvi, 1:xxviii; and "middle path" between Plotinus and Proclus, 1:xxv–xxviii; and Neoplatonism, 1:xiv–xvi, 1:xxxvii; and Pico (see Pico-Ficino controversy); and scholasticism, 1:xxxi–xxxviii; as teacher of philosophy, 1:xvi n31; as translator, 1:xiii–xiv; use of Plotinus, 1:xxv–xxxi; use of Proclus, 1:xvi–xx, 1:xxv–xxxi; working methods, 1:xv–xvi

Ficino, Marsilio, *Argumentum on Ion*, 1:xl

Ficino, Marsilio, commentaries on various Neoplatonic texts, 1:xli, 1:105, 2:107, 2:149, 2:257, 2:265

Ficino, Marsilio, *Commentary on the Divine Names*, 1:xli, 1:163n116

Ficino, Marsilio, *Commentary on Parmenides*, 1:xiii–xvi; character and themes, 1:xvi–xx; composition and publication, 1:xv; and Pico-Ficino controversy, 1:xx–xxv

Ficino, Marsilio, *Commentary on Symposium*, 1:xl

Ficino, Marsilio, *De amore 2.3*, 2:197n190

Ficino, Marsilio, *De Christiana religione*, 2:35n34

Ficino, Marsilio, *De numero fatali 6.46–47*, 2:251n224

Ficino, Marsilio, *De sole 8*, 2:267n240

Ficino, Marsilio, *De vita*, 1:xli, 1:xlii, 1:xliv, 2:267; *3*, 1:85; *3.1–2*, 1:99n48; *3.6*, 2:267n240; *3.9–10*, 1:xliv n106, 2:251n221; *3.14*, 1:xliii n104, 1:85n39; *3.16*, 1:53n8; *3.17*, 1:xliv n106

Ficino, Marsilio, *De voluptate*, 1:217n178

Ficino, Marsilio, *Di Dio et anima*, 1:3n5

Ficino, Marsilio, *In Phaedrum*, 1:xl; *7.1–2*, 1:xviii n35; *Argumentum*, 1:xl n101

Ficino, Marsilio, *In Philebum*, 1:197, 2:71, 2:105; *2.1*, 1:xxxi n75, 1:73n27, 1:167n120, 1:195n158; *2.1–4*, 2:71n77; *2.2*, 1:209n168, 2:105n105, 2:189n186; *2.3*, 2:107n106; *2.4*, 2:73n80; *11*, 1:xlv n107, 1:75n33; *26*, 2:95n101, 2:201n192

Ficino, Marsilio, *In Plotinum*, 1:xv n24, 1:45, 1:131; *ad Enn. 2.2*, 2:267n239; *ad Enn. 3.1*, 1:131n80; *ad Enn. 3.6*, 1:xxxi n75, 1:73n27; *ad Enn. 3.7*, 2:139n132; *ad Enn. 5.5*, 1:209n168, 2:189n186; *ad Enn. 5.7*, 1:45n6; *ad Enn. 5.8*, 2:221n198; *ad Enn. 5.9*, 1:45n6; *ad Enn. 6.1–3*, 2:105n105; *ad Enn. 6.7*, 1:45n6

Ficino, Marsilio, *In Sophistam*: *17–18*, 1:157n105; *21*, 1:169n126; *26*, 1:169n126; *30–31*, 2:107n106; *30–32*, 1:169n126; *31*, 2:39n41; *34*, 1:209n168, 2:105n105, 2:189n186; *37–38*, 1:169n126; *46*, 1:xxxi n75, 1:73n27

Ficino, Marsilio, *In Timaeum*: *9*, 1:xxxi n75, 1:73n27, 1:73n29; *15–16*, 2:265n237; *27*, 2:257n233–2:257n234

Ficino, Marsilio, *On Christian Religion*, 2:35

Ficino, Marsilio, *On the Sun and Light*, 2:267

Ficino, Marsilio, *Platonic Theology*, 1:xl, 1:45, 1:75, 1:89, 1:109, 1:131, 1:141, 2:91, 2:155–57, 2:239, 2:257, 2:265, 2:285; *1.5–6*, 1:137n87; *1.6.7*, 1:193n156; *1.12*, 1:7n12; *1.29*, 1:75n33; *2.2*, 2:157n148; *2.2–3*, 1:41n3; *2.13*, 1:109n57, 1:125n74; *2.13.10–11*, 1:131n80; *3.2*, 2:257n233; *3.9*, 2:295n253; *3.21*, 1:173n130; *3.28*, 1:xxxvi n88; *4.1*, 2:241n206, 2:255n230; *4.2*, 2:267n239; *4.2.5*, 2:261n235, 2:265n237; *4.17–22*, 1:141n91; *4.34*, 1:xliv n105; *5.7*, 2:285n245; *5.13.6*, 1:85n38; *5.13.7*, 2:91n97; *6.1.6*, 1:49n7; *6.1.7*, 1:123n73; *6.14*, 2:243n211; *8.9.2*, 1:113n62, 1:211n171; *8.12.1*, 1:75n31; *11.3*, 1:89n44, 1:141n91; *11.4*, 1:xxxi n75; *11.4–5*, 1:45n6;

11.4.17–22, 1:89n44; 12.3, 1:xxxvi
n88, 2:197n188; 12.3.2, 2:93n100;
12.3.5, 2:93n100; 12.3.7, 1:213n175;
14.9.2, 1:205n164; 16.1.9–15,
2:239n203; 17.2.11, 1:167n120;
17.3, 2:253n226; 18.8.6, 2:93n100
fifth essence, 2:257n233
final cause, 1:xxi, 1:63, 1:205n65,
1:213n174, 1:223n183, 1:225n184,
2:101
fingers, as example, 2:219
first being, 1:xxvii, 1:xxxvi, 1:41,
1:167, 1:169, 1:171, 1:193, 1:221;
and differentiae, 2:39
first composition, 2:49, 2:73
first essence, 1:97, 1:173, 2:57–59;
identical to first life and first
mind, 2:49–59
first form, 1:47–49; one being as,
2:219. See also total form (forma
totalis)
first infinite, 1:167
first infinity, 2:249–51
first intellect, 1:47–49, 2:57–59,
2:179; circular motion of,
2:199–201; existence of, 1:73;
and first principle, 1:171, 1:201,
1:229–35; and Ideas, 1:95, 1:113,
1:115, 1:119, 1:137, 2:187; and intelligence, 1:97, 1:129, 1:131, 1:167;
as subject of second hypothesis,
2:9, 2:177, 2:179, 2:193, 2:211,
2:221, 2:239, 2:253
first intelligible, 2:37, 2:179
first life, 2:57–59; in relation to
first essence and first mind,
2:37, 2:49–59

first limit, 1:167, 2:249
first matter, 1:7, 2:19
first mind, in relation to first essence and first life, 2:49–59
first motion, 2:267
first principle, 1:173–75; absolute
Unity as, 2:33; all things depend on, 1:223; all things disposed toward, 1:223–25; and
being, 1:205n163; and character
common to all things, 1:187–91;
contains perfections of all
things, 2:103; extends to lowest
degree, 1:193; function proper
to, 1:187–91; Ideas within, 1:137,
1:139; naming of, 1:207–9; nature of, 1:109; prerogatives of,
2:101; rational principle of,
1:231; superior to intellect, life,
and essence, 1:229–35; transcends all beings, 1:177; two
Platonic ways of ascent to,
1:175–79; uniqueness of, 1:45;
unity and simplicity of, 1:191–
93; universal being denied of,
2:37–47
first principles (henads) of light,
generation, knowledge, 1:227–29
first species: God's knowledge of,
1:113, 1:133; human knowledge
of, 1:113, 1:147; as intelligible objects, 1:95–97; knowledge of,
1:113; prior to intelligences,
1:93–95; in themselves, 1:113–15
first time, 2:267
five genera of being, 2:39, 2:105–11
five levels of realities, 2:257

five principles of all things, 2:9–11
Florence, University of, 1:xvi n31
flux, soul and, 2:317
form: and matter, 2:73–75; of the whole, 2:289
formless matter, 1:7, 1:57, 1:69; is absolutely not, 2:327; and not-being, 1:177, 1:193n157, 1:195, 1:233; as object of fifth hypothesis, 2:11, 2:295–303; participates in unity and goodness, 1:235
formlessness, and matter, 1:149, 1:151, 1:197
forms, 1:137–39; in art, 1:49; and intellect, 1:69; not directly created by Ideas, 1:85; and one being, 2:233; variety of, 1:193. See also first form; material forms; natural forms, mutual likeness to Ideas; total form (forma totalis)
forms-in-matter: designated by the term "others," 1:9; as subject of fourth hypothesis, 1:7
formulae, ideal, 1:139–43, 1:147, 1:201
fortune, 1:125
four elements, 2:91, 2:185, 2:257
future, 2:147–51. See also time

Ganay, Germain de, 1:xv
Garin, Eugenio, 1:xxiii
gaze: of God, 1:113; of intellect, 1:69, 1:97, 1:119, 1:127, 1:133, 1:143, 1:145, 1:147, 1:151, 1:201; primary and direct, 1:xxxii, 1:113, 1:121, 1:133. See also actus directus/actus reflectus; divine gaze
genera, five: of being, 1:xxvii, 1:159, 1:161, 1:169; 1:171; in first being, 1:41; in intelligible world, 2:37–39, 2:49, 2:197; not in One, 2:105–11, 2:117; and the One, 1:xxxvii; and one being, 2:193; present in first intellect, 2:187. See also Great Kinds, five
generation, 1:55, 1:85, 1:103, 1:149, 1:169, 1:175; distinguished from essence, 1:189; Ideas as principles of, 1:55; One as principle of, 1:229; power of, 2:87–89
Gentile, Sebastiano, 1:xiv n20
geocentrism, 1:75n30
George of Trebizond, 1:xiii, 1:xiii n16
Gerard of Cremona, 1:xii
Giles of Viterbo, 1:xvi
Glaucon (character), 1:39
God: assertions and negations about, 2:27–29, 2:49, 2:59–63, 2:181; as both final cause and prime mover, 1:213n174, 1:225; as both immanent and transcendent, 1:3n5, 1:175; contains all Ideas, 1:141; contains all things but cannot contain them individually, 1:209n170; has no Idea of evil, 1:65–67; inferential knowledge of lower things, 1:113n61; as infinite sphere, 1:3n5; and Intellect, 1:229, 1:231–33, 2:177; is nameless,

1:209n169; knowledge of human things, 1:121, 1:125, 1:133–37; knowledge of Ideas, 1:113; negations about, 1:179; as One and Good, 1:175, 1:203, 1:223, 2:21; perception of, 2:165–67, 2:175; simplicity of, 2:57; as subject of first hypothesis, 2:9, 2:19, 2:23; as unity, 2:3–5

goddess Soul, 2:19n16, 2:179, 2:257n231

gods: Dionysius and, 1:xii; Ficino and, 1:xxvi; intellects as, 1:135, 1:231; invocation of, 1:xlii, 1:xliv, 1:75n33; knowledge of human things, 1:121; multiple and secondary, 2:5; Neoplatonic hierarchy of, 1:ix–x, 1:xii, 1:xvii, 1:xxvi–xxvii; orders of, 1:7, 1:57, 1:73, 1:119, 2:3–9, 2:17–19, 2:17n13, 2:23, 2:41, 2:111, 2:179–81, 2:239–41, 2:243–55; and sense perception, 2:161; souls as, 2:179. See also celestial souls; cosmic gods; henads; hypercosmic gods; intellects

Good/good: Aristotle's definition of, 1:205n165; and being, 1:xxxii–xxxiii, 1:211n172, 1:213, 1:215–25; degrees of, 1:221; describing, 1:205; and desirable, 1:213; does not precede One, 2:165; as end and object of desire for all things, 1:205; and essence, 1:215; Idea of, 1:173–75; and matter, 1:197–99; as name for first principle, 1:177, 1:209;

Neoplatonic definition of, 1:205n165; rational principle of, 1:217; as source of unity, goodness, and essence, 1:69; superior to being, 1:223–25, 1:223n183. See also absolute Good; highest Good, three properties of; ideal good; One-and-Good

goodness: is double, 1:219; as summit of intelligible world, 2:197; and unity, as first principle, 1:229–35

grace, and nature, 1:35, 1:35n1

Great Kinds, five, 1:169n125

greatness: Idea of, 1:79–83; and not-being, 2:317–21; and one being, 2:223–25; and soul, 2:269

Greece, Neoplatonists in, 1:x; prisca theologia in, 1:xx

Gregory of Nazianzus, 2:55

Grosseteste, Robert, 1:xii

heat, 2:189; degrees of, 1:221; Idea of, 1:117

heavens: and change, 2:265; and circular motion, 2:267; matter proper to, 1:59

heavy and light, 2:163

henads, 1:xvii–xx, 1:xxvii–xxviii, 1:xxxvi, 1:xxxvii, 1:187n150, 1:229n186–87, 2:17–19, 2:23, 2:23n22, 2:25, 2:53–55, 2:57n59. See also first principles (henads) of light, generation, knowledge

Hermes Trismegistus, 1:xxi, 1:3n5, 2:175n171

Hermias, 1:xl, 1:173

hidden sense, and striving toward first principle, 2:163–65

hidden truths, 2:225

hierarchy of beings, 2:173

highest Good, three properties of, 1:167

Homer, 2:161

Homer, *Iliad*: 3.172, 1:159n110; 14.344–45, 2:161n152

Horace, *Ars Poetica* 139, 2:69n76

Horace, *Epistles* 1.12.19–20, 2:293n250

Horace, *Satires* 2.2.3, 2:239n204

Hugh of St. Victor, 1:xii

humanity, 1:45–47; Idea of, 1:87

human knowledge, and human truth, 1:119–23

human logic, 2:57n59

human mind, and formulae, 1:141

humidity, Idea of, 1:117

Hymn of Proteus (Orphic hymn 25), 2:261n235

hypercosmic gods, 2:239–41, 2:243, 2:243n211, 2:253–55

hypotheses, of *Parmenides*: arrangement of, 2:9–15; general purpose, 2:3–9. *See also separate entries for hypotheses*

hypothesis, first, 2:43–45, 2:49–177; and absolute One, 2:15; dialectic in, 2:169; negations in, 2:35, 2:41–43; purpose, truth, and structure of, 2:21–27; validity of, 2:167–77

hypothesis, second, 2:79, 2:85,

2:89, 2:111, 2:151, 2:155, 2:167–69, 2:171, 2:177–255, 2:179n177, 2:257n231; and one being, 2:15–17, 2:33; purpose of, 2:177–81; summary of, 2:239–55

hypothesis, third, 2:17n14, 2:19n16, 2:169, 2:179, 2:179n177, 2:255–83, 2:257n231, 2:313; and divine soul, 2:17–19; summary of, 2:275–83

hypothesis, fourth, 2:283–93, 2:305–7

hypothesis, fifth, 2:295–303, 2:295n253, 2:305–7

hypothesis, sixth, 2:45, 2:303–25

hypothesis, seventh, 2:309, 2:325–27

hypothesis, eighth, 2:329–37

hypothesis, ninth, 2:337–39

Iamblichus, 1:viii n1; 1:ix, 1:xv, 1:xxxiii n82, 1:173, 2:39, 2:57n59, 2:59n65, 2:105n105, 2:169n163, 2:181n182

ideal good, 1:175

ideal species: consequences of denial of existence of, 1:139–47; denied of first principle, 2:109; and inferior things, 1:105; as objects of study, 1:149

Ideas, 1:xxx–xxxi, 2:39, 2:127; and age, 2:139; are natural species with paradigmatic and efficient force, 1:101–3; are not aligned with material things in nature or condition, 1:83–85; are not

intelligences but intelligible objects, 1:95–97; and associations between things, 1:87; and beauty, 2:197; of body as a whole, 1:61, 1:67; can and cannot be known by us, 1:111–15, 1:121–23; can be totally and simultaneously present to many different things, 1:77; different from but joined to each other, 1:51–55; as efficient cause, 1:65; existence and nature of, 1:45–51; as first intelligible objects, 1:89; and formulae, 1:141–43; four questions on, 1:5; general and intermediate, 1:49–51; and knowledge, 2:165; and mutual likeness to natural forms, 1:105–7; neither mixed nor opposed, 1:49–51; and number, 2:227; numbers of, 1:47, 1:87; objects' participation in, 1:71–75; and One, 1:xxxvii, 2:77–79; and one being, 2:193, 2:233; order of effects, 1:55; participation in, 1:55, 1:75–79, 1:83, 1:103, 1:105–7; participation in divine, 1:135–37; parts lacking, 1:61; power of, 1:77, 1:99; precede intelligences, 1:95–97; present in first intellect, 2:187; as principles of both contemplation and action, 1:49; Proclus' critique of, 1:x; properties of, 1:77, 1:99, 1:107–11; and quantity, 1:79–83; and rational principles, 1:73,

1:145; of rational souls, 1:57; relationship to earthly realities, 1:115–19; relationship to one another, 1:117; six orders of, 1:137–39; as species, 1:57; things that have or have not, 1:57–67; Xenocrates' definition of, 1:63. See also ideal species; intellectual Ideas; natural Ideas; psychic Ideas

Ideas, Platonic theory of, 1:vii–viii; and magical notions, 1:xlii–xliii

imagination, 1:127–29; and absence of soul, 2:339; and One, 2:161; Parmenides' use of, 2:305; and soul, 2:329–33; untruthful, 2:333–37

imitation: soul and, 2:261–63

impression, 1:73, 1:129. See also seal impression

inchoation of forms, 1:193n156

"in contact," and one being, 2:217–19. See also contact

incorporeal motion, denied of One, 2:99

"Indefinite Dyad," 2:155

inequality, absence of, 2:223. See also equal and unequal

inferential knowledge, 1:113n61, 1:121, 1:133–35. See also actus reflexus/actus directus

inferential mode of relationship, 1:115–19, 1:121

infinite: being and, 1:167, 2:193–95; as consequence of postulating absence of unity, 1:181, 1:187,

infinite *(continued)*
2:47, 2:55, 2:157, 2:291, 2:333–
37; as consequence of postulating an Idea for each object,
1:87, 1:89; definition of term,
1:193–95, 2:249; and limit, 1:167,
2:71–75, 2:197; matter as, 1:193–
95; in multitude, 2:251; and
number, 2:193–95, 2:243–51;
One as, 1:197, 2:69–75
infinites, two, 1:195n158
infinity: denied of One, 2:127; as
element of beings, 2:291–93;
and limit, 1:167; and matter,
1:193–95; and multitude, 2:247–
51
initiation, 1:xi, 1:xiv; maieutic, 1:x,
1:xl
in reference to, and One, 2:171–73
intellect, 1:xxxv–xxxviii, 1:3, 1:127–
29, 1:189, 1:225–29; and age,
2:139; and alteration, 2:95; can
produce quasi-Ideas of artificial
objects, 1:63; created by Good,
1:73; differs formally from essence and life, 1:221; and first
principle, 1:229–35; and forms,
1:69; and nature, 1:55, 1:63; as
origin of numbers, 1:xliii; participation in divine, 1:135–37;
possesses forces and forms of
all things, 1:49; rational principle of, 1:231; relation to intelligible good, 1:211; relation to
sense perception, 1:217–19; and
time, 2:139n132, 2:145n137; and

will, 1:137n86. *See also* first intellect
intellection, and perception, 1:141
intellects: called gods, 2:179; relation to Ideas, 1:51
intellectual essence: and differentiae, 2:39; and unity, 2:25
intellectual forms, 1:149–51, 1:215
intellectual formulae, 1:147
intellectual Ideas, 1:137
intellectuality, 1:xxxiii–xxxiv, 2:61
intellectual nature, 1:55
intellectual order, 1:xxvii–xxviii
intellectual substances, are produced by themselves and in
themselves, 2:89
intellectual world, and sensible
world, 2:235
intelligence: as action and motion,
1:97; cannot constitute the
good, 1:167; cannot reach One,
2:165; and distinction between
things, 2:247; as first cognition,
1:189, 1:231; and motion, 2:89–
91; as name for first principle,
1:207–9; and *noemata*, 1:89; and
One, 2:159–67; and rectilinear
procession, 2:99. *See also* actualized intelligence; natural intelligence
intelligences, preceded by Ideas,
1:95–97
intelligible, and first principle, 1:231
intelligible appellations, 2:181
intelligible nature, attributes of,
2:77

intelligible object, 1:89–91, 2:25n24; and age, 2:139; and *noemata*, 1:89; prior to intelligences, 1:93–95

intelligible order, 1:xxvii–xxviii

intelligible powers, 2:181

intelligible realities: do not contain accidents, 2:109; do not contain species and genera, 2:109; do not contain substance, 2:109

intelligibles, 1:3

intelligible species, 1:123, 1;149–51

intelligible world, 2:37–39, 2:177, 2:243; as composite, 2:203–5; and motion, 2:205–7; one being as, 2:295; produced by creator, 2:205–7; and rest, 2:205; and sensible world, 2:227–29; as son of Good, 2:179; and universe, 2:227. *See also* one being

irrational souls, as one species, 1:57

"is," and One, 2:149, 2:153

is/is not, 1:viii, 1:151–57

"is-not," 2:309. *See also* not-being

-itas, Latin words ending in, 1:xxxiii–xxxiv, 1:xxxiv n83, 2:61n66

John Sarracenus, 1:xii

John Scotus Eriugena, 1:xii, 1:xxxvii

Jupiter, 1:101, 2:161, 2:267

justice, Idea of, 1:145

knowledge, 1:131; Idea of, 1:123; and One, 2:159–67; of one being and not-being, 2:311, 2:315–17; related to object of knowledge, 2:159–61; varies according to nature of object of knowledge, 1:111–15, 1:113n60, 1:113n62. *See also* absolute knowledge, and absolute truth; divine knowledge; human knowledge, and human truth; inferential knowledge; scientific knowledge

language, Parmenides' use of, 2:305. *See also specific terms*

last/lowest degree, fecundity of, 1:193

law of continuity (Proclus), 2:199n191

left, Idea of, 1:117

Liber de causis, 1:xii

life, 1:209–11; differs formally from essence and intellect, 1:221; and essence, 1:217–19; and first principle, 1:229–35; as name for first principle, 1:207–9; precedes intellect, 2:139

light: and Beauty, 2:197; of Good, 1:201; Idea compared to, 1:77–79; image of, 2:201, 2:247, 2:305; inner *(lux)*, 1:xxxvi; outer *(splendor)*, 1:xxxvi; of stars and sun, 2:211; of sun, 1:201; sun as principle of, 1:227–29. *See also* divine light; henads; shadow; sun

like and unlike, 1:181–83, 2:123–27, 2:141; and "in contact," 2:217–19; and matter, 2:301; and not-being, 2:317–21; and one being, 2:213–15

likeness, 1:105–7, 2:181

limit, 2:73n78–2:73n80, 2:197–99; and being, 2:193–95; of beings, 1:167, 2:291–93; denied of One, 2:75, 2:127; and infinity, 1:167, 2:71–75; and number, 2:193–95. *See also* first limit

line and point, 2:25n26, 2:65–67, 2:185, 2:233; as example, 2:25; and touching/touched, 2:219

lion, Idea of, 1:85

to live, as name for first principle, 1:207–9

Macrobius, *Dream of Scipio 1.14.14*, 2:239n202

Magi, 2:251

magical numbers, 1:xliii–xliv, 2:251n221

magical practice, theoretical justification for, 1:69n23

manuscripts: Canon. lat. class. 163, 1:xiv n18; Laurentianus Conv. Soppr. 103, 1:xv; Laurentianus Pluteus 85.8, 1:xv, 1:xv n25; Pal. gr. 63, 1:xx n39; Riccardianus 70, 1:xiv; Vat. lat. 11600, 1:xv n26

mastership: Idea of, 1:115–19; and slavery, 1:115–19. *See also* divine mastership

material forms, 1:47–49, 1:137–39;

and being, 1:195; and essence, 1:197; as most imperfect form, 1:149; not directly created by Ideas, 1:85

matter: all things denied of, 2:299; and being, 1:195; and change, 2:265; as component of corporeal world, 1:53; contains no multiplicity, 1:193; created by Good, 1:73; expressed by the terms "other" and "others," 1:9, 2:11; and form, 1:193, 1:197, 2:73–75; and good, 1:197–99; and infinity, 1:193–95, 2:49; lacking Idea, 1:57–59, 1:177, 1:193–99; as not-being, 1:153–55; as one, 2:3, 2:93; and one being, 2:295–303; participation in Ideas, 1:73; as subject of fifth hypothesis, 1:7, 2:11–13, 2:19, 2:295–303; and unity, 1:195. *See also* first matter; formless matter

Maximus the Confessor, 1:xii n13

mean: between extremes, 2:199, 2:243; of motion, 2:273–75; between motions, 2:265–75; between opposites, 2:275, 2:281

measurement, 2:129, 2:133, 2:135

mèden, 1:185, 2:159

Medici, Cosimo de', 1:xiv

Medici family, 1:3n1

medicine, 1:65

Melissus (disciple of Parmenides), 1:xxix, 1:159n109, 1:163, 1:173n130, 2:21, 2:33

men, multitude of, 1:87

Mercury (Hermes), 2:175

mereology, 1:xxxvi, 1:xxxvi n90

metaballein, 2:271

metals, 1:85

metaphor, Parmenides' use of, 2:305. *See also specific images*

middle, denied of One, 2:65–69

"middle path," Ficino's, 1:xxv–xxviii

mind: as name for first principle, 1:207–9; and soul, 2:329–33; of soul, 2:259

mirror reflection, 1:73, 1:73n27, 2:195, 2:301, 2:331; and body, 1:195–97; earthly objects as, 1:103; of man, 1:197; and third unity, 1:85

mixed shape, 2:201

moment: and motion, 2:187, 2:271–75; and soul, 2:145, 2:275–83

monad, and intelligible world, 2:109, 2:127, 2:205

moon, Idea of, 1:85, 1:99

moral virtues, Ideas of, 1:65

motion, 1:55, 1:169, 1:183, 1:189, 2:137–41, 2:181, 2:265–75; attributed to intelligence, 2:89–91; and celestial soul, 2:265–75; denied of One, 2:91, 2:103; exists in all things but first principle, 2:89–95; formulae and, 1:141; linear/circular, 1:211n171; and matter, 2:301; necessarily in every being, 2:229; and one being, 2:203–7, 2:229–35, 2:237–39; precedes same and other,

2:109; and soul, 2:255, 2:257, 2:275–83, 2:317–25; and time, 2:275n244. *See also* circular motion; oblique motion; rectilinear motion; straight motion

multiplicity, 1:viii; and unity, 1:179–81, 1:183–85. *See also* henads

multitude, 1:195, 1:201, 2:243–55; continuous, 2:245; created by One, 2:29; denied of One, 2:37–47, 2:49–59; and infinity, 2:247–51; limited or infinite, 2:193–95; and not-being, 2:315–17; and not-multitude, 1:185; and number, 2:245–47; and one, 1:189, 1:199, 2:291–93; and one being, 2:43–47; origin of, 2:53–55; partakes of unity, 2:49–59; participation in unity, 1:43–45; precedes being, 2:53; precedes whole and parts, 2:51; and second principle, 2:45; separate, 2:245; and soul, 2:275–83; and touching/touched, 2:219; and unity, 2:329–33, 2:335. *See also* not-multitude

Muses, 2:303

Mussato, Albertino, 1:xxxix

names and naming, 1:105n53; of first principle, 1:173–1:179, 1:207–9; and One, 2:159–67. *See also* divine names

natural forms, mutual likeness to Ideas, 1:105–7

natural Ideas, 1:137
natural intelligence, 1:55
natural philosophers, 2:271–75, 2:281
natural realities, 2:283–93
natural species, Ideas as, 1:101–3
nature, 1:101, 1:225–29; and art, 2:287; and creation of material forms, 1:85; and grace, 1:35, 1:35n1; as guide, 1:41–43; and intellect, 1:55, 1:63; seminal reasons, 1:49
negations, 2:169, 2:173–75; about God, 1:xxxiv–xxxv, 1:137, 1:175–79, 1:195, 2:59–63; Dionysius on, 1:63; do not reach One, 2:173; in hypotheses, 2:15–19; and One, 2:27–31; opposites in, 2:77; order of, in first hypothesis, 2:35; purpose and summary of, 2:31–35; signifying excess not defect, 1:137, 2:29; three levels of, 1:177, 2:105–11
negative theology, 1:xii, 1:137n85, 2:29n29; Pico and, 1:xxxiii–xxxv
Neoplatonic ritual, 1:xl
Neoplatonism, 1:113n61
Neoplatonists, 1:viii–xi, 1:xiv, 1:173n131, 1:179n143, 2:175; Ficino and, 1:xiv–xvi, 1:xxxvii; and Parmenides' Poem, 1:xxxviii–xxxix; on Plato's Sophist, 1:xxix. See also Platonists
Nicholas of Cusa, 1:xiii, 1:xxxvii
Nicholas of Methone, 2:47, 2:47n47, 2:55
noemata, 1:89, 1:89n43, 1:91n45

not-being, 1:185, 1:191, 1:215, 2:159; all things denied of, 2:325–27; and being, 1:169, 1:177, 1:199, 2:257, 2:303–13; degrees of, 2:325–27; and matter, 2:301; as opposite of being, 1:41–43, 1:215; as opposite of essence, 1:221; and soul, 2:275–83; two senses of, 1:5, 1:151–55. See also matter; One
not-good, 1:215
nothing, 1:189–91
notion, 1:89, 1:93
not-knowing, as opposite of intellect, 1:221
not-living, as opposite of life, 1:221
not-multitude, 1:185
not-one, 1:185, 1:191, 2:159; as opposite of one, 1:41
nous, 1:89
nulla proportio inter deum et hominem, 1:125n76
number: contained in one being, 2:189–93; created by One, 2:29; and differentiae, 2:191; infinite, 2:243–55; and matter, 2:301; and multitude, 2:245–47; and one being, 2:227–29; origin of, 2:39; partakes of essence, 2:193; perfect, 2:251n222; precedes beings, 2:49–59, 2:191–93; and sameness, 2:121
number two, 2:189–93
number three, 2:189–93, 2:251
number five, 2:257
number nine, 2:303

numbers, odd and even, 2:191,
2:251–53

objects: of desire, 1:205; participation in Ideas, 1:71–75
oblique motion, 2:95, 2:95n101
Olympiodorus, 1:173
Olympiodorus, *In Phaedonem 1.9,*
1:213n175
omniform being, 2:295–303
One, 1:vii–viii, 1:3–5; above essence, 2:21–23; all things denied
of, 2:299; and assertion, 2:27;
and being, 1:xxiv–xxv, 1:169–73,
1:185, 1:187, 1:193; beyond all
things, 2:33–35; cannot be any
of the things it creates, 2:29–31;
cannot be apprehended by
knowledge, 2:165; cannot be apprehended by opinion, 2:165;
cannot be apprehended by
sense perception, 2:165; cannot
be known or named, 2:159–67;
cannot be younger or older
than, or of equal age with, itself and others, 2:137–41; and
conversion, 2:89; conversion denied of, 2:81; as creator of all,
2:29–31; does not participate in
anything, 2:113; does not participate in essence, 2:149–57; does
not precede the Good, 2:165;
and essence, 1:171–73, 1:185–87;
essence denied of, 2:43; and exists/existence, 2:31; in first hypothesis, 2:21–27; genera and
properties of being denied of,

2:105; as God, 1:viii; has no beginning, end, or middle, 2:65–
69; hidden concept of, 2:163; as
"Idea of the Good," 2:125–27;
and Ideas, 1:xxxvii, 2:77–79; as
infinite, 2:69–75; and "is," 2:149,
2:153, 2:159; is above eternity,
time, and motion, 2:141–45; is
commonly within all things,
1:187–91; is neither at rest nor
in motion, 2:89–95; is neither
in itself nor in another, 2:83–
89; is not equal or unequal to
itself or the others, 2:127–31; is
not in time, 2:141–45; is not
like or unlike itself or another,
2:123–27; is not moved in circle
or straight line, 2:97–101; is not
other than itself nor same as
another, 2:111–15; is not other
than the others, 2:115–19; is not
the same as itself, 2:119–21; is
separate from all conditions,
2:111–15; is unique, singular, and
separate, 2:113; limit denied of,
2:75; as limit of all things,
2:69–75; and multitude, 1:189,
1:199; multitude denied of,
2:37–47, 2:49–59; as name for
first principle, 1:179, 1:209; and
negation, 2:27–31; nine hypotheses on, 1:5–6; and not-one,
1:185; and opposition, 2:103;
and others, 1:xxxv–xxxviii (*see
also* henads); parts and whole
denied of, 2:49–59, 2:65–69;
place denied of, 2:101; Plotinus

One *(continued)*

on, 1:ix; precedes universal being, 2:105; as principle of beings, 2:159; as principle of universe, 2:23, 2:81; procession denied of, 2:81; rational principle of, 2:183–89; rest denied of, 2:101–3; shape denied of, 2:75–81; superior to being, 2:167–77; as supreme God, 2:21; ten categories denied of, 2:105–11; transcendent being denied of, 2:109; transcends equality and inequality, 2:133; transcends first intellect, 1:171–73; transcends infinite and limit, 2:71; transcends temporal conditions, 2:147–49; transcends temporal realities, 2:147–49; transcends time, 2:147–49. *See also* absolute One; first principle; God; not-one; One-and-Good; unity

one: degrees of, 2:325–27; our own innermost, 2:163; and soul, 2:275–83; within us, 2:27

One-and-Good, 1:165–73, 1:179, 1:179n142, 1:203, 1:225n184; and creation, 2:91; as principle of all things, 1:235, 2:3, 2:47; related to all levels of beings, 2:125; superior to being, 1:179–87

one being, 2:31–35, 2:243–55; and age, 2:229–35; all numbers contained in, 2:189–93; all things denied of, 2:325–27; can be known and named, 2:239; de-

nial of existence of, 2:303–9; distributed in intelligible world, 2:193–95; has and has not contact with itself and others, 2:217–19; intelligible world as, 2:37–39; is all things, 2:35; is always at rest and in movement, 2:203–7; is equal and unequal to itself and others, 2:221–25; is everywhere, 2:83–85; is in itself and in another than itself, 2:201–3; is like and unlike itself and others, 2:213–15; is within One-and-Good, 2:85–87; and matter, 2:295–303; and multitude, 2:43–47; and not-being, 2:309–13, 2:315–17; not same as essence, 2:189; and One, 2:105–7; and otherness, 2:191; rational principle of, 2:189, 2:191, 2:311; same as and different from itself, 2:207–13; same as and different from others, 2:207–13; as second principle, 2:33; and soul, 2:311–13; use of term, 2:179. *See also* first intellect

"one in the soul" (Proclean/Plotinian doctrine), 1:xviii–xx

One/one (term), 1:9, 1:165, 2:5–9, 2:11, 2:23, 2:163–65, 2:241, 2:295, 2:297, 2:305; three senses of, 1:5, 1:39–41

ontology, 2:57n59

opinion: and One, 2:161, 2:165; related to object of opinion, 2:159–61

opposite conditions, combinations of, 1:73–75

opposites, 2:309–11, 2:327; and matter, 2:301; in negations, 2:77; and rational principles, 2:209; union of, 2:293

opposition: One and, 2:87, 2:103; relative, 2:145–47; and soul, 2:275–83

order of universe, 1:191. *See also* intellectual order

Origen, 1:xxix n69

Origen the Platonist, 2:9n7, 2:21n20, 2:167n158

Orpheus, 1:xiv, 1:xxi

otherness, 1:55, 1:153, 1:169, 1:189; and not-being, 2:315–21; nowhere and never exists totally, 2:209–11; and one being, 2:191; rational principle of, 2:189

other/others, 1:vii–viii, 1:9, 2:11; and one, 2:283–93; opposed to one another, 2:291–93; use of term, 2:285, 2:295–303. *See also* henads; multiplicity; multitude

oudèn, 1:191

oud'hen (not-one), 2:31

oud'on (not-being), 2:31

Pachymeres, George, 1:xii n11

painting, 1:73, 1:73n27

paradigm, and cause, 1:59

paradigmatic power, 1:103, 1:105

paradox, 2:175–77, 2:269, 2:305, 2:305n261

Parmenides (character), 1:vii, 1:x

Parmenides (historical), 2:19, 2:33; *fgmt 3,* 2:89n95; *fgmt 8.4,* 2:89n94; *fgmt 8.29,* 2:111n110; *fgmt. 8.29,* 2:83n87; *fgmt 8.34–36,* 2:89n95; *fgmt 8.41,* 2:89n96; *fgmt 8.43–44,* 2:79n85, 2:305n259; in *Parmenides,* 1:xxxviii; as poet, 1:xxxix, 2:303–9

participation, 1:73n27; corporeal mode of, 1:77, 1:77n34; denied of One, 2:113; in essence, 2:149–57; in Ideas, 1:55, 1:71–79, 1:83, 1:103, 1:105–7; noncorporeal, 1:77; and one being, 2:211–13; in unity, 1:41, 1:43–45. *See also* division

particulars, lacking Ideas, 1:59

parts, lacking Ideas, 1:61

parts and whole, 2:97, 2:197–201, 2:245, 2:283–93; denied of One, 2:49–59, 2:65–69; and matter, 2:301; neither same nor different, 2:207; and one being, 2:185–87, 2:201–3; preceded by multitude, 2:51

past, 2:147–51. *See also* time

Patrizi, Francesco, 1:xvi

Paul, Saint, 1:xii

perception, and intellection, 1:141

per consequentiam, 1:xxxii

perfection, double, 1:219

Peripatetics, 1:41, 1:109, 1:131–33, 2:53

per reflexionem, 1:xxxii

per se, 1:47

Petrarca, Francesco, 1:xxxix–xl

Philolaus, 1:xiv, 1:167

philosophy, and divine species, 1:147

Philostratus, *Life of Apollonius of Tyana* 1.1, 2:175n171

Phoebe, 2:267, 2:267n240

Phoebus, 1:65, 2:267, 2:267n240

Phoenix, 2:269

Pico della Mirandola, Giovanni, 1:xx–xxv

Pico della Mirandola, Giovanni, *Commento sopra una Canzone d'Amore*, 1:xxiii

Pico della Mirandola, Giovanni, *De ente et uno*, 1:xxiii, 1:157n106, 1:187n152, 1:207n167, 1:213n175; 2, 1:xxiv n53, 1:163n117; 3–4, 1:xxiv n52; 4, 1:225n184; 5, 1:xxxiv n84, 2:61n66; 6, 1:191n154; 7, 1:179n143; 8, 1:215n176, 1:221n181; 8–9, 1:223n183

Pico-Ficino controversy, 1:xx–xxv, 1:xxix–xxxi, 1:xxxii–xxxiv

Pierleone da Spoleto, 1:xv n26

place, denied of One, 2:101

planets, retrograde motion of, 1:75n30

Plato, 1:xxi, 1:35, 1:65–67, 1:159, 1:189; on dialectic, 1:35n4; and Parmenides, 1:159

Plato, *Cratylus*, 2:253; *404d*, 2:253n227; *421c*, 1:75n33

Plato, *Laws*, 2:67, 2:135; *3.685a*, 1:163n118; *4.715e–16a*, 2:67n74; *716c*, 2:135n128

Plato, *Letters*, 1:173, 2:43, 2:165; *1.313a*, 2:171n164; *2*, 2:179n176;

2.312e, 1:175n133; *2.312e–13a*, 2:173n167; *2.313a*, 2:43n44; *2.313a3–4*, 2:63n70; *2.314a*, 1:161n111; *6*, 2:179n176; *6.323d*, 2:167n157; *6.323d4*, 2:179n176; *7.342a–44b*, 1:147n96, 2:161n151; *7.342b*, 2:173n168; *7.343a–44c*, 2:165n156; *7.344c–d*, 1:161n111; *Letter to Dionysius*, 1:161, 2:63, 2:171, 2:173; *Letter to Prince Hermias*, 2:165–67; *Letter to the Syracusans*, 1:147, 1:161, 2:161, 2:173

Plato, *Parmenides*, 1:3, 1:177–79, 1:235; *127e*, 1:41n3; *130e*, 1:75n33; *132A–33A*, 1:85n41; *132d*, 1:103n51; *133b*, 1:3n4; *134a–c*, 1:119n68; *141d8–e5*, 2:181n183; *142d9–43a3*, 2:177n175; *159d–60b*, 2:295n252; arrangement of, 1:39; logical reading of, 1:ix; medieval transmission of, 1:xii–xiii; place in history of philosophy, 1:vii–xvi; and *Sophist*, 1:xxix–xxxi, 1:xi, 1:xxix n69; subject of, 1:35–37; theological reading of, 1:viii–xi; transmission of, 1:xii–xiii, 1:xii n10. *See also* Ficino, Marsilio, *Commentary on Parmenides*

Plato, *Phaedo*, 2:11, 2:47; *96a–99d*, 2:11n9; *99c*, 2:47n49

Plato, *Phaedrus*, 1:xxxix, 1:xl, 1:35, 1:121, 1:123, 1:161, 2:77; *247c–d*, 2:77n83; *247d*, 1:119n68; *248a3*, 1:xviii n35; *275e*, 1:161n111

Plato, *Philebus*, 1:35, 1:101, 1:149,

1:165, 1:167, 1:173, 1:193, 2:135,
2:157, 2:213, 2:293n248; *15c*,
1:149n97; *16c–e*, 2:213n196; *20d*,
1:167n122; *23c*, 1:167n120; *23c9–
10*, 2:73n80; *23c–30e*, 2:303n257;
23e9–d1, 2:157n149; *24b*,
1:195n158; *26d–e*, 1:167n121; *30d*,
1:101n50; *66a–c*, 2:135n128

Plato, *Republic*, 1:3, 1:35, 1:149,
1:173, 1:175, 1:177, 1:189, 2:47,
2:125, 2:169, 2:177, 2:253;
4.445c4, 2:25n25; *6*, 2:179n176;
6.7.502c–21c, 2:127n122; *6.506d8–
e7*, 2:177n173; *6.508c*, 2:177n174;
6.508c–9c, 1:169n124; *6.508e–9b*,
1:175n134, 1:175n136; *6.509b*,
1:189n153, 2:169n161; *6.509c*,
2:47n48; *7.514a–18b*, 1:75n32;
7.518c, 1:175n135; *7.533b*, 1:xxii
n47, 1:35n4; *7.533b–34d*,
2:169n160; *8.546b–e*, 2:251n222;
10.567b, 1:63n16; *10.617–18*,
2:253n226; *507e–8c*, 1:177n141;
509d, 2:25n26; *537e*, 1:149n97;
549d, 2:25n26; Book VI, 1:169;
Book VII, 1:75; Book VIII, 1:xliv;
Book X, 1:63

Plato, *Sophist*, 1:35, 1:45, 1:71, 1:155,
1:159n109, 1:163, 1:169, 1:171,
1:173n130, 1:177, 1:189, 2:33, 2:37,
2:39, 2:105, 2:135, 2:167; *216b*,
1:163n117; *217b*, 1:159n109; *237a–
b*, 1:155n102; *237b–38d*, 1:157n104;
239d–40b, 1:73n26; *239d–240b*,
1:xxxi n74; *242c–45e*, 2:21n20;
243c–45b, 2:169n126; *243d–e*,
1:xxx n73, 1:171n127; *244b–245b*,

1:xxx n73, 1:171n128; *244e*,
2:135n130; *245a–b*, 2:167n159;
245a–c, 2:33n33, 2:37n37; *245a–e*,
2:21n19; *245d*, 1:189n153; *248a*,
1:45n5; *248e*, 2:57n59, 2:57n63;
249a–c, 2:39n39; *249e–250d*,
1:xxx n73, 1:171n127; *256a*,
2:105n105; *258b*, 1:177n138; and
Parmenides, 1:xi, 1:xxix–xxxi,
1:xxix n69

Plato, *Statesman*, 1:35; *272e5*, 2:25n25

Plato, *Theaetetus*, 1:41, 1:159, 1:163,
2:135, 2:305; *148e–51d*, 1:69n24;
176c, 2:135n128; *183e–84a*, 1:41n2,
1:159n109–1:159n110; *184a*,
2:305n260

Plato, *Timaeus*, 1:xxx–xxxi, 1:3,
1:35, 1:71, 1:75, 1:189, 1:197, 2:11,
2:179n176, 2:257n233; *27d*,
1:189n153; *28a–29b*, 2:227n200;
28a–29d, 1:75n32; *28a–c*, 1:xxxi
n74, 1:73n26; *29b–c*, 2:173n169;
29e–30a, 1:67n20; *46d–e*, 2:11n9;
48e–51b, 1:195n159; *50b–52b*,
1:xxxi n74, 1:73n26; *51a–b*,
1:197n160; *55c–d*, 1:139n88; and
Parmenides, 1:xi

Platonism: as theology, 1:ix; truths
of, 1:71–73

Platonists, 1:163, 1:195, 2:19n16,
2:89, 2:109, 2:151, 2:175, 2:179,
2:181, 2:221, 2:239, 2:243, 2:257,
2:289, 2:299, 2:315; and absolute
assertions about God, 2:59–63;
and hierarchy of world, 1:85;
"later," 2:63n69; "more ancient,"
2:59n65; and not-being, 1:153

Pletho, George Gemistus, 1:xxi

Plotinus, 1:xv, 1:xxxi, 1:xl, 1:73, 1:173, 2:57, 2:77, 2:105n105, 2:181n182, 2:191, 2:263, 2:301; and Ficino's "middle path," 1:xxv–xxviii; and theological reading of *Parmenides*, 1:ix; on unity and multiplicity, 1:xxxv–xxxvi

Plotinus, *Enneads*, 1:xxv; 1.6.7, 2:57n59, 2:57n63; 1.7.1, 2:211n195; 1.8.2.2–3, 1:205n165; 2.2.1, 2:79n84; 2.2.1–2, 2:265n237; 2.4.1.8–14, 2:303n257; 2.4.5, 2:73n79, 2:295n253; 2.4.15, 2:295n251; 2.7.6–24, 2:183n184; 3.6.6–13, 1:xxxi n76, 1:1:73n27, 1:193n156; 3.6.7–8, 2:301n256; 3.7.11–13, 2:139n132; 4.1–2, 2:263n236; 5.1.8.1–27, 2:179n176; 5.2.1.7–9, 1:xxxv n86; 5.3.33–44, 1:xxvii n63, 2:37n36; 5.4, 1:xxxvi n90, 2:189n186; 5.4.2, 2:57n59, 2:57n63, 2:191n187; 5.5, 2:25n24; 5.5.6.27–28, 2:303n258; 5.5.12, 2:197n188; 5.6.6, 2:57n63; 5.8.4, 2:187n185; 5.9.8, 2:57n59; 5.9.10, 2:49n52; 6.1–2, 2:53n56; 6.2.7.9, 2:57n61; 6.2.8.11, 2:57n62; 6.2.8.32–37, 2:209n194; 6.4–5, 1:79n35; 6.5.5, 1:115n65; 6.6.5–6, 2:289n247; 6.6.8.17–18, 2:59n64; 6.6.9, 2:191n187; 6.7, 1:233n192; 6.7.17, 2:73n79; 6.7.17.11, 1:xxv n56; 6.7.25, 1:175n137; 6.7.32, 1:xxxvi n88; 6.7.35.19, 1:xxv n58; 6.7.36.6, 1:xxxi n76, 1:73n27; 6.8.16, 1:xxxv n87; "On the Three Hypostases" (V.I.8), 1:ix

Plotinus, *On Numbers*, 2:51

Plotinus, *On the Genera of Beings*, 2:51

Plotinus, *On the Ideas*, 2:51

Plutarch of Athens, 1:ix, 1:7n14, 1:173n131, 2:9–15, 2:9n8, 2:63n69

Plutarch of Chaeronea, 1:173, 1:173n131, 2:9n8

pneuma, Stoic doctrine of, 1:109n55

Poem (Parmenides), 1:xxxviii

poet: and dialectician, 2:305; and divine inspiration, 1:xxxix–xl; Parmenides as, 1:xxxix, 2:303–9

poetic license, Parmenides' use of, 2:307

poetry, dialectic as, 1:xxxviii–xli

point: on continuum, 2:271; and dimension, 1:195; as infinite, 2:69–71. *See also* line and point

Poliziano, Angelo, 1:35n3

Porphyry, 1:ix, 1:xv, 1:xxxiii n82, 1:173, 2:105n105, 2:181n182

Porphyry, *Life of Plotinus*, 1:173n131

posteriority, 2:257–59

potentiality: denied of One, 2:91; precedes operation, 2:139

power, 1:131; of Idea, 1:77, 1:99; as name for first principle, 1:207–9; and one being, 2:201–3; as one of four elements, 2:91; proceeds from essence, 2:99

premise, and consequent, 2:51

Prenninger, Martin, 1:xiv n20

present, 2:147–51. *See also* time

prime matter, 2:295, 2:295n251
prime mind, and matter, 2:303
privations, 1:215; and rational principle of being, 1:213
procession: denied of One, 2:81; as principle of distinction, 2:79–81
Proclus, 1:ix–x, 1:xv, 1:xxxi, 1:xxxiv, 1:xl, 1:59, 1:63, 1:129, 1:131–33, 1:143, 1:173, 1:187n150, 1:195n158, 2:17, 2:17n13, 2:23, 2:39, 2:41, 2:63n69, 2:71, 2:77, 2:91–93, 2:105n105, 2:121, 2:155, 2:163, 2:171, 2:177, 2:181, 2:239, 2:241, 2:251; on development of multiplicity, 1:xxxvii; Ficino and, 1:xiv; and Ficino's "middle path," 1:xxv–xxviii; on hypotheses, 2:5–9; on Trinity, 2:57; on unity and multiplicity, 1:xxxv–xxxvi
Proclus, *Elements of Theology*, 1:xii, 1:161; *prop. 1–3*, 2:61n67; *prop. 28–29*, 2:199n191; *prop. 54*, 2:141n135; *prop. 57 and 72*, 1:193n156; *prop. 67–69*, 1:xxxvi n90, 2:189n186, 2:287n246; *prop. 90*, 2:73n78; *prop. 97–102*, 1:xlii n103, 1:99n49; *prop. 101–3*, 2:57n59; *prop. 103*, 1:xxviii n68, 2:57n63; *prop. 110–12*, 1:xlii n103, 1:99n49; *prop. 124*, 1:119n68; *prop. 135*, 2:3n1
Proclus, *In Alcibiadem*: 246.21–248.4, 1:xx n39; 326.13–15, 1:193n156
Proclus, *In Parmenidem*, 1:viii, 1:xii n11, 1:xv, 1:xvi–xx; *1.617–18*,

1:3n3; *1.633.24*, 1:157n107; *1.635.2–17*, 1:xxii n47, 1:35n4; *1.646*, 1:xlv n107; *1.648.13–649.2*, 1:35n4; *1.648.14–649.2*, 1:xxii n47; *1.653.1–3*, 1:35n4; *1.653.4–654.10*, 1:xxii n46; *1.672*, 1:5n6, 1:173n130; *2.725*, 1:41n3; *2.726–27*, 1:45n4; *2.729.20–26*, 1:45n5; *2.755–57*, 1:55n9; *3.784.12–18*, 1:5n7; *3.812–13*, 1:55n10; *3.817–20*, 1:57n11; *3.822–23*, 1:59n12; *3.824–25*, 1:59n13; *3.826*, 1:61n14; *3.826–27*, 1:61n15; *3.828–29*, 1:63n17, 1:65n19; *3.829–31*, 1:67n21; *3.831–33*, 1:67n22; *3.835–38*, 1:69n23; *4.637*, 1:35n2; *4.838–39*, 1:71n25; *4.839–42*, 1:xxxi n76, 1:73n27; *4.842–45*, 1:73n29; *4.845–48*, 1:xxxi n76, 1:73n28; *4.846–48*, 1:73n28; *4.847.5–6*, 1:73n28; *4.851–53*, 1:xlv n107, 1:75n33; *4.865–66*, 1:79n35; *4.866–73*, 1:83n37; *4.871.10–20*, 1:81n36; *4.873.16–26*, 1:85n38; *4.873–75*, 1:xliii n104, 1:85n39; *4.878–79*, 1:85n40; *4.888*, 1:63n18; *4.893–98*, 1:89n44; *4.895–96*, 1:91n45; *4.903–4*, 1:99n49; *4.905*, 1:97n47; *4.906*, 1:103n51; *4.906–11*, 1:103n52; *4.912*, 1:107n54; *4.920–23*, 1:109n58; *4.921.11–19*, 1:109n56; *4.923–25*, 1:113n62; *4.924*, 1:xxxii n79; *4.926–28*, 1:3n4, 1:111n59; *4.930*, 1:115n63; *4.933–34*, 1:119n67; *4.943*, 1:117n65; *4.943.21*, 1:115n64; *4.944*, 1:123n72; *4.945*, 1:121n69; *4.948*,

Proclus, *In Parmenidem* (*continued*)
I:xxvii n63; *4.950.39–951.7*,
I:xxxvi n88; *4.954–55*, I:125n74;
4.956, I:127n77; *4.956–57*,
I:125n75; *4.957*, I:119n68,
I:121n70; *4.957–59*, I:129n78;
4.958–59, I:129n79; *4.963*,
I:135n82; *4.964*, I:133n81; *4.966*,
I:135n83; *4.967–68*, I:137n84;
4.969–70, I:139n89; *4.1062*,
2:17n13; *4.1071.4–1072.11*, I:xviii
n34; *5.980*, I:143n92; *5.980–83*,
I:143n93; *5.982*, I:35n2; *5.982.19*,
I:147n95; *5.992*, I:149n98; *5.995–
96*, I:151n99; *5.999–1000*,
I:155n101; *5.1009.1–12*, 2:241n210;
5.1035.1–5, I:5n9; *5.1035.5–15*,
I:7n11; *5.1035.7–9*, I:7n10;
5.1035.11–12, I:5n9; *6.903–4*, I:xlii
n103; *6.1039*, 2:309n263;
6.1039.19–22, I:5n8; *6.1039–40*,
2:305n262; *6.1041*, I:163n118;
6.1043.24–1045.19, I:229n187;
6.1043.30–1047.24, I:xix n37;
6.1044–51, I:227n186; *6.1045.20–
1046.10*, I:229n188; *6.1046.11–
1047.19*, I:229n189; *6.1047*,
I:231n191; *6.1048.5–7*, I:9.15;
6.1048.9–27, 2:5n2; *6.1050*, 2:7n3;
6.1050–51, 2:7n4–2:7n5; *6.1056.3–
1057.4*, 2:9n6; *6.1058–60*, 2:9n8;
6.1059.3–15, I:7n14; *6.1059.15–17*,
2:11n10; *6.1062.17–26*, 2:17n12;
6.1063.4–10, 2:19n16; *6.1063.4–
1064.10*, 2:179n177, 2:257n231;
6.1063.5–9, 2:19n15; *6.1063.14–
1064.10*, 2:19n17; *6.1064.17–

1065.11*, 2:9n7; *6.1064.21–1066.16*,
I:xxv n56; *6.1065.12–20*, 2:21n20;
6.1065.15–34, I:xxix n69; *6.1065–
66*, 2:21n21; *6.1066.13–21*, 2:23n22;
6.1069.18–1070.12, 2:23n23;
6.1070.1–12, 2:25n24; *6.1071.16–
19*, I:xxv n58; *6.1071–72*, 2:27n27;
6.1072.3–5, I:xxv n58; *6.1074*,
2:29n28; *6.1075–77*, 2:31n31,
2:299n255; *6.1077–79*, I:xxxviii
n95; *6.1078–83*, 2:35n35;
6.1085.11–1086.7, 2:41n42; *6.1088–
89*, 2:43n43, 2:43n45; *6.1089–90*,
2:45n46; *6.1089–92*, 2:39n38;
6.1097, 2:47n50; *6.1098*, 2:51n53;
6.1099, 2:51n54, 2:57n60; *6.1101*,
2:55n58; *6.1106.2–24*, I:xxxiii
n82; *6.1107.8–16*, I:xxxiii n82,
2:59n65; *6.1107.16–1108.15*,
2:63n71; *6.1107.20–29*, I:xxxv
n85; *6.1109.4–14*, I:xxxv n85;
6.1110.24–1111.15, 2:65n72; *6.1111–
12*, 2:67n73; *6.1113–15*, 2:69n75;
6.1118, I:195n158; *6.1119–20*,
2:303n257; *6.1119–23*, 2:73n78;
6.1126, 2:75n81; *6.1127–28*,
2:77n83; *6.1129*, 2:75n82; *6.1129–
30*, 2:79n85, 2:305n259; *6.1130–
31*, 2:79n86; *7.500.1–27*,
2:155n147; *7.500.27–501.15*,
2:155n146; *7.503.18–504.7*,
2:159n150; *7.506.19–28*, 2:161n153;
7.509.10–24, 2:165n154; *7.509.10–
26*, I:205n165; *7.514.9–35*,
2:165n155; *7.515.4–30*, 2:167n158;
7.515.21–24, 2:169n160; *7.515.26*,
2:169n162; *7.516.33–517.21*,

2:169n163; *7.518.21–28,*
2:173n166; *7.519.8–521.25,*
2:173n170, 2:175n171; *7.1134,*
2:83n87; *7.1134–35,* 2:85n88;
7.1140–41, 2:85n89; *7.1142,*
2:85n90; *7.1145–46,* 2:87n91;
7.1148, 2:87n92; *7.1149,* 2:89n93;
7.1152, 2:89n94; *7.1154,* 2:93n98;
7.1155, 2:93n99; *7.1165,* 2:99n102;
7.1167–69, 2:101n103; *7.1171–72,*
2:103n104; *7.1175–77,* 2:111n111;
7.1177–78, 2:111n112; *7.1179–80,*
2:113n113; *7.1180–81,* 2:115n114;
7.1182–85, 2:119n115; *7.1187.13–29,*
2:119n116; *7.1187.30–1188.14,*
2:121n118; *7.1188.24–1189.2,*
2:121n119; *7.1191.10–1201.12,*
2:243n211; *7.1191.10–1201.21,*
2:241n205; *7.1192,* 2:109n108;
7.1193–95, 2:111n109; *7.1198,*
2:123n121; *7.1198.2–9,* 2:123n120;
7.1198–2–11, 2:293n249; *7.1198.9–
21,* 2:129n123; *7.1199–1200,*
2:127n122; *7.1201.22–1239.21,*
2:241n207; *7.1206,* 2:129n124;
7.1207, 2:131n125; *7.1208.21–29,*
2:133n127; *7.1208.29–1209.2,*
2:133n126; *7.1209.11–20,*
2:135n129; *7.1209.20–29,*
2:135n130; *7.1209.29–1210.18,*
2:135n128; *7.1211.18–1212.4,*
2:137n131; *7.1217.11–22,*
2:257n231; *7.1217–18,* 2:139n133;
7.1221, 2:141n134; *7.1225.30–
1228.18,* 2:145n136; *7.1228.23–
1229.6,* 2:145n138; *7.1229,*
2:147n140; *7.1233–39,* 2:181n183;

7.1240.5–1241.6, 2:151n144;
1106.2–24, 2:59n65; *1209.4–11,*
2:133n127
Proclus, *In Rem Publicam 2,*
2:229n201, 2:251n222
Proclus, *In Timaeum: 1.177,* 1:xxxvi
n90; *3.334,* 1:xxvii n63; *28,*
2:105n105
Proclus, *Platonic Theology,* 1:x, 1:xi,
1:xvi–xx, 1:xxviii, 1:157n106,
1:161n113, 2:177n172; *1.1,* 1:3n3–
1:3n4, 1:173n131; *1.3,* 1:187n150,
2:25n25; *1.4,* 1:xxix n69,
2:21n20; *1.8,* 1:3n2, 1:161n112; *1.9,*
1:xxii n47, 1:35n4, 1:159n108–
1:159n110; *1.10,* 1:xxvii n63, 1:5n8,
2:41n42, 2:245n217; *1.11,*
2:179n177, 2:181n182, 2:257n231;
1.12, 1:3n5, 1:7n13–1:7n14,
2:19n18, 2:29n30; *2.1,* 1:41n3,
1:179n144, 1:183n146–1:183n147,
1:185n148; *2.1–2,* 1:179n143; *2.2,*
1:45n4, 1:187n149, 1:187n151,
1:205n163; *2.3,* 1:187n152,
1:191n154; *2.4,* 2:9n7; *2.4,* 1:xxv
n56, 1:xxx n73, 1:167n120,
1:167n123, 1:169n124, 1:171n127–
1:171n129, 1:217n178; *2.5,*
1:177n139–1:177n140; *2.6,*
1:179n141; *2.7,* 1:175n137,
1:205n163, 1:205n166; *2.10,*
2:241n205; *2.11,* 1:203n162,
2:175n171; *3.4,* 2:183n184; *3.8,*
1:167n120, 2:249n220; *3.8–9,*
2:73n78; *3.8–10,* 1:195n158; *3.9,*
2:73n80; *3.9–10,* 2:49n52,
2:303n257; *3.21,* 1:xxix n70; *3.24,*

Proclus, *Platonic Theology*
(*continued*)
2:243n212, 2:245n213; *3.24–26*,
1:xxviii n67; *3.25–26*, 2:245n215;
3.26, 2:177n175, 2:247n218–
2:247n219; *3.28*, 2:197n188;
4.1.16, 2:303n258; *4.28*, 2:39n40,
2:245n214, 2:247n218, 2:251n223;
4.28–30, 2:245n216; *4.28–36*,
1:xxviii n67; *4.29*, 2:251n222,
2:253n225; *4.31*, 2:251n224; *4.32*,
2:37n36; *4.34*, 2:251n221; *5.37–39*,
1:xxviii n67; *6*, 2:241n207; *6.12*,
2:303n258; *6.14*, 1:xxviii n67;
6.24, 2:253n226–2:253n228,
2:255n229; Balbi's translation
of, 1:xiv n20; manuscripts, 1:xiv
Proteus, 2:261, 2:261n235, 2:263
protosubordinationist model,
1:xxxviii n93
providence, 1:131. *See also* communicable providence; divine providence
Psellos, Michael, 1:xv
pseudo-Plato, *Epinomis*, 2:257n233
psychic Ideas, 1:137
psychic one, 2:275–83
Ptolemy of Alexandria, 1:175n30
Pythagoras, 1:xiv, 1:xxi, 1:35, 2:251
Pythagoreans, 1:35, 1:71, 2:151; as
"lovers of Ideas," 1:45
Pythodorus (character), 1:39

quantity, 1:79–83

radial species, 1:53, 1:53n8
Raphael, *School of Athens*, 1:xxi

rational power, of soul, 2:259
rational principle, 1:53–55, 1:137; of
essence, 2:189, 2:191; and Ideas,
1:73, 1:145; and intellect, 2:221;
of intellect and of first principle, 1:231; of One, 2:183–89; of
one being, 2:183–2:189, 2:191,
2:311; opposite, 2:209; of otherness, 2:189
rational souls, Ideas of, 1:57
"ready and eternal formation," 1:73
reason, 1:127–29; as guide, 1:41–43
rectilinear motion, 2:143–45; denied of One, 2:97–101; in soul,
2:93
reflection: intellect's use of, 2:79,
2:83; intelligible essence and,
2:87
relative assertions, 2:145–47; about
God, 2:63
resolutio, 1:147n95, 1:193n155
rest, 1:55, 1:169, 1:183, 1:189, 2:181;
denied of One, 2:101–3; exists
in all things but first principle,
2:89–95; and matter, 2:301; and
one being, 2:203–7; precedes
same and other, 2:109; and
soul, 2:275–83, 2:323
right, Idea of, 1:117
Rome, Neoplatonists in, 1:x
roundness, denied of One, 2:75–
81
rule of relative terms, 2:145–47

Salutati, Coluccio, 1:xl
same and different, 1:181–83,
2:105–21, 2:127–31; and like/un-

like, 2:123–2:127; and matter, 2:301; and one being, 2:207–15

sameness, 1:55, 1:169, 1:189; in all things, 2:209; consists of at least three elements, 2:121

scholasticism: Ficino and, 1:xxxi–xxxviii; Pico's defense of, 1:xxiii

scientific knowledge, 1:111–15

sculpture, 1:73n27

Scutellius, Nicolaus, 1:xvi

seal impression, 1:xxxi, 1:73n27

second principle: and multitude, 2:45; one being as, 2:33

seminal reasons, 1:49, 1:61, 1:69, 1:137

sense object, 1:89–91

sense perception, 1:127–29, 1:145n94; and One, 2:161, 2:165; and one being, 2:239; related to sense object, 2:159–61; relation to life, 1:217–19; relation to sensible good, 1:211. *See also* divine sense perception

sensible being, 2:325

sensible matter, 2:303n257

sensibles, 1:3

sensitive power, of soul, 2:259

separateness, ways of, 2:117–19

shadow: and body, 1:197; and third unity, 1:85

shadowy innumerable masses, and not-being, 2:333–37

shape: created by One, 2:29; use of term, 2:77

shaped, denied of One, 2:75–81

shapes, 2:199–201

ship, image of, 1:129

signa indicativa, 1:xxxviii, 1:xxxviii n94, 2:315n264

silence: and approach to One, 2:161, 2:173–77; of Aristotle toward Plato, 1:xxi, 1:225

similitude, 2:181

simplicity: of first and last degrees, 1:191–99; of first principle, 1:193

Simplicius, 1:xxiii

slave and master, image of, 2:145–47

slavery, 1:115–19

smallness: and not-being, 2:317–21; and one being, 2:223–25; and soul, 2:269

smallness, Idea of, 1:79–83, 1:81n36

Socrates (character), 1:vii, 1:x

Socrates (historical), 1:35

soul, 2:309–13, 2:317–21; absence of, 2:337–39; and age, 2:139, 2:145; ascent of, 1:xvii–xviii, 1:xli–xlv, 1:203n162; and being/not-being, 2:255, 2:313, 2:321–25; change in, 2:259–61; and circular motion, 2:93, 2:265–75, 2:323; comes into existence and ceases to exist, 2:269; formulates own concept *in reference to* One, 2:173; and imagination, 2:329–33; and imitation, 2:261–63; is rarefied and becomes dense, 2:269; and mind, 2:329–33; and motion, 2:313; mystic union with God, 1:203n162; and naming of "One," 2:163–65; and *noemata*, 1:91n45, 1:93n46;

soul *(continued)*
number of motions in, 2:265–75; and principle of motion, 2:315–17; as principle of universal motion, 2:261; and rectilinear motion, 2:93, 2:99; and sharing of itself, 2:255; spatial motions in, 2:269–75; species in, 1:89–91. *See also* celestial souls; divine soul
souls, orders of, 2:255
spatial motion (term), 2:93–95
species, 1:89–91; as essence, power, and limit, 1:97; Ideas as, 1:57; Ideas of, 1:57; of irrational souls, 1:57; as many and one, 1:45–47; produced by the soul, 1:89–91. *See also* ideal species; intelligible species; natural species, Ideas as; third species
species formation, 1:85n38
speculative sciences, Ideas of, 1:65
Speusippus (nephew of Plato), 2:155
sphere, 2:247, 2:305; one being as, 2:79
square, as geometric shape, 2:75
stability, soul and, 2:317
stars, 1:85
Stoics, 1:109
stones, 1:85
straight, denied of One, 2:75–81
straight motion: pertains to intelligence, 2:79–81; and soul, 2:323
straight shape, 2:199
studiositas, 1:xxvi n61

subcelestial gods, 1:73
substance: and accident, 1:213n173; precedes potentiality, 2:139; use of term, 2:109
succession, in divine soul, 2:259
succession Zeno-Socrates-Parmenides, 1:5n6
suicide, 1:213, 1:213n175
sun, 1:169, 1:175, 1:225–29, 2:211n195, 2:247; Idea of, 1:85; as principle of all light, 1:227; as proximate cause of sublunary generation, 1:127n77
supercelestial gods, 1:73
superessential unity, 2:243
superior realities, 1:227
superlatives, and the One, 2:137
sympathy, 1:85
Syrianus, 1:viii, 1:ix, 1:x, 1:161, 2:17n13, 2:39, 2:41, 2:63n69, 2:71, 2:85, 2:143–45, 2:171, 2:177, 2:239, 2:241, 2:245–47, 2:245n217; Neoplatonists in, 1:x; on Trinity, 2:57

temporal conditions, 2:147–49, 2:151
temporal differences, and one being, 2:237–39
temporal realities, 2:147–49
ten categories: are inferior to intelligible realities, 2:109; denied of One, 2:105–11
Theodorus, 1:173
theology: ancient *(prisca theologia)*, 1:xx–xxi, 1:xxii; and dialectic, 1:157–63

theurgy, 1:viii, 1:xli–xlv; theoretical justification for, 1:69n23, 1:75n33

things: that exist or are produced by themselves, 2:83–89; that produce and contain themselves, 2:87

Third Man argument, 1:85n41, 1:87n42

third principle (intermediary power), 2:243

third species, 1:87

third unity, 1:85

three levels of negations, 2:105–11

thunderstorm, image of, 2:259

time, 2:137–41, 2:147–49, 2:179, 2:181; and intellect, 2:139n132, 2:145n137; and motion, 2:275n244; motion and rest in, 2:265–75; necessarily in every being, 2:229; and one being, 2:229–35, 2:237–39; and soul, 2:255, 2:257, 2:275–83. *See also* age

total form (*forma totalis*), 1:xxxvi–xxxviii, 2:189n186; and intelligible world, 2:205; of one being, 2:201–3

touching and touched, and one being, 2:217–19

traces (*sunthemata, symbola, characteres*), 1:xlii

transcendence, 1:107–11, 1:135

transcendentals, doctrine of, 1:xxxiv n84, 2:319n267

transcendent being, denied of One, 2:109

transparent body, 2:263

tree, image of, 2:163, 2:201

triad: beginning-end-middle, 2:65; being-life-intellect, 2:57n59, 2:61, 2:61n68; being-life-intelligence, 1:xxviii n68; *essentialitas-vitalitas-intellectualitas*, 2:61n67; *essentia-vita-intellectus*, 2:61n67; one-intellect-soul, 1:xxxviii; *sapientia-veritas-virtus*, 2:61n68; wisdom-truth-power, 2:61

triangle, as geometric shape, 2:75

trinity: Christian, 2:47, 2:55–57, 2:239; Platonic, 2:239; related to first being and intelligible, 2:251

truth, as name for first principle, 1:207–9. *See also* absolute truth, and absolute knowledge

una totius forma, 2:49n51

union, 1:225; and conversion, 2:79–81

unities: in essence, 2:3–9; joined yet distinct, 2:5

Unity: as proper name of God, 2:3–5. *See also* absolute Unity, as first principle

unity, 1:viii; above being, 2:31–33; above essence, 2:3–9; absolutely transcendent, 1:41–43; in all things, 2:209; differs from sameness, 2:119; and essence, 1:203; of first principle, 1:193; and goodness, as first principle, 1:229–35; and intellectual essence, 2:25; and multiplicity, 1:xxxv–xxxviii, 1:179–81, 1:183–85

unity (*continued*)
(*see also* henads); and multitude, 2:329–33, 2:335; and number, 2:289; Parmenides' use of term, 1:43; participation in, 1:41, 1:43–45; precedes being, 2:53; as principle of universe, 1:225–29; of privation and of disposition, 2:3; rational principle of, 1:41; related to absolute One, 2:251; as unifying principle of being, 2:3. *See also* third unity
unity, mathematical, as infinite, 2:69–71
Unity and Goodness, supra-essential, 2:197
universal being, properties, 2:37–47
"universal or all," 1:39–41
universal souls, 2:179
universal sympathy, 1:xli–xlii, 1:xliii
universe: and intelligible world, 2:227; order of, 1:191
untruthfulness, and soul, 2:329–33
unum in nobis, 1:229n187

Valla, Lorenzo, 1:xii n13
Valla, Lorenzo, *Annotations to the New Testament*, 1:xii n13
Valla, Lorenzo, *Retractatio totius dialecticae 1.4*, 1:xxxiv n83

Valori, Filippo, 1:xv
Valori, Niccolò, 1:3, 1:3n1
vegetative power, of soul, 2:259
vehicle of the soul, 2:257n233
Vergil, *Aeneid 6.726–27*, 2:239n202
vile things, Ideas of, 1:67
vitality, 2:61
"vitality," 1:xxxiii–xxxiv
Vulcan, 1:65

wandering, Platonic notion of, 1:151
watchtower, image of, 2:25, 2:25n25
weaving, 1:65
well-being, 1:215
whole: and one being, 2:185–87; use of term, 2:287–89. *See also* parts and whole
will, and intellect, 1:137n86
William of Moerbeke, 1:xiii, 1:xiii n15, 1:xv, 2:155n146, 2:177n172
world soul, and matter, 2:303
world spirit, 2:257n233

Xenocrates, 1:63

Zeno (character), 1:3–5
Zeno (historical), 1:43
Zoroaster, 1:xxi

Publication of this volume has been made possible by

The Myron and Sheila Gilmore Publication Fund at I Tatti
The Robert Lehman Endowment Fund
The Jean-François Malle Scholarly Programs and Publications Fund
The Andrew W. Mellon Scholarly Publications Fund
The Craig and Barbara Smyth Fund
for Scholarly Programs and Publications
The Lila Wallace–Reader's Digest Endowment Fund
The Malcolm Wiener Fund for Scholarly Programs and Publications